Lazy Functional Languages: Abstract
Interpretation and Compilation

TITLES IN THIS SERIES

Optimizing Supercompilers for Supercomputers, Michael Wolfe, 1989

Reconfigurable Processor-Array: A Bit-Sliced Parallel Computer, Andrew Rushton, 1989

Partitioning and Scheduling Parallel Programs for Execution on Multiprocessors, Vivek Sarkar, 1989

Functional Programming for Loosely-coupled Multiprocessors, Paul H. J. Kelly, 1989

Algorithmic Skeletons: Structured Management of Parallel Computation, Murray I. Cole, 1989

Execution Models of Prolog for Parallel Computers, Péter Kacsuk, 1990

Languages and Compilers for Parallel Computing, David Gelernter, Alexandru Nicolau and David Padua (Editors), 1990

Massively Parallel Computing with the DAP, Dennis Parkinson and John Litt (Editors), 1990

Implementation of a General-Purpose Dataflow Multiprocessor, Gregory M. Papadopoulos, 1991

Implementation of Non-Strict Functional Programming Languages, Kenneth R. Traub, 1991

Advances in Languages and Compilers for Parallel Processing, Alexandru Nicolau, David Gelernter, Thomas Gross and David Padua (Editors), 1991

Parallel Processing for Computer Graphics, Stuart Green, 1991

Lazy Functional Languages: Abstract Interpretation and Compilation, Geoffrey Burn, 1991

RESEARCH MONOGRAPHS IN PARALLEL AND DISTRIBUTED COMPUTING

Geoffrey Burn
Imperial College of Science, Technology and Medicine

Lazy Functional Languages: Abstract Interpretation and Compilation

Pitman, London
The MIT Press, Cambridge, Massachusetts

PITMAN PUBLISHING
128 Long Acre, London WC2E 9AN

First published 1991

Available in the Western Hemisphere and Israel from
The MIT Press
Cambridge, Massachusetts (and London, England)

ISSN 0953-7767

British Library Cataloguing in Publication Data
Burn, Geoffrey
Lazy functional languages : abstract interpretation and compilation.—(Research monographs in parallel and distributed computing)
1. Computer systems. Functional programming. Programming languages
I. Title II. Series
005.13

ISBN 0-273-08832-7

Library of Congress Cataloging-in-Publication Data
Burn, Geoffrey.
Lazy functional languages : abstract interpretation and compilation / Geoffrey Burn.
p. cm.—(Research monographs in parallel and distributed computing)
Includes bibliographical references and index.
ISBN 0-262-52160-1
1. Functional programming languages. I. Title. II. Series.
QA76.7.B87 1991
005.1—dc20

Reproduced and printed by photolithography
in Great Britain by Biddles Ltd, Guildford

MIT Press
0262521601
BURN
LAZY FUNCTIONAL LANG

Preface

This book studies the analysis and implementation of lazy functional languages. By *functional* languages we mean those in the style of Standard ML[1] [HMT88, MTH90, Wik87], Miranda[2] [Tur85, Tur86], LML [Aug87], Haskell [HWe90] and HOPE [FH88, Per87]. In particular, we will be studying *lazy* functional languages.

Popular mythology about implementations of lazy functional languages is that they are slow when compared with more traditional languages such as C and Pascal. Early implementations *were* slow, for two reasons:

- they were largely interpretive; and
- the semantics of such languages requires that arguments to functions are not evaluated until their values are needed, imposing time and memory overheads, and restricting any parallelism in an implementation.

Compiler technology has advanced sufficiently so that lazy functional programs now run respectably fast when compared with those written in more traditional languages, solving the first problem.

This book tackles the second problem. Specifically we:

- describe a more efficient implementation model, the *evaluation transformer model*, that can be used when information is known about how functions use their arguments;
- develop a semantically sound analysis technique, *abstract interpretation*, which can determine this information; and
- show how to use the information to compile more efficient code for *sequential* and *parallel* machines.

In more detail, the story-line of the book is as follows.

Lazy evaluation is restrictive evaluation mechanism in two ways. Firstly, it only ever knows the next step that must be performed in executing a program. Secondly, it only ever evaluates expressions to *head normal form.*

The evaluation transformer model of reduction lifts both of these restrictions. It introduces the concept of an *evaluator*, which specifies the amount of evaluation to do to an expression. With each argument to a function, we associate an *evaluation transformer*, which says how much evaluation of that argument expression can be done, given that a certain amount of evaluation is allowed of the function application. Using this information, we may know that there are several expressions which must be evaluated, and that they need more evaluation than to head normal form.

Functional languages can be studied from both *operational* and *denotational* viewpoints. The operational viewpoint tells us how they can be implemented, and the freedom

[1]Standard ML has some non-functional features, but the hope is that programmers will use it in a mainly functional way.

[2]Miranda is a trademark of Research Software Ltd.

we have in the implementation, whilst the denotational viewpoint gives the meanings of programs in terms of mathematical structures called domains.

There is an important relationship between the operational and denotational viewpoints, which must be preserved in any implementation model.

We ensure that the evaluation transformer model of reduction preserves this relationship by developing a semantically sound analysis technique, called *abstract interpretation*, to determine evaluation transformers.

Finally, we show how to use the evaluation transformer information to generate more efficient code for sequential and parallel machines. It is used in a sequential machine to know when arguments to functions can be evaluated immediately, rather than incurring the cost of building a data structure to hold a representation of the unevaluated argument. In a parallel machine it is used to generate code which will initiate parallel processes to evaluate parts of the program.

Our theoretical development is done in terms of the *typed lambda calculus.* All functional programs written in the languages mentioned above can be translated into the typed lambda calculus, and so it allows us to study the properties of functional languages without worrying about the concrete syntax of a particular language.

An index of symbols can be found at the end of the book.

Prerequisites

It has been our intention to make this book essentially self-contained, with introductions to the necessary concepts from the typed lambda calculus, domain theory, denotational semantics, functional programming and the implementation of functional languages being given in the body of the text. All five topics are rather large fields in themselves, and so a background in one or more of them would help make the book more accessible. A fair degree of mathematical maturity is needed to understand this book, and the book is probably most suited to postgraduates.

Some texts containing background material on the typed lambda calculus are [Bar84, Bar91b, Gor88], on domain theory is [GS90], on denotational semantics are [Mos90, Sch86, Sto77], on functional programming are [BW88, FH88, Rea89], and on the implementation of lazy functional languages are [FH88, Pey87, Rea89].

Acknowledgements

This book brings together much of the research I have been doing over the past six years.

My first foray into the field was the development of a strictness analysis for higher-order functions in conjunction with Chris Hankin and Samson Abramsky (Imperial College). In generalising this work to deal with abstract domains for structured data types, such as lists, I discovered evaluation transformers. Thus, evaluation transformers are an example of an implementation concept which arose from a study of the denotational semantics of functional programming languages. These two pieces of work formed the backbone of my PhD thesis from Imperial College, which was supervised by Chris Hankin. I am most grateful for all the time Chris spent with me when I was doing my PhD, and for his continuing support.

Following the study of abstract interpretation, I worked on the implementation of functional languages on sequential and parallel machines. During that time I benefited greatly from discussions with David Bevan, Raju Karia, David Lester and John Robson (GEC Hirst Research Centre), Simon Peyton Jones (now at the University of Glasgow), Lennart Augustsson and Thomas Johnsson (University of Göteborg), Dick Kieburtz (Oregon Graduate Center), Werner Damm (University of Oldenburg), and Pier Giorgio Bosco and Corrado Moiso (CSELT).

All of the above work, including my PhD, was completed whilst working at the GEC Hirst Research Centre, Wembley, Middlesex, UK, and was partially funded by ESPRIT Project 415 – "Parallel Languages and Architectures: A VLSI-Directed Approach". I am grateful also for all of the things I learnt from the rest of my many colleagues on that project, and for the way discussions with them helped direct my work.

Since joining Imperial College in October 1989, two of the things I have done are tightening up the definition of evaluators and putting the theory of the evaluation transformer model on a sounder footing. Some of the contents of this book are the results of new research that has not been published elsewhere. Discussions with Sebastian Hunt, Thomas Jensen and David Sands have been particularly helpful in this endeavour. Correspondence with Roger Hindley helped me prove that leftmost reduction was head normalising for the language of this book, and I thank Henk Barendregt for suggesting I should contact him. During this time, my research has received some financial support from the ESPRIT Basic Research Action 3124 ("Semantique").

I give my thanks to David Turner for sending me a complimentary copy of Miranda Version 2.

Many thanks to those people who have read various drafts of this book and made many helpful suggestions. In alphabetical order they are: Guy Argo (University of Glasgow), Gebreselassie Baraki (University of Glasgow), Lennart Edblom (University of Umea), John Farrel (University of Queensland), Chris Hankin (Imperial College), John Launchbury (University of Glasgow), David Lester (University of Manchester), and David Wright (University of Tasmania). Alan Mycroft gave me many helpful suggestions on producing a book, using my thesis as a basis, for which I give my thanks.

The camera-ready copy of this book was prepared using the LaTeXdocument preparation system, and the diagrams on pages 12, 14, 24, 68 and 69 were produced using the diagrams macros designed and written by Paul Taylor of Imperial College.

Finally I would like to thank my parents, whose support through my education, and in many ways afterwards is most appreciated, which in part provided the foundations enabling this work to be done, and Helen, with whom it is a privilege and a joy to share married life.

Geoffrey Burn
September, 1990

Contents

List of Figures

To Helen

Chapter 1

Introduction

To set the scene for this book, this chapter discusses functional programming languages and lazy evaluation, the evaluation transformer model of reduction and abstract interpretation. The first section gives a way of thinking about the execution of functional programs in terms of *rewriting* function applications. This enables us to discuss the importance of the order in which function applications are evaluated, and to motivate the need for *laziness*. We argue in the second section that lazy evaluation is restrictive when we know that some functions need to evaluate their arguments, and so develop the *evaluation transformer model* of reduction. For those unfamiliar with *abstract interpretation*, the third section gives an example of an abstract interpretation – the 'rule of signs' – of a simple arithmetic language, to introduce the main concepts of abstract interpretation. The example is closely modelled on the way that we will discuss the abstract interpretation of functional languages in the rest of the book. Finally, we give an outline of the book in the fourth section.

1.1 Functional Programming Languages and Lazy Evaluation

In this section we address the issues of what a functional program looks like, and what it means to *execute* a functional program. The discussion will necessarily be informal; all of the concepts described will be formally defined in the next chapter in the context of the typed lambda calculus.

1.1.1 Functional Programs and Reduction

A functional program consists of two parts, a series of function definitions, and an expression to be evaluated in the environment of the function definitions. We will write our examples in the language Miranda, using the *inverse comment convention*, where lines of program text are highlighted by beginning them with a >, rather than highlighting comments. The following is a simple functional program:

```
> f x y = x + y
> f 1 2
```

The function defined is called `f`. It has two formal parameters, `x` and `y`, and the result of applying the function to two arguments is to return their sum. So the application `f 1 2` returns the value 3. Note that function application is represented by textual juxtaposition of the function and its arguments, a convention that has been adopted in all lazy functional languages. When arguments to functions are complex expressions, then bracketing is used in the normal way to remove ambiguities. For example, the application `f (1+3) (2*5)` is the application of `f` to the arguments `1+3` and `2*5`.

How are functional programs executed? The execution of functional languages is often described in terms of rewriting: given some subexpression which is a function application, it is replaced by the right-hand side of the definition of the function, with the formal parameters of the function being appropriately replaced by the actual parameters. For the example `f 1 2`, this would be written:

$$\mathtt{f\ 1\ 2} \rightarrow \mathtt{1+2} \rightarrow \mathtt{3}.$$

The notation

$$\mathtt{expression1} \rightarrow \mathtt{expression2}$$

should be read "`expression1` *rewrites* (or *reduces*) to `expression2`" and a function applied to enough arguments is called a *redex*.

As a more complex example, consider the functions defined by:

```
> f x = g x x
> g a b = a + b
```

The application `(f (5 * 2))` is reduced as follows:

$$\begin{array}{lll} \mathtt{f\ (5\ *\ 2)} & \rightarrow & \mathtt{g\ (5\ *\ 2)\ (5\ *\ 2)} \\ & \rightarrow & \mathtt{+\ (5\ *\ 2)\ (5\ *\ 2)} \\ & \rightarrow & \mathtt{+\ 10\ (5\ *\ 2)} \\ & \rightarrow & \mathtt{+\ 10\ 10} \\ & \rightarrow & \mathtt{20} \end{array}$$

In the above example, there was often more than one function application which could have been reduced at each step. Which one should we have chosen? Consider the following functional program:

```
> g x = g x
> h x y = x
> h 5 (g 2)
```

What should the value of `h 5 (g 2)` be? Intuitively, it should give the value 5, because the function `h` ignores its second argument. However, a naïve rewriting algorithm may fail to terminate if it does not do the reduction steps in a sensible order. Consider the sequence:

$$\begin{array}{ll} \mathtt{f\ 5\ (g\ 2)} & \rightarrow \mathtt{f\ 5\ (g\ 2)} \\ & \rightarrow \mathtt{f\ 5\ (g\ 2)} \\ & \rightarrow \mathtt{f\ 5\ (g\ 2)} \\ & \rightarrow \mathtt{f\ 5\ (g\ 2)} \end{array}$$

where (g 2) is repeatedly rewritten to itself using the definition of g. What we need is some mechanical way of choosing the next function application to reduce so that the expected answer from a program is obtained.

Systems such as these have been studied extensively. It turns out that if an *outermost* function application is always chosen for reduction, then the expected answer is obtained from executing a program. A function application is *outermost* if it is not included in any other function application. For example, in (f 5 (g 2)), the application of f is outermost, and the application of g is not. Using outermost reduction, the above example reduces in one step to the value 5. In an application of +, where there is more than one outermost redex,

(f 5 (g 2))+(f 3 4),

it does not matter which one is done first. Usually an implementation will reduce the leftmost one first, and so often authors write of *leftmost outermost* reduction. In fact, if expressions are fully bracketed, and the leftmost redex is defined to be the one whose opening bracket is leftmost in the expression, then the leftmost outermost redex is just the leftmost redex, and so in Chapter 2 we will refer to the leftmost redex.

Sometimes this choice of the leftmost redex is called *call-by-name*, terminology introduced for Algol60, where call-by-name parameters were passed to a function unevaluated.

Notice one more thing about the second example. In the body of f, the arguments to g are both bound to the same expression. We wrote out the example so that a copy of the actual parameter was made for each occurrence of the parameter of f in its body, so that two copies were made of the argument expression (* 5 2). In general, this will lead to the recomputation of the actual parameters to a function. Wadsworth developed a technique for avoiding recomputation of expressions [Wad71, Chapter 4]. Expressions are stored as graphs. When a function application is reduced, a copy of its body is made, with the formal parameters being replaced by pointers to the graphs of the respective arguments. This implementation technique has become known as *graph reduction*, and will be discussed further in Chapter 6.

1.1.2 Algebraic Data Types and Lazy Evaluation

Many functional languages have the facility to define algebraic data types. For example, a data type for lists of integers could be defined by:

```
> listnum ::= Nil | Cons num listnum
```

where integers are called num in Miranda. This declaration says that a list is either empty, written as Nil, or is of the form (Cons n l) where n is of type num and l is of type listnum. The first argument to Cons is usually called the *head* of the list, and the second argument its *tail*. Lists are actually a predefined data type in Miranda, with nil being written [] and Cons being written as an infix colon. For the purposes of uniformity with the rest of this book, we will use Nil and Cons.

Miranda allows functions over algebraic data types to be written using patterns. Consider for example the function sumlist defined by:

```
> sumlist Nil          = 0
> sumlist (Cons x xs) = x + (sumlist xs)
```

which calculates the sum of the elements in an object of type `listnum`. If an application of the function `sumlist` is being reduced, its argument is matched against `Nil`; if it is `Nil`, then the result of the application is `0`, otherwise it is must be of the form `(Cons u l)`, and the result of the reduction is `(u + (sumlist l))`, where `x` and `xs` have been bound to the head (`u`) and the tail (`l`) of the argument list respectively. This process is called *pattern matching*. An example of this is the reduction of the following application:

$$\begin{aligned} \texttt{sumlist (Cons 1 Nil)} &\rightarrow 1 + (\texttt{sumlist Nil}) \\ &\rightarrow 1 + 0 \\ &\rightarrow 1 \end{aligned}$$

In this book we will assume that only simple patterns are used; there is a case for each of `Nil` and `Cons`, and that the arguments to these in the pattern are variables, not other patterns. More complex patterns can be translated into these simple cases; see [Pey87, Chapter 5] and [FH88, Section 8.4] for example.

With the introduction of structured data types like lists, we have a new problem. When should we stop evaluating an expression? For the examples we have considered so far, reductions were continually performed until no more reduction could be done. Consider now the program:

```
> ints_from n       = Cons n (ints_from (n+1))
> head (Cons x xs) = x
> head (ints_from 0)
```

Given a value for `n`, the value of `(ints_from n)` is the infinite list of integers starting from `n`. For example, `(ints_from 0)` is the infinite list:

```
Cons 0 (Cons 1 (Cons 2 ....
```

The function `head` returns the first element of its argument list. An application of `head` cannot be reduced until its argument has been evaluated. What do we mean by evaluating `(ints_from 0)`? Our intuition is that the application `(head (ints_from 0))` should return the value `0`. This can only happen if evaluating an infinite list does not cause an infinite computation. A simple way of ensuring this is that an expression of type `listnum` should only be evaluated as far as either being `Nil` or of the form `(Cons e1 e2)`, where no evaluation has been done to `e1` nor `e2`. This idea was independently suggested in [FW76] and [HM76]. Formally, we say that expressions are only evaluated to *head normal form (HNF)*, defined in Chapter 2. For the discussion of this chapter, the informal idea that an expression of the form `Nil` or `(Cons e1 e2)` is in head normal form suffices.

Lazy evaluation is an execution mechanism that consists of three things:

1. Reductions are performed in a leftmost order.

2. Reduction of an expression proceeds only as far as head normal form[1]; application of base functions such as `head` may force further evaluation of an expression.

[1]In passing, we note that texts on implementing lazy functional languages often speak of *weak* head normal form, rather than head normal form. In the lambda calculus, a term of the form $\lambda x.e$ is in weak head normal form, but is not necessarily in head normal form, as e may be a redex. Our implementations will be based on combinator reduction, and we will only consider reduction to head normal form.

3. Any expression which is bound to a formal parameter in a function application must only be evaluated once.

Notice that the third condition is a much lower-level implementation detail than the first two.

Throughout the book, we will use lists and binary trees as prototypical examples of structured data types. The type `treenum` is defined by the declaration:

```
> treenum ::= Empty | Node treenum num treenum
```

which says that objects of type `treenum` are either `Empty`, the empty tree, or are a node with containing a number and two subtrees. Example functions over the two data types are given in Figure 1.1. It is worth making sure that they are understood, for they will be used throughout the rest of the book.

1.1.3 Polymorphic and Monomorphic Typing

We have skirted around a very important issue in functional programming – the issue of typing. Consider the function `sumlist` defined in Figure 1.1. Given some argument of type `listnum`, it returns an integer, of type `num`. We write this as:

```
> sumlist :: listnum -> num.
```

Given an argument of type `listnum`, the function `length`, defined in Figure 1.1, also returns a result of type `num`. However, the function `length` is more general than that. Observe that in the definition of `length`, no use is made of the elements of the list, and so it should be possible to use `length` to calculate the length of lists of elements of any type. The function `length` is called *polymorphic* because it can have many types, and its type could be written:

```
> length :: (list *) -> num
```

where `*` is a *type variable*, that is, `length` has the type `(list t) -> num` for any type `t`. The type `(list *)` can be defined by the declaration:

```
> list * ::= Nil | Cons * (list *)
```

which says that a list of elements of type `*` is either `Nil` or the `Cons` of an element of type `*` and a list of elements of type `*`. Note that all of the elements of the list have the same type (unlike 'lists' in Lisp). In a similar way, the type of binary trees of elements of any type is defined by:

```
> tree * ::= Empty | Node (tree *) * (tree *)
```

Of the functions in Figure 1.1, `append`, `reverse`, `map`, `size` and `join` are also polymorphic.

For technical reasons, the abstract interpretation framework developed in Chapter 3 can only deal with *monomorphic* functions, that is, functions with only one type, like `sumlist`. However, this is no theoretical restriction on the work, as any polymorphically

```
> length :: list * -> num
> length Nil          = 0
> length (Cons x xs) = 1 + (length xs)

> sumlist :: list num -> num
> sumlist Nil         = 0
> sumlist (Cons x xs) = x + (sumlist xs)

> append :: list * -> list * -> list *
> append Nil ys          = ys
> append (Cons x xs) ys = Cons x (append xs ys)

> reverse :: list * -> list *
> reverse Nil         = Nil
> reverse (Cons x xs) = append (reverse xs) (Cons x Nil)

> before0 :: list num -> list num
> before0 Nil         = Nil
> before0 (Cons x xs) = if (x=0) then Nil else (Cons x (before0 xs))

> doubles :: list num -> list num
> doubles Nil         = Nil
> doubles (Cons x xs) = Cons (2*x) (doubles xs)

> map :: (* -> **) -> list * -> list **
> map f Nil         = Nil
> map f (Cons x xs) = Cons (f x) (map f xs)

> size :: tree * -> num
> size Empty          = 0
> size (Node t1 n t2) = (size t1) + 1 + (size t2)

> sumtree :: tree num -> num
> sumtree Empty          = 0
> sumtree (Node t1 n t2) = (sumtree t1) + n + (sumtree t2)

> join :: tree * -> * -> tree * -> tree *
> join t1 n t2 = Node t1 n t2
```

Figure 1.1: Definitions of Some Example Functions

typed program can be translated into a monomorphic one [Hol83]. We return to the issue of polymorphism in Chapter 7.

As an aside, we note that most lazy functional languages allow the programmer to write programs without providing the types of functions. The types of functions are then inferred using some type inference algorithm, commonly by some form of *Hindley-Milner* type inference system. Details can be found in one of [FH88, Chapter 7], [Pey87, Chapters 8 and 9] and [Rea89, Chapter 11]. Nevertheless, most functional programmers find it a powerful programming methodology to work out the types of functions before writing them.

1.2 The Evaluation Transformer Model of Reduction

Leftmost reduction to head normal form produces the expected answers from programs. This section argues informally that some functions need to evaluate their arguments, so that the leftmost strategy can be changed, and that they may need to evaluate them more than to HNF, giving rise to the evaluation transformer model of reduction.

1.2.1 Evaluators

In some function applications, the argument will need more reduction than just to HNF. Consider the data type for binary trees defined in the previous section, `tree *`, and the functions defined over it in Figure 1.1. The function `size` counts the number of `Node`s in a tree. The size of an empty tree, `Empty`, is zero, whilst the size of a tree which is `(Node t1 n t2)` is is one more than the the sum of the sizes of its two subtrees, `t1` and `t2`. To evaluate an application of `size`, the whole of the structure of the argument tree will need to be traversed, but the values which are the second argument to the constructor `Node` will never have to be evaluated. The function `sumtree` however, also has to evaluate the second argument to the constructor `Node` for each node in the tree.

We will say that we can evaluate an expression using a particular *evaluator*, and call an evaluator which evaluates tree-valued expressions to HNF $\xi_{\perp}^{(tree\ \tau)}$, an evaluator which evaluates the structure of the tree data type $\xi_{\infty}^{(tree\ \tau)}$, and an evaluator which evaluates the structure of the tree data type and the second field in every node of the tree to HNF $\xi_{\perp\!\in}^{(tree\ \tau)}$. The reason for the names of the evaluators will be made clear when they are defined formally in Chapter 5. Informally, the ξ is supposed to remind us of *evaluator* because it looks a bit like a curly E, the superscript $(tree\ \tau)$ gives the type of the expressions it evaluates, and the subscript says how much evaluation has to be done to an expression. For completeness, the evaluator $\xi_{NO}^{(tree\ \tau)}$ does no evaluation.

As with trees, functions over lists may require some evaluation of their argument expressions. For example, consider the functions defined in Figure 1.1. The function `length` needs to evaluate the structure of its argument list, whilst `sumlist` needs to evaluate the structure of its argument and every element of the list to HNF. We will call the first evaluator $\xi_{\infty}^{(list\ \tau)}$ and the second $\xi_{\perp\!\in}^{(list\ \tau)}$. There is also $\xi_{\perp}^{(list\ \tau)}$, which evaluates lists to HNF, and $\xi_{NO}^{(list\ \tau)}$ which does no evaluation.

The data types (`list *`) and (`tree *`) are called *recursive* data types because they are defined in terms of themselves. For any recursive data type, there are two very natural evaluators: the first one evaluates the structure of an expression, and the second evaluates the structure of an expression and each element in the structure to HNF. By evaluating the structure of an expression, we mean firstly evaluating it to HNF, and then recursively evaluating any subterms which are also of the same type as the expression. For lists this means evaluating the second argument to `Cons` if an expression reduces to an application of `Cons`, and for trees it means evaluating the first and third arguments to `Node`. The process will only terminate if the structure of the data object is finite. Throughout the book we will use lists and trees as our example data types, leaving the adaptation of the techniques to other data types to the reader. Note that both $\xi_{NO}^{(tree\ \tau)}$ and $\xi_{NO}^{(list\ \tau)}$ do no evaluation, so we will drop the superscripts.

When the second field of a `Node` or the elements in a list are themselves complex data structures, then more complex evaluators could be defined. The theory we develop in later chapters is able to deal with this situation. For simplicity, we will give all examples in terms of these three types of evaluation – evaluation to HNF, evaluating the structure of an expression, and evaluating the structure of an expression and each element in the structure to HNF.

Note that although we have written of evaluating the structure of a data item, it need not be implemented so that the whole structure is evaluated at once. We discuss the implementation of evaluators in Chapter 6.

1.2.2 Evaluation Transformers

Not only do some functions require more evaluation of their argument than to HNF, but the amount of evaluation of an argument may depend on the amount of evaluation required of an application of a function. Consider for example the function `join` defined in Figure 1.1. Normally no arguments to `join` need to be evaluated because a result in HNF is required. However, if one was to require that an application of `join` was to deliver the structure of a tree, such as in the application `size (join e1 e2 e3)`, then clearly it can only do this if the structures of its first and third arguments are created.

For each argument of a function therefore, we have to determine an *evaluation transformer.* An evaluation transformer for an argument is a mapping that gives the evaluator which may be used for evaluating the argument, given the evaluator for an application of the function. For example, the evaluation transformers for `join` are given in Figure 1.2. $JOIN_i$ is the evaluation transformer for the ith argument of `join`. If an application of `join` is being evaluated with the evaluator $\xi_{\infty}^{(tree\ \tau)}$, then the second argument can be evaluated with the evaluator ($JOIN_2\ \xi_{\infty}^{(tree\ \tau)}$) which, from the figure, is ξ_{NO}. Similarly, the first and third arguments can be evaluated with $\xi_{\infty}^{(tree\ \tau)}$ in this case. We will see further examples of evaluation transformers in Chapter 5.

1.2.3 The Evaluation Transformer Model

Evaluation transformers say how much evaluation can be done to an argument expression in a function application, given the amount of evaluation that can be done to the appli-

E	$JOIN_1\ E$	$JOIN_2\ E$	$JOIN_3\ E$
ξ_{NO}	ξ_{NO}	ξ_{NO}	ξ_{NO}
$\xi_{\perp}^{(tree\ \tau)}$	ξ_{NO}	ξ_{NO}	ξ_{NO}
$\xi_{\infty}^{(tree\ \tau)}$	$\xi_{\infty}^{(tree\ \tau)}$	ξ_{NO}	$\xi_{\infty}^{(tree\ \tau)}$
$\xi_{\perp\in}^{(tree\ \tau)}$	$\xi_{\perp\in}^{(tree\ \tau)}$	$\xi_{\perp_{A_\tau}}^{\tau}$	$\xi_{\perp\in}^{(tree\ \tau)}$

Figure 1.2: Evaluation Transformers for `join`

cation. In a sequential implementation, this information is used to evaluate the argument to that extent before applying the function, so saving the cost of building a closure for the argument in the heap. The information is used in a parallel implementation by creating a parallel process to evaluate the argument in parallel with the function application. This will be discussed further in Chapter 6.

1.3 An Introduction to Abstract Interpretation

We are all familiar in everyday life with the idea that often we do not require the exact answer to a question – a distance of order of magnitude of ten kilometres can be cycled, whereas a distance of order of magnitude one hundred kilometres may require some automated form of transport. To answer the question "Do I ride my bicycle or do I go by train?", one needs only to know an approximation (order of magnitude) of the distance.

In a similar manner, we are taught at school that to tell whether a number is odd or even, all we need to do is see if the least significant digit is odd or even – a task which requires less computational effort than dividing the whole number by two (unless it is a single digit number!).

What is the key concept lying behind the answering of these and similar questions? The idea is that there is some property in which we are interested, and about which we can find information without having the exact answer, or doing the whole calculation.

Suppose that we wanted to know if the value of an arithmetic expression involving positive numbers, negative numbers and zero, and applications of addition and multiplication was positive, negative or zero. Instead of having to completely evaluate the expression, we can use the properties of how such numbers behave under the operations of addition and multiplication to determine the result much more easily. For example, the value of the expression

$$29 \times -33 \times 64$$

is negative, since the sign of a positive number multiplied by a negative number is negative and vice versa. This calculation uses what is often called 'the rule of signs', and can be formalised as an abstract interpretation. To do so, we begin by giving an abstract syntax for a language of arithmetic expressions:

$$Exp \ ::= c_n | Exp \boxed{+} Exp | Exp \boxed{\times} Exp$$

There is one constant, c_n for each integer n, and an arithmetic *Expression* is either a constant or the $\boxed{+}$ of two *Expressions*, or the $\boxed{\times}$ of two *Expressions*. By writing c_n, $\boxed{+}$ and $\boxed{\times}$ for what would normally be interpreted as integers, addition and multiplication, we are making explicit the fact that any language needs to have some interpretation, and that there may be several ways of interpreting the language. The *standard* way to interpret such a language is to firstly interpret the set of constants $\{c_n\}$ as the integers, which we will denote by $\mathbf{S}_{int}$, so that the constant c_n is interpreted to be the integer n. The symbols $\boxed{+}$ and $\boxed{\times}$ are then interpreted as integer addition and multiplication respectively. These induce a *standard interpretation* function, which we will denote by S:

$$\begin{array}{l} \mathsf{S} : Exp \rightarrow \mathbf{S}_{int} \\ \mathsf{S} [\![c_n]\!] = n \\ \mathsf{S} [\![Exp_1 \boxed{+} Exp_2]\!] = \mathsf{S} [\![Exp_1]\!] + \mathsf{S} [\![Exp_2]\!] \\ \mathsf{S} [\![Exp_1 \boxed{\times} Exp_2]\!] = \mathsf{S} [\![Exp_1]\!] \times \mathsf{S} [\![Exp_2]\!] \end{array}$$

where $+$ and $\times$ are integer addition and multiplication respectively.

To find out if the value of the expression is positive, negative or zero, the standard interpretation of the language could be used to determine the answer by doing the calculation, and then seeing whether the result was positive or negative or zero. For example, for the expression

$$c_{29} \boxed{\times} c_{-33} \boxed{\times} c_{64}$$

we could calculate the answer to be

$$\mathsf{S} [\![c_{29}]\!] \times \mathsf{S} [\![c_{-33}]\!] \times \mathsf{S} [\![c_{64}]\!]$$

which is

$$29 \times -33 \times 64 = -61248$$

and then see that the answer is negative. However, there is a much simpler way of finding the answer to this question, using the properties of the multiplication of positive and negative numbers. The way we normally answer the question about the sign of the the answer is to do the 'calculation'

$$\mathbf{+ve} \boxed{\times} \mathbf{-ve} \boxed{\times} \mathbf{+ve} = \mathbf{-ve}$$

where **+ve** represents the property of being positive, and similarly **-ve** the property of being negative, and then say that the answer to the real calculation would have been negative.

What have we done? The first step is that we have said that the important property of the constant c_n is not its magnitude, but its sign, and provided an abstract interpretation for the constants c_n, which we will denote by **A**, that says

$$\mathbf{A} [\![c_n]\!] = sign(\mathsf{S} [\![c_n]\!])$$

where

$$sign\ n = \begin{cases} \mathbf{+ve} & \text{if } n > 0 \\ \mathbf{zero} & \text{if } n = 0 \\ \mathbf{-ve} & \text{if } n < 0 \end{cases}$$

Secondly, we have given different interpretations to the functional constants, $\boxed{+}$ and $\boxed{\times}$, in the language *Exp*. We will write the interpretations of $\boxed{+}$ and $\boxed{\times}$ under this abstract interpretation (the rule of signs) as $\overline{+}$ and $\overline{\times}$ respectively. For the abstract interpretation of $\boxed{\times}$, we have the following rules:

$$
\begin{array}{llll}
\mathbf{+ve}\ \overline{\times}\ \mathbf{+ve} = \mathbf{+ve} & \qquad & \mathbf{zero}\ \overline{\times}\ \mathbf{+ve} & = \mathbf{zero} \\
\mathbf{+ve}\ \overline{\times}\ \mathbf{-ve} = \mathbf{-ve} & & \mathbf{+ve}\ \overline{\times}\ \mathbf{zero} & = \mathbf{zero} \\
\mathbf{-ve}\ \overline{\times}\ \mathbf{+ve} = \mathbf{-ve} & & \mathbf{zero}\ \overline{\times}\ \mathbf{-ve} & = \mathbf{zero} \\
\mathbf{-ve}\ \overline{\times}\ \mathbf{-ve} = \mathbf{+ve} & & \mathbf{-ve}\ \overline{\times}\ \mathbf{zero} & = \mathbf{zero} \\
\mathbf{zero}\ \overline{\times}\ \mathbf{zero} = \mathbf{zero} & & &
\end{array}
$$

For the abstract interpretation of $\boxed{+}$, some of the rules are obvious, for example,

$$
\begin{array}{llll}
\mathbf{+ve}\ \overline{+}\ \mathbf{+ve} = \mathbf{+ve} & \qquad & \mathbf{zero}\ \overline{+}\ \mathbf{+ve} & = \mathbf{+ve} \\
\mathbf{-ve}\ \overline{+}\ \mathbf{-ve} = \mathbf{-ve} & & \mathbf{+ve}\ \overline{+}\ \mathbf{zero} & = \mathbf{+ve} \\
\mathbf{zero}\ \overline{+}\ \mathbf{zero} = \mathbf{zero} & & \mathbf{zero}\ \overline{+}\ \mathbf{-ve} & = \mathbf{-ve} \\
\mathbf{-ve}\ \overline{+}\ \mathbf{zero} = \mathbf{-ve} & & &
\end{array}
$$

A result cannot be given for either $(\mathbf{+ve}\ \overline{+}\ \mathbf{-ve})$ or $(\mathbf{-ve}\ \overline{+}\ \mathbf{+ve})$ because the sign of the result depends on the magnitude of the two values, and this information has been abstracted away. To cope with this situation, we thus introduce the value $\top$ (pronounced "top") to represent the idea that the sign of the calculation is unknown. Another way of representing this would be to use the set $\{\mathbf{-ve}, \mathbf{zero}, \mathbf{+ve}\}$, but we prefer to use $\top$ so that sets are not introduced into the abstract interpretation. The rules for $\top$ are :

$$
\begin{array}{lllll}
\mathbf{+ve}\ \overline{\times}\ \top = \top & \qquad & \top\ \overline{\times}\ \mathbf{+ve} & = & \top \\
\mathbf{zero}\ \overline{\times}\ \top = \mathbf{zero} & & \top\ \overline{\times}\ \mathbf{zero} & = & \mathbf{zero} \\
\mathbf{-ve}\ \overline{\times}\ \top = \top & & \top\ \overline{\times}\ \mathbf{-ve} & = & \top \\
\mathbf{+ve}\ \overline{+}\ \top = \top & & \top\ \overline{+}\ \mathbf{+ve} & = & \top \\
\mathbf{zero}\ \overline{+}\ \top = \top & & \top\ \overline{+}\ \mathbf{zero} & = & \top \\
\mathbf{-ve}\ \overline{+}\ \top = \top & & \top\ \overline{+}\ \mathbf{-ve} & = & \top
\end{array}
$$

For uniformity with the rest of the book, we have to introduce one more technicality. Readers familiar with *domain theory* will know $\mathbf{S}_{int}$ is in fact a domain, with an object called $\perp_{\mathbf{S}_{int}}$, the bottom element of the domain, which represents non-terminating computations (although there is no way of writing such an expression in the simple language we have been discussing). It is called the *bottom* element because there is a *partial order* on $\mathbf{S}_{int}$ called $\sqsubseteq$, and defined by $z_1 \sqsubseteq z_2$ if and only if either $z_1 = \perp_{\mathbf{S}_{int}}$, or $z_1 = z_2$, that is, $\perp_{\mathbf{S}_{int}}$ is the lowest object in the ordering. This is shown diagrammatically by:

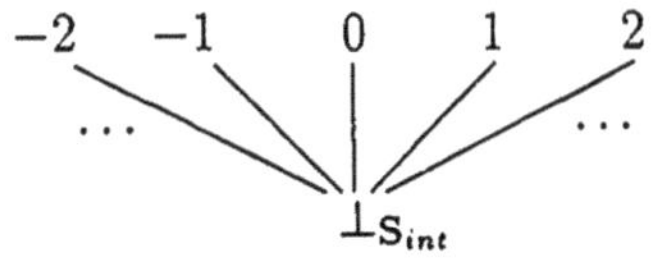

where $\perp_{\mathbf{S}_{int}}$ is drawn at the bottom of the diagram, with a line from it to each other integer, to indicate that $\perp_{\mathbf{S}_{int}}$ is lower in the ordering than any other integer. All the other integers are on the same level, with no lines between them, because they are equally defined. For those unfamiliar with partial orders and domain theory, an introduction to the relevant concepts is given in Section 2.2.

We also add a bottom point to the set of signs, so that the set which is used for the abstract interpretation of the constants c_n, which we will call $\mathbf{A}_{int}$, contains the elements:

$$\mathbf{A}_{int} = \{\bot, \mathbf{-ve}, \mathbf{zero}, \mathbf{+ve}, \top\}.$$

It also has an ordering on it, shown diagramatically by:

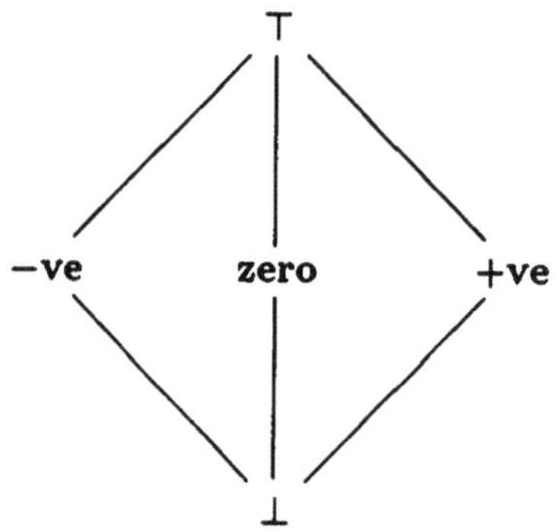

Note that $\mathbf{A}_{int}$ is a finite *lattice*. We also have to extend the definitions of $\overline{+}$ and $\overline{\times}$. We do this in the natural way, so that if either argument to either function is $\bot$, then result of the application is $\bot$.

In the same way that we defined a standard interpretation for our language, we can provide an abstract interpretation, the semantic function being called $\mathbf{A}$:

$$\begin{array}{l}\mathbf{A} \ : \ Exp \rightarrow \mathbf{A}_{int} \\ \mathbf{A} \ [\![c_n]\!] = sign(\mathrm{S} \ [\![c_n]\!]) \\ \mathbf{A} \ [\![Exp_1 \boxed{+} Exp_2]\!] = \mathbf{A} \ [\![Exp_1]\!] \ \overline{+} \ \mathbf{A} \ [\![Exp_2]\!] \\ \mathbf{A} \ [\![Exp_1 \boxed{\times} Exp_2]\!] = \mathbf{A} \ [\![Exp_1]\!] \ \overline{\times} \ \mathbf{A} \ [\![Exp_2]\!]\end{array}$$

Notice that the form of the abstract interpretation is the same as that of the standard interpretation; all that has changed is the interpretation of the constants c_n, $\boxed{+}$ and $\boxed{\times}$.

We now have two interpretations :

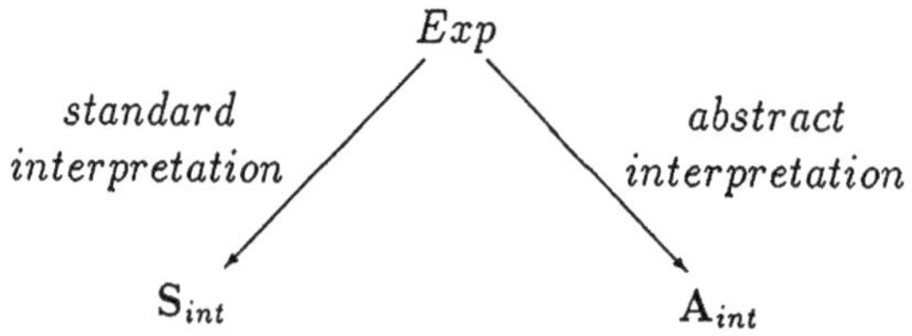

How can we say that if we get the answer $\mathbf{-ve}$ in the abstract interpretation, that the answer in the standard interpretation was really negative? That is, we must find a notion of *correctness*, and prove that the abstract interpretation is correct. We begin by noting that the symbol $\mathbf{+ve}$ "represents" any positive integer. To capture this notion, we define a *concretisation* map:

$$\gamma_{int} \ : \ \mathbf{A}_{int} \rightarrow \mathbf{P} \ \mathbf{S}_{int}$$

where (**P** X) is the powerset of X. Concretisation returns an element in the powerset because each element in $\mathbf{A}_{int}$ represents (possibly) many elements of $\mathbf{S}_{int}$.

Rather than define this map directly, we will define it in a manner which is similar to the way we will define such maps in Chapter 3. An *abstraction* map :

$$\alpha_{int} \;:\; \mathbf{S}_{int} \rightarrow \mathbf{A}_{int}$$

can be defined, which relates the standard interpretation and the abstract interpretation of the constants. In this case, the abstraction map is just the *sign* map defined earlier, augmented with a rule for $\perp_{\mathbf{S}_{int}}$:

$$\alpha_{int}\ n = \begin{cases} \perp & \text{if } n = \perp_{\mathbf{S}_{int}} \\ \mathbf{+ve} & \text{if } n > 0 \\ \mathbf{zero} & \text{if } n = 0 \\ \mathbf{-ve} & \text{if } n < 0 \end{cases}$$

We can now define a map

$$Abs_{int} \;:\; \mathbf{P}\ \mathbf{S}_{int} \rightarrow \mathbf{A}_{int}$$

which will allow us to find the abstract interpretation of sets of elements. A set of integers may contain integers of differing sign. Suppose that the set $\{-3, 4\}$ had to be abstracted. Then we can apply the abstraction map α_{int} to each element in the set to obtain the set $\{\mathbf{-ve}, \mathbf{+ve}\}$. The point $\top$ was introduced to represent uncertainty about the sign of a result of a computation. Here we can give it another reading: it represents sets of elements which have more than one sign in them. Because of the ordering on $\mathbf{A}_{int}$, this is obtained by taking the least upper bound of the set of elements we get by abstracting each element in the set. (Note that $\bigsqcup\{\mathbf{-ve}, \mathbf{+ve}\}$ is $\top$.) Thus we define Abs_{int} by

$$Abs_{int}\ S = \bigsqcup\{\alpha_{int}\ n | n \in S\}.$$

Finally we are able to define the concretisation map. For $z \in \mathbf{A}_{int}$,

$$\gamma_{int}\ z = \{n | (\alpha_{int}\ n) \sqsubseteq z\}$$

The concretisation map collects together all of the elements which abstract to something at most as defined as z. If we calculate what this means for each of the elements of $\mathbf{A}_{int}$, then we find that :

$$\begin{array}{ll} \gamma_{int}\ \perp & = \{\perp_{\mathbf{S}_{int}}\} \\ \gamma_{int}\ \mathbf{-ve} & = \{n | n < 0\} \cup \{\perp_{\mathbf{S}_{int}}\} \\ \gamma_{int}\ \mathbf{zero} & = \{0, \perp_{\mathbf{S}_{int}}\} \\ \gamma_{int}\ \mathbf{+ve} & = \{n | n > 0\} \cup \{\perp_{\mathbf{S}_{int}}\} \\ \gamma_{int}\ \top & = \mathbf{S}_{int} \end{array}$$

and so that indeed concretisation captures our notion of an element "representing" a set of values.

We can now state what we mean by correctness: for any expression e, if

$$\mathbf{A}\ [\![e]\!] = z$$

then we have that $\mathbf{S}\ [\![e]\!] \in (\gamma_{int}\ z)$. It can be shown that the abstract interpretation we have defined satisfies this property.

As an example of this, let us return to the previous example and ask the sign of the expression :

$$c_{29} \boxed{\times} c_{-33} \boxed{\times} c_{64}.$$

Our previous calculation showed that the real answer was -61248 and so the answer is negative. Doing the calculation in the abstract domain we obtain :

$$\mathbf{A}\ [\![c_{29}]\!] \mathbin{\overline{\times}} \mathbf{A}\ [\![c_{-33}]\!] \mathbin{\overline{\times}} \mathbf{A}\ [\![c_{64}]\!]$$

which is

$$\mathbf{+ve} \mathbin{\overline{\times}} \mathbf{-ve} \mathbin{\overline{\times}} \mathbf{+ve} = \mathbf{-ve}$$

If we concretise $\mathbf{-ve}$, we obtain the set of negative integers (plus $\bot_{\mathbf{S}_{int}}$), and so we are able to conclude (because of the correctness of the abstract interpretation) that the result really was negative.

There is another feature of abstract interpretation that can be shown using the rule of signs, that it does not give exact answers. For example,

$$\begin{aligned} \mathbf{A}\ [\![c_{-10} \boxed{+} c_{11}]\!] &= \mathbf{A}\ [\![c_{-10}]\!] \mathbin{\overline{+}} \mathbf{A}\ [\![c_{11}]\!] \\ &= \mathbf{-ve} \mathbin{\overline{+}} \mathbf{+ve} \\ &= \top \end{aligned}$$

whereas the sign of the real answer

$$\alpha_{int}\ (\mathbf{S}\ [\![c_{-10} \boxed{+} c_{11}]\!]) = \alpha_{int}\ 1$$

is $\mathbf{+ve}$, and so the abstract interpretation loses information, but in a safe way; the abstract interpretation may not be able to determine the sign of the answer, but does not wrongly conclude that it is negative (or some other wrong answer).

Those familiar with universal algebra will notice that we almost have that α_{int} is a homomorphism:

$$\begin{array}{ccc} \mathbf{S}_{int} \times \mathbf{S}_{int} & \xrightarrow{\ op\ } & \mathbf{S}_{int} \\ \Big\downarrow{\scriptstyle \alpha_{int} \times \alpha_{int}} & \sqsubseteq & \Big\downarrow{\scriptstyle \alpha_{int}} \\ \mathbf{A}_{int} \times \mathbf{A}_{int} & \xrightarrow[\ \overline{op}\ ]{} & \mathbf{A}_{int} \end{array}$$

where in the middle we have $\sqsubseteq$ to indicate that the path going along the top and down the right gives a value which is less defined than going down the left and along the bottom, that is

$$\alpha_{int} \circ op \sqsubseteq \overline{op} \circ (\alpha_{int} \times \alpha_{int}),$$

where op is one of $+$ and $\times$. The abstraction map, α_{int}, is then a *semi-homomorphism*, rather than a homomorphism (c.f. Proposition 3.2.12).

We can now summarise the key features of abstract interpretation:

- Given any language, meanings, or *interpretations*, must be given to terms constructed in the language.

- There may be several different interpretations of a language, and often these different interpretations are obtained by just changing the meanings of the constants in the language.

- Usually a language designer has one particular interpretation in mind, which we call the *standard* interpretation.

- By giving an *abstract* interpretation of the language, we may be able to answer questions about the standard interpretation with less computational effort.

- An abstract interpretation may not give exact answers, but the answers will be correct in the sense that they do not give any wrong information.

- To establish the correctness of an abstract interpretation, an abstraction map from the standard interpretation to the abstract interpretation of the language is defined, which induces the definition of a concretisation map that is used to define correctness.

1.4 Outline of Book

This book tells a complete story from the semantic foundations of lazy functional languages to their implementation on sequential and parallel machines. It is organised into the following chapters:

- **Chapter 2. Operational and Denotational Semantics of the Typed Lambda Calculus:** Functional programming languages can be translated into the typed lambda calculus, and so the typed lambda calculus is, in some sense, the canonical functional programming language. Moreover, it allows us to discuss properties of functional languages without being concerned about the concrete syntax of any particular language. The *operational* semantics of the typed lambda calculus tells us how functional languages can be implemented, and the freedom we have in their implementation. The *denotational* semantics gives the meanings of functional programs in terms of mathematical structures called *domains*. We provide a parameterised denotational semantics, so that different *interpretations* of the language can be given by changing some of the parameters. There is an important relationship between the two types of semantics, and we will ensure that this relationship is preserved when the evaluation transformer information is used to modify the operational semantics of programs. An introduction to the concepts of domain theory is provided; experts may find it worth scanning to pick up our notation.

- **Chapter 3. A Framework for the Abstract Interpretation of Functional Languages:**

  An abstract interpretation is defined to be *correct* if the inferences that can be made using it are correct with respect to the standard interpretation of the language (its usual denotational semantics). A framework is developed for defining correct abstract interpretations. By giving some specified items, a particular abstract interpretation can be defined to capture some property of interest.

- **Chapter 4. Some Example Abstract Interpretations:**

  We give examples of using the framework to define a number of particular abstract interpretations. One of them can be used to determine the evaluation transformers motivated in this chapter. We also show how two abstract interpretations can be combined to make a new one which captures more information.

- **Chapter 5. Evaluation Transformers:**

  The important property of an *evaluator* is that it divides the expressions of a particular type into two classes: those for which it terminates when evaluating an expression in the class, and those for which it does not. In an abstract interpretation, abstract domain points represent a particular class of expressions. Evaluators are therefore formally defined with respect to their behaviour on the class of expressions represented by an abstract domain point. Although it results in quite an abstract definition, the evaluators we discussed informally in this chapter arise naturally from one of the abstract interpretations that will be presented in Chapter 4. We are then able to show how evaluation transformers can be determined from any correct abstract interpretation, and that the resulting evaluation model preserves the important relationship between the operational and denotational semantics that is established in Chapter 2. It turns out that we need two different types of evaluation transformer information in an implementation – that true in any context in which a function is used, and that which is true in a particular application context.

- **Chapter 6. Implementing Functional Languages on Sequential and Parallel Machines:**

  The chapter begins by designing a graphical data structure and an algorithm so that lazy evaluation can be implemented on a computer. It then develops an abstract machine, and shows how to compile code to implement the reduction process. With this abstract machine as a basis, we show how to use the evaluation transformer information to generate more efficient code for *sequential* and *parallel* machines. The information is used in a sequential implementation to save the cost of building the graphs for some expressions, and to allow the parallel evaluation of expressions in a parallel implementation.

  This chapter brings to an end the main story-line of the book.

- **Chapter 7. Relationship to Other Work:**

  Here we give pointers to the wider literature on the subjects covered by this book.

- **Chapter 8. Epilogue:**

  Now that all the work has been done, this draws together all the threads, and makes the story-line explicit once again.

Two appendices are also included in this book. The first contains proofs omitted from Chapters 2–4, which are fairly technical, and would otherwise interrupt the flow of the book. It does, however, contain the proofs of a couple of important theorems about the operational semantics of the typed lambda calculus, which will be of interest to those who wish to know more about this subject. The second appendix contains a complete, executable specification of an abstract machine to execute lazy functional programs, and compilation rules to produce code for this machine. This can be used as a basis for incorporating the evaluation transformer information into sequential and parallel implementations, as discussed in Chapter 6.

An extensive index of symbols is given at the end of the book.

Chapter 2

Operational and Denotational Semantics of the Typed Lambda Calculus

The typed lambda calculus with constants plays an important role in the theory of functional programming. Programs in any functional language can be translated into the typed lambda calculus, and so it is, in a sense, the canonical functional programming language; it allows us to study properties of functional languages without referring to the specific concrete syntax of any particular language.

There are two viewpoints from which the typed lambda calculus can be studied. The first is as a term rewriting system, much as the way we introduced the execution of functional languages in Section 1.1. Such a viewpoint is essentially an *operational* semantics (or a proof theoretic viewpoint), showing how programs can be executed. Important questions that are asked of this semantics are: What is an answer from a program?; Do different execution orders give the same answer?; Can we be guaranteed to always get an answer from a program? The second viewpoint is model-theoretic, often associated with *denotational* semantics. Until the work of Scott in the late sixties [Sco70], the (untyped) lambda calculus was viewed with suspicion, as it was a formal system with no non-trivial mathematical model. If there had been no non-trivial model, then all the work on the lambda calculus from the operational view point would have been vacuous. Fortunately, Scott managed to construct a model.

Both ways of studying the typed lambda calculus are important to us in this book. The operational viewpoint tells us how we can implement the typed lambda calculus, and by analogy, lazy functional languages. Theorems about changing the execution order and terminating execution sequences give us the freedom we have in varying the implementation. Section 2.1 introduces the concepts that are important for this book. Conversely, the denotational viewpoint uses *domain theory* to give meanings to programs written in the typed lambda calculus. Various mathematical structures used in this book are introduced in Section 2.2. Most works on denotational semantics give descriptions of languages which model the standard meaning of the language, at whatever level the language is being studied, see for example [MS76, Sch86, Sto77]. The purpose of abstract interpretation is to find out information about a program without running it. We will therefore work with *interpretations* of a language, where the *standard* interpretation is the usual denotational semantics given to programs, whilst an *abstract* interpretation is obtained by giving different meanings to the symbols in the language, and is used to find properties of the standard interpretation. Interpretations are introduced in Section 2.3.

The Computational Adequacy Theorem establishes an important relationship between the operational and denotational viewpoints, and is crucial in using abstract interpretation information to change the operational behaviour of a program.

Proofs of theorems that have not been taken directly from the literature can be found in Section A.2.

2.1 The Typed Lambda-Calculus

This introduction to the concepts of the typed lambda calculus necessary for this book has been heavily influenced by the presentation of [Bar84], which we recommend for the serious student of the lambda calculus. Those who do not want to tackle [Bar84] may find [Gor88, Chapters 4–7] more accessible.

We will begin by introducing a typed lambda calculus with one base type and no constants. Executing programs is formalised by β-reduction. The Church-Rosser Theorem states that reduction order does not matter for terminating reduction sequences. Some typed lambda calculi have programs which allow infinite reduction sequences. It can be proved, for this first language, that choosing the leftmost redex at each reduction step produces an answer from a program in a finite number of steps, if an answer exists.

Most functional languages have a number of built-in types and typed constants, such as integers and plus. These can be added to the typed lambda calculus. The behaviour of functional constants, such as plus, can be modelled by special reduction rules, often called δ-rules (pronounced "delta-rules").

A particular typed lambda calculus is defined by giving its types, its typed constants and the delta-rules for the constants. In Section 2.1.6 we define the language Λ_T which will be used throughout the rest of the book. The language Λ_T is sufficiently powerful to encode most functional programs[1].

With each typed lambda calculus that is defined, we must ask again whether it satisfies the Church-Rosser Theorem, and whether there is a strategy for choosing the redexes which is guaranteed to produce an answer from a program, if one exists. The language Λ_T satisfies the Church-Rosser Theorem, and the leftmost reduction strategy has the desired property of producing answers from programs.

2.1.1 Syntax of a First Typed Lambda Calculus

Let B denote an arbitrary base type. Initially we will consider a language we will call Λ_1, whose set of types is the least set containing B and $(\sigma \rightarrow \tau)$ whenever it contains σ and τ. Intuitively, an expression of type $\sigma \rightarrow \tau$ is a function that takes an argument of type

[1]We say *most* for two reasons. Firstly, we restrict ourselves to programs which can be given (polymorphic) types by some sort of Hindley-Milner type checker. Secondly, we do not treat recursive types in a general way, but suggest how they can be dealt with by analogy with our treatment of lists and trees.

σ and returns a result of type τ. We adopt the convention that $\rightarrow$ associates to the right, and so we write:

$$\sigma_1 \rightarrow \sigma_2 \ldots \rightarrow \sigma_n$$

for

$$(\sigma_1 \rightarrow (\sigma_2 \rightarrow (\ldots \rightarrow \sigma_n) \ldots)).$$

Note that each type is of the form:

$$\sigma_1 \rightarrow \sigma_2 \ldots \rightarrow \sigma_n \rightarrow B$$

where $n \geq 0$. We will use σ and τ, possibly with subscripts, to stand for arbitrary types throughout this book.

Terms in the language are built from the following alphabet:

$x^\sigma, y^\sigma, z^\sigma \ldots$	variables for each type σ
$\lambda, (,), .$	auxiliary symbols

We will often drop the superscript from variables when it is clear from the context (or irrelevant).

The syntax of the language Λ_1 is defined inductively in Figure 2.1. If e is a term in the language and τ a type, the notation

$$e : \tau$$

means that e is a term of the language, and has type τ. Rules of the form:

$$(n)\ \frac{conditions}{conclusion}$$

mean that if the *conditions* are satisfied, then we can conclude the *conclusion*. For example, the rule labelled (3) can be read: "If e_1 is a term of the language with type $\sigma \rightarrow \tau$, and e_2 is a term of the language with type σ, then $(e_1\ e_2)$ is a term of the language with type τ". The numbers labelling the rules are so that they can be referred to later in the book. Label (2) is reserved for when typed constants are added to the language.

The term $(e_1\ e_2)$ means that the term e_1 is applied to e_2. This convention, that application is denoted by juxtaposition, is standard in all literature on the lambda calculus, and has been adopted by designers of lazy functional languages. We will adopt the further convention that application associates to the left, so that

$$e_1\ e_2\ \ldots\ e_n$$

is understood to mean

$$((\ldots(e_1\ e_2)\ \ldots)\ e_n).$$

Terms of the form $(\lambda x^\sigma.e)$ are called *lambda abstractions* (or λ-abstractions), and represent functions. More commonly in mathematics, such a function would be given a name, say f, and would have been written:

$$f\ x = e$$

The set T of types is the least set defined by:

$$\{B\} \subseteq T$$
$$\sigma, \tau \in T \Rightarrow \sigma \rightarrow \tau \in T$$

The type system of Λ_1

$$(1) \quad x^\sigma \; : \; \sigma$$

$$(3) \quad \frac{e_1 \; : \; \sigma \rightarrow \tau, \; e_2 \; : \; \sigma}{(e_1 \; e_2) \; : \; \tau}$$

$$(4) \quad \frac{e \; : \; \tau}{(\lambda x^\sigma . e) \; : \; \sigma \rightarrow \tau}$$

The syntax of Λ_1

Figure 2.1: The Language Λ_1 - A First Typed Lambda Calculus

We adopt the convention that λ's associate to the right, so that

$$\lambda x_1^{\sigma_1} . \lambda x_2^{\sigma_2} . \ldots . \lambda x_n^{\sigma_n} . e$$

means

$$(\lambda x_1^{\sigma_1} . (\lambda x_2^{\sigma_2} . (\ldots (\lambda x_n^{\sigma_n} . e) \ldots))).$$

Note that the association of $\rightarrow$ matches the association of λ.

Sometimes this language is called the *simple-* or *monomorphic*-typed lambda calculus in order to distinguish it from the *polymorphic-* or *second-order* typed lambda calculus. The polymorphically-typed lambda calculus allows type variables in the type of expressions.

2.1.2 Computation in the Typed Lambda Calculus

What does it mean to 'execute' a program written in the typed lambda calculus? Abstraction and application work together in the following intuitive way:

$$\begin{aligned} (\lambda x^\sigma . (\lambda y^\sigma . y^\sigma) \; x^\sigma) \; z^\sigma &= (\lambda y^\sigma . y^\sigma) \; z^\sigma \\ &= z^\sigma \end{aligned}$$

In the first step, the 'function' $(\lambda x^\sigma . (\lambda y^\sigma . y^\sigma) \; x^\sigma)$ is applied to the argument z^σ. Recalling our intuition that writing $(\lambda x^\sigma . (\lambda y^\sigma . y^\sigma) \; x^\sigma)$ is like defining the function:

$$f \; x^\sigma = (\lambda y^\sigma . y^\sigma) \; x^\sigma,$$

the application would be written in more familiar notation as $f\ z^\sigma$, and the result of the application is obtained by replacing all the (free) occurrences of x^σ in $(\lambda y^\sigma.y^\sigma)\ x^\sigma$ with z^σ, to get $(\lambda y^\sigma.y^\sigma)\ z^\sigma$. There is still another application in this term, so we apply the same rule again to get z^σ, and then there are no more applications. Computation therefore consists of repeatedly 'doing applications' until 'no more work needs to be done'. Let us formalise these concepts.

In order to formalise application, we need to define how an argument is *substituted* for a formal parameter, and to do this we need the concept of *free* and *bound* variables. An abstraction $\lambda x^\sigma.e$ is said to *bind* the variable x^σ, just as $\forall x.P$ binds x in predicate logic, and $\int_a^b e\ dx$ binds x in integral calculus. Given some term e, the set of free variables of e, denoted by $FV(e)$ is defined as follows:

$$\begin{aligned}
&FV(x^\sigma) = \{x^\sigma\}\\
&FV(e_1\ e_2) = FV(e_1) \bigcup FV(e_2)\\
&FV(\lambda x^\sigma.e) = FV(e) - \{x^\sigma\}
\end{aligned}$$

The term e *closed* (or is a *combinator*) if $FV(e) = \emptyset$. For example, in the term:

$$(\lambda z^{((\sigma\to\tau)\to\sigma\to\sigma)\to\sigma}.y^\sigma)\ (\lambda x^{\sigma\to\tau}.\lambda y^\sigma.x^{\sigma\to\tau}\ y^\sigma)$$

$x^{\sigma\to\tau}$ is a bound variable, and y^σ is free in its first occurrence and bound in its second. The term $(\lambda x^{\sigma\to\tau}.\lambda y^\sigma.x^{\sigma\to\tau}\ y^\sigma)$ is closed. Just as with variables in logic and integral calculus, the name of the bound variable is not significant; the terms

$$(\lambda z^{((\sigma\to\tau)\to\sigma\to\sigma)\to\sigma}.z^\sigma)\ (\lambda x^{\sigma\to\tau}.\lambda y^\sigma.x^{\sigma\to\tau}\ y^\sigma)$$

and

$$(\lambda r^{((\sigma\to\tau)\to\sigma\to\sigma)\to\sigma}.r^\sigma)\ (\lambda p^{\sigma\to\tau}.\lambda q^\sigma.p^{\sigma\to\tau}\ q^\sigma)$$

are regarded as equivalent.

The result of substituting e for all the free occurrences of x^σ in e', denoted by

$$e'[x^\sigma := e],$$

is defined as follows:

$$\begin{aligned}
x^\sigma[x^\sigma := e] &= e\\
y^\tau[x^\sigma := e] &= y^\tau \text{ if } y^\tau \neq x^\sigma\\
(e_1\ e_2)[x^\sigma := e] &= (e_1[x^\sigma := e])\ (e_2[x^\sigma := e])\\
(\lambda x^\sigma.e_1)[x^\sigma := e] &= (\lambda x^\sigma.e_1)\\
(\lambda y^\tau.e_1)[x^\sigma := e] &= \lambda y^\tau.(e_1[x^\sigma := e]),\\
&\quad \text{provided } y^\tau \text{ is not } x^\sigma \text{ and } y^\tau \text{ does not occur free in e.}\\
(\lambda y^\tau.e_1)[x^\sigma := e] &= \lambda z^\tau.((e_1[y^\tau := z^\tau])[x^\sigma := e]),\\
&\quad \text{provided } y^\tau \text{ is not } x^\sigma \text{ and } y^\tau \text{ occurs free in e and}\\
&\quad z^\tau \text{ is a new variable.}
\end{aligned}$$

We can now define the process of application. The application $(\lambda x^\sigma.e_1)\ e_2$ *one-step β reduces* to $e_1[x^\sigma := e_2]$, and this is written as:

$$(\lambda x^\sigma.e_1)\ e_2 \to_\beta e_1[x^\sigma := e_2].$$

The term $(\lambda x^\sigma.e_1)\ e_2$ is called a *redex*. More generally, if $(\lambda x^\sigma.e_1)\ e_2$ occurs as a subterm of some term e, and e' is obtained from e by replacing the term $(\lambda x^\sigma.e_1)\ e_2$ with $e_1[x^\sigma := e_2]$, then we will also say that $e \rightarrow_\beta e'$[2].

Now that we know how to perform applications, there are still a number of questions unanswered. For example, in the term:

$$(\lambda x^\sigma.(\lambda y^\sigma.y^\sigma)\ x^\sigma)\ z^\sigma,$$

there are two redexes, the whole term:

$$(\lambda x^\sigma.(\lambda y^\sigma.y^\sigma)\ x^\sigma)\ z^\sigma$$

and:

$$(\lambda y^\sigma.y^\sigma)\ x^\sigma.$$

Which one should we reduce first? Do we get different 'answers' depending on the choice that is made? What do we mean by an answer, that is, when should we stop performing reductions? These questions are addressed in the next section.

2.1.3 The Church-Rosser Property, Normal Forms and Reduction Strategies

Following the notation of [Bar84], we denote the reflexive, transitive closure of $\rightarrow_\beta$ by $\twoheadrightarrow_\beta$, that is, $e_1 \twoheadrightarrow_\beta e_2$ if e_2 can be obtained from e_1 by zero or more uses of one-step β-reduction, and say that e_1 *β-reduces* to e_2.

The *Church-Rosser property* is a very important property that holds for some reduction systems.

Definition 2.1.1

> Suppose that $\rhd$ denotes some sort of one-step reduction on a language Λ, and that $\rhd^*$ is its reflexive, transitive closure, then $\rhd^*$ has the Church-Rosser property for the language Λ if for all terms e of Λ, if $e \rhd^* e_1$ and $e \rhd^* e_2$, then there exists an e_3 such that $e_1 \rhd^* e_3$ and $e_2 \rhd^* e_3$.
>
> Sometimes it is called the *diamond property* as it can be represented diagrammatically by:

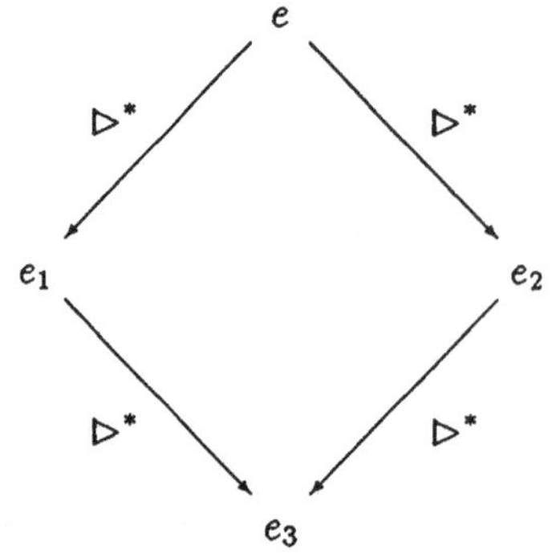

[2] This notion can be formalised using a language of *contexts* and the interested reader is referred to [Bar84, Definition 2.1.18 and pages 50ff.] or [BCL85].

Informally, the Church-Rosser property is important because it says that, for any finite one-step reduction sequence, the choice of redex does not matter, for if any other choice is made, then there is a common term to which the results of both reduction sequences can be reduced.

Theorem 2.1.2 (Church-Rosser Theorem)

> *The language Λ_1 with β-reduction has the Church-Rosser property, that is, if $e \twoheadrightarrow_\beta e_1$ and $e \twoheadrightarrow_\beta e_2$, then there exists an e_3 such that $e_1 \twoheadrightarrow_\beta e_3$ and $e_2 \twoheadrightarrow_\beta e_3$.*

The proof of this theorem can be found in [Bar84, Appendix A].

When should a computation stop? One obvious criterion is when there are no more redexes in the expression being reduced. Such an expression is called a *normal form*, and if a term e_1 has e_2 as a normal form, we have that there is some reduction sequence such that $e_1 \twoheadrightarrow_\beta e_2$ [Bar84, Corollary 3.1.13]. If we are to model the implementation of lazy functional languages, we have already seen in Section 1.1.2 that attempting to reduce terms to normal form may result in an undesired infinite reduction sequence. Moreover, there are sound theoretical reasons for not considering normal forms to be the result of computations (because this implies identifying all terms without normal forms, and doing so results in an inconsistent theory – see Section 2.2 of [Bar84], especially Proposition 2.2.4 and the discussion on pages 41–43). Therefore the notion of *head normal form* is defined.

Definition 2.1.3

A term e is a *head normal form*[3] (abbreviated *HNF*), if it is of the form:

$$\lambda x_1^{\sigma_1}. \ldots \lambda x_n^{\sigma_n}.y^\tau \; e_1 \; \ldots \; e_m$$

where $m \geq 0$, $n \geq 0$ and y^τ is some variable (maybe one of the $x_i^{\sigma_i}$).

The function *inHNF* is defined by:

$$inHNF\; e = \begin{cases} true & \text{if e is an HNF} \\ false & \text{otherwise} \end{cases}$$

If e is of the form:

$$\lambda x_1^{\sigma_1}. \ldots \lambda x_n^{\sigma_n}.(\lambda x^\tau.e_0) \; e_1 \; \ldots \; e_n$$

then $(\lambda x^\tau.e_0)\; e_1$ is called the *head-redex* of e.

Head normal forms are not necessarily unique. For example,

$$\lambda x^{\sigma\to\tau}.x^{\sigma\to\tau} \; ((\lambda y^\sigma.y^\sigma) \; z^\sigma)$$

and

$$\lambda x^{\sigma\to\tau}.x^{\sigma\to\tau} \; z^\sigma$$

[3] We will revise this definition in Section 2.1.6 after the full language Λ_T has been introduced.

are both head normal forms of the term

$$(\lambda p^{\tau}.(\lambda x^{\sigma\to\tau}.x^{\sigma\to\tau}\ ((\lambda y^{\sigma}.y^{\sigma})\ z^{\sigma})))\ q^{\tau}.$$

Nevertheless, we will say that the reduction of a term should proceed until a term in HNF is reached, and ask whether there is a some strategy for choosing redexes such that, if a term has an HNF, then an HNF will be found using this strategy.

Definition 2.1.4

A *one-step reduction strategy* for a language Λ is a map, $F : \Lambda \to \Lambda$, if for all $e \in \Lambda$ not in HNF,

$$e \to_{\beta} F(e).$$

A *reduction strategy* is a map $F : \Lambda \to \Lambda$, if for all $e \in \Lambda$,

$$e \twoheadrightarrow_{\beta} F(e).$$

In words, a one-step reduction strategy is a way of choosing the next redex to reduce at each stage of a reduction sequence. The condition that $e \to_{\beta} F(e)$ means that e must actually reduce to the term $F(e)$ in one step, that is, $F(e)$ must be obtained from e by reducing one redex. Because F is a mapping, for each $e \in \Lambda$ not in HNF, there is a unique redex it chooses. Clearly we will only be interested in computable reduction strategies, that is, given some term e in Λ, $F(e)$ can be computed. Moreover, we are interested in reduction strategies which will find an HNF of a term if one exists.

Definition 2.1.5

We will say that a reduction strategy, F, is *head-normalising* if for all e in some language Λ which have an HNF, $F^n(e)$ is an HNF for some finite integer n.

We now define the *head-reduction* strategy, which will always terminate with an HNF for a term if it exists.

Definition 2.1.6

The one-step head-reduction strategy, F_h, is defined as follows:

$$\begin{aligned} F_h(e) &= e \quad \text{if } e \text{ is an HNF} \\ &= e' \quad \text{if } e \to_{\beta} e' \text{ is the head-reduction} \end{aligned}$$

Theorem 2.1.7

F_h is a head-normalising one-step reduction strategy for Λ_1 [Bar84, Theorem 13.2.2].

In other words, if some term e has a head normal form, then we are guaranteed to be able to find one if at each reduction step we always reduce the head redex.

2.1.4 The Untyped Lambda Calculus

There are also many flavours of untyped lambda calculi, usually just referred to as the lambda calculi, dropping the 'untyped'. Terms in a lambda calculus are built in the same way as terms from the typed language, from variables, applications and abstractions, except that variables and abstractions are not decorated with types, and applications do not have to satisfy any type constraints. This allows terms to be written which could not be written in the typed calculus, The classic example of such a term is one involving the self-application of a variable, $(x\ x)$ for example, which cannot be given any (finite) type.

All the concepts we have introduced so far, such as β-reduction and head normal forms are the same for the untyped theory. In effect, the typed lambda calculus imposes a restriction on the set of terms that can be built – that they be typed correctly – but once the terms have been built, calculations are performed in the same way. There is a rich body of knowledge about the lambda calculus, see [Bar84] for example. Although the typed and untyped lambda calculus have some subtle differences, we will be able to carry over some theorems about reduction from the untyped calculus to the typed calculus since β-reduction of a typed term can be mimicked by the β-reduction of an equivalent untyped term.

2.1.5 Adding Constants to the Typed Lambda-Calculus

We have used the language Λ_1 to introduce a number of important concepts. It does not look like the functional languages we are familiar with. Where, for example, are all the constants like the integers and arithmetic operators, and how do we express recursion? Not only is the language unfamiliar, but it is theoretically weak in terms of the class of functions that can be written in it [Bar84, Appendix A],[Bar91b]. In fact, β-reduction is *strongly normalising* for Λ_1, that is, every reduction sequence starting from some term is guaranteed to terminate in its unique normal form [Bar84, Theorem A.1.7]. Any computer programmer knows that it is easy to write programs which do not terminate, and so intuitively Λ_1 does not provide us with the power to describe every computer program. To make the language sufficiently powerful, we need to add constants and recursion.

As an illustration of adding constants and recursion to Λ_1, the language Λ_2 is defined in Figures 2.2 and 2.3. It has *bool* and *int* as base types, and a few typed constants: the boolean constants, $\mathbf{true}_{bool}$ and $\mathbf{false}_{bool}$, an integer constant, m_{int}, for each integer m, a conditional on each type σ, $\mathbf{if}_{bool \to \sigma \to \sigma \to \sigma}$, and $+_{int \to int \to int}$ for integer addition. Rule (2) in Figure 2.2 is an abbreviation for saying that, if c_σ is any constant from Figure 2.3, then it is a term in Λ_2. Recursion is encoded using $\mathbf{fix}_{(\sigma \to \sigma) \to \sigma}$. Λ_2 is sufficient for writing programs which do not terminate, and for discussing the issues concerning computation in a typed lambda calculus with constants.

The notion of reduction must be modified to include applications of $+_{int \to int \to int}$, $\mathbf{if}_{bool \to \sigma \to \sigma \to \sigma}$ and $\mathbf{fix}_{(\sigma \to \sigma) \to \sigma}$. Reduction rules for constants are usually called δ-rules. If e_1 reduces to e_2 using a δ-rule, and e' is obtained from e by replacing one occurrence of e_1 with e_2, then we will write $e \to_\delta e'$ and say that e_1 one-step δ-reduces to e'.

Let us see how we might define the δ-rules for the constant $+_{int \to int \to int}$. Clearly, if $e_1 : int$ and $e_2 : int$ are arbitrary terms in Λ_2, it is not possible in general to reduce the

The set T of types is the least set defined by:

$$\{bool, int\} \subseteq T$$
$$\sigma, \tau \in T \Rightarrow \sigma \to \tau \in T$$

The type system of Λ_2

$$(1)\quad x^\sigma : \sigma$$

$$(2)\quad c_\sigma : \sigma$$

$$(3)\quad \frac{e_1 : \sigma \to \tau,\ e_2 : \sigma}{(e_1\ e_2) : \tau}$$

$$(4)\quad \frac{e : \tau}{(\lambda x^\sigma.e) : \sigma \to \tau}$$

$$(5)\quad \frac{e : \sigma \to \sigma}{\mathbf{fix}_{(\sigma\to\sigma)\to\sigma}\ e : \sigma}$$

The syntax of Λ_2

Figure 2.2: The Language Λ_2 - A Typed Lambda Calculus with Constants

$\mathbf{true}_{bool}$	$\mathbf{false}_{bool}$	$\mathbf{if}_{bool\to\sigma\to\sigma\to\sigma}$
$\{\mathbf{0}_{int}, \mathbf{1}_{int}, \mathbf{2}_{int}, \ldots\}$	$+_{int\to int\to int}$	

Figure 2.3: The Constants Used In Λ_2

$$+_{int\to int\to int}\ \mathrm{m}_{int}\ \mathrm{n}_{int} \to_\delta (\mathrm{m} + \mathrm{n})_{int}$$
$$\mathbf{if}_{bool\to\sigma\to\sigma\to\sigma}\ \mathbf{true}_{bool}\ e_1\ e_2 \to_\delta e_1$$
$$\mathbf{if}_{bool\to\sigma\to\sigma\to\sigma}\ \mathbf{false}_{bool}\ e_1\ e_2 \to_\delta e_2$$

Figure 2.4: δ-rule Schemata for the Constants in Λ_2

application:

$$+_{int \to int \to int}\ e_1\ e_2.$$

Such an application can only be reduced if e_1 and e_2 have been reduced to integer constants, say $\mathbf{0}_{int}$ and $\mathbf{1}_{int}$, and then

$$+_{int \to int \to int}\ \mathbf{0}_{int}\ \mathbf{1}_{int} \rightarrow_\delta (\mathbf{0} + \mathbf{1})_{int} = \mathbf{1}_{int}.$$

So the δ-rules for $+_{int \to int \to int}$ are going to be of the form:

$$\begin{array}{llll} +_{int \to int \to int}\ \mathbf{0}_{int}\ \mathbf{0}_{int} & \rightarrow_\delta\ \mathbf{0}_{int} & +_{int \to int \to int}\ \mathbf{0}_{int}\ \mathbf{1}_{int} & \rightarrow_\delta\ \mathbf{1}_{int} \\ +_{int \to int \to int}\ \mathbf{1}_{int}\ \mathbf{0}_{int} & \rightarrow_\delta\ \mathbf{1}_{int} & +_{int \to int \to int}\ \mathbf{0}_{int}\ \mathbf{2}_{int} & \rightarrow_\delta\ \mathbf{2}_{int} \\ \ldots & & & \end{array}$$

In fact, there are going to be an infinite number of δ-rules for $+_{int \to int \to int}$, one for each possible pair of integer constants. All the rules can be loosely represented by the schema given in Figure 2.4, where $\mathbf{m}_{int}$ and $\mathbf{n}_{int}$ are understood to range over all integer constants, and $(\mathbf{m} + \mathbf{n})_{int}$ is $\mathbf{k}_{int}$ if $(m + n) = k$. The δ-rules for the constant $\mathbf{if}_{bool \to \sigma \to \sigma \to \sigma}$ are also given in Figure 2.4.

The term constructor $\mathbf{fix}_{(\sigma \to \sigma) \to \sigma}$ is added to encode recursion. It has the reduction rule:

$$\mathbf{fix}_{(\sigma \to \sigma) \to \sigma}\ e \rightarrow_\delta e\ (\mathbf{fix}_{(\sigma \to \sigma) \to \sigma}\ e)$$

that is, given some expression e, $(\mathbf{fix}_{(\sigma \to \sigma) \to \sigma}\ e)$ is a *fixed point* of e. With the introduction of $\mathbf{fix}_{(\sigma \to \sigma) \to \sigma}$, it is possible to write terms in Λ_2 without HNFs. For example, the term

$$\mathbf{fix}_{(\sigma \to \sigma) \to \sigma}\ (\lambda x^\sigma . x^\sigma)$$

can be proved to have no HNF using the Head-Normalisation Theorem. Sometimes $\mathbf{fix}_{(\sigma \to \sigma) \to \sigma}$ is called $\mathbf{Y}$ in combinatory logic. It is possible to define $\mathbf{Y}$ in the untyped lambda calculus:

$$\mathbf{Y} = \lambda f.(\lambda x.f\ (x\ x))\ (\lambda x.f\ (x\ x))$$

but it is not possible in the typed lambda calculus as it involves the self-application of x, which cannot be given a (finite) type. In fact, it is not possible to define any term in Λ_2 which has the behaviour of $\mathbf{fix}_{(\sigma \to \sigma) \to \sigma}$ without using $\mathbf{fix}_{(\sigma \to \sigma) \to \sigma}$.

In the language Λ_2, there are two types of reduction steps that can be done, either a one-step β-reduction, or a one-step δ-reduction. We will say that e_1 *one-step $\beta\delta$-reduces* to e_2, written as $e_1 \rightarrow_{\beta\delta} e_2$, if either $e_1 \rightarrow_\beta e_2$ or $e_1 \rightarrow_\delta e_2$, and that e_1 $\beta\delta$-reduces to e_2, written $e_1 \twoheadrightarrow_{\beta\delta} e_2$, if e_2 results from e_1 by performing zero or more one-step $\beta\delta$-reductions.

It is necessary to consider whether Λ_2 with $\twoheadrightarrow_{\beta\delta}$ has the Church-Rosser property. That it does is not trivial, for the property is fragile. For the untyped lambda calculus, the classical example of the violation of this property is *surjective pairing*. It is obtained by adding constants P, P_1 and P_2 and δ-rules:

$$\begin{array}{ll} P_i\ (P\ e_1\ e_2) \rightarrow_\delta e_i, & i \in \{1, 2\} \\ P\ (P_1\ e)\ (P_2\ e) \rightarrow_\delta e & \end{array}$$

This example is extensively discussed in [Bar84, p. 403ff]. The fact that Λ_2 with $\twoheadrightarrow_{\beta\delta}$ has the Church-Rosser property follows from the theorem below, due originally to [Mit76], but cited as Theorem 15.3.3 of [Bar84], which gives sufficient conditions for a typed lambda calculus with constants to be Church-Rosser.

Theorem 2.1.8

Let c_σ be some constant. Let $R_1, \ldots, R_m \subseteq (\Lambda^n)$ be n-ary relations on Λ, a typed lambda calculus with constants, and let $N_1, \ldots, N_m$ be arbitrary. Suppose that the δ-rules for the constant c_σ are given by:

$$\begin{array}{l} c_\sigma\ M_1\ \ldots\ M_n \rightarrow_\delta N_1 \text{ if } R_1(M_1,\ldots,M_n) \\ \vdots \\ c_\sigma\ M_1\ \ldots\ M_n \rightarrow_\delta N_m \text{ if } R_m(M_1,\ldots,M_n) \end{array}$$

Then $\twoheadrightarrow_{\beta\delta}$ is Church-Rosser provided that

1. *The R_i are disjoint.*
2. *The R_i are closed under $\rightarrow_{\beta\delta}$ and substitution, that is,*

   $$R_i(M_1,\ldots,M_{j-1},M_j,M_{j+1},\ldots,M_n) \Rightarrow R_i(M_1,\ldots,M_{j-1},M_j',M_{j+1},\ldots,M_n)$$

   if $M_j \rightarrow_{\beta\delta} M_j'$ or $M_j' = M_j[x := M']$ for some variable x and term M'.

This theorem is actually stated for the untyped lambda calculus, but carries over to the typed lambda calculus by the observations we made in Section 2.1.4. Note that, for the untyped lambda calculus, the δ-rules for surjective pairing fail to satisfy the conditions of the above theorem because for each term e, there is a δ-rule

$$P\ (P_1\ e)\ (P_2\ e) \rightarrow_\delta e,$$

where the implicit relation is $R(e, e')$ if and only if e is syntactically equal to e', which is not preserved under $\rightarrow_{\beta\delta}$.

Corollary 2.1.9

$\beta\delta$-reduction for Λ_2 has the Church-Rosser property.

2.1.6 The Language Λ_T

The language to be used throughout the rest of the book is defined in Figures 2.5–2.7. We have called it Λ_T, where the Λ reminds us that it is a lambda calculus, and the subscript T that it is a *typed* lambda calculus. Note that the δ-rules for the constants in Λ_T are an integral part of the language definition, as changing them can alter the behaviour of the language. The language has been designed so that most functional programs can be translated into it. Some important features of the language are discussed in the following paragraphs.

Λ_T allows types to be constructed using product, smash product, smash sum[4] and lifting[5], has syntactic constructs which give terms of these constructed types ($\mathbf{tuple}_{(\sigma_1,\ldots,\sigma_k)}$,

[4]We shall see that sum can be defined using smash sum and lifting, and so there is no loss in generality in omitting it from the types in Λ_T.

[5]A lifted type typically arises in an algebraic type declaration:

```
> newtype ::= Tag oldtype
```

The set T of types is the least set defined by:

$$\{bool, int\} \subseteq T$$
$$\sigma, \tau \in T \Rightarrow (\sigma \rightarrow \tau) \in T$$
$$\sigma_1, \ldots, \sigma_k \in T \Rightarrow (\sigma_1 \times \ldots \times \sigma_k) \in T$$
$$\sigma_1, \ldots, \sigma_k \in T \Rightarrow (\sigma_1 \otimes \ldots \otimes \sigma_k) \in T$$
$$\sigma_1, \ldots, \sigma_k \in T \Rightarrow (\sigma_1 \oplus \ldots \oplus \sigma_k) \in T$$
$$\sigma \in T \Rightarrow (lift\ \sigma) \in T$$
$$\sigma \in T \Rightarrow (list\ \sigma) \in T$$
$$\sigma \in T \Rightarrow (tree\ \sigma) \in T$$

The type system of Λ_T

(1) $x^\sigma : \sigma$

(2) $c_\sigma : \sigma$

(3) $$\frac{e_1 : \sigma \rightarrow \tau,\ e_2 : \sigma}{(e_1\ e_2) : \tau}$$

(4) $$\frac{e : \tau}{(\lambda x^\sigma . e) : \sigma \rightarrow \tau}$$

(5) $$\frac{e : \sigma \rightarrow \sigma}{\mathbf{fix}_{(\sigma\rightarrow\sigma)\rightarrow\sigma}\ e : \sigma}$$

(6) $$\frac{e_1 : \sigma,\ e_2 : \tau}{(\mathbf{let}\ x^\sigma = e_1\ \mathbf{in}\ e_2) : \tau}$$

(7) $$\frac{\forall i \in \{1, \ldots, k\} : e_i : \sigma_i}{\mathbf{tuple}_{(\sigma_1,\ldots,\sigma_k)}(e_1, \ldots, e_k) : \sigma_1 \times \ldots \times \sigma_k}$$

(8) $$\frac{\forall i \in \{1, \ldots, k\} : e_i : \sigma_i}{\mathbf{tuples}_{(\sigma_1,\ldots,\sigma_k)}(e_1, \ldots, e_k) : \sigma_1 \otimes \ldots \otimes \sigma_k}$$

(9) $$\frac{e : \sigma_i}{\mathbf{ins}_{\mathbf{i}(\sigma_1,\ldots,\sigma_k)}\ e : \sigma_1 \oplus \ldots \oplus \sigma_k}$$

(10) $$\frac{e : \sigma}{\mathbf{lift}_\sigma\ e : lift\ \sigma}$$

The syntax of Λ_T

Figure 2.5: The Language Λ_T - A Typed Lambda Calculus with Constants

$\mathbf{true}_{bool}$ $\mathbf{false}_{bool}$
$\mathbf{and}_{bool \to bool \to bool}$ $\mathbf{or}_{bool \to bool \to bool}$
$\mathbf{if}_{bool \to \sigma \to \sigma \to \sigma}$

$\{\mathbf{0}_{int}, \mathbf{1}_{int}, \mathbf{2}_{int}, \ldots\}$
$+_{int \to int \to int}$ $*_{int \to int \to int}$
$-_{int \to int \to int}$ $/_{int \to int \to int}$

$<_{int \to int \to bool}$ $\leq_{int \to int \to bool}$
$<_{int \to int \to bool}$ $\leq_{int \to int \to bool}$
$=_{int \to int \to bool}$

$\mathbf{nil}_{(list\ \tau)}$ $\mathbf{cons}_{\tau \to (list\ \tau) \to (list\ \tau)}$
$\mathbf{head}_{(list\ \tau) \to \tau}$ $\mathbf{tail}_{(list\ \tau) \to (list\ \tau)}$
$\mathbf{lcase}_{(list\ \tau) \to \sigma \to (\tau \to (list\ \tau) \to \sigma) \to \sigma}$

$\mathbf{empty}_{(tree\ \tau)}$ $\mathbf{node}_{(tree\ \tau) \to \tau \to (tree\ \tau) \to (tree\ \tau)}$
$\mathbf{value}_{(tree\ \tau) \to \tau}$ $\mathbf{left}_{(tree\ \tau) \to (tree\ \tau)}$
$\mathbf{right}_{(tree\ \tau) \to (tree\ \tau)}$
$\mathbf{tcase}_{(tree\ \tau) \to \sigma \to ((tree\ \tau) \to \tau \to (tree\ \tau) \to \sigma) \to \sigma}$

$\mathbf{take}_{\mathbf{i}\, \sigma_1 \times \ldots \times \sigma_k \to \sigma_i}$
$\mathbf{takes}_{\mathbf{i}\, \sigma_1 \otimes \ldots \otimes \sigma_k \to \sigma_i}$
$\mathbf{outs}_{\mathbf{i}\, \sigma_1 \oplus \ldots \oplus \sigma_k \to \sigma_i}$ $\mathbf{iss}_{\mathbf{i}\, \sigma_1 \oplus \ldots \oplus \sigma_k \to bool}$

Figure 2.6: The Constants Used In Λ_T

$\mathbf{tuples}_{(\sigma_1,\ldots,\sigma_k)}$, $\mathbf{ins}_{i(\sigma_1,\ldots,\sigma_k)}$ and $\mathbf{lift}_\sigma$ respectively), and a number of constants are defined over these types. Most functional languages have a number of built-in types, such as boolean and integer, and allow new types to be constructed using products, sums, lifting and recursion. Often recursive data types, such as lists, are also given as primitives in the language. The only feature missing from Λ_T is the ability to define recursive types. The reason for this restriction is that the standard way of interpreting recursive types often results in infinite sets containing infinite objects of that type. We want to give finite abstract interpretations to all types, as this guarantees the computability of an abstract interpretation, and so recursive types need to be treated in a somewhat ad-hoc manner. Instead, we treat two examples of recursive types, namely lists and binary trees. Nevertheless, we are able to give intuitions about defining abstract interpretations of such types, and use lists and trees as examples.

Expressions such as

$$\mathbf{head}_{(list\ \tau)\to\tau}\ \mathbf{nil}_{(list\ \tau)}$$

are normally treated as errors in an implementation, causing the execution of a program to stop with some error message like "Tried to take head of nil". Unfortunately, most denotational semantic definitions do not handle such errors in a clean way, and will typically give $\bot_{\mathbf{S}_\tau}$ as the meaning of the above expression, as we will in fact do. We shall see that there is a very important relationship between the operational and denotational viewpoints of Λ_T, namely that there is a reduction strategy (the leftmost reduction reduction strategy to be defined later) which, for any term $e : \sigma$, fails to terminate if and only if the denotational semantics of e is $\bot_{\mathbf{S}_\sigma}$. The reason for curious δ-rules like:

$$\mathbf{head}_{(list\ \tau)\to\tau}\ \mathbf{nil}_{(list\ \tau)} \to_\delta \mathbf{head}_{(list\ \tau)\to\tau}\ \mathbf{nil}_{(list\ \tau)}$$

is that they ensure that leftmost reduction of such a term will fail to terminate, preserving the relationship between the two viewpoints of Λ_T.

There is one other new syntactic construct in Λ_T:

$$\mathbf{let}\ x^\sigma = e_1\ \mathbf{in}\ e_2,$$

often called a *let-expression*. Primarily we have added it so that we can give a δ-rule for $\mathbf{tuples}_{(\sigma_1,\ldots,\sigma_k)}(e_1,\ldots,e_k)$ which forces each of the e_i to be evaluated to HNF. It also allows the programmer to write terms in a more structured way by naming particular subexpressions. Just as the λ in $\lambda x^\sigma.e$ binds all the free occurrences of x^σ in e, the let-expression binds all the free occurrences of x^σ in e_2. The intended meaning of the let-expression is that it should first try to evaluate e_1 to HNF. If the reduction terminates, then the HNF of e_1 is substituted for all the free occurrences of x_σ in e_2. Leftmost reduction and the only δ-rule for the let-expression:

$$\mathbf{let}\ x^\sigma = e_1\ \mathbf{in}\ e_2 \to_\delta e_2[x^\sigma := e_1], \quad \text{if } (inHNF\ e_1)$$

where all the terms of type `newtype` are just terms of type `oldtype`, but with the tag `Tag`. The head normal form of an expression of type `newtype` is a term of the form `Tag e`, where no evaluation has been done to `e`, so if $\mathbf{S}\ [\![e]\!]\ \{\}$ was bottom, then the evaluation of the expression to `Tag e` would terminate, whereas the evaluation of `e` (of type `oldtype`) would not. Lifting is modelled in domain theory by adding a new bottom element, and tagging all the elements from the old domain.

$$+_{int\to int\to int}\ \mathrm{m}_{int}\ \mathrm{n}_{int} \to_\delta (\mathrm{m}+\mathrm{n})_{int} \qquad *_{int\to int\to int}\ \mathrm{m}_{int}\ \mathrm{n}_{int} \to_\delta (\mathrm{m}*\mathrm{n})_{int}$$

$$-_{int\to int\to int}\ \mathrm{m}_{int}\ \mathrm{n}_{int} \to_\delta (\mathrm{m}-\mathrm{n})_{int} \qquad /_{int\to int\to int}\ \mathrm{m}_{int}\ \mathrm{n}_{int} \to_\delta (\mathrm{m}/\mathrm{n})_{int}$$

$$<_{int\to int\to bool}\ \mathrm{m}_{int}\ \mathrm{n}_{int} \to_\delta \begin{cases} \mathbf{true}_{bool} & \text{if } (\mathrm{m}<\mathrm{n}) \\ \mathbf{false}_{bool} & \text{otherwise} \end{cases}$$

and similarly for $\leq_{int\to int\to bool}$, $<_{int\to int\to bool}$, $\leq_{int\to int\to bool}$ and $=_{int\to int\to bool}$

$$\mathbf{and}_{bool\to bool\to bool}\ \mathbf{true}_{bool}\ \mathbf{true}_{bool} \to_\delta \mathbf{true}_{bool}$$

and similarly for the 3 other cases and for $\mathbf{or}_{bool\to bool\to bool}$

$$\mathbf{if}_{bool\to\sigma\to\sigma\to\sigma}\ \mathbf{true}_{bool}\ e_2\ e_3 \to_\delta e_2$$
$$\mathbf{if}_{bool\to\sigma\to\sigma\to\sigma}\ \mathbf{false}_{bool}\ e_2\ e_3 \to_\delta e_3$$

$$\mathbf{head}_{(list\ \tau)\to\tau}\ \mathbf{nil}_{(list\ \tau)} \to_\delta \mathbf{head}_{(list\ \tau)\to\tau}\ \mathbf{nil}_{(list\ \tau)}$$
$$\mathbf{head}_{(list\ \tau)\to\tau}\ (\mathbf{cons}_{\tau\to(list\ \tau)\to(list\ \tau)}\ e_1\ e_2) \to_\delta e_1$$
$$\mathbf{tail}_{(list\ \tau)\to(list\ \tau)}\ \mathbf{nil}_{(list\ \tau)} \to_\delta \mathbf{tail}_{(list\ \tau)\to(list\ \tau)}\ \mathbf{nil}_{(list\ \tau)}$$
$$\mathbf{tail}_{(list\ \tau)\to(list\ \tau)}\ (\mathbf{cons}_{\tau\to(list\ \tau)\to(list\ \tau)}\ e_1\ e_2) \to_\delta e_2$$
$$\mathbf{lcase}_{(list\ \tau)\to\sigma\to(\tau\to(list\ \tau)\to\sigma)\to\sigma}\ \mathbf{nil}_{(list\ \tau)}\ e_1\ e_2 \to_\delta e_1$$
$$\mathbf{lcase}_{(list\ \tau)\to\sigma\to(\tau\to(list\ \tau)\to\sigma)\to\sigma}\ (\mathbf{cons}_{\tau\to(list\ \tau)\to(list\ \tau)}\ e_1\ e_2)\ e_3\ e_4 \to_\delta e_4\ e_1\ e_2$$

$$\mathbf{value}_{(tree\ \tau)\to\tau}\ \mathbf{empty}_{(tree\ \tau)} \to_\delta \mathbf{value}_{(tree\ \tau)\to\tau}\ \mathbf{empty}_{(tree\ \tau)}$$
$$\mathbf{value}_{(tree\ \tau)\to\tau}\ (\mathbf{node}_{(tree\ \tau)\to\tau\to(tree\ \tau)\to(tree\ \tau)}\ t_1\ n\ t_2) \to_\delta n$$
$$\mathbf{left}_{(tree\ \tau)\to(tree\ \tau)}\ \mathbf{empty}_{(tree\ \tau)} \to_\delta \mathbf{left}_{(tree\ \tau)\to(tree\ \tau)}\ \mathbf{empty}_{(tree\ \tau)}$$
$$\mathbf{left}_{(tree\ \tau)\to(tree\ \tau)}\ (\mathbf{node}_{(tree\ \tau)\to\tau\to(tree\ \tau)\to(tree\ \tau)}\ t_1\ n\ t_2) \to_\delta t_1$$
$$\mathbf{right}_{(tree\ \tau)\to(tree\ \tau)}\ \mathbf{empty}_{(tree\ \tau)} \to_\delta \mathbf{right}_{(tree\ \tau)\to(tree\ \tau)}\ \mathbf{empty}_{(tree\ \tau)}$$
$$\mathbf{right}_{(tree\ \tau)\to(tree\ \tau)}\ (\mathbf{node}_{(tree\ \tau)\to\tau\to(tree\ \tau)\to(tree\ \tau)}\ t_1\ n\ t_2) \to_\delta t_2$$
$$\mathbf{tcase}_{(tree\ \tau)\to\sigma\to((tree\ \tau)\to\tau\to(tree\ \tau)\to\sigma)\to\sigma}\ \mathbf{empty}_{(tree\ \tau)}\ e_1\ e_2 \to_\delta e_1$$
$$\mathbf{tcase}_{(tree\ \tau)\to\sigma\to((tree\ \tau)\to\tau\to(tree\ \tau)\to\sigma)\to\sigma}\ (\mathbf{node}_{(tree\ \tau)\to\tau\to(tree\ \tau)\to(tree\ \tau)}\ e_1\ e_2\ e_3)\ e_4\ e_5 \\ \to_\delta e_5\ e_1\ e_2\ e_3$$

$$\mathbf{let}\ x^\sigma = e_1\ \mathbf{in}\ e_2 \to_\delta e_2[x^\sigma := e_1], \quad \text{if } (inHNF\ e_1)$$

$$\begin{aligned} \mathbf{tuples}_{(\sigma_1,\ldots,\sigma_k)}(e_1,\ldots,e_k) \to_\delta\ & \mathbf{let}\ x_1 = e_1\ \mathbf{in} \\ & \mathbf{let}\ x_2 = e_2\ \mathbf{in} \\ & \quad \ddots \\ & \qquad \mathbf{let}\ x_k = e_k\ \mathbf{in}\ \mathbf{tuples}_{(\sigma_1,\ldots,\sigma_k)}(x_1,\ldots,x_k) \\ & \qquad \text{if } \exists i \in \{1,\ldots,k\} : \neg(inHNF\ e_i) \end{aligned}$$

$$\mathbf{take}_{\mathbf{i}\,\sigma_1\times\ldots\times\sigma_k\to\sigma_i}(\mathbf{tuple}_{(\sigma_1,\ldots,\sigma_k)}(e_1\ \ldots\ e_k)) \to_\delta e_i$$
$$\mathbf{takes}_{\mathbf{i}\,\sigma_1\otimes\ldots\otimes\sigma_k\to\sigma_i}(\mathbf{tuples}_{(\sigma_1,\ldots,\sigma_k)}(e_1\ \ldots\ e_k)) \to_\delta e_i \text{ if } \forall j \in \{1,\ldots k\},\ (inHNF\ e_j)$$

$$\mathbf{outs}_{\mathbf{i}\,\sigma_1\oplus\ldots\oplus\sigma_k\to\sigma_i}(\mathbf{ins}_{\mathbf{j}(\sigma_1,\ldots,\sigma_k)}\ e) \\ \to_\delta \begin{cases} e & \text{if } \mathrm{i}=\mathrm{j} \text{ and } (inHNF\ e) \\ \mathbf{outs}_{\mathbf{i}\,\sigma_1\oplus\ldots\oplus\sigma_k\to\sigma_i}(\mathbf{ins}_{\mathbf{j}(\sigma_1,\ldots,\sigma_k)}\ e) & \text{if } \mathrm{i}\neq\mathrm{j} \text{ and } (inHNF\ e) \end{cases}$$

$$\mathbf{iss}_{\mathbf{i}\,\sigma_1\oplus\ldots\oplus\sigma_k\to bool}(\mathbf{ins}_{\mathbf{j}(\sigma_1,\ldots,\sigma_k)}\ e) \to_\delta \begin{cases} \mathbf{true}_{bool} & \text{if } \mathrm{i}=\mathrm{j} \text{ and } (inHNF\ e) \\ \mathbf{false}_{bool} & \text{if } \mathrm{i}\neq\mathrm{j} \text{ and } (inHNF\ e) \end{cases}$$

Figure 2.7: δ-rule Schemata for Constants in Λ_T

achieve this effect. Whilst e_1 is not in HNF, the leftmost redex is in e_1. Once e_1 has been reduced to HNF, the leftmost redex is the let-expression.

We shall see that the denotational semantics of a term of the form

$$\mathbf{tuples}_{(\sigma_1,\ldots,\sigma_k)}(e_1,\ldots,e_k)$$

is non-bottom if and only if $\forall i \in \{1,\ldots,k\}$, e_i has an HNF. Appealing again to the theorem relating the operational and denotational viewpoints of Λ_T, an attempt must be made to evaluate each of the e_i to HNF in an expression of the form $\mathbf{tuples}_{(\sigma_1,\ldots,\sigma_k)}(e_1,\ldots,e_k)$. If one of them is has no HNF, then its evaluation will fail to terminate, meaning that the evaluation of the entire expression will fail to terminate, which is what is required. Conversely, if they all have HNFs, then the process will terminate, and an HNF can be given to the expression. By using the **let** construct in giving a δ-rule for the case when some of the e_i in the expression $\mathbf{tuples}_{(\sigma_1,\ldots,\sigma_k)}(e_1,\ldots,e_k)$ are not in HNF, we force each of the e_i to be evaluated in turn, terminating if and only if each of the e_i have an HNF.

The δ-rules for $\mathbf{and}_{bool\to bool\to bool}$ and $\mathbf{or}_{bool\to bool\to bool}$ require both arguments to be reduced to HNF (i.e. they are strict functions).

With the new syntactic constructs, we must extend the definition of free variables and substitution with the following:

$$\begin{array}{lcl}
FV(\mathbf{fix}_{(\sigma\to\sigma)\to\sigma}\ e) & = & FV(e) \\
FV(\mathbf{let}\ x^\sigma = e_1\ \mathbf{in}\ e_2) & = & FV(e_1)\bigcup(FV(e_2) - \{x^\sigma\}) \\
FV(\mathbf{tuple}_{(\sigma_1,\ldots,\sigma_k)}(e_1,\ldots,e_k)) & = & \bigcup_{i=1}^{k} FV(e_i) \\
FV(\mathbf{tuples}_{(\sigma_1,\ldots,\sigma_k)}(e_1,\ldots,e_k)) & = & \bigcup_{i=1}^{k} FV(e_i) \\
FV(\mathbf{ins}_{\mathbf{i}(\sigma_1,\ldots,\sigma_k)}\ e) & = & FV(e) \\
FV(\mathbf{lift}_\sigma\ e) & = & FV(e)
\end{array}$$

$$\begin{array}{lcl}
(\mathbf{fix}_{(\sigma\to\sigma)\to\sigma}\ e)[x^\sigma := e'] & = & \mathbf{fix}_{(\sigma\to\sigma)\to\sigma}\ (e[x^\sigma := e']) \\
(\mathbf{let}\ x^\sigma = e_1\ \mathbf{in}\ e_2)[x^\sigma := e'] & = & \mathbf{let}\ x^\sigma = (e_1[x^\sigma := e'])\ \mathbf{in}\ e_2 \\
(\mathbf{let}\ x^\sigma = e_1\ \mathbf{in}\ e_2)[y^\tau := e'] & = & \mathbf{let}\ x^\sigma = (e_1[y^\tau := e'])\ \mathbf{in}\ e_2[y^\tau := e'] \\
 & & \text{provided } y^\tau \not\equiv x^\sigma \\
(\mathbf{tuple}_{(\sigma_1,\ldots,\sigma_k)}(e_1,\ldots,e_k))[x^\sigma := e'] & = & \mathbf{tuple}_{(\sigma_1,\ldots,\sigma_k)}(e_1[x^\sigma := e'],\ldots,e_k[x^\sigma := e']) \\
(\mathbf{tuples}_{(\sigma_1,\ldots,\sigma_k)}(e_1,\ldots,e_k))[x^\sigma := e'] & = & \mathbf{tuples}_{(\sigma_1,\ldots,\sigma_k)}(e_1[x^\sigma := e'],\ldots,e_k[x^\sigma := e']) \\
(\mathbf{ins}_{\mathbf{i}(\sigma_1,\ldots,\sigma_k)}\ e)[x^\sigma := e'] & = & \mathbf{ins}_{\mathbf{i}(\sigma_1,\ldots,\sigma_k)}\ (e[x^\sigma := e']) \\
(\mathbf{lift}_\sigma\ e)[x^\sigma := e'] & = & \mathbf{lift}_\sigma\ (e[x^\sigma := e'])
\end{array}$$

All the important properties of the typed lambda calculus that have been discussed so far remain true of this extended language, and are recorded in this section for future reference.

The notion of HNF needs to be modified in any typed lambda calculus with constants.

Definition 2.1.10

A term in Λ_T is in head normal form if it is in one of the forms:

- $\lambda x_1^{\sigma_1} \ldots \lambda x_n^{\sigma_n}.v\ e_1\ \ldots\ e_k, k \geq 0,\ n \geq 0$
  where:
  1. v is a variable; or
  2. v is a constant c_σ and either
     (a) all δ-rules for c_σ require more than k arguments; or
     (b) there are no δ-rules for c_σ

- $\lambda x_1^{\sigma_1}.\ldots.\lambda x_n^{\sigma_n}.\mathbf{tuples}_{(\sigma_1,\ldots,\sigma_k)}(s_1,\ldots s_k), n \geq 0, \forall i \in \{1,\ldots,k\} : inHNF\ s_i$
- $\lambda x_1^{\sigma_1}.\ldots.\lambda x_n^{\sigma_n}.\mathbf{ins}_{\mathbf{i}(\sigma_1,\ldots,\sigma_k)}\ s_i, n \geq 0, inHNF\ s_i$
- $\lambda x_1^{\sigma_1}.\ldots.\lambda x_n^{\sigma_n}.\mathbf{lift}_\sigma\ s, n \geq 0$

Note that this definition means that an object of type $\sigma_1 \times \ldots \times \sigma_k$ cannot be in HNF. We will return to this issue in Section 2.4, after we have discussed the denotational semantics of Λ_T.

Theorem 2.1.11 (Church-Rosser Theorem)

For the language Λ_T and the δ-rules given in Figure 2.7, the notion of reduction $\twoheadrightarrow_{\beta\delta}$ has the Church-Rosser property.

This can be proved using Theorem 2.1.8, in the same way as for Λ_2.

For Λ_T, we need a more general notion than head-reduction in order to define a head-normalising $\beta\delta$-reduction strategy. The reason for this can be seen by considering the example:

$$+_{int\rightarrow int\rightarrow int}\ (+_{int\rightarrow int\rightarrow int}\ \mathbf{0}_{int}\ \mathbf{1}_{int})\ \mathbf{5}_{int}$$

where there is no head redex, and the term is not in HNF. In order to define a head-normalising reduction strategy, we need a concept analogous to the head-redex.

Definition 2.1.12

If e_1 and e_2 are two subterms of some term e, then we will say that e_1 is *to the left of* to e_2 if either e_1 occurs entirely to the left of e_2 in e, or e_2 is a proper subterm of e_1.

For example, in the expression from above:

$$+_{int\rightarrow int\rightarrow int}\ (+_{int\rightarrow int\rightarrow int}\ \mathbf{0}_{int}\ \mathbf{1}_{int})\ \mathbf{5}_{int}$$

$(+_{int\rightarrow int\rightarrow int}\ \mathbf{0}_{int}\ \mathbf{1}_{int})$ is to the left of $\mathbf{0}_{int}$, and $\mathbf{0}_{int}$ is to the left of $\mathbf{5}_{int}$. "To the left of" is a non-reflexive linear ordering on the occurrences of subterms in e. If terms in Λ_T were fully bracketed, then a subterm e_1 is to the left of e_2 if its leftmost bracket is to the left of the leftmost bracket of e_2.

$$
\begin{array}{l}
\mathit{length} = \textbf{fix}\ (\lambda g.\lambda l.\textbf{lcase}\ l\ \textbf{0}\ (\lambda x.\lambda xs.\textbf{1} + (g\ xs))) \\
\mathit{sumlist} = \textbf{fix}\ (\lambda g.\lambda l.\textbf{lcase}\ l\ \textbf{0}\ (\lambda x.\lambda xs.x + (g\ xs))) \\
\mathit{append} = \textbf{fix}\ (\lambda g.\lambda l_1.\lambda l_2.\textbf{lcase}\ l_1\ l_2\ (\lambda x.\lambda xs.\textbf{cons}\ x\ (g\ xs\ l_2))) \\
\mathit{reverse} = \textbf{fix}\ (\lambda g.\lambda l.\textbf{lcase}\ l\ \textbf{nil}\ (\lambda x.\lambda xs.\mathit{append}\ (g\ xs)\ (\textbf{cons}\ x\ \textbf{nil}))) \\
\mathit{before0} = \textbf{fix}\ (\lambda g.\lambda l.\textbf{lcase}\ l\ \textbf{nil}\ (\lambda x.\lambda xs.\textbf{if}\ (=\ x\ \textbf{0})\ \textbf{nil}\ (\textbf{cons}\ x\ (g\ xs)))) \\
\mathit{doubles} = \textbf{fix}\ (\lambda g.\lambda l.\textbf{lcase}\ l\ \textbf{nil}\ (\lambda x.\lambda xs.\textbf{cons}\ (\textbf{2} * x)\ (g\ xs))) \\
\mathit{map} = \textbf{fix}\ (\lambda g.\lambda f.\lambda l.\textbf{lcase}\ l\ \textbf{nil}\ (\lambda x.\lambda xs.\textbf{cons}\ (f\ x)\ (g\ f\ xs))) \\
\mathit{size} = \textbf{fix}\ (\lambda g.\lambda t.\textbf{tcase}\ t\ \textbf{0}\ (\lambda t_1.\lambda n.\lambda t_2.(g\ t_1) + \textbf{1} + (g\ t_2))) \\
\mathit{sumtree} = \textbf{fix}\ (\lambda g.\lambda t.\textbf{tcase}\ t\ \textbf{0}\ (\lambda t_1.\lambda n.\lambda t_2.(g\ t_1) + n + (g\ t_2))) \\
\mathit{join} = \lambda t_1.\lambda n.\lambda t_2.\textbf{node}\ t_1\ n\ t_2
\end{array}
$$

Figure 2.8: Translation of Functions in Figure 1.1 into Λ_T

Definition 2.1.13

The *leftmost* redex in a term e is a subterm of e that is a redex and is to the left of any other subterm of e which is also a redex.

The one-step reduction strategy F_ℓ is defined by

$$
\begin{array}{lll}
F_\ell(e) & = e & \text{if } e \text{ is an HNF} \\
 & = e' & \text{if } e \rightarrow_{\beta\delta} e' \text{ by reducing the leftmost redex}
\end{array}
$$

Theorem 2.1.14 (Head-Normalisation Theorem)

For Λ_T with $\beta\delta$-reduction, F_ℓ is head-normalising.

The proof of this theorem can be found in Appendix A, Section A.2, and is non-trivial. Many books on functional programming gloss over this fact, saying that the *typed* lambda calculus *with* constants can be translated into the *untyped* calculus *without* constants, that F_ℓ is head-normalising for this latter calculus, and so it is for Λ_T. This lacks rigour because functional languages are not implemented by translating them into the untyped lambda calculus without constants and doing only β-reduction, but effectively use a typed lambda calculus with constants and δ-rules. The proof is non-trivial precisely because it is possible to introduce δ-rules for which the above theorem is not true (see [Hin78b, pp. 255, 261] for example).

2.1.7 Translating Functional Programs into Λ_T

As stated in the introduction to this chapter, the typed lambda calculus can be regarded as the canonical functional programming language. The example functions from Figure 1.1 can be translated into Λ_T, and the results are given in Figure 2.8, where we have omitted the type information so that the programs can fit on the page.

There are four major stages in the translation process, which we will demonstrate using the function `length`:

1. uses of pattern matching are rewritten using **lcase** and **tcase**. For example,

```
> length Nil          = 0
> length (Cons x xs) = 1 + length xs
```

becomes

$$\begin{aligned}&\mathit{length}\ l\\ &\quad = \mathbf{lcase}_{(list\ \tau)\to int\to(\tau\to(list\ \tau)\to int)\to int}\ l\ \mathbf{0}\ (\lambda x^{\tau}.\lambda xs^{(list\ \tau)}.\mathbf{1} + (\mathit{length}\ xs))\end{aligned}$$

2. The definition:

$$f\ x_1\ \ldots\ x_n = e$$

is changed to:

$$f = \lambda x_1^{\sigma_1}.\ldots.\lambda x_n^{\sigma_n}.e.$$

so that the definition of `length` becomes:

$$\begin{aligned}&\mathit{length} =\\ &\quad \lambda l^{(list\ \tau)}.\mathbf{lcase}_{(list\ \tau)\to int\to(\tau\to(list\ \tau)\to int)\to int}\ l\ \mathbf{0}\ (\lambda x^{\tau}.\lambda xs^{(list\ \tau)}.\mathbf{1} + (\mathit{length}\ xs)).\end{aligned}$$

3. Explicit recursion using named variables is removed by using $\mathbf{fix}_{(\sigma\to\sigma)\to\sigma}$, where $\sigma = (list\ \tau) \to int$, so that

$$\begin{aligned}\mathit{length} = \mathbf{fix}_{(\sigma\to\sigma)\to\sigma}(\lambda g^{\sigma\to\sigma}.\lambda l^{(list\ \tau)}.\ &\mathbf{lcase}_{(list\ \tau)\to int\to(\tau\to(list\ \tau)\to int)\to int}\ l\ \mathbf{0}\\ &(\lambda x^{\tau}.\lambda xs^{(list\ \tau)}.\mathbf{1} + (g\ xs))).\end{aligned}$$

4. At this stage, functions may still be polymorphic. Work by Holmstrom shows that any polymorphically typed program can be translated into a monomorphically typed one [Hol83]. For functions like `length`, this will result in several versions of the function, one for each type of list to which it is applied.

A more rigorous approach to the translation of functional languages into the lambda calculus (typed or untyped) can be found in a number of books, [FH88, Gor88, Pey87, Rea89] for example.

This completes our discussion of the operational viewpoint of the typed lambda calculus. Before we can proceed to the denotational one, we must introduce the mathematical objects which are used to give the denotational semantics. Those familiar with the background may still like to skim through the next section to pick up the notation that is being used, and properties (P1) to (P11) of functions over powerdomains which are used in Chapter 3. The reader is also reminded that an Index of Symbols can be found at the end of the book.

2.2 Sets With Structure

The theory underlying the denotational method of giving semantics, usually called *domain theory*, uses sets with a number of different structures imposed on them. In this section we introduce some of these, functions on them, and some of their properties. It is possible to understand the technical details of this book using only basic concepts from domain theory [Sco81, Sco82], category theory [AM75] and powerdomains [Plo76, Smy78].

The main results about that we use about powerdomains can be summarised as a set of algebraic rules given in Section 2.2.6. The proofs of the basic facts cited in that section are either directly in the literature, or obtainable by minor modifications therefrom; see [HP79, Plo76].

We will sometimes represent functions which are defined on a finite set of arguments using the notation:

$$\{x_1 \mapsto v_1, \ldots, x_n \mapsto v_n\}$$

which is the function f such that $f\ x_i = v_i$ and is undefined for any argument not in $\{x_1, \ldots, x_n\}$. The function $\{\}$ is undefined everywhere.

2.2.1 Partial Orders

Definition 2.2.1

> A *partial order* is a pair $(S, \sqsubseteq)$ where S is a set of elements, and $\sqsubseteq$ is an ordering relation which satisfies the following three axioms:
>
> 1. $\forall\, a \in S,\ a \sqsubseteq a$ (reflexivity);
> 2. $\forall\, a, b \in S,\ a \sqsubseteq b$ and $b \sqsubseteq a \ \Rightarrow\ a = b$ (antisymmetry);
> 3. $\forall\, a, b, c \in S,\ a \sqsubseteq b$ and $b \sqsubseteq c \ \Rightarrow\ a \sqsubseteq c$ (transitivity).
>
> We will sometimes write $a \sqsupseteq b$, which is true if and only if $b \sqsubseteq a$. If $a \sqsubseteq b$ is false, then we will also write $a \not\sqsubseteq b$.

We will often write "the partial order P" where the ordering relation $\sqsubseteq$ on P is contextually implicit.

When partial orders are used in giving semantics to programming languages, the ordering represents *information content*, that is, $a \sqsubseteq b$ if b has at least as much information as a. The three properties that must be possessed by a partial ordering relation can be understood in terms of this intuition: the first one says that an object has at least as much information as itself, the second says that if one object has at least as much information as another, and vice versa, then they must have the same amount of information, and the third says that if there are three objects such that the second has more information than the first, and the third more than the second, then the third must have more information than the first.

It is called a *partial* rather than a *total* order because some pieces of information may be mutually exclusive. In terms of the above definition, this means that there may be some a and some b for which neither $a \sqsubseteq b$ nor $b \sqsubseteq a$.

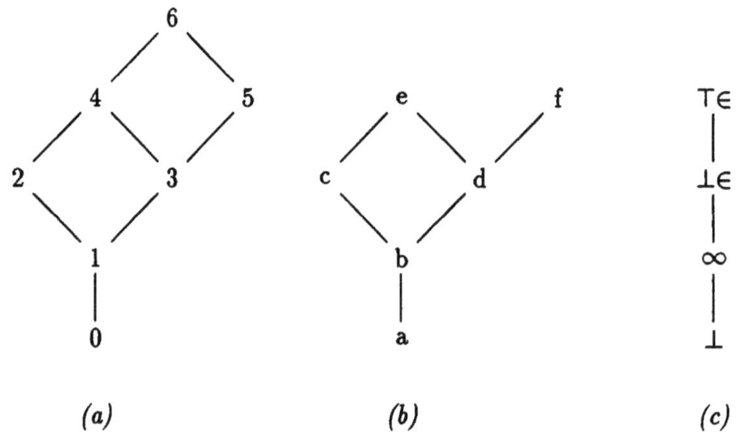

Figure 2.9: Diagrams of Some Partial Orders

Partial orders can be presented in diagrammatic form. Figure 2.9 gives examples of three (finite) partial orders. If $x \sqsubseteq z$, and there is no y such that $x \sqsubseteq y$ and $y \sqsubseteq z$, then x is written on the page below z, and a line is drawn from x to z to indicate that $x \sqsubseteq z$. In general, $a \sqsubseteq b$ in some partial order if there is some path along zero or more lines (following them up the page) starting from a and ending in b in the diagram of the partial order. For example, in Figure 2.9*(a)*, $2 \sqsubseteq 4$, $1 \sqsubseteq 6$, and $2 \not\sqsubseteq 3$.

Example 2.2.2

Three further examples of partial orders are:

1. If S is some set, and $\mathcal{P}\ S$ is the powerset of S, then $(\mathcal{P}\ S, \subseteq)$ is a partial order.
2. If $\mathbf{Z}$ is the set of integers, then $(\mathbf{Z}, \leq)$ is a partial order. This is an example of a partial order which also happens to be total. Note that $(\mathbf{Z}, <)$ is not a partial order, as $<$ is not reflexive.
3. Any set S can be turned into a partial order $(S, \sqsubseteq)$ by defining $\sqsubseteq$ by

$$s_1 \sqsubseteq s_2 \text{ if and only if } s_1 = s_2.$$

Definition 2.2.3

A *chain* is a subset $X = \{x_1, x_2, \ldots\}$ of some partial order $(S, \sqsubseteq)$ such that $\forall i,\ x_i \sqsubseteq x_{i+1}$.

We wrote $X = \{x_1, x_2, \ldots\}$ to indicate that, in partial orders containing an infinite number of objects, it is possible for chains to be infinite. Some examples of chains from

Figure 2.9 are {0,1}, {0,1,3,4,6} and {a,b,d}. The partial order in Figure 2.9*(c)* a chain.

Functions over structured sets should preserve the structure in some way. A natural restriction on functions over partial orders is that if we have more information about an argument, then we must get at least as much information about the result of applying the function to that argument. Such functions are called *monotonic.*

Definition 2.2.4

A function $f : D \to E$ is *monotonic* if whenever $d_1, d_2 \in D$ and $d_1 \sqsubseteq d_2$ we have that $f\ d_1 \sqsubseteq f\ d_2$.

Example 2.2.5

Suppose that D and E are the partial orders given in Figure 2.9*(a)* and *(b)* respectively. Then the function defined by:

$$\{0 \mapsto \mathrm{a}, 1 \mapsto \mathrm{b}, 2 \mapsto \mathrm{d}, 3 \mapsto \mathrm{c}, 4 \mapsto \mathrm{e}, 5 \mapsto \mathrm{e}, 6 \mapsto \mathrm{e}\}$$

is monotonic, whilst the function defined by:

$$\{0 \mapsto \mathrm{b}, 1 \mapsto \mathrm{a}, 2 \mapsto \mathrm{d}, 3 \mapsto \mathrm{c}, 4 \mapsto \mathrm{e}, 5 \mapsto \mathrm{e}, 6 \mapsto \mathrm{e}\}$$

is not monotonic because $0 \sqsubseteq 1$, but $b \not\sqsubseteq a$.

2.2.2 Lattices

Definition 2.2.6

An *upper bound* of two elements a and b is an element c such that $a \sqsubseteq c$ and $b \sqsubseteq c$. The *least upper bound* of two elements a and b, written $a \sqcup b$, is an object c such that c is an upper bound of a and b, and if there is any other upper bound c', then $c \sqsubseteq c'$. Given some partially ordered set S, the least upper bound of S, written as $\bigsqcup S$, is the least element s' such that $\forall s \in S,\ s \sqsubseteq s'$.

In terms of the intuition that $x \sqsubseteq y$ if y contains at least as much information as x, an upper bound of a and b contains at least as much information as both a and b, and the least upper bound is the least element which contains the information from both a and b; it adds the least extra information.

The point 6 is an upper bound of 2 and 3 in the partial order given in Figure 2.9*(a)*, and 4 is the least upper bound of 2 and 3. It is possible that either upper bounds or least upper bounds do not exist. In Figure 2.9*(b)*, the points e and f do not have an upper bound.

Lower bounds are a dual concept to upper bounds.

Definition 2.2.7

> A *lower bound* of two elements a and b is an element c such that $c \sqsubseteq a$ and $c \sqsubseteq b$. The *greatest lower bound* of two elements a and b, written $a \sqcap b$, is a lower bound c such that if there is any other lower bound c', then $c \sqsupseteq c'$. Given some partially ordered set S, the greatest lower bound of S, written as $\bigsqcap S$, is the greatest element s' such that $\forall s \in S$, $s \sqsupseteq s'$.

It is easy to prove that when either the least upper bound or greatest lower bound exists, then it is unique.

Definition 2.2.8

> A *lattice* is a partially ordered set such that every pair of objects has both a least upper bound and a greatest lower bound contained in the set. Equivalently, a partially ordered set $(L, \sqsubseteq)$ is a lattice if for all finite, non-empty subsets X of L, both $\bigsqcup X$ and $\bigsqcap X$ exist in L.

Out of the partial orders given in Figure 2.9, *(a)* and *(c)* are lattices, but *(b)* is not.

Definition 2.2.9

> The lattice L is *complete* if for all subsets X of L (including any infinite ones), both $\bigsqcup X$ and $\bigsqcap X$ exist in L.

Note that any finite lattice is necessarily complete.

Complete lattices are of interest to us because the framework of Chapter 3 requires that abstract domains be complete lattices. We require that the lattices be finite so that abstract interpretations can be computed in finite time.

2.2.3 Complete Partial Orders

Definition 2.2.10

> A *complete partial order (cpo)* is a partial order $(S, \sqsubseteq)$ with a least element, and the property that every non-empty, countable chain has a least upper bound in S.

The least element of the complete partial order D is often written as $\bot_D$ (or just $\bot$ when D is clear from the context), and is pronounced "bottom". It represents no information, and is often used to model non-terminating computations which produce no output, and hence give no information.

Sometimes partial orders have a top element, written $\top$, or $\top_D$ to indicate that it is from the partial order D. The element $\top$ is pronounced "top", because it is the top element in the ordering, that is, $\forall d \in D, d \sqsubseteq \top$.

Example 2.2.11

1. All the partial orders in Figure 2.9 are complete.
2. Given any set S, a complete partial order $(S^{\perp}, \sqsubseteq)$ can be defined by adding a new element, $\perp$, to S to give $S^{\perp} = \{\perp\} \bigcup S$, and defining the ordering $\sqsubseteq$ by

$$s_1 \sqsubseteq s_2 \text{ iff } s_1 = \perp \text{ or } s_1 = s_2.$$

Such a partial order is said to be *flat* since all the non-bottom elements are at the same level in the ordering.

Definition 2.2.12

A subset X of some partial order D is *directed* if every finite subset of X has an upper bound in X.

The subset $X = \{0, 2, 3, 6\}$ of the partial order in Figure 2.9*(a)* is directed, but the set $Y = \{3, 4, 5\}$ is not because the subset $\{4, 5\}$ has no upper bound in the set Y.

Definition 2.2.13

Let D and E be complete partial orders. A monotonic function $f : D \rightarrow E$ is *strict* if $f \perp_D = \perp_E$.

Definition 2.2.14

Let D and E be complete partial orders. A monotonic function $f : D \rightarrow E$ is *bottom-reflecting* if $f\ d = \perp_E$ implies $d = \perp_D$.

Note that a function f being bottom-reflecting does not necessarily mean that it is strict, as $f \perp_D$ may not be $\perp_E$, that is, there may be no d such that $f\ d = \perp_E$.

Definition 2.2.15

Let D and E be complete partial orders. A function $f : D \rightarrow E$ is *continuous* if it is monotonic, and for all chains $X \subseteq D$, $f\ (\bigsqcup X) = \bigsqcup\{f\ x | x \in X\}$.

As an aside, it is not coincidental that such functions are called continuous. A topology can be defined on a cpo, and functions continuous by this definition are continuous with respect to the topology [GHK+80, Vic89].

Definition 2.2.16

The value $d \in D$ is a *fixed point* of a function $f : D \rightarrow D$ if $f\ d = d$. It is the *least fixed point* if whenever d' is any other fixed point, $d \sqsubseteq d'$.

Theorem 2.2.17 (Fixed Point Theorem)

Any continuous function $f : D \rightarrow D$ over a complete partial order D has a least fixed point, given by the formula:

$$\bigsqcup_{i \geq 0} f^i \perp_D$$

where $f^0 \perp_D = \perp_D$ and $f^{i+1}\ d = f\ (f^i\ d)$.

It is easy to prove that $\bigsqcup_{i \geq 0} f^i \perp_D$ is indeed the least fixed point of f. This formula was first proved to be true by Tarski for the restricted class of complete partial orders that are also complete lattices [Tar55].

2.2.4 Domains

A domain is a cpo with some extra properties, which are required to guarantee the existence of solutions to recursive domain equations. For completeness, we define these properties in this section, but none of them are used explicitly in the book.

Definition 2.2.18

An element d of a cpo D is *compact* (or *finite*) if and only if for all chains $X \subseteq D$, $X = \{x_1, x_2, \ldots\}$, $d \sqsubseteq \bigsqcup X$ implies $\exists n$ such that $d \sqsubseteq x_n$.

Definition 2.2.19

A cpo D is *algebraic* (or *ω-algebraic*) if the set of compact elements is countable and each $d \in D$ may be written as $d = \bigsqcup X$ of some chain X of compact elements.

Definition 2.2.20

A cpo D is *consistently complete* if and only if every subset Y of D which has an upper bound in D also has a least upper bound in D.

Definition 2.2.21

A *domain* is a consistently complete ω-algebraic cpo.

2.2.5 Constructions on Domains

In set theory, sets can be constructed by taking products, disjoint unions and powersets of other sets. Analogous constructions can be defined on domains. We leave powerdomains until the next section. Because domains have an ordering structure, we can define two different sorts of product and disjoint union, which vary in the way they treat the $\bot$ elements from the constituent domains. Moreover, we can define a new construction called *lifting*.

Product Domains

Definition 2.2.22

Given domains D_1 to D_k, the *product* of D_1 to D_k, written

$$D_1 \times \ldots \times D_k$$

has as elements:

$$\{(d_1, \ldots, d_k) | \forall i \in \{1, \ldots, k\} : d_i \in D_i\}$$

and the ordering is defined by:

$$(d_1, \ldots, d_k) \sqsubseteq (d_1', \ldots, d_k') \text{ if and only if } \forall i \in \{1, \ldots, k\} : d_i \sqsubseteq d_i'$$

Smash Product Domains

Definition 2.2.23

Given domains D_1 to D_k, the *smash product* of D_1 to D_k, written

$$D_1 \otimes \ldots \otimes D_k$$

has as elements:

$$\{< d_1, \ldots, d_k > | \forall i \in \{1, \ldots, k\} : d_i \in D_i, d_i \neq \perp_{D_i}\} \bigcup \{\perp_{D_1 \otimes \ldots \otimes D_k}\}$$

and the ordering is defined by:

$$\perp_{D_1 \otimes \ldots \otimes D_k} \sqsubseteq d, \forall d \in D_1 \otimes \ldots \otimes D_k$$
$$< d_1, \ldots, d_k > \sqsubseteq < d'_1, \ldots, d'_k > \text{ if and only if } \forall i \in \{1, \ldots, k\} : d_i \sqsubseteq d'_i$$

This construction is called the *smash* product because no tuples are allowed with $\perp_{D_i}$ elements; they all get 'smashed' to $\perp_{D_1 \otimes \ldots \otimes D_k}$. Angle brackets are used in this book to distinguish elements of a smash product from those of an ordinary product, which are written using round brackets.

Sum Domains

Definition 2.2.24

Given domains D_1 to D_k, the *sum* of D_1 to D_k, written

$$D_1 + \ldots + D_k$$

has as elements:

$$\{(in_i\ d_i) | \forall i \in \{1, \ldots, k\} : d_i \in D_i\} \bigcup \{\perp_{D_1 + \ldots + D_k}\}$$

and the ordering is defined by:

$$\perp_{D_1 + \ldots + D_k} \sqsubseteq d, \forall d \in D_1 + \ldots + D_k$$
$$(in_i\ d) \sqsubseteq (in_j\ d') \text{ if and only if } i = j \text{ and } d \sqsubseteq d'$$

Smash Sum Domains

Definition 2.2.25

Given domains D_1 to D_k, the *smash sum* (or *coalesced sum*) of D_1 to D_k, written

$$D_1 \oplus \ldots \oplus D_k$$

has as elements:

$$\{(ins_i\ d_i) | \forall i \in \{1, \ldots, k\} : d_i \in D_i, d_i \neq \perp_{D_i}\} \bigcup \{\perp_{D_1 \oplus \ldots \oplus D_k}\}$$

and the ordering is defined by:

$$\perp_{D_1 \oplus \ldots \oplus D_k} \sqsubseteq d, \forall d \in D_1 \oplus \ldots \oplus D_k$$
$$(ins_i\ d) \sqsubseteq (ins_j\ d') \text{ if and only if } i = j \text{ and } d \sqsubseteq d'$$

Again the 'smash' indicates that the bottom object in the constructed domain corresponds to all the bottom elements of the constituent domains. Note that the s in ins_i is to indicate that it gives a result in the smash sum.

Lifted Domains

Definition 2.2.26

Given a domain D, the *lifted* domain is written as $lift\ D$, has as elements:

$$\{(0,d)|d \in D\}$$

and the ordering is defined by:

$$\perp_{lift\ D} \sqsubseteq d, \forall d \in (lift\ D)$$
$$(0,d) \sqsubseteq (0,d') \text{ if and only if } d \sqsubseteq d'$$

Proposition 2.2.27

$$D_1 + \ldots + D_k \cong (lift\ D_1) \oplus \ldots \oplus (lift\ D_k)$$

(where $\cong$ means 'is isomorphic to').

The proof of this proposition is an easy exercise.

> *Because ordinary sum can be defined in terms of smash sum and lifting, we will not consider the ordinary sum any further in this book. This makes the presentation of theorems and proofs shorter, without any loss of power.*

Function Domains

Definition 2.2.28

Given domains D and E, the domain of continuous functions from D to E, is written as $D \to E$, and its ordering defined by:

$$f \sqsubseteq g \text{ if and only if } \forall d \in D: \ (f\ d) \sqsubseteq (g\ d)$$

For every domain D, the identity function on D, written id_D, is defined by

$$\forall d \in D: \ id_D\ d = d.$$

If $f \in D \to E$ and $g \in E \to F$, then their *composition*, written as $g \circ f$, is defined by:

$$\forall d \in D: \ (g \circ f)\ d = g\ (f\ d).$$

$$(d_1, \ldots, d_k) \downarrow i = d_i$$

$$\perp_{D_1 \otimes \ldots \otimes D_k} \downarrow i = \perp_{D_i}$$
$$< d_1, \ldots, d_k > \downarrow i = d_i$$

$$mk\_sum_i \ e = \begin{cases} \perp_{D_1 \oplus \ldots \oplus D_k} & \text{if } e = \perp_{D_i} \\ ins_i \ e & \text{otherwise} \end{cases}$$

$$outs_i \perp_{D_1 \oplus \ldots \oplus D_k} = \perp_{D_i}$$
$$outs_i \ (ins_j \ e) = \begin{cases} e & if \ i = j \\ \perp_{D_i} & if \ i \neq j \end{cases}$$

$$iss_i \perp_{D_1 \oplus \ldots \oplus D_k} = \perp_{bool}$$
$$iss_i \ (ins_j \ e) = \begin{cases} true & if \ i = j \\ false & if \ i \neq j \end{cases}$$

Figure 2.10: Functions Defined on Constructed Domains

Functions Defined on Constructed Domains

A number of operators are defined on these constructed domains, and are given in Figure 2.10.

Combining Continuous Functions

Each of the constructions we have defined are functors over the category of domains, and so operate on continuous functions (the morphisms in the category) as well. Their actions are given in the following definition.

Definition 2.2.29

In this definition, D, D_1 to D_k and E, E_1 to E_k are domains.

If $f_i : D_i \rightarrow E_i$ are continuous functions for all $i \in \{1, \ldots, k\}$, we define the following continuous functions:

$$f_1 \times \ldots \times f_k : D_1 \times \ldots \times D_k \rightarrow E_1 \times \ldots \times E_k$$
$$(f_1 \times \ldots \times f_k) \ (d_1, \ldots, d_k) = (f_1 \ d_1, \ldots, f_k \ d_k)$$

$$f_1 \otimes \ldots \otimes f_k : D_1 \otimes \ldots \otimes D_k \rightarrow E_1 \otimes \ldots \otimes E_k$$
$$(f_1 \otimes \ldots \otimes f_k) \perp_{D_1 \otimes \ldots \otimes D_k} = \perp_{E_1 \otimes \ldots \otimes E_k}$$
$$(f_1 \otimes \ldots \otimes f_k) \ (d_1, \ldots, d_k) = \begin{cases} \perp_{E_1 \otimes \ldots \otimes E_k} & \text{if } \exists i \in \{1, \ldots, k\} : f_i \ d_i = \perp_{E_i} \\ < f_1 \ d_1, \ldots, f_k \ d_k > & \text{otherwise} \end{cases}$$

If $f_i : D_i \rightarrow E$ are continuous functions for all $i \in \{1, \ldots, k\}$, we define the following continuous function:

$$f_1 \oplus \ldots \oplus f_k : D_1 \oplus \ldots \oplus D_k \rightarrow E$$
$$(f_1 \oplus \ldots \oplus f_k)\ d = \begin{cases} \perp_E & \text{if } d = \perp_{D_1 \oplus \ldots \oplus D_k} \\ f_i\ d_i & \text{if } d = ins_i\ d_i \end{cases}$$

If $f \quad D \rightarrow E$ is a continuous function, we define the following continuous function:

$$lift\ f : lift\ D \rightarrow lift\ E$$
$$(lift\ f)\ d = \begin{cases} \perp_{lift\ E} & \text{if } d = \perp_{lift\ D} \\ (0, f\ d') & \text{if } d = (0, d') \end{cases}$$

2.2.6 Powerdomains

Given some set S, the powerset of S is the set of subsets of S. We need an analogous construction on domains for the work of this book. Just as the powerset is a set, we would like a powerdomain to be a domain. The construction of the powerdomain of some domain D requires some non-trivial mathematics, see [Plo76, Smy78] for example. It is beyond the scope of this book to discuss powerdomain constructions. One of the problems with the construction is to define an ordering on the subsets of the domain which are to be the elements of the powerdomain. There are at least three sensible candidates for the ordering:

1. (*Egli-Milner*):

$$X \sqsubseteq Y \quad \text{iff } \forall x \in X,\ \exists y \in Y : x \sqsubseteq y \text{ and } \forall y \in Y,\ \exists x \in X : x \sqsubseteq y$$

2. (*Hoare* or *Partial Correctness* or *Safety*):

$$X \sqsubseteq Y \quad \text{iff } \forall x \in X,\ \exists y \in Y : x \sqsubseteq y$$

3. (*Smyth* or *Total Correctness* or *Liveness*):

$$X \sqsubseteq Y \quad \text{iff } \forall y \in Y,\ \exists x \in X : x \sqsubseteq y$$

Each of these orderings capture a different intuition about the semantics that should be given to non-deterministic or parallel programs. It is easy to see that, with any of these possible orderings, the elements of a powerdomain will not be all of the subsets of some domain. This is because it is possible for two different sets, X and Y, with different elements, to satisfy $X \sqsubseteq Y$ and $Y \sqsubseteq X$, and so by the antisymmetry condition in the definition of a partial order (Definition 2.2.1), they must be declared "equal". For example, the subsets $\{3,4\}$ and $\{3,5\}$ of the domain given in Figure 2.9*(a)* are equivalent under the Smyth ordering.

In the subsequent chapters of this book, we require a powerdomain construction where a set of objects represents the idea of a computation giving a result which is at most as defined as something. This is captured conveniently by the so-called Hoare powerdomain.

Definition 2.2.30

A subset $X \subseteq D$ is *Scott-closed*[6]. if

1. If $Y \subseteq X$ and Y is directed, then $\bigsqcup Y \in X$.
2. If $y \sqsubseteq x \in X$ then $y \in X$.

The least Scott-closed set containing X is written X^*.

A set is *left-closed* if it satisfies (2).

Definition 2.2.31

Given a domain D, then $\mathbf{P}D$, the *Hoare* (or *partial correctness*) *powerdomain* is formed by taking as elements all non-empty Scott-closed sets, ordered by subset inclusion.

In terms of category theory, $\mathbf{P}$ is a *functor*, and so can also be applied to a continuous function between domains (a morphism in the category of domains) to give a continuous function between powerdomains. If $f : D \rightarrow E$, then $\mathbf{P}f : \mathbf{P}D \rightarrow \mathbf{P}E$ is defined thus:

$$\forall X \in \mathbf{P}D : (\mathbf{P}f)\ (X) \ = \ \{f\ x | x \in X\}^*$$

Some continuous functions over powerdomains are given in the following definition.

Definition 2.2.32

1. $\{\!\!\{.\}\!\!\}_D : D \rightarrow \mathbf{P}\ D$
   $\{\!\!\{d\}\!\!\}_D = \{d' \in D | d' \sqsubseteq d\}$
2. $\biguplus_D$: $\mathbf{PP}D \rightarrow \mathbf{P}D$
   $\biguplus_D \ \Theta = \{x | \text{for some } X \in \Theta,\ x \in X\} = \bigcup \Theta$
3. $\bigsqcup\!\!\!\!-_D : \mathbf{P}D \rightarrow D$
   $\bigsqcup\!\!\!\!-_D = \bigsqcup$

The symbol $\{\!\!\{.\}\!\!\}$ is called "singleton", $\biguplus_D$ is called "big union", and $\bigsqcup\!\!\!\!-_D$ is just called "least upper bound". We will drop the subscripts from these functions as they can be deduced from the context.

For the Hoare powerdomain, as noted in parts (2) and (3) of the above definition, $\biguplus$ is just $\bigcup$ and $\bigsqcup\!\!\!\!-$ is $\bigsqcup$, so we will use $\bigcup$ and $\bigsqcup$ in this book.

The properties of these functions that we use in this book are:

(P1) If D is a domain, $\mathbf{P}D$ is a domain.

(P2) If $f : D \rightarrow E$, $\mathbf{P}f : \mathbf{P}D \rightarrow \mathbf{P}E$ is a continuous function.

[6] This terminology is due to the fact that these are the closed sets with respect to the Scott topology (c.f. for example [GHK+80]).

(P3) $\mathbf{P}(f \circ g) \;=\; (\mathbf{P}f) \circ (\mathbf{P}g)$.

(P4) $\mathbf{P}id_D \;=\; id_{\mathbf{P}D}$.

(P5) $\{\!\!\{.\}\!\!\}_D$ is continuous.

(P6) For $f : D \to E$, $\mathbf{P}f \circ \{\!\!\{.\}\!\!\}_D = \{\!\!\{.\}\!\!\}_E \circ f$.

(P7) $\bigcup_D$ is continuous.

(P8) for $f : D \to E$, $\bigcup_E \circ \mathbf{PP}f = \mathbf{P}f \circ \bigcup_D$.

(P9) $\bigsqcup$ is continuous.

(P10) $\bigsqcup \circ \{\!\!\{.\}\!\!\}_D = id_D$.

(P11) When X is a subset of a finite lattice, $\bigsqcup X^* = \bigsqcup X$.

By using *function-level reasoning* with the equations in the above, we are able to give simple, algebraic proofs of many results.

(P1)–(P4) arise because $\mathbf{P}$ is a functor on the category of domains; (P5) and (P6) say that $\{\!\!\{.\}\!\!\}$ is a natural transformation from the identity functor on the category of domains to $\mathbf{P}$; and (P7) and (P8) say that $\bigcup$ is a natural transformation from $\mathbf{P}$ to $\mathbf{P}^2$. As well, we have that $(\mathbf{P}, \{\!\!\{.\}\!\!\}, \bigcup)$ is a monad.

2.3 Interpretations

In Figures 2.5 and 2.6 we gave the syntax for Λ_T, and in Section 2.2 we gave the semantic domains in which we will give the semantics of this language. Usually only one semantics is given for a language, but in abstract interpretation, we are intertested in giving some other semantics with which we can reason about properties of the usual semantics of the language. These different semantics are called *interpretations.* In particular, we will be considering the *standard* interpretation of Λ_T, its usual denotational semantics, and a number of *abstract* interpretations.

An interpretation for Λ_T has two parts:

1. a domain must be given as the interpretation of each type; and

2. an interpretation of the syntactic constructs of the language must be given.

Much of the form of each interpretation, be it the standard or an abstract interpretation, is the same. In our work for example, product types are always interpreted as a product domain, and lambda terms as functions. To emphasise this common structure, we first discuss a general interpretation of Λ_T. A specific interpretation can then be defined by supplying the variable parts of the interpretation.

2.3.1 A General Interpretation of Λ_T

Interpreting the Types in Λ_T

Suppose that we are defining any interpretation of Λ_T, which we will refer to as the I-interpretation. The first step in interpreting the type structure is to give interpretations for each of the base types, *bool* and *int*. We will denote the I-interpretation of the type σ by $\mathbf{I}_\sigma$, so that $\mathbf{I}_{bool}$ is the I-interpretation of the type *bool*. Different interpretations may require various properties of the interpretations of the types; all will require that they be at least domains.

Constructed types are usually added to a functional language with the intention that objects of these types take their meanings in domains constructed using the corresponding domain constructors, so that the product type is interpreted as the product domain constructor, and so on. An abstract interpretation however, captures certain properties of the standard interpretation, and so it may not be appropriate to interpret the domain constructors in this way in an abstract interpretation. Nielson therefore provides an interpretation framework where type constructors can be interpreted differently in each interpretation - see [Nie89] and its references. This is more general than is necessary for our purposes. We need a framework where the interpretations of booleans, integers, lists and trees can be varied, and hence the interpretation of types constructed from them. The interpretations of the other constructed types have to be defined in such a way that any abstract interpretation can capture as much information about the standard interpretation as possible. It turns out that for product, smash product and lifting, the corresponding domain constructors are sufficient for the abstract interpretations we consider. For products, we express this by the rule:

$$\mathbf{I}_{\sigma_1 \times \ldots \times \sigma_k} = \mathbf{I}_{\sigma_1} \times \ldots \times \mathbf{I}_{\sigma_k}$$

which can be read as saying that the I-interpretation of the type $\sigma_1 \times \ldots \times \sigma_k$ is the (domain) product of the I-interpretations of each of the σ_i. This, and the similar interpretation rules for smash product and lifting can be found in Figure 2.11. In order to capture as much information as possible, smash sumwill be interpreted as product in the abstract interpretations we consider[7]. We will give an example of how this gives more information after giving the abstract interpretation of $\mathbf{if}_{bool \to \sigma \to \sigma \to \sigma}$. For this reason, the interpretation of the type $\sigma_1 \oplus \ldots \oplus \sigma_k$ is given in Figure 2.11 as:

$$\mathbf{I}_{(\sigma_1 \oplus \ldots \oplus \sigma_k)} = (\mathbf{I}\ \oplus)\ (\mathbf{I}_{\sigma_1}, \ldots, \mathbf{I}_{\sigma_k})$$

to indicate that the interpretation of the smash sum will vary according to the interpretation being defined.

Finally, we note that lists and trees, our examples of recursively defined types, are also special cases. We discuss their standard interpretation in the next section, and in Chapter 4, we give a number of finite lattices as interpretations of these types. To indicate

[7] As an aside, we note that abstract domains will be required to be finite lattices, and that the smash sum of k finite lattices is not a finite lattice, as it has no top element. This can be rectified by defining a new type of smash sum, either by adding a new top element, or coalescing all the top elements of the constituent lattices. Further discussion of this issue can be found in [Bur87b].

$$\mathbf{I}_{(\sigma \to \tau)} = (\mathbf{I}_\sigma) \to (\mathbf{I}_\tau)$$
$$\mathbf{I}_{(\sigma_1 \times \ldots \times \sigma_k)} = (\mathbf{I}_{\sigma_1}) \times \ldots \times (\mathbf{I}_{\sigma_k})$$
$$\mathbf{I}_{(\sigma_1 \otimes \ldots \otimes \sigma_k)} = (\mathbf{I}_{\sigma_1}) \otimes \ldots \otimes (\mathbf{I}_{\sigma_k})$$
$$\mathbf{I}_{(\sigma_1 \oplus \ldots \oplus \sigma_k)} = (\mathbf{I} \oplus)\ (\mathbf{I}_{\sigma_1}, \ldots, \mathbf{I}_{\sigma_k})$$
$$\mathbf{I}_{(\mathit{lift}\ \sigma)} = \mathit{lift}\ (\mathbf{I}_\sigma)$$
$$\mathbf{I}_{(\mathit{list}\ \sigma)} = (\mathbf{I}\ \mathit{list})\ \mathbf{I}_\sigma$$
$$\mathbf{I}_{(\mathit{tree}\ \sigma)} = (\mathbf{I}\ \mathit{tree})\ \mathbf{I}_\sigma$$

Interpretation of the Types

$$\mathbf{I}\ [\![x^\sigma]\!]\ \rho^{\mathbf{I}} = \rho^{\mathbf{I}}\ x^\sigma$$

$$\mathbf{I}\ [\![c_\sigma]\!]\ \rho^{\mathbf{I}} = \mathbf{K}^{\mathbf{I}}\ [\![c_\sigma]\!]$$

$$\mathbf{I}\ [\![e_1\ e_2]\!]\ \rho^{\mathbf{I}} = (\mathbf{I}\ [\![e_1]\!]\ \rho^{\mathbf{I}})\ (\mathbf{I}\ [\![e_2]\!]\ \rho^{\mathbf{I}})$$

$$\mathbf{I}\ [\![\lambda x^\sigma.e]\!]\ \rho^{\mathbf{I}} = \lambda y \epsilon \mathbf{I}_\sigma.(\mathbf{I}\ [\![e]\!]\ \rho^{\mathbf{I}}[y/x^\sigma])$$

$$\mathbf{I}\ [\![\mathbf{fix}_{(\sigma\to\sigma)\to\sigma}\ e]\!]\ \rho^{\mathbf{I}} = \bigsqcup_{i\geq 0}\ (\mathbf{I}\ [\![e]\!]\ \rho^{\mathbf{I}})^i\ \bot_{\mathbf{I}_\sigma}$$

$$\mathbf{I}\ [\![\mathbf{let}\ x^\sigma = e_1\ \mathbf{in}\ e_2]\!]\ \rho^{\mathbf{I}} = (\mathbf{I}\ \mathit{let})\ (\mathbf{I}\ [\![e_1]\!]\ \rho^{\mathbf{I}})\ (\mathbf{I}\ [\![e_2]\!]\ \rho^{\mathbf{I}}[(\mathbf{I}\ [\![e_1]\!]\ \rho^{\mathbf{I}})/x^\sigma])$$

$$\mathbf{I}\ [\![\mathbf{tuple}_{(\sigma_1,\ldots,\sigma_k)}(e_1,\ldots,e_k)]\!]\ \rho^{\mathbf{I}} = (\mathbf{I}\ [\![e_1]\!]\ \rho^{\mathbf{I}},\ldots,\mathbf{I}\ [\![e_k]\!]\ \rho^{\mathbf{I}})$$

$$\mathbf{I}\ [\![\mathbf{tuples}_{(\sigma_1,\ldots,\sigma_k)}(e_1,\ldots,e_k)]\!]\ \rho^{\mathbf{I}} = \begin{cases} \bot_{\mathbf{I}_{\sigma_1}\otimes\ldots\otimes\mathbf{I}_{\sigma_k}}, & \text{if } \exists i \in \{1,\ldots,k\} : (\mathbf{I}\ [\![e_i]\!]\ \rho^{\mathbf{I}}) = \bot_{\mathbf{I}_{\sigma_i}} \\ <\mathbf{I}\ [\![e_1]\!]\ \rho^{\mathbf{I}},\ldots,\mathbf{I}\ [\![e_k]\!]\ \rho^{\mathbf{I}}>, & \text{otherwise} \end{cases}$$

$$\mathbf{I}\ [\![\mathbf{ins}_{\mathbf{i}(\sigma_1,\ldots,\sigma_k)}\ e]\!]\ \rho^{\mathbf{I}} = (\mathbf{I}\ \mathbf{ins}_{\mathbf{i}})\ (\mathbf{I}\ [\![e]\!]\ \rho^{\mathbf{I}})$$

$$\mathbf{I}\ [\![\mathbf{lift}_\sigma\ e]\!]\ \rho^{\mathbf{I}} = \mathit{lift}\ (\mathbf{I}\ [\![e]\!]\ \rho^{\mathbf{I}})$$

Interpretation of the Language Constructs

Figure 2.11: The **I** Interpretation for Λ_T

$$\mathbf{I}\ [\![\mathbf{take}_i\ e]\!]\ \rho^{\mathbf{I}} = (\mathbf{I}\ [\![e]\!]\ \rho^{\mathbf{I}}) \downarrow i$$
$$\mathbf{I}\ [\![\mathbf{takes}_i\ e]\!]\ \rho^{\mathbf{I}} = (\mathbf{I}\ [\![e]\!]\ \rho^{\mathbf{I}}) \downarrow i$$

Figure 2.12: The I-Interpretation of Constants which are the Same in all Interpretations

that the type constructors *list* and *tree* are treated differently in the standard and abstract interpretations, their **I**-interpretation equation in Figure 2.11 is written in the same way as that for smash sum.

Interpreting the Syntactic Constructs of Λ_T

The **I**-interpretation of the expression e will be denoted by $\mathbf{I}\ [\![e]\!]\ \rho^{\mathbf{I}}$. As with the interpretations of the types, the interpretations of some of the syntactic constructs of Λ_T remain constant in all interpretations. For example, the interpretation of an application is always the application of the interpretations of the two terms being applied. We will now explain the **I**-interpretation of each of the syntactic constructs of Λ_T, also given in Figure 2.11.

An interpretation of Λ_T is given in terms of an environment $\rho^{\mathbf{I}}$, where the superscript **I** indicates it is an environment for the **I**-interpretation. The environment gives a mapping from identifier names to the values which have been bound to the identifiers, and $\{\}$ is the empty environment. A modified environment is denoted by

$$\rho^{\mathbf{I}}[e/x^\sigma],$$

and is defined by:

$$\rho^{\mathbf{I}}[e/x^\sigma]\ y^\tau = if\ (y^\tau = x^\sigma)\ then\ e\ else\ (\rho^{\mathbf{I}}\ y^\tau).$$

Thus the interpretation rule for variables:

$$\mathbf{I}\ [\![x^\sigma]\!]\ \rho^{\mathbf{I}} = \rho^{\mathbf{I}}\ x^\sigma$$

says that the meaning of a variable is the value stored in the environment.

We assume that for each interpretation, there is an interpretation function $\mathbf{K}^{\mathbf{I}}$ for the constants, so that the **I**-interpretation of the constant c_σ is given by $(\mathbf{K}^{\mathbf{I}}\ [\![c_\sigma]\!])$. The interpretations of some constants are the same in all interpretations, and are given in Figure 2.12.

The rule for applications says that the interpretation of an application is just the application of the interpretations of the two terms being applied. It is usual in domain theory to represent functions using a notation like the typed lambda calculus. The rule:

$$\mathbf{I}\ [\![\lambda x^\sigma.e]\!]\ \rho^{\mathbf{I}} = \lambda y_\epsilon \mathbf{I}_\sigma.(\mathbf{I}\ [\![e]\!]\ \rho^{\mathbf{I}}[y/x^\sigma])$$

means that the **I**-interpretation of the term $(\lambda x^\sigma.e)$ is a function which takes an argument from the domain $\mathbf{I}_\sigma$, the **I**-interpretation of the type σ, and returns as a result the value of $(\mathbf{I}\ [\![e]\!]\ \rho^{\mathbf{I}}[y/x^\sigma])$, recalling that $\rho^{\mathbf{I}}[y/x^\sigma]$ denotes the environment where x^σ is bound to the value which was passed as an argument.

In general, expressions may have many fixed points. For example, the **I**-interpretation of $\lambda x^\sigma.x^\sigma$ has an infinite number of fixed points. Which one should be chosen? Programming language semantic theory says that we should choose the *least* fixed point, and the Fixed Point Theorem stated that the least fixed point of $f : \sigma \to \sigma$ is given by the formula:

$$\bigsqcup_{i \geq 0} f^i \perp_{\mathbf{I}_\sigma}.$$

This explains the interpretation of $\mathbf{fix}_{(\sigma\to\sigma)\to\sigma}$.

The let-expression:

$$(\mathbf{let}\ x^\sigma = e_1\ \mathbf{in}\ e_2) : \tau$$

was introduced with the intention that its standard interpretation should be bottom if the meaning of e_1 is bottom, otherwise it should be that of e_2 with all the free occurrences of x^σ in e_2 bound to the value of e_1. We could therefore have expected the **I**-interpretation of the let-expression to be defined by:

$$\mathbf{I}\ [\![(\mathbf{let}\ x^\sigma = e_1\ \mathbf{in}\ e_2) : \tau]\!]\ \rho^{\mathbf{I}} = \begin{cases} \perp_{\mathbf{I}_\tau} & \text{if } \mathbf{I}\ [\![e_1]\!]\ \rho^{\mathbf{I}} = \perp_{\mathbf{I}_\sigma} \\ \mathbf{I}\ [\![e_2]\!]\ \rho^{\mathbf{I}}[\mathbf{I}\ [\![e_1]\!]\ \rho^{\mathbf{I}}/x^\sigma] & \text{otherwise} \end{cases}$$

Unfortunately, this definition is not correct for some abstract interpretations, and a safe approximation to this value has to be given. For this reason, we write the **I**-interpretation of the let-expression as:

$$\mathbf{I}\ [\![\mathbf{let}\ x^\sigma = e_1\ \mathbf{in}\ e_2]\!]\ \rho^{\mathbf{I}} = (\mathbf{I}\ let)\ (\mathbf{I}\ [\![e_1]\!]\ \rho^{\mathbf{I}})\ (\mathbf{I}\ [\![e_2]\!]\ \rho^{\mathbf{I}}[(\mathbf{I}\ [\![e_1]\!]\ \rho^{\mathbf{I}})/x^\sigma]).$$

In passing, note that the occurrences of x^σ in e_1 are looked up in the environment $\rho^{\mathbf{I}}$, and so there is no recursion in the binding of x^σ.

The **I**-interpretation of $\sigma_1 \times \ldots \times \sigma_k$ is just $\mathbf{I}_{\sigma_1} \times \ldots \times \mathbf{I}_{\sigma_k}$, and so the **I**-interpretation of $\mathbf{tuple}_{(\sigma_1,\ldots,\sigma_k)}(e_1,\ldots,e_k)$ is the natural element of $\mathbf{I}_{\sigma_1} \times \ldots \times \mathbf{I}_{\sigma_k}$. For the construct $\mathbf{tuples}_{(\sigma_1,\ldots,\sigma_k)}(e_1,\ldots,e_k)$,the situation is similar, the only complication being that its interpretation must be the bottom of $\mathbf{I}_{\sigma_1} \otimes \ldots \otimes \mathbf{I}_{\sigma_k}$ if the interpretation of any of the e_i is the bottom of the interpretation of σ_i.

Because the interpretation of $\sigma_1 \oplus \ldots \oplus \sigma_k$ can vary, an interpretation for $\mathbf{ins}_{\mathbf{i}(\sigma_1,\ldots,\sigma_k)}$ has to provided for each interpretation. This is indicated by writing the **I**-interpretation of $\mathbf{ins}_{\mathbf{i}(\sigma_1,\ldots,\sigma_k)}$ as $(\mathbf{I}\ \mathbf{ins}_\mathbf{i})\ (\mathbf{I}\ [\![e]\!]\ \rho^{\mathbf{I}})$.

Finally, the **I**-interpretation of $\mathbf{lift}_\sigma$ gives a value which is in the lifted domain.

Summary

The forms of both the standard and any abstract interpretations we will consider have much in common, which is why we have written of the **I**-interpretation of Λ_T, and given the interpretation rules in Figure 2.11. To define a particular interpretation, the following need to be given:

1. the interpretation of $\oplus$;

2. the interpretation of $\mathbf{ins}_{\mathrm{i}(\sigma_1,\ldots,\sigma_k)}$, which depends on the interpretation given to $\oplus$;

3. domains as interpretations of the types *bool*, *int*, and for each type τ, $(list\ \tau)$ and $(tree\ \tau)$;

4. an interpretation of each of the constants given in Figure 2.6; and

5. an interpretation of the let-expression.

2.3.2 The Standard Interpretation of Λ_T

We will use $\mathbf{S}$ to denote the standard interpretation of Λ_T, so that $\mathbf{S}_\sigma$ is the standard interpretation of the type σ, and $\mathbf{S}\ [\![e]\!]\ \rho^{\mathbf{S}}$ is the standard interpretation of the expression e. The standard interpretation is specified by providing each of the items mentioned in the above summary. To see how Figure 2.11 gives a general interpretation for Λ_T, we give the standard interpretation of Λ_T in Figure 2.13.

The Standard Interpretation of $\oplus$ and $\mathbf{ins}_{\mathrm{i}(\sigma_1,\ldots,\sigma_k)}$

standard interpretation!smash sum

In the standard interpretation, $\oplus$ is interpreted as smash sum, so

$$\mathbf{S}_{\sigma_1\oplus\ldots\oplus\sigma_k} = \mathbf{S}_{\sigma_1} \oplus \ldots \oplus \mathbf{S}_{\sigma_k}.$$

As $\oplus$ is being interpreted as smash sum, the standard interpretation of $(\mathbf{ins}_{\mathrm{i}(\sigma_1,\ldots,\sigma_k)}\ e)$ must be an element of $\mathbf{S}_{\sigma_1} \oplus \ldots \oplus \mathbf{S}_{\sigma_k}$. We cannot define

$$\mathbf{S}\ [\![\mathbf{ins}_{\mathrm{i}(\sigma_1,\ldots,\sigma_k)}\ e]\!]\ \rho^{\mathbf{S}} = ins_i\ (\mathbf{S}\ [\![e]\!]\ \rho^{\mathbf{S}})$$

since $(\mathbf{S}\ [\![e]\!]\ \rho^{\mathbf{S}})$ may be $\perp_{\mathbf{S}_{\sigma_i}}$, and the smash sum does not contain elements of the form $(ins_i\ \perp_{\mathbf{S}_{\sigma_i}})$ (Definition 2.2.25). Therefore we define

$$\mathbf{S}\ [\![\mathbf{ins}_{\mathrm{i}(\sigma_1,\ldots,\sigma_k)}\ e]\!]\ \rho^{\mathbf{S}} = mk\_sum_i\ (\mathbf{S}\ [\![e]\!]\ \rho^{\mathbf{S}})$$

where mk_sum_i is defined in Figure 2.10.

The Standard Interpretation of *bool*, *int*, $(list\ \tau)$ and $(tree\ \tau)$

The standard interpretations of the types *bool* and *int*, denoted by $\mathbf{S}_{bool}$ and $\mathbf{S}_{int}$, are the usual flat domains. For *bool*, this is the domain containing *true*, *false*, and $\perp_{\mathbf{S}_{bool}}$, ordered by

$$a \sqsubseteq b \text{ if and only if } a = \perp_{\mathbf{S}_{bool}} \text{ or } a = b,$$

with

$$\mathbf{K}^{\mathbf{S}}\ [\![\mathbf{true}_{bool}]\!] = true \qquad \mathbf{K}^{\mathbf{S}}\ [\![\mathbf{false}_{bool}]\!] = false.$$

For *int*

$$\mathbf{K}^{\mathbf{S}}\ [\![\mathrm{n}_{int}]\!] = n$$

$$S_{(\sigma \rightarrow \tau)} = (S_\sigma) \rightarrow (S_\tau)$$
$$S_{(\sigma_1 \times \ldots \times \sigma_k)} = (S_{\sigma_1}) \times \ldots \times (S_{\sigma_k})$$
$$S_{(\sigma_1 \otimes \ldots \otimes \sigma_k)} = (S_{\sigma_1}) \otimes \ldots \otimes (S_{\sigma_k})$$
$$S_{(\sigma_1 \oplus \ldots \oplus \sigma_k)} = (S_{\sigma_1}) \oplus \ldots \oplus (S_{\sigma_k})$$
$$S_{(lift\ \sigma)} = lift\ (S_\sigma)$$
$$S_{(list\ \sigma)} = list\ (S_\sigma)$$
$$S_{(tree\ \sigma)} = tree\ (S_\sigma)$$

Interpretation of the Types

$$S\ [\![x^\sigma]\!]\ \rho^S = \rho^S\ x^\sigma$$

$$S\ [\![c_\sigma]\!]\ \rho^S = K^S\ [\![c_\sigma]\!]$$

$$S\ [\![e_1\ e_2]\!]\ \rho^S = (S\ [\![e_1]\!]\ \rho^S)\ (S\ [\![e_2]\!]\ \rho^S)$$

$$S\ [\![\lambda x^\sigma.e]\!]\ \rho^S = \lambda y \epsilon S_\sigma.(S\ [\![e]\!]\ \rho^S[y/x^\sigma])$$

$$S\ [\![\mathbf{fix}_{(\sigma\rightarrow\sigma)\rightarrow\sigma}\ e]\!]\ \rho^S = \bigsqcup_{i\geq 0}\ (S\ [\![e]\!]\ \rho^S)^i\ \perp_{S_\sigma}$$

$$S\ [\![(\mathbf{let}\ x^\sigma = e_1\ \mathbf{in}\ e_2) : \tau]\!]\ \rho^S = \begin{cases} \perp_{S_\tau} & \text{if } S\ [\![e_1]\!]\ \rho^S = \perp_{S_\sigma} \\ S\ [\![e_2]\!]\ \rho^S[S\ [\![e_1]\!]\ \rho^S/x^\sigma] & \text{otherwise} \end{cases}$$

$$S\ [\![\mathbf{tuple}_{(\sigma_1,\ldots,\sigma_k)}(e_1,\ldots,e_k)]\!]\ \rho^S = (S\ [\![e_1]\!]\ \rho^S,\ldots,S\ [\![e_k]\!]\ \rho^S)$$

$$S\ [\![\mathbf{tuples}_{(\sigma_1,\ldots,\sigma_k)}(e_1,\ldots,e_k)]\!]\ \rho^S$$

$$= \begin{cases} \perp_{S_{\sigma_1}\otimes\ldots\otimes S_{\sigma_k}}, & \text{if } \exists i \in \{1,\ldots,k\} : (S\ [\![e_i]\!]\ \rho^S) = \perp_{S_{\sigma_i}} \\ < S\ [\![e_1]\!]\ \rho^S,\ldots,S\ [\![e_k]\!]\ \rho^S >, & \text{otherwise} \end{cases}$$

$$S\ [\![\mathbf{ins}_{i(\sigma_1,\ldots,\sigma_k)}\ e]\!]\ \rho^S = mk\_sum_i\ (S\ [\![e]\!]\ \rho^S)$$

$$S\ [\![\mathbf{lift}_\sigma\ e]\!]\ \rho^S = lift\ (S\ [\![e]\!]\ \rho^S)$$

Interpretation of the Language Constructs

Figure 2.13: The Standard Interpretation of Λ_T

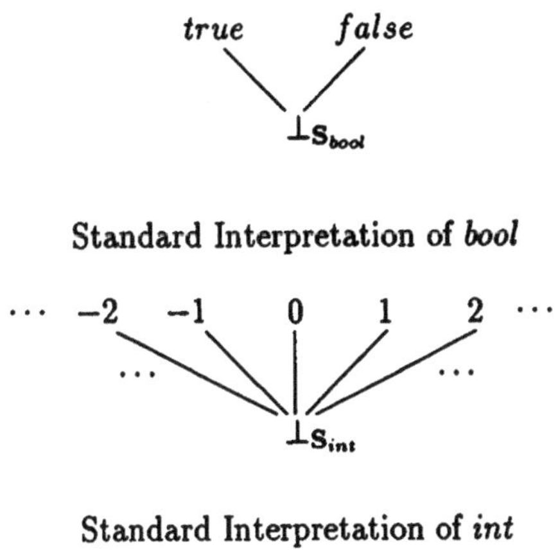

Figure 2.14: The Standard Interpretation of the Types *bool* and *int*

where n is any integer, with the ordering defined by

$$a \sqsubseteq b \text{ if and only if } a = \perp_{\mathbf{S}_{int}} \text{ or } a = b.$$

These domains are shown diagrammatically in Figure 2.14. Note that they are both *flat* domains (and hence flat complete partial orders).

The situation is more complex for the types ($list\ \tau$) and ($tree\ \tau$). If D is a domain, then the domain of lists of elements from D is the solution of the recursive domain isomorphism:

$$list\ D \cong 1 + D \times (list\ D).$$

so that, if $\mathbf{S}_\tau$ is the standard interpretation of the type τ, then the domain of lists of elements of type τ is given by the solution of the isomorphism:

$$list\ \mathbf{S}_\tau \cong 1 + \mathbf{S}_\tau \times (list\ \mathbf{S}_\tau).$$

In the case that D is $\mathbf{S}_{bool}$, compare this with how we could define the type list of booleans in a functional language:

```
> list bool ::= Nil | Cons bool (list bool)
```

Intuitively, the domain isomorphism can be read as saying that an element in $list\ D$ is either an element from the one point domain (that is, `Nil`), or is a pair of objects, the first of which is an element of D, the second of $list\ D$ (that is, the `Cons` of an element from D and one from $list\ D$). Effectively, `Nil` and `Cons` are the tags in_1 and in_2. This isomorphism can be solved over the category of domains to give the standard interpretation of the type (*list* τ) [SP82]. The domain given as the solution of the above isomorphism has as elements:

$$\mathbf{S}_{(list\ \tau)} = \{\bot_{\mathbf{S}_{(list\ \tau)}}\} \bigcup \{nil\} \bigcup \{cons\ u\ l | u \in \mathbf{S}_\tau, l \in \mathbf{S}_{(list\ \tau)}\}$$

with the ordering:

$$\begin{array}{l} \bot_{\mathbf{S}_{(list\ \tau)}} \sqsubseteq l, \forall l \in \mathbf{S}_{(list\ \tau)} \\ (cons\ u\ l) \sqsubseteq (cons\ u'\ l') \text{ if } u \sqsubseteq u' \text{ and } l \sqsubseteq l' \\ nil \sqsubseteq nil \end{array}$$

The difference between this list domain and the lists in a strict language like ML is that this domain contains infinite lists, lists which are terminated in $\bot_{\mathbf{S}_{(list\ \tau)}}$, and lists containing $\bot_{\mathbf{S}_\tau}$.

Trees can be treated in the same way as lists. In Section 1.1.2 we introduced the data type declaration:

```
> tree * ::= Empty | Node (tree *) * (tree *)
```

If τ is any type, the standard interpretation of the type (*tree* τ) is the solution of the domain isomorphism:

$$tree\ \mathbf{S}_\tau \cong 1 + (tree\ \mathbf{S}_\tau) \times \mathbf{S}_\tau \times (tree\ \mathbf{S}_\tau)$$

which has $\mathbf{S}_{(tree\ \tau)}$ as a solution, where

$$\mathbf{S}_{(tree\ \tau)} = \{\bot_{\mathbf{S}_{(tree\ \tau)}}\} \bigcup \{empty\} \bigcup \{node\ t_1\ n\ t_2 | t_1 \in \mathbf{S}_{(tree\ \tau)}, n \in \mathbf{S}_\tau, t_2 \in \mathbf{S}_{(tree\ \tau)}\}$$

with the ordering:

$$\begin{array}{l} \bot_{\mathbf{S}_{(tree\ \tau)}} \sqsubseteq t, \forall t \in \mathbf{S}_{(tree\ \tau)} \\ (node\ t_1\ n\ t_2) \sqsubseteq (node\ t_1'\ n'\ t_2') \text{ if } t_1 \sqsubseteq t_1' \text{ and } n \sqsubseteq n' \text{ and } t_2 \sqsubseteq t_2' \\ empty \sqsubseteq empty \end{array}$$

A number of functions on the domains $\mathbf{S}_{(list\ \tau)}$ and $\mathbf{S}_{(tree\ \tau)}$, that are used in defining the standard semantics of constants, are given in Figure 2.15.

The Standard Interpretation of the Functional Constants in Λ_T.

The standard interpretations of the functional constants in Λ_T are given in Figure 2.16, where $\wedge$ and $\vee$ are respectively the strict boolean functions *and* and *or*, and the rest of the functions used in giving the interpretations are defined in Figures 2.10 and 2.15. The S-interpretation of the constants $\mathbf{take_i}$ and $\mathbf{takes_i}$ can be deduced from the general definitions given in Figure 2.12.

The Standard Interpretation of the Let-Expression

The standard interpretation of the let-expression is:

$$\mathrm{S}\ [\![(\text{let } x^\sigma = e_1 \text{ in } e_2) : \tau]\!]\ \rho^{\mathrm{S}} = \begin{cases} \bot_{\mathbf{S}_\tau} & \text{if S } [\![e_1]\!]\ \rho^{\mathrm{S}} = \bot_{\mathbf{S}_\sigma} \\ \mathrm{S}\ [\![e_2]\!]\ \rho^{\mathrm{S}}[\mathrm{S}\ [\![e_1]\!]\ \rho^{\mathrm{S}}/x^\sigma] & \text{otherwise} \end{cases}$$

as expected.

$$head : \mathbf{S}_{(list\ \tau)} \rightarrow \mathbf{S}_{\tau}$$
$$head\ \bot_{\mathbf{S}_{(list\ \tau)}} = \bot_{\mathbf{S}_{\tau}}$$
$$head\ nil = \bot_{\mathbf{S}_{\tau}}$$
$$head\ (cons\ e_1\ e_2) = e_1$$

$$tail : \mathbf{S}_{(list\ \tau)} \rightarrow \mathbf{S}_{(list\ \tau)}$$
$$tail\ \bot_{\mathbf{S}_{(list\ \tau)}} = \bot_{\mathbf{S}_{(list\ \tau)}}$$
$$tail\ nil = \bot_{\mathbf{S}_{(list\ \tau)}}$$
$$tail\ (cons\ e_1\ e_2) = e_2$$

$$lcase : \mathbf{S}_{(list\ \tau)} \rightarrow \mathbf{S}_{\sigma} \rightarrow \mathbf{S}_{\tau \rightarrow (list\ \tau) \rightarrow \sigma} \rightarrow \mathbf{S}_{\sigma}$$
$$lcase\ \bot_{\mathbf{S}_{(list\ \tau)}}\ e_1\ e_2 = \bot_{\mathbf{S}_{\sigma}}$$
$$lcase\ nil\ e_1\ e_2 = e_1$$
$$lcase\ (cons\ e_1\ e_2)\ e_3\ e_4 = e_4\ e_1\ e_2$$

$$value : \mathbf{S}_{(tree\ \tau)} \rightarrow \mathbf{S}_{\tau}$$
$$value\ \bot_{\mathbf{S}_{(tree\ \tau)}} = \bot_{\mathbf{S}_{\tau}}$$
$$value\ empty = \bot_{\mathbf{S}_{\tau}}$$
$$value\ (node\ t_1\ n\ t_2) = n$$

$$left : \mathbf{S}_{(tree\ \tau)} \rightarrow \mathbf{S}_{(tree\ \tau)}$$
$$left\ \bot_{\mathbf{S}_{(tree\ \tau)}} = \bot_{\mathbf{S}_{(tree\ \tau)}}$$
$$left\ empty = \bot_{\mathbf{S}_{(tree\ \tau)}}$$
$$left\ (node\ t_1\ n\ t_2) = t_1$$

$$right : \mathbf{S}_{(tree\ \tau)} \rightarrow \mathbf{S}_{(tree\ \tau)}$$
$$right\ \bot_{\mathbf{S}_{(tree\ \tau)}} = \bot_{\mathbf{S}_{(tree\ \tau)}}$$
$$right\ empty = \bot_{\mathbf{S}_{(tree\ \tau)}}$$
$$right\ (node\ t_1\ n\ t_2) = t_2$$

$$tcase : \mathbf{S}_{(tree\ \tau)} \rightarrow \mathbf{S}_{\sigma} \rightarrow \mathbf{S}_{(tree\ \tau) \rightarrow \tau \rightarrow (tree\ \tau) \rightarrow \sigma} \rightarrow \mathbf{S}_{\sigma}$$
$$tcase\ \bot_{\mathbf{S}_{(tree\ \tau)}}\ e_1\ e_2 = \bot_{\mathbf{S}_{\sigma}}$$
$$tcase\ empty\ e_1\ e_2 = e_1$$
$$tcase\ (node\ e_1\ e_2\ e_3)\ e_4\ e_5 = e_5\ e_1\ e_2\ e_3$$

Figure 2.15: Definitions of Functions Which Operate on Lists and Trees

$$\mathbf{K}^{\mathbf{S}}\ [\![\mathbf{true}_{bool}]\!] = true \qquad \mathbf{K}^{\mathbf{S}}\ [\![\mathbf{false}_{bool}]\!] = false$$
$$\mathbf{K}^{\mathbf{S}}\ [\![\mathbf{and}_{bool \to bool \to bool}]\!] = \lambda x \epsilon \mathbf{S}_{bool}.\lambda y \epsilon \mathbf{S}_{bool}.x \wedge y$$
$$\mathbf{K}^{\mathbf{S}}\ [\![\mathbf{or}_{bool \to bool \to bool}]\!] = \lambda x \epsilon \mathbf{S}_{bool}.\lambda y \epsilon \mathbf{S}_{bool}.x \vee y$$
$$\mathbf{K}^{\mathbf{S}}\ [\![\mathbf{if}_{bool \to \sigma \to \sigma \to \sigma}]\!]\ x\ y\ z = \begin{cases} \bot_{\mathbf{S}_\sigma} & \text{if } x = \bot_{\mathbf{S}_{bool}} \\ y & \text{if } x = true \\ z & \text{if } x = false \end{cases}$$

$$\mathbf{K}^{\mathbf{S}}\ [\![\mathbf{0}_{int}]\!] = 0 \qquad \mathbf{K}^{\mathbf{S}}\ [\![\mathbf{1}_{int}]\!] = 1 \qquad \ldots$$
$$\mathbf{K}^{\mathbf{S}}\ [\![+_{int \to int \to int}]\!] = \lambda x \epsilon \mathbf{S}_{int}.\lambda y \epsilon \mathbf{S}_{int}. +\ x\ y$$
$$\mathbf{K}^{\mathbf{S}}\ [\![*_{int \to int \to int}]\!] = \lambda x \epsilon \mathbf{S}_{int}.\lambda y \epsilon \mathbf{S}_{int}. *\ x\ y$$
$$\mathbf{K}^{\mathbf{S}}\ [\![-_{int \to int \to int}]\!] = \lambda x \epsilon \mathbf{S}_{int}.\lambda y \epsilon \mathbf{S}_{int}. -\ x\ y$$
$$\mathbf{K}^{\mathbf{S}}\ [\![/_{int \to int \to int}]\!] = \lambda x \epsilon \mathbf{S}_{int}.\lambda y \epsilon \mathbf{S}_{int}. /\ x\ y$$

$$\mathbf{K}^{\mathbf{S}}\ [\![>_{int \to int \to bool}]\!] = \lambda x \epsilon \mathbf{S}_{int}.\lambda y \epsilon \mathbf{S}_{int}. >\ x\ y$$
$$\mathbf{K}^{\mathbf{S}}\ [\![\geq_{int \to int \to bool}]\!] = \lambda x \epsilon \mathbf{S}_{int}.\lambda y \epsilon \mathbf{S}_{int}. \geq\ x\ y$$
$$\mathbf{K}^{\mathbf{S}}\ [\![<_{int \to int \to bool}]\!] = \lambda x \epsilon \mathbf{S}_{int}.\lambda y \epsilon \mathbf{S}_{int}. <\ x\ y$$
$$\mathbf{K}^{\mathbf{S}}\ [\![\leq_{int \to int \to bool}]\!] = \lambda x \epsilon \mathbf{S}_{int}.\lambda y \epsilon \mathbf{S}_{int}. \leq\ x\ y$$
$$\mathbf{K}^{\mathbf{S}}\ [\![=_{int \to int \to bool}]\!] = \lambda x \epsilon \mathbf{S}_{int}.\lambda y \epsilon \mathbf{S}_{int}. =\ x\ y$$

$$\mathbf{K}^{\mathbf{S}}\ [\![\mathbf{nil}_{(list\ \tau)}]\!] = nil$$
$$\mathbf{K}^{\mathbf{S}}\ [\![\mathbf{cons}_{\tau \to (list\ \tau) \to (list\ \tau)}]\!] = cons$$
$$\mathbf{K}^{\mathbf{S}}\ [\![\mathbf{head}_{(list\ \tau) \to \tau}]\!] = head$$
$$\mathbf{K}^{\mathbf{S}}\ [\![\mathbf{tail}_{(list\ \tau) \to (list\ \tau)}]\!] = tail$$
$$\mathbf{K}^{\mathbf{S}}\ [\![\mathbf{lcase}_{(list\ \tau) \to \sigma \to (\tau \to (list\ \tau) \to \sigma) \to \sigma}]\!] = lcase$$

$$\mathbf{K}^{\mathbf{S}}\ [\![\mathbf{empty}_{(tree\ \tau)}]\!] = empty$$
$$\mathbf{K}^{\mathbf{S}}\ [\![\mathbf{node}_{(tree\ \tau) \to \tau \to (tree\ \tau)}]\!] = node$$
$$\mathbf{K}^{\mathbf{S}}\ [\![\mathbf{value}_{(tree\ \tau) \to \tau}]\!] = value$$
$$\mathbf{K}^{\mathbf{S}}\ [\![\mathbf{left}_{(tree\ \tau) \to (tree\ \tau)}]\!] = left$$
$$\mathbf{K}^{\mathbf{S}}\ [\![\mathbf{right}_{(tree\ \tau) \to (tree\ \tau)}]\!] = right$$
$$\mathbf{K}^{\mathbf{S}}\ [\![\mathbf{tcase}_{(tree\ \tau) \to \sigma \to ((tree\ \tau) \to \tau \to (tree\ \tau) \to \sigma) \to \sigma}]\!] = tcase$$

$$\mathbf{K}^{\mathbf{S}}\ [\![\mathbf{outs}_{\mathbf{i}_{\sigma_1 \oplus \ldots \oplus \sigma_k \to \sigma_i}}]\!] = outs_i$$
$$\mathbf{K}^{\mathbf{S}}\ [\![\mathbf{iss}_{\mathbf{i}_{\sigma_1 \oplus \ldots \oplus \sigma_k \to bool}}]\!] = iss_i$$

Figure 2.16: The Standard Interpretation of the Constants in Λ_T

2.4 A Result Relating the Operational Semantics and Standard Interpretation of Λ_T

We would hope that there is a strong relationship between the operational semantics and the standard interpretation of Λ_T, and in fact there is one.

Not all types are suitable as the type of a program. We have said that reduction of an expression should terminate when an HNF has been obtained for the expression. The concept of HNF is not defined for terms of some types, $\sigma_1 \times \ldots \times \sigma_k$ for example, and so such types should not be considered as valid types for programs. Moreover, it is normal functional programming practice to restrict programs to being terms of *ground* type, that is, containing no function types. Of course subexpressions in the program can have one of these types, as long as the final type of a program does not. Formally, we define the predicates *valid* and ground on types by:

$$
\begin{array}{llllll}
\textit{valid bool} & = & \textit{true} & \textit{ground bool} & = & \textit{true} \\
\textit{valid int} & = & \textit{true} & \textit{ground int} & = & \textit{true} \\
\textit{valid}\ (\sigma \rightarrow \tau) & = & \textit{false} & \textit{ground}\ (\sigma \rightarrow \tau) & = & \textit{false} \\
\textit{valid}\ (\sigma_1 \times \ldots \times \sigma_k) & = & \textit{false} & \textit{ground}\ (\sigma_1 \times \ldots \times \sigma_k) & = & \bigwedge_{i=1}^{k} \textit{ground}\ \sigma_i \\
\textit{valid}\ (\sigma_1 \otimes \ldots \otimes \sigma_k) & = & \bigwedge_{i=1}^{k} \textit{valid}\ \sigma_i & \textit{ground}\ (\sigma_1 \otimes \ldots \otimes \sigma_k) & = & \bigwedge_{i=1}^{k} \textit{ground}\ \sigma_i \\
\textit{valid}\ (\sigma_1 \oplus \ldots \oplus \sigma_k) & = & \bigwedge_{i=1}^{k} \textit{valid}\ \sigma_i & \textit{ground}\ (\sigma_1 \oplus \ldots \oplus \sigma_k) & = & \bigwedge_{i=1}^{k} \textit{ground}\ \sigma_i \\
\textit{valid}\ (\textit{lift}\ \sigma) & = & \textit{ground}\ \sigma & \textit{ground}\ (\textit{lift}\ \sigma) & = & \textit{ground}\ \sigma \\
\textit{valid}\ (\textit{list}\ \sigma) & = & \textit{ground}\ \sigma & \textit{ground}\ (\textit{list}\ \sigma) & = & \textit{ground}\ \sigma \\
\textit{valid}\ (\textit{tree}\ \sigma) & = & \textit{ground}\ \sigma & \textit{ground}\ (\textit{tree}\ \sigma) & = & \textit{ground}\ \sigma
\end{array}
$$

We now define a *program* to be any closed term of Λ_T which has a valid type.

Theorem 2.4.1 (Computational Adequacy Theorem)

Given any program $e : \sigma$, F_ℓ, the leftmost reduction strategy, fails to terminate if and only if $\mathsf{S}\ [\![e]\!]\ \{\} = \bot_{\mathsf{S}_\sigma}$. *Moreover, if the reduction sequence terminates in some HNF e', then*

$$\mathsf{S}\ [\![e]\!]\ \{\} = \mathsf{S}\ [\![e']\!]\ \{\}.$$

As we saw in Theorem 2.1.14, the leftmost strategy terminates if and only if the expression has an HNF, otherwise it continues forever. The semantic domain point $\bot_{\mathsf{S}_\sigma}$ represents no information, and a non-terminating computation that produces no HNF can certainly be regarded as producing no information. So the theorem says that the two ways of giving semantics agree when a program gives no information. Furthermore, the second part of the theorem assures us that when the head-normalising reduction sequence terminates with a HNF, then it has preserved the semantics of the original program. This theorem is used in Chapter 5 as an example of what we will call a *safe* reduction strategy.

The theorem also indicates why there is no sensible notion of HNF for an object of type $\sigma_1 \times \ldots \times \sigma_k$. Reduction to HNF should fail to terminate if and only if the semantics of the term is the $\bot$ of the appropriate type. For the type $\sigma_1 \times \ldots \times \sigma_k$ there is no *sequential* reduction strategy which will achieve this. We can see that this is the case because the bottom element of $\mathsf{S}_{\sigma_1 \times \ldots \times \sigma_k}$ is $(\bot_{\mathsf{S}_{\sigma_1}}, \ldots, \bot_{\mathsf{S}_{\sigma_k}})$. Evaluation must terminate if and only if at least one of the elements of the tuple does not have the bottom element of the corresponding domain as its standard interpretation. In general, this can only be achieved by reducing all of the expressions which are arguments to $\textbf{tuple}_{(\sigma_1,\ldots,\sigma_k)}$ in *parallel*, and terminating when one of them reaches an HNF. We return to this problem when evaluators are defined formally in Section 5.2.

2.5 Drawing it Together

In introducing the operational and denotational semantics of the typed lambda calculus, we have covered a lot of ground. The important results for the rest of the book are summarised below:

Operational Semantics:

- The Church-Rosser Theorem says that the order of choosing redexes in a terminating reduction sequence does not matter, for if some other reduction sequence is chosen, which gives a different result, there is always another term to which both results can be reduced in a finite number of reduction steps. This will allow us to change the evaluation order of a program if we preserve its termination properties.
- The reduction strategy of reducing the leftmost redex at each reduction step will produce an answer, that is, a result in HNF, if one exists. Otherwise, it will not terminate.

Interpretations:

- Any formal language must be given an interpretation.
- For the typed lambda calculus, giving an interpretation involves defining domains as interpretations of the types and giving the meaning of the syntactic constructs of the language.
- We require a framework where a *standard* interpretation, the normal denotational semantics, and a number of *abstract* interpretations can be given.
- For our purposes, it is sufficient to interpret most of the type constructors the same way in any interpretation. This means that the interpretation of many of the syntactic constructs in the language have the same form in any interpretation. Because of this, we were able to give a parameterised interpretation, which can be specialised to give a particular interpretation.
- Using the parameterised interpretation, we gave the standard interpretation of the language Λ_T.

Relating the Operational and Denotational Views:

- The reduction strategy F_ℓ fails to terminate when reducing an expression if and only if the standard interpretation of the expression is bottom (from the appropriate domain). In defining other evaluation strategies later in the book, we will preserve this termination property.

Chapter 3

A Framework for the Abstract Interpretation of Functional Languages

In Section 2.3 we gave a general interpretation for Λ_T. To specialise it to a particular interpretation, the following things need to be given:

1. the interpretation of $\oplus$;
2. the interpretation of $\mathbf{ins}_{\mathbf{i}(\sigma_1,\ldots,\sigma_k)}$, which depends on the interpretation given to $\oplus$;
3. domains as interpretations of the types *bool*, *int*, (*list* τ) and (*tree* τ) for any type
4. an interpretation of each of the constants from Λ_T; and
5. an interpretation of the let-expression.

The purpose of an *abstract* interpretation is to capture some property of interest, to use this to make inferences about programs, and to be assured that conclusions drawn are correct. In our case, we develop a framework for the abstract interpretation of Λ_T in order to find out evaluation transformer information. It is a *framework* because we only fix (1), (2) and (5) above, but do not fix (3) or (4); it is in varying the abstract interpretations of booleans, integers, lists and trees, and consequently of the functional constants over these types, that we get different abstract interpretations. To use the framework, we place restrictions on what can be given for (3) and (4), so that to specify a particular abstract interpretation, the following have to be given:

- *finite lattices* as the abstract interpretation of the types *bool*, *int*, (*list* τ) and (*tree* τ) for any type τ;
- an abstract interpretation for each of the constants in Λ_T *which satisfies a safety condition*; and
- *a strict, continuous abstraction map for each of the types bool, int,* (*list* τ) *and* (*tree* τ), *from the standard interpretation of the type to its abstract interpretation.*

Why these extra conditions?

Lattices are needed for abstract domains because the abstraction maps that will be defined for functional types require the existence of least upper bounds. We will also see that the abstract interpretation of $\mathbf{if}_{bool \to \sigma \to \sigma \to \sigma}$ is defined using least upper bound. The lattices need to be *finite* because recursive functions are translated into Λ_T using $\mathbf{fix}_{\sigma \to \sigma \to \sigma}$, and we saw in Figure 2.11 and Section 2.3.1 that the interpretation of $\mathbf{fix}_{(\sigma \to \sigma) \to \sigma}$ involves finding a least fixed point. This is guaranteed to be computable in finite time if the abstract domains are finite[1]. Given finite lattices for booleans, integers, lists and trees, the interpretation of constructed types using the rules given in Figure 2.11 results in finite lattices for the abstract interpretations of all types.

The other two conditions, that the abstract interpretations of the constants must satisfy a safety condition, and that strict, continuous abstraction maps must be given from the standard interpretations of booleans, integers, lists and trees to their abstract interpretations, are to do with ensuring the *correctness* of the abstract interpretation framework. When should we say that an abstract interpretation is *correct*? Let us denote the abstract interpretation of the type σ by $\mathbf{A}_\sigma$, and the abstract interpretation of an expression e by $\mathbf{A}\ [\![e]\!]\ \rho^{\mathbf{A}}$ (so that $\mathbf{A}$ stands for 'abstract'). Each abstract domain point 'represents' a set of objects from the standard interpretation of a type (roughly the set of objects which abstract to a point no more defined than that point). If an abstract interpretation is correct, then we would expect that for all $f : \sigma \to \tau$,

$$(\mathbf{A}\ [\![f]\!]\ \rho^{\mathbf{A}})\ \overline{s} = \overline{t}$$

implies that $\overline{t}$ 'represents'

$$(\mathbf{S}\ [\![f]\!]\ \rho^{\mathbf{S}})\ s$$

for all $s \in \mathbf{S}_\sigma$ which are 'represented' by $\overline{s} \in \mathbf{A}_\sigma$. In Section 3.2 we will formalise 'represents' in terms of concretisation. Using this notion, we formally define correctness in Section 3.3, and there prove the correctness of the framework we develop in this chapter.

The importance of this chapter is that the framework allows the specification of particular abstract interpretations, that are guaranteed to be correct, by just giving some simple pieces of information. Our program is to give the abstract interpretation of Λ_T in Section 3.1, parameterised on the three points above. In Section 3.2 we define abstraction and concretisation maps for all types, and give some useful properties that they have, then in Section 3.3 we prove that the framework we have developed is correct.

Most of the proofs are given in Appendix A, Section A.3, rather than in the body of the chapter.

[1]The reader may then ask how a computer ever manages to implement a recursive function if it is defined as the least fixed point of some expression over an infinite domain. The point is that it does not calculate the *whole* fixed point, but only the fixed point at the value where it is needed. In abstract interpretation we must calculate the entire fixed point.

3.1 The Abstract Interpretation of Λ_T

The Abstract Interpretation of $\oplus$ and $\mathbf{ins}_{\mathbf{i}(\sigma_1,\ldots,\sigma_k)}$

In the standard interpretation, $\oplus$ is interpreted as smash sum, so

$$\mathbf{S}_{\sigma_1\oplus\ldots\oplus\sigma_k} = \mathbf{S}_{\sigma_1} \oplus \ldots \oplus \mathbf{S}_{\sigma_k}.$$

To use some sort of sum in the abstract interpretation loses a lot of information - which we will demonstrate in Section 4.1.2 - so we interpret $\oplus$ as product in the abstract interpretation, that is,

$$\mathbf{A}_{\sigma_1\oplus\ldots\oplus\sigma_k} = \mathbf{A}_{\sigma_1} \times \ldots \times \mathbf{A}_{\sigma_k}.$$

The idea is that the abstract domain point $(\bar{s}_1, \ldots, \bar{s}_k)$ 'represents' the set

$$\bigcup_{i=1}^{k} \{ins_i\ s_i | \bar{s}_i \text{ 'represents' } s_i\} \bigcup \{\perp_{\mathbf{S}_{\sigma_1\oplus\ldots\oplus\sigma_k}}\}.^2$$

Therefore we define

$$(\mathbf{A}\ [\![\mathbf{ins}_{\mathbf{i}(\sigma_1,\ldots,\sigma_k)}]\!]\ \rho^{\mathbf{A}})\ \bar{s} = (\perp_{\mathbf{A}_{\sigma_1}}, \ldots, \perp_{\mathbf{A}_{\sigma_{i-1}}}, \bar{s}, \perp_{\mathbf{A}_{\sigma_{i+1}}}, \ldots, \perp_{\mathbf{A}_{\sigma_k}}).$$

We shall see that in all the abstract interpretations we will define, the only object that is represented by $\perp_{\mathbf{A}_{\sigma_j}}$ is $\perp_{\mathbf{S}_{\sigma_j}}$, and so the abstract domain point

$$(\perp_{\mathbf{A}_{\sigma_1}}, \ldots, \perp_{\mathbf{A}_{\sigma_{i-1}}}, \bar{s}, \perp_{\mathbf{A}_{\sigma_{i+1}}}, \ldots, \perp_{\mathbf{A}_{\sigma_k}})$$

does only represent objects of the form $(ins_i\ s)$, where $\bar{s}$ represents s (plus the point $\perp_{\mathbf{S}_{\sigma_1\oplus\ldots\oplus\sigma_k}}$.

Abstract Interpretation of *bool*, *int*, (*list* τ) and (*tree* τ)

As discussed in the introduction to this chapter, we assume that finite lattices have been given as abstract interpretations of each of these types. Then we have the following.

Proposition 3.1.1

For all types σ, $\mathbf{A}_\sigma$ is a finite lattice.

[2] This formula is not entirely correct, as 'represents' is formalised by concretisation, concretisation returns sets which contain bottom, and objects of the form $(ins_i\ \perp_{\mathbf{S}_{\sigma_i}})$ do not occur in domains formed using the smash sum. The formula given in Proposition 3.2.8 is correct.

$\mathbf{A}_{(\sigma\to\tau)} = (\mathbf{A}_\sigma) \to (\mathbf{A}_\tau)$
$\mathbf{A}_{(\sigma_1\times\ldots\times\sigma_k)} = (\mathbf{A}_{\sigma_1}) \times \ldots \times (\mathbf{A}_{\sigma_k})$
$\mathbf{A}_{(\sigma_1\otimes\ldots\otimes\sigma_k)} = (\mathbf{A}_{\sigma_1}) \otimes \ldots \otimes (\mathbf{A}_{\sigma_k})$
$\mathbf{A}_{(\sigma_1\oplus\ldots\oplus\sigma_k)} = (\mathbf{A}_{\sigma_1}) \times \ldots \times (\mathbf{A}_{\sigma_k})$
$\mathbf{A}_{(lift\ \sigma)} = lift\ (\mathbf{A}_\sigma)$
$\mathbf{A}_{(list\ \sigma)} = (\mathbf{A}\ list)\ \mathbf{A}_\sigma$
$\mathbf{A}_{(tree\ \sigma)} = (\mathbf{A}\ tree)\ \mathbf{A}_\sigma$ } For each specific abstract interpretation, finite lattices must be given for these.

Interpretation of the Types

$\mathbf{A}\ [\![x^\sigma]\!]\ \rho^{\mathbf{A}} = \rho^{\mathbf{A}}\ x^\sigma$

$\mathbf{A}\ [\![c_\sigma]\!]\ \rho^{\mathbf{A}} = \mathbf{K}^{\mathbf{A}}\ [\![c_\sigma]\!]$ - Must be given for each specific abstract interpretation.

$\mathbf{A}\ [\![e_1\ e_2]\!]\ \rho^{\mathbf{A}} = (\mathbf{A}\ [\![e_1]\!]\ \rho^{\mathbf{A}})\ (\mathbf{A}\ [\![e_2]\!]\ \rho^{\mathbf{A}})$

$\mathbf{A}\ [\![\lambda x^\sigma.e]\!]\ \rho^{\mathbf{A}} = \lambda y \epsilon \mathbf{A}_\sigma.(\mathbf{A}\ [\![e]\!]\ \rho^{\mathbf{A}}[y/x^\sigma])$

$\mathbf{A}\ [\![\mathrm{fix}_{(\sigma\to\sigma)\to\sigma}\ e]\!]\ \rho^{\mathbf{A}} = \bigsqcup_{i\geq 0}\ (\mathbf{A}\ [\![e]\!]\ \rho^{\mathbf{A}})^i\ \bot_{\mathbf{A}_\sigma}$

$\mathbf{A}\ [\![(\mathrm{let}\ x^\sigma = e_1\ \mathrm{in}\ e_2) : \tau]\!]\ \rho^{\mathbf{A}}$

$$= \begin{cases} \bot_{\mathbf{A}_\tau} & \text{if } \alpha_\sigma \text{ is bottom-reflecting and } \mathbf{A}\ [\![e_1]\!]\ \rho^{\mathbf{A}} = \bot_{\mathbf{A}_\sigma} \\ \mathbf{A}\ [\![e_2]\!]\ \rho^{\mathbf{A}}[\mathbf{A}\ [\![e_1]\!]\ \rho^{\mathbf{A}}/x^\sigma] & \text{otherwise} \end{cases}$$

$\mathbf{A}\ [\![\mathrm{tuple}_{(\sigma_1,\ldots,\sigma_k)}(e_1,\ldots,e_k)]\!]\ \rho^{\mathbf{A}} = (\mathbf{A}\ [\![e_1]\!]\ \rho^{\mathbf{A}},\ldots,\mathbf{A}\ [\![e_k]\!]\ \rho^{\mathbf{A}})$

$\mathbf{A}\ [\![\mathrm{tuples}_{(\sigma_1,\ldots,\sigma_k)}(e_1,\ldots,e_k)]\!]\ \rho^{\mathbf{A}}$

$$= \begin{cases} \bot_{\mathbf{A}_{\sigma_1}\otimes\ldots\otimes\mathbf{A}_{\sigma_k}} & \text{if } \exists i \in \{1,\ldots,k\} : (\mathbf{A}\ [\![e_i]\!]\ \rho^{\mathbf{A}}) = \bot_{\mathbf{A}_{\sigma_i}} \\ < \mathbf{A}\ [\![e_1]\!]\ \rho^{\mathbf{A}},\ldots,\mathbf{A}\ [\![e_k]\!]\ \rho^{\mathbf{A}} > & \text{otherwise} \end{cases}$$

$\mathbf{A}\ [\![\mathrm{ins}_{i(\sigma_1,\ldots,\sigma_k)}\ e]\!]\ \rho^{\mathbf{A}} = (\bot_{\mathbf{A}_{\sigma_1}},\ldots,\bot_{\mathbf{A}_{\sigma_{i-1}}},\mathbf{A}\ [\![e]\!]\ \rho^{\mathbf{A}},\bot_{\mathbf{A}_{\sigma_{i+1}}},\ldots\bot_{\mathbf{A}_{\sigma_k}})$

$\mathbf{A}\ [\![\mathrm{lift}_\sigma\ e]\!]\ \rho^{\mathbf{A}} = lift\ (\mathbf{A}\ [\![e]\!]\ \rho^{\mathbf{A}})$

Interpretation of the Language Constructs

Figure 3.1: The Abstract Interpretation of Λ_T

The Abstract Interpretation of the Let-Expression

In the next section, we will see that the standard and abstract interpretations of the types in Λ_T are related by an abstraction map for each type. If we denote the abstraction map for the type σ by α_σ, then the correctness of the abstract interpretation framework depends on being able to prove that

$$\mathbf{A}\ [\![e]\!]\ \rho^{\mathbf{A}} \sqsupseteq \alpha_\sigma\ (\mathbf{S}\ [\![e]\!]\ \rho^{\mathbf{S}})$$

for any expression e in Λ_T. If we were to define the abstract interpretation of the let-expression to be:

$$\mathbf{A}\ [\![(\text{let } x^\sigma = e_1 \text{ in } e_2) : \tau]\!]\ \rho^{\mathbf{A}} = \begin{cases} \perp_{\mathbf{A}_\tau} & \text{if } \mathbf{A}\ [\![e_1]\!]\ \rho^{\mathbf{A}} = \perp_{\mathbf{A}_\sigma} \\ \mathbf{A}\ [\![e_2]\!]\ \rho^{\mathbf{A}}[\mathbf{A}\ [\![e_1]\!]\ \rho^{\mathbf{A}}/x^\sigma] & \text{otherwise} \end{cases}$$

then the required relationship does not necessarily hold for abstract interpretations where the abstraction map for the type σ is not bottom-reflecting. However, it does hold when the abstraction map is bottom-reflecting, so we define:

$$\mathbf{A}\ [\![(\text{let } x^\sigma = e_1 \text{ in } e_2) : \tau]\!]\ \rho^{\mathbf{A}} = \begin{cases} \perp_{\mathbf{A}_\tau}, \text{if } \alpha_\sigma \text{ is bottom-reflecting and } \mathbf{A}\ [\![e_1]\!]\ \rho^{\mathbf{A}} = \perp_{\mathbf{A}_\sigma} \\ \mathbf{A}\ [\![e_2]\!]\ \rho^{\mathbf{A}}[\mathbf{A}\ [\![e_1]\!]\ \rho^{\mathbf{A}}/x^\sigma], \text{ otherwise} \end{cases}$$

Summary

For completeness, we give the abstract interpretation of Λ_T in Figure 3.1. This should be compared with the general interpretation given in Figure 2.11 and the standard interpretation given in Figure 2.13. We postpone giving specific examples of lattices as abstract interpretations of booleans, integers, lists and trees until the next chapter, and therefore cannot give any abstract interpretations of constants at this stage.

3.2 Abstraction and Concretisation Maps

Abstraction and *concretisation* maps have to be defined in order to relate the standard and abstract interpretations. We will denote the abstraction map for the type σ by α_σ, and the concretisation map by γ_σ. The functionalities of these maps are:

$$\begin{aligned} \alpha_\sigma &: \mathbf{S}_\sigma \to \mathbf{A}_\sigma \\ \gamma_\sigma &: \mathbf{A}_\sigma \to \mathbf{PS}_\sigma. \end{aligned}$$

In this section we assume that strict, continuous abstraction maps have been given for *bool* and *int*, and if τ is any type, for (*list* τ) and (*tree* τ).

3.2.1 Definition of the Abstraction and Concretisation Maps

Abstraction maps for the constructed types are defined by induction over the type structure. For all type constructors except the function space, the abstraction maps are defined by in the following.

Definition 3.2.1

$$\alpha_{\sigma_1 \times \ldots \times \sigma_k} = (\alpha_{\sigma_1} \times \ldots \times \alpha_{\sigma_k})$$

$$\alpha_{\sigma_1 \otimes \ldots \otimes \sigma_k} = (\alpha_{\sigma_1} \otimes \ldots \otimes \alpha_{\sigma_k})$$

$$\alpha_{\sigma_1 \oplus \ldots \oplus \sigma_k}\ \bot_{\mathbf{S}_{\sigma_1 \oplus \ldots \oplus \sigma_k}} = (\bot_{\mathbf{A}_{\sigma_1}}, \ldots, \bot_{\mathbf{A}_{\sigma_k}})$$
$$\alpha_{\sigma_1 \oplus \ldots \oplus \sigma_k}\ (ins_i\ e) = (\bot_{\mathbf{A}_{\sigma_1}}, \ldots, \bot_{\mathbf{A}_{\sigma_{i-1}}}, \alpha_{\sigma_i}\ e, \bot_{\mathbf{A}_{\sigma_{i+1}}}, \ldots, \bot_{\mathbf{A}_{\sigma_k}})$$

$$\alpha_{(lift\ \sigma)} = lift\ \alpha_\sigma$$

where the product, smash product and lifting of functions are defined in Definition 2.2.29.

How can we define an abstraction map for the type $\sigma \rightarrow \tau$, that is, given some $f \in \mathbf{S}_{\sigma\rightarrow\tau}$:

$$\mathbf{S}_\sigma \xrightarrow{f} \mathbf{S}_\tau,$$

how can we define:

$$\mathbf{A}_\sigma \xrightarrow{\alpha_{\sigma\rightarrow\tau}\ f} \mathbf{A}_\tau?$$

For any such $f \in \mathbf{S}_{\sigma\rightarrow\tau}$, and some $\overline{s} \in \mathbf{A}_\sigma$, $((\alpha_{\sigma\rightarrow\tau}\ f)\ \overline{s})$ is supposed to 'represent' the action of f on all the values 'represented' by $\overline{s}$. Suppose that a representation (or concretisation) function, $\gamma_\sigma : \mathbf{A}_\sigma \rightarrow \mathbf{P}\ \mathbf{S}_\sigma$, has been defined for the type σ, so that $(\gamma_\sigma\ \overline{s})$ is the set of objects that $\overline{s}$ represents. Then the value of f on all of the objects in $(\gamma_\sigma\ \overline{s})$ is obtained by applying f to all of the values in the set. Since $(\gamma_\sigma\ \overline{s})$is an element of $\mathbf{P}\ \mathbf{S}_\sigma$ (the Hoare powerdomain of $\mathbf{S}_\sigma$), the application of f to all the elements in $(\gamma_\sigma\ \overline{s})$ is written $(\mathbf{P}\ f)\ (\gamma_\sigma\ \overline{s})$, and the process is shown diagrammatically as:

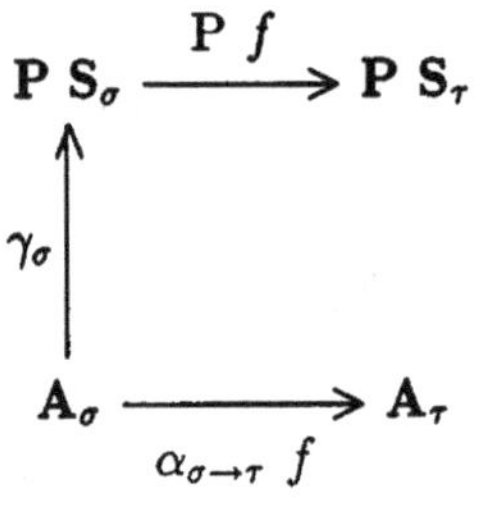

The value of $((\alpha_{\sigma\rightarrow\tau}\ f)\ \overline{s})$ is to be some $\overline{t} \in \mathbf{A}_\tau$. How can this be chosen so that it represents the set $(\mathbf{P}\ f)\ (\gamma_\sigma\ \overline{s})$? The set $(\mathbf{P}\ f)\ (\gamma_\sigma\ \overline{s})$ can be abstracted using $\mathbf{P}\ \alpha_\tau$, to give a set of elements in $\mathbf{P}\ \mathbf{A}_\tau$. Which one should we choose as the representative of the whole set? We choose the least upper bound of all of the abstract values because this is the least element which captures all of the information from each of the abstract values in the set. Thus we make the following definition.

Definition 3.2.2

For all types σ and τ,

$$\alpha_{\sigma\to\tau}\ f = \bigsqcup \circ (\mathbf{P}\ \alpha_\tau) \circ (\mathbf{P}\ f) \circ \gamma_\sigma.$$

which is shown diagrammatically by:

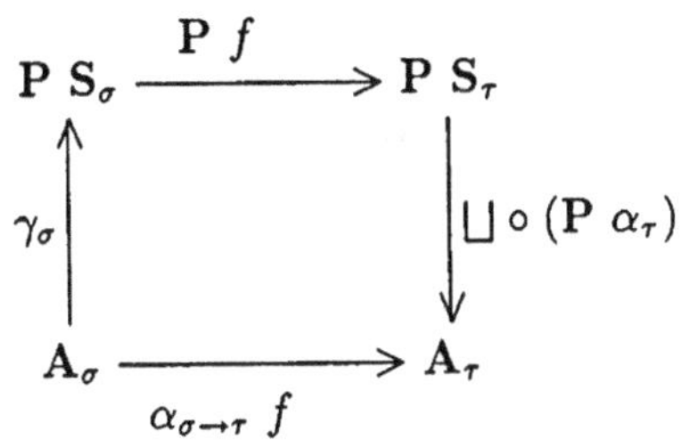

The composition $\bigsqcup \circ (\mathbf{P}\ \alpha_\sigma)$ occurs so often that we give it a separate name.

Definition 3.2.3

$$\begin{aligned} Abs_\sigma &: \mathbf{P}\ \mathbf{S}_\sigma \to \mathbf{A}_\sigma \\ Abs_\sigma &= \bigsqcup \circ \mathbf{P}\ \alpha_\sigma \end{aligned}$$

With this definition we will sometimes write:

$$\alpha_{\sigma\to\tau}\ f = Abs_\tau \circ (\mathbf{P}\ f) \circ \gamma_\sigma.$$

It only remains to define γ_σ. We define it so that γ_σ and Abs_σ are *adjoined* functions (see Proposition 3.2.11) [GHK+80].

$$\begin{aligned} \gamma_\sigma &: \mathbf{A}_\sigma \to \mathbf{P}\ \mathbf{S}_\sigma \\ \gamma_\sigma\ \overline{s} &= \bigcup\{S|(Abs_\sigma\ S) \sqsubseteq \overline{s}\} \end{aligned}$$

The reason for requiring adjointness is that it guarantees that the abstraction maps on higher types lose as little information as possible. In fact, Abramsky has shown that the abstraction map for higher types, that we have defined above, is the most accurate one that could be defined [Abr90].

As an aside, in Section 2.2.1 we gave the intuition that domain points are pieces of information, and the domain ordering tells us which objects have at least as much information as others. The information abstract domains points contain is the set of objects from the standard interpretation of a type that they represent, so that for any $\overline{s}_1, \overline{s}_2 \in \mathbf{A}_\sigma$, $\overline{s}_1 \sqsubseteq \overline{s}_2$ if and only if $\overline{s}_2$ represents at least as many objects as $\overline{s}_1$.

We must now show that the maps we have defined are well-defined and continuous.

Lemma 3.2.4

If for each of the types bool, int, and if τ is any type, for (list τ) and (tree τ), strict and continuous abstraction maps from the standard interpretation of the type to the abstract interpretation of the type are given, then for all types σ

1. *α_σ and Abs_σ are continuous.*
2. *α_σ and Abs_σ are strict.*
3. *γ_σ is well-defined and continuous.*

The proof of Lemma 3.2.4 makes use of all the properties we have insisted upon for the abstraction maps and abstract domains for the types *bool*, *int*, (*list* τ) and (*tree* τ). Firstly, continuity is needed for the abstraction maps so that all of the maps used in the framework are continuous, which is needed for proving the safety of the framework. The strictness of the abstraction maps, which is preserved by the abstraction maps on constructed types, is needed to prove the well-definedness of the concretisation maps. To guarantee the existence of least upper bounds for the definition of the abstraction maps, we need the property that the abstract domains are complete lattices. Finally, finiteness of the abstract domains is needed, not only so that an effective analysis can be developed, but because it ensures that the concretisation maps are continuous. Abramsky [Abr90] has shown that if the abstract domains are arbitrary complete lattices (including infinite ones), then the concretisation maps induced from the abstraction maps are not in general continuous. If the abstraction maps also map finite elements (Definition 2.2.18) to finite elements, then the concretisation maps will be continuous [Abr90]. Since our abstract domains are finite, this condition trivially holds.

We have the following useful relationship between α_σ and γ_σ.

Proposition 3.2.5

For all types σ, $(\alpha_\sigma\ s) \sqsubseteq \overline{s}$ if and only if $s \in (\gamma_\sigma\ \overline{s})$.

3.2.2 Alternative Definitions

Sometimes other forms of the definitions of the abstraction and concretisation maps are easier to work with in the theory. Proposition 3.2.6 gives two alternative forms for the abstraction map $\alpha_{\sigma\to\tau}$ when τ is a function space, and Proposition 3.2.7 gives an alternative definition of the map γ_σ, for any type σ. When σ is a constructed type such as a product, sum or lifted domain, then Proposition 3.2.8 gives definitions of γ_σ in terms of the concretisation maps for each of the components of the constructed type. In any use of the framework concretisation maps for constructed types can then be constructed inductively from the concretisation maps on the base types.

Proposition 3.2.6

Suppose $f \in \mathbf{S}_{\sigma_1} \to \ldots \to \mathbf{S}_{\sigma_n} \to \mathbf{S}_\tau$. Then

1. $(\alpha_{\sigma_1\to\ldots\to\sigma_n\to\tau}\ f)\ \overline{s}_1\ \ldots\ \overline{s}_n = \bigsqcup\{\alpha_\tau(f\ s_1\ \ldots\ s_n) | \forall i \in \{1,\ldots,n\} : (\alpha_{\sigma_i}\ s_i) \sqsubseteq \overline{s}_i\}$
2. $(\alpha_{\sigma_1\to\ldots\to\sigma_n\to\tau}\ f)\ \overline{s}_1\ \ldots\ \overline{s}_n = \bigsqcup\{\alpha_\tau(f\ s_1\ \ldots\ s_n) | \forall i \in \{1,\ldots,n\} : s_i \in (\gamma_{\sigma_i}\ \overline{s}_i)\}$.

Proposition 3.2.7

For all types σ, $\gamma_\sigma\ \overline{s} = \{s|(\alpha_\sigma\ s) \sqsubseteq \overline{s}\}$.

Proposition 3.2.8

For all types $\sigma, \sigma_1, \ldots, \sigma_k$,

1. $\gamma_{\sigma_1 \times \ldots \times \sigma_k}\ (\overline{s_1}, \ldots, \overline{s_k}) = (\gamma_{\sigma_1}\ \overline{s_1}) \times \ldots \times (\gamma_{\sigma_k}\ \overline{s_k})$.
2. $\gamma_{\sigma_1 \otimes \ldots \otimes \sigma_k}\ < \overline{s_1}, \ldots, \overline{s_k} >= (\gamma_{\sigma_1}\ \overline{s_1}) \otimes \ldots \otimes (\gamma_{\sigma_k}\ \overline{s_k})$.
3. $\gamma_{\sigma_1 \oplus \ldots \oplus \sigma_k}\ (\overline{s_1}, \ldots, \overline{s_k}) = inject\ (\gamma_{\sigma_1}\ \overline{s_1}, \ldots, \gamma_{\sigma_k}\ \overline{s_k})$ *where*
   $inject\ (S_1, \ldots, S_k) = \{mk\_sum_1\ s_1 | s_1 \in S_1\} \bigcup \ldots \bigcup \{mk\_sum_k\ s_k | s_k \in S_k\}$
4. *If* γ_σ *is strict, then*

$$\gamma_{(lift\ \sigma)}\ \overline{a} = \begin{cases} \{\bot_{\mathbf{S}_{(lift\ \sigma)}}\} & if\ \overline{a} = \bot_{\mathbf{A}_{(lift\ \sigma)}} \\ (\mathbf{P}\ lift)\ (\gamma_\sigma\ \overline{s}) & if\ \overline{a} = (0, \overline{s}) \end{cases}$$

3.2.3 Properties of Abstraction and Concretisation Maps

Here we record some useful properties of the abstraction and concretisation maps that have been defined.

Bottom Reflexivity of α_σ

Lemma 3.2.9

If for each of the types bool, int, and if τ *is any type, for (list* τ*) and (tree* τ*) the abstraction maps are bottom-reflecting, then* α_σ *and* Abs_σ *are bottom-reflecting for each type* σ.

Strictness of γ_σ

The following Lemma is often useful in the applications for which we will use this framework.

Lemma 3.2.10

If for all types σ, α_σ *is strict and bottom-reflecting, then* γ_σ *is strict for all types* σ, *that is,* $\gamma_\sigma\ \bot_{\mathbf{A}_\sigma} = \bot_{\mathbf{P}\ \mathbf{S}_\sigma} = \{\bot_{\mathbf{S}_\sigma}\}$.

Adjointness of Abs_σ and γ_σ

The maps Abs_σ and γ_σ are adjoined functions. **This ensures that the abstract domain closely models the sets of elements of equal definedness in the standard interpretation.**

Proposition 3.2.11

Abs_σ and γ_σ are a pair of adjoined functions. i.e.

1. $\gamma_\sigma \circ Abs_\sigma \sqsupseteq id_{\mathbf{P}\ \mathbf{S}_\sigma}$; ***and***
2. $Abs_\sigma \circ \gamma_\sigma \sqsubseteq id_{\mathbf{A}_\sigma}$.

Semi-homomorphic Properties of α_σ and *fix*

For each type σ we have that α_σ **is a semi-homomorphism of function application**, that is, if $f \in \mathbf{S}_{\sigma\to\tau}$ then

$$\alpha_{\sigma\to\tau}\ f \circ \alpha_\sigma \ \sqsupseteq\ \alpha_\tau \circ f$$

or, in terms of elements, if $s \in \mathbf{S}_\sigma$ then

$$(\alpha_{\sigma\to\tau}\ f)\ (\alpha_\sigma\ s) \sqsupseteq \alpha_\tau\ (f\ s)$$

We will need this to prove Theorem 3.3.2. It can be seen to be intuitively true by looking at the definition of $(\alpha_{\sigma\to\tau}\ f)\ (\alpha_\sigma\ s)$:

$$(\alpha_{\sigma\to\tau}\ f)\ (\alpha_\sigma\ s) = \bigsqcup\{\alpha_\tau\ (f\ s') | \alpha_\sigma\ s' \sqsubseteq \alpha_\sigma\ s\} \qquad \text{(Proposition 3.2.6)}$$

We see that $(\alpha_{\sigma\to\tau}\ f)\ (\alpha_\sigma\ s)$ applies f to all the values in $\mathbf{S}_\sigma$ which abstract to something less than or equal to what s abstracts to, some of which may give a more defined answer, and hence may be abstracted to a greater value than $(f\ s)$ would. For example, using the abstract interpretation that will be given in Chapter 4, we find that if $e : int$ is a term such that $(\mathrm{S}\ [\![e]\!]\ \rho^{\mathrm{S}}) = \perp_{\mathrm{S}_{int}}$, then

$$\alpha_{int\to int}(\mathrm{S}\ [\![\lambda x^{int}.\mathbf{if}_{bool\to int\to int\to int}\ (=_{int\to int\to bool}\ x^{int}\ \mathbf{5}_{int})\ e\ \mathbf{1}_{int}]\!]\ \rho^{\mathrm{S}}) = \lambda x \epsilon \mathbf{A}_{int}.x$$

and $\alpha_{int}\ 5 = \top_{\mathbf{A}_{int}}$, so that

$$(\alpha_{int\to int}(\mathrm{S}\ [\![\lambda x^{int}.\mathbf{if}_{bool\to int\to int\to int}\ (=_{int\to int\to bool}\ x^{int}\ \mathbf{5}_{int})\ e\ \mathbf{1}_{int}]\!]\ \rho^{\mathrm{S}}))\ (\alpha_{int}\ 5) = \top_{\mathbf{A}_{int}},$$

whilst

$$\begin{aligned} &\alpha_{int}\ ((\mathrm{S}\ [\![\lambda x^{int}.\mathbf{if}_{bool\to int\to int\to int}\ (=_{int\to int\to bool}\ x^{int}\ \mathbf{5}_{int})\ e\ \mathbf{1}_{int}]\!]\ \rho^{\mathrm{S}})\ 5) \\ &= \alpha_{int}\ (\mathrm{S}\ [\![e]\!]\ \rho^{\mathrm{S}}) \\ &= \alpha_{int}\ \perp_{\mathrm{S}_{int}} \\ &= \perp_{\mathbf{A}_{int}} \\ &\quad \text{since } \alpha_{int} \text{ was required to be strict.} \end{aligned}$$

Proposition 3.2.12

For all types σ, α_σ is a semi-homomorphism of function application.

As a consequence of the semi-homomorphic property of abstraction, and the fact that the abstraction maps are continuous, we have that taking fixed points is a semi-homomorphism of abstraction, which is also needed in the proof of Theorem 3.3.2.

Proposition 3.2.13

Taking fixed points is a semi-homomorphism of abstraction, that is,

$$(\lambda F \epsilon \mathbf{A}_{\sigma\to\sigma}.\bigsqcup_{i\geq 0} F^i\ \perp_{\mathbf{A}_\sigma}) \circ \alpha_{\sigma\to\sigma} \sqsupseteq \alpha_\sigma \circ (\lambda F \epsilon \mathbf{S}_{\sigma\to\sigma}.\bigsqcup_{i\geq 0} F^i\ \perp_{\mathbf{S}_\sigma})$$

A Relationship Between $\alpha_{\sigma_1 \to \ldots \to \sigma_k \to \tau}$ and $\alpha_{\sigma_1 \times \ldots \times \sigma_k \to \tau}$

The domains $\mathbf{I}_{\sigma_1 \to \ldots \to \sigma_k \to \tau}$ and $\mathbf{I}_{\sigma_1 \times \ldots \times \sigma_k \to \tau}$ are isomorphic:

$$\mathbf{I}_{\sigma_1 \to \ldots \to \sigma_k \to \tau} \cong \mathbf{I}_{\sigma_1 \times \ldots \times \sigma_k \to \tau}.$$

The map from left to right is often called *uncurry*, and its inverse *curry*. They are defined by:

$$\begin{aligned} \mathit{uncurry}\ f &= \lambda(s_1, \ldots, s_k).f\ s_1\ \ldots\ s_k \\ \mathit{curry} f &= \lambda s_1 \ldots \lambda s_k.f\ (s_1, \ldots, s_k) \end{aligned}$$

Proposition 3.2.14

1. $\alpha_{\sigma_1 \to \ldots \to \sigma_k \to \tau} = \mathit{curry} \circ \alpha_{\sigma_1 \times \ldots \times \sigma_k \to \tau} \circ \mathit{uncurry}$
2. $\alpha_{\sigma_1 \times \ldots \times \sigma_k \to \tau} = \mathit{uncurry} \circ \alpha_{\sigma_1 \to \ldots \to \sigma_k \to \tau} \circ \mathit{curry}$

3.3 Correctness of the Framework

3.3.1 A Result Relating the Abstract and Standard Interpretations

The correctness of the abstract interpretation framework relies on abstract interpretations being given for constants which satisfy the *constant safety condition.*

Definition 3.3.1

The abstract interpretation of a constant c_σ, $\mathbf{K^A}\ [\![c_\sigma]\!]$, satisfies the *constant safety condition* if

$$\mathbf{K^A}\ [\![c_\sigma]\!] \sqsupseteq \alpha_\sigma\ (\mathbf{K^S}\ [\![c_\sigma]\!])$$

For each functional constant c_σ in Λ_T, the abstract interpretation given for it in the next chapter was determined by using the definition of α_σ and trying to calculate $\alpha_\sigma\ (\mathbf{K^S}\ [\![c_\sigma]\!])$. Approximations sometimes had to be made in the calculation, using the semi-homomorphic property of abstraction. Abstract interpretations determined in this way are often called *induced* interpretations, because they are induced from the standard interpretation, using the abstraction map. This is discussed further in Section 4.1.2.

If the abstract interpretations of all of the constants satisfy this condition, then the following theorem shows that a similar condition holds for all expressions in Λ_T, which is crucial for proving the correctness of the framework.

Theorem 3.3.2

Suppose that the abstract interpretations of all constants satisfy the constant safety condition. Then for all $\rho^{\mathbf{S}}, \rho^{\mathbf{A}}$ such that for all x^τ, $(\rho^{\mathbf{A}}\ x^\tau) \sqsupseteq \alpha_\tau\ (\rho^{\mathbf{S}}\ x^\tau)$, we have for all $e\ :\ \sigma$:

$$\mathbf{A}\ [\![e]\!]\ \rho^{\mathbf{A}} \sqsupseteq \alpha_\sigma(\mathbf{S}\ [\![e]\!]\ \rho^{\mathbf{S}}).$$

3.3.2 Correctness of the Framework

In the introduction to this chapter, we motivated what we meant by the correctness of an abstract interpretation. Here we define *correctness* formally, and prove that the framework we have developed is in fact correct.

Definition 3.3.3

The abstract interpretation framework is *correct* if whenever

$$(\mathbf{A}\ [\![f]\!]\ \rho^{\mathbf{A}})\ \bar{s} \sqsubseteq \bar{t},$$

we have that

$$\forall s \in (\gamma_\sigma\ \bar{s}), ((\mathbf{S}\ [\![f]\!]\ \rho^{\mathbf{S}})\ s) \in (\gamma_\tau\ \bar{t}).$$

Theorem 3.3.4 (Correctness Theorem for Abstract Interpretation)

The abstract interpretation we have developed is correct. That is, given $f : \sigma \rightarrow \tau$, abstract interpretations of constants which satisfy the safety condition, and environments satisfying the conditions of Theorem 3.3.2, we have that if $\bar{s} \in \mathbf{A}_\sigma$ and $(\mathbf{A}\ [\![f]\!]\ \rho^{\mathbf{A}})\ \bar{s} \sqsubseteq \bar{t}$, then for all $s \in (\gamma_\sigma\ \bar{s})$, $((\mathbf{S}\ [\![f]\!]\ \rho^{\mathbf{S}})\ s) \in (\gamma_\tau\ \bar{t})$.

Proof

$$\begin{array}{lll}
\bar{t} & \sqsupseteq & (\mathbf{A}\ [\![f]\!]\ \rho^{\mathbf{A}})\ \bar{s} & \\
& \sqsupseteq & (\alpha_{\sigma\rightarrow\tau}\ (\mathbf{S}\ [\![f]\!]\ \rho^{\mathbf{S}}))\ \bar{s} & \text{Theorem 3.3.2} \\
& \sqsupseteq & (\alpha_{\sigma\rightarrow\tau}\ (\mathbf{S}\ [\![f]\!]\ \rho^{\mathbf{S}}))\ (\alpha_\sigma\ s) & \forall s \in (\gamma_\sigma\ \bar{s}) \text{ by Proposition 3.2.7} \\
& \sqsupseteq & \alpha_\tau\ ((\mathbf{S}\ [\![f]\!]\ \rho^{\mathbf{S}})\ s) & \text{Proposition 3.2.12} \\
& \Rightarrow & ((\mathbf{S}\ [\![f]\!]\ \rho^{\mathbf{S}})\ s) \in (\gamma_\tau\ \bar{t}) & \text{Proposition 3.2.5}
\end{array}$$

□

When a function f has the type $\sigma_1 \rightarrow \ldots \rightarrow \sigma_n \rightarrow \tau$, then the following theorem gives a useful result about an application of the function.

Theorem 3.3.5

Suppose that $f : \sigma_1 \rightarrow \ldots \rightarrow \sigma_n \rightarrow \tau$ and $(\mathbf{A}\ [\![f]\!]\ \rho^{\mathbf{A}})\ \bar{s}_1\ \ldots\ \bar{s}_n \sqsubseteq \bar{t}$. Then $\forall j \in \{1,\ldots,n\}, j \neq i, \forall e_j : \sigma_j$ such that $(\mathbf{A}\ [\![e_j]\!]\ \rho^{\mathbf{A}}) \sqsubseteq \bar{s}_j$, $\forall s_i \in (\gamma_{\sigma_i}\ \bar{s}_i)$,

$$(\mathbf{S}\ [\![f]\!]\ \rho^{\mathbf{S}})\ (\mathbf{S}\ [\![e_1]\!]\ \rho^{\mathbf{S}})\ \ldots\ (\mathbf{S}\ [\![e_{i-1}]\!]\ \rho^{\mathbf{S}})\ s_i\ (\mathbf{S}\ [\![e_{i+1}]\!]\ \rho^{\mathbf{S}})\ \ldots\ (\mathbf{S}\ [\![e_n]\!]\ \rho^{\mathbf{S}}) \in (\gamma_\tau\ \bar{t}).$$

3.4 Drawing It Together

The main points covered in this chapter are as follows:

- For an abstract interpretation to be of any use, the conclusions drawn from a calculation using it must be correct with respect to the standard interpretation of a language.
- To formalise our notion of correctness, we had to define an abstraction and concretisation map for each type, relating the standard and abstract interpretations of Λ_T.
- Abstract domain points represent sets of objects from the standard interpretation of a type, and this notion was formalised using concretisation, so that the set of elements represented by $\overline{s} \in \mathbf{A}_\sigma$ was defined to be $(\gamma_\sigma\ \overline{s})$.
- We were then able to say that an abstract interpretation is correct if for all $\overline{s} \in \mathbf{A}_\sigma$, if $(\mathbf{A}\ [\![f]\!]\ \rho^{\mathbf{A}})\ \overline{s} \sqsubseteq \overline{t}$, then for all $s \in (\gamma_\sigma\ \overline{s})$, $((\mathbf{S}\ [\![f]\!]\ \rho^{\mathbf{S}})\ s) \in (\gamma_\tau\ \overline{t})$. The intuition is that $\overline{t}$ represents all the results of applying the standard interpretation of f to each of the s represented by $\overline{s}$.
- It would be of little use if an abstract interpretation had to be proved correct every time the abstract interpretation of a particular type was changed. Therefore, this chapter has provided a framework for the abstract interpretation of Λ_T, which can be used to generate a particular, correct abstract interpretation if given the following:
  - finite lattices as the abstract interpretation of the types *bool*, *int*, (*list* τ) and (*tree* τ) for any type τ;
  - an abstract interpretation for each of the constants given in Λ_T which satisfies the constant safety condition; and
  - a strict, continuous abstraction map for each of the types *bool*, *int*, (*list* τ) and (*tree* τ), from the standard interpretation of the type to its abstract interpretation.

  We stated that suitable abstract interpretations for the constants could be induced from their standard interpretation, and will give examples of doing this in the next chapter.

A number of properties of abstraction and concretisation maps were given which are useful in the application of the framework.

Chapter 4

Some Example Abstract Interpretations

The purpose of this chapter is to exemplify a number of issues concerning the use of the framework from the previous chapter in defining particular abstract interpretations for Λ_T.

Our first, and major example, demonstrates all the steps needed to define a particular abstract interpretation, and using it to determine the abstract interpretation of user-defined functions. Specifically it covers:

- Giving finite lattices as interpretations of booleans, integers, lists and trees, and strict, continuous abstraction maps which capture some property of interest. In this case the property is the behaviour of the evaluators introduced in Section 1.2.
- Defining abstract interpretations of the constants which satisfy the constant safety condition. This demonstrates a general methodology for giving abstract interpretations to constants: for each constant c_σ, calculate α_σ ($\mathbf{K}^{\mathbf{S}}$ $[\![c_\sigma]\!]$), making approximations as necessary. Three constants are treated in the body of the chapter; the rest can be found in Appendix A, Section A.4.
- Determining the abstract interpretation of recursive functions. As we have seen, recursive functions are translated into Λ_T using $\mathbf{fix}_{(\sigma\to\sigma)\to\sigma}$, and the interpretation of $\mathbf{fix}_{(\sigma\to\sigma)\to\sigma}$ is defined as the least upper bound of a chain of values. We will show how this least upper bound can be determined for one particular function, and then give the abstract interpretations of all of the functions from Figure 1.1, which were determined in the same way.

This example is covered in Section 4.1, and will be used in the next chapter for giving examples of evaluation transformers.

In Section 4.2 we discuss some other approaches to, and issues concerning the defining of abstract domains, concentrating on lists. As an example, we show how an abstract domain can be defined to capture the property of one-level head-strictness (defined in that section). Not all one-level head-strict functions can be determined to be so by this abstract interpretation, as having this property may depend on some other property not captured by the one-level head-strictness abstract interpretation. This leads us to showing how two different abstract interpretations, capturing different properties, can be combined to get a new abstract interpretation capturing both properties. In general, such combined abstract interpretations are more powerful than using the constituent ones separately.

All the abstract interpretations of lists discussed in the first two sections ignore the type of the elements in a list, giving a constant abstract interpretation for (*list* τ) for all types τ. However, the general interpretation of (*list* τ) is given as

$$\mathbf{I}_{(list\ \tau)} = (\mathbf{I}\ list)\ \mathbf{I}_\tau$$

in Figure 2.11. Section 4.3 gives an abstract interpretation for lists which takes into account the types of elements in the list. A similar technique can be used for giving abstract interpretations for other recursive data types.

For all of the abstract domains discussed in Sections 4.2 and 4.3, we give abstract interpretations, which satisfy the constant safety condition, for all the constants over lists. They were determined by calculating the abstraction of the standard interpretation of the constants. Using them, the reader can experiment with the different abstract interpretations defined in this chapter.

As a notational convention, we will denote the abstract interpretation of a function by putting a bar over the name of the function. For example, if f is a function, then $\overline{f}$ is its abstract interpretation, and is equivalent to writing $\mathbf{A}\ [\![f]\!]\ \{\}$.

4.1 An Abstract Interpretation for Evaluation Transformers

The purpose of an abstract interpretation is to capture some property in which we are interested. For example, in the 'rule of signs' the property of interest was whether the result of a calculation was positive, negative or zero. Our desire is to design an abstract interpretation so that we can calculate the evaluation transformers for a function. Abstract domains should therefore capture the important properties of evaluators. Then the abstract interpretation of a function is in some sense a mapping from evaluators to evaluators, which is close to our idea of evaluation transformers.

The important property of an evaluator is that all the expressions of a particular type can be divided into two classes – those for which the evaluator terminates and those for which it fails to terminate. Our intuitions about the class of expressions for which an evaluator fails to terminate will be used to define abstract domains for the types *bool* and *int*, and (*list* τ) and (*tree* τ) for each type τ.

4.1.1 The Abstract Interpretation of Booleans, Integers, Lists and Trees

Abstract Interpretation of *bool* and *int*

For any type, such as *bool* or *int*, which has a flat domain as its standard interpretation, there is only one amount of evaluation of any interest, and that is evaluating an expression to HNF. By the Computational Adequacy Theorem, a reduction strategy can be defined which fails to terminate if and only if the standard interpretation of the expression it is evaluating is the bottom element from the appropriate domain, and so the abstract domain for such a type should contain a point which represents the bottom of the standard interpretation of the type. Seeing as there are no other evaluators to make further distinctions between the other elements of the standard interpretation of these two types, only one other abstract domain point is needed, to represent 'could be any value'. We therefore make the following definition.

Definition 4.1.1

If B is *bool* or *int*, then $\mathbf{A}_B = \mathbf{2}$, where $\mathbf{2} = \{0,1\}$ with the ordering defined by $0 \sqsubseteq 1$.

The abstraction map is defined by:

$$\alpha_B : \mathbf{S}_B \rightarrow \mathbf{2}$$
$$\alpha_B\ u = \begin{cases} 0 & \text{if } u = \bot_{\mathbf{S}_B} \\ 1 & \text{otherwise} \end{cases}$$

This abstract domain was first introduced by Alan Mycroft [Myc80, Myc81].

Abstract Interpretation of $(list\ \tau)$

In Section 1.2.1 we introduced three different evaluators for lists: $\xi_{\bot}^{(list\ \tau)}$, $\xi_{\infty}^{(list\ \tau)}$ and $\xi_{\bot\in}^{(list\ \tau)}$. The evaluator $\xi_{\bot}^{(list\ \tau)}$ tries to evaluate an expression to HNF, and so must fail to terminate only if the expression has no HNF, that is, has $\bot_{\mathbf{S}_{(list\ \tau)}}$ as its standard interpretation (Computational Adequacy Theorem). Intuitively, the evaluator $\xi_{\infty}^{(list\ \tau)}$ evaluates the structure of a list, and so fails to terminate when an expression has as its standard interpretation the undefined list, or an infinite list, or a list whose tail is undefined at some point. Finally, the evaluator $\xi_{\bot\in}^{(list\ \tau)}$ will only terminate if it is evaluating an expression whose standard interpretation is a finite list with no bottom elements in it. An abstract domain for $(list\ \tau)$ should therefore have points 'representing' each of these subsets of $\mathbf{S}_{(list\ \tau)}$, plus one point for the whole of $\mathbf{S}_{(list\ \tau)}$, which also contains the standard interpretation of all the expressions for which every evaluator terminates. This domain was first described by Wadler, who named the abstract domain points $\bot$, ∞, $\bot\in$ and $\top\in$, with the ordering $\bot \sqsubseteq \infty \sqsubseteq \bot\in \sqsubseteq \top\in$ [Wad87], and is shown diagrammatically in Figure 2.9*(c)*. It is rather unfortunate that the symbol $\bot$ was chosen for the bottom of the abstract domain for $(list\ \tau)$, as it is also used as the bottom element of a general complete partial order. Nevertheless, we will stick to these names for the abstract domain points, and the meaning of $\bot$ should be clear from the context in which it is being used.

How should the abstraction map $\alpha_{(list\ \tau)}$ be defined? Each abstract domain point represents a set of elements, and the abstraction of a list must be the point which represents the smallest subset of the standard interpretation which contains the list. In order to define this map, and for ease of referring to particular subsets of $\mathbf{S}_{(list\ \tau)}$ subsequently, we single out three subsets of $\mathbf{S}_{(list\ \tau)}$ in the following definition.

Definition 4.1.2

$$
\begin{aligned}
&List_\tau^{\infty} = \{u \mid T\ u = \bot_{\mathbf{S}_{(list\ \tau)}}\} - \{\bot_{\mathbf{S}_{(list\ \tau)}}\}\\
&List_\tau^{\bot\in} = \{u \mid F\ u = \bot_{\mathbf{S}_{(list\ \tau)}}\} - List_\tau^{\infty}\\
&List_\tau^{\top\in} = \mathbf{S}_{(list\ \tau)} - List_\tau^{\bot\in}\\
&\quad where\\
&\quad \begin{array}{lll@{\qquad}lll}
T\ \bot_{\mathbf{S}_{(list\ \tau)}} & = & \bot_{\mathbf{S}_{(list\ \tau)}} & F\ \bot_{\mathbf{S}_{(list\ \tau)}} & = & \bot_{\mathbf{S}_{(list\ \tau)}}\\
T\ nil & = & nil & F\ nil & = & nil\\
T\ (cons\ u\ l) & = & T\ l & F\ (cons\ u\ l) & = & \begin{cases} \bot_{\mathbf{S}_{(list\ \tau)}} & \text{if } u = \bot_{\mathbf{S}_\tau}\\ F\ l & \text{otherwise}\end{cases}
\end{array}
\end{aligned}
$$

$List_\tau^{\infty}$ are lists (of type τ) which have at least one element in them, and are either infinite in length, or have an undefined tail at some point (sometimes called *partial lists*); $List_\tau^{\bot\in}$ are finite lists containing at least one bottom element; and $List_\tau^{\top\in}$ are finite lists containing no bottom elements. Using these subsets, we can define the abstraction map for the type $(list\ \tau)$.

Definition 4.1.3

For all types τ, the domain $\mathbf{A}_{(list\ \tau)}$ contains the four elements $\{\bot, \infty, \bot\in, \top\in\}$, where the ordering is defined by $\bot \sqsubseteq \infty \sqsubseteq \bot\in \sqsubseteq \top\in$.

The abstraction map is defined by:

$$
\begin{aligned}
&\alpha_{(list\ \tau)} : \mathbf{S}_{(list\ \tau)} \rightarrow \mathbf{A}_{(list\ \tau)}\\
&\alpha_{(list\ \tau)}\ u = \begin{cases} \bot & \text{if } u = \bot_{\mathbf{S}_{(list\ \tau)}}\\ \infty & \text{if } u \in List_\tau^{\infty}\\ \bot\in & \text{if } u \in List_\tau^{\bot\in}\\ \top\in & \text{if } u \in List_\tau^{\top\in}\end{cases}
\end{aligned}
$$

The names of the abstract domain points are chosen to be partly mnemonic - a list abstracts to ∞ (pronounced "infinite") if it is infinite or ends in $\bot_{\mathbf{S}_{(list\ \tau)}}$, to $\bot\in$ (pronounced "botmem") if it is finite but contains at least one bottom element, and $\top\in$ (pronounced "topmem") if it is finite and contains no bottom elements.

Recalling that, at the beginning of Chapter 3, we introduced the concept of concretisation to capture what we mean by 'represents', and using the definition of $\gamma_{(list\ \tau)}$ given in Section 3.2 or Proposition 3.2.7, it can be seen that each of the above abstract domain points describes the standard interpretations of a class of expressions for which one of the (intuitively defined) evaluators fails to terminate.

Abstract Interpretation of $(tree\ \tau)$

The intuitions for the abstract domain for trees are similar to those of lists, and as for lists, we single out three subsets of $\mathbf{S}_{(tree\ \tau)}$ in the following definition.

Definition 4.1.4

$$
\begin{aligned}
&Tree_\tau^\infty = \{u \mid T\ u = \bot_{\mathbf{S}_{(tree\ \tau)}}\} - \{\bot_{\mathbf{S}_{(tree\ \tau)}}\}\\
&Tree_\tau^{\bot\in} = \{u \mid F\ u = \bot_{\mathbf{S}_{(tree\ \tau)}}\} - Tree_\tau^\infty\\
&Tree_\tau^{\top\in} = \mathbf{S}_{(tree\ \tau)} - Tree_\tau^{\bot\in}\\
&\quad where\\
&\quad \begin{array}{lcl}
T\ \bot_{\mathbf{S}_{(tree\ \tau)}} & = & \bot_{\mathbf{S}_{(tree\ \tau)}}\\
T\ empty & = & empty\\
T\ (node\ t_1\ n\ t_2) & = & (T\ t_1) \sqcap (T\ t_2)\\
 & & \\
F\ \bot_{\mathbf{S}_{(tree\ \tau)}} & = & \bot_{\mathbf{S}_{(tree\ \tau)}}\\
F\ empty & = & empty\\
F\ (node\ t_1\ n\ t_2) & = & \begin{cases} \bot_{\mathbf{S}_{(tree\ \tau)}} & \text{if } n = \bot_{\mathbf{S}_\tau}\\ (F\ t_1) \sqcap (F\ t_2) & \text{otherwise} \end{cases}
\end{array}
\end{aligned}
$$

The abstraction map for the type $(tree\ \tau)$ can now be defined.

Definition 4.1.5

The domain $\mathbf{A}_{(tree\ \tau)}$ contains the four elements $\{\bot, \infty, \bot\in, \top\in\}$, where the ordering is defined by $\bot \sqsubseteq \infty \sqsubseteq \bot\in \sqsubseteq \top\in$. The abstraction map is defined by:

$$
\begin{aligned}
&\alpha_{(tree\ \tau)} : \mathbf{S}_{(tree\ \tau)} \rightarrow \mathbf{A}_{(tree\ \tau)}\\
&\alpha_{(tree\ \tau)}\ u = \begin{cases} \bot & \text{if } u = \bot_{\mathbf{S}_{(tree\ \tau)}}\\ \infty & \text{if } u \in Tree_\tau^\infty\\ \bot\in & \text{if } u \in Tree_\tau^{\bot\in}\\ \top\in & \text{if } u \in Tree_\tau^{\top\in} \end{cases}
\end{aligned}
$$

where $Tree_\tau^\infty$, $Tree_\tau^{\bot\in}$ and $Tree_\tau^{\top\in}$ are defined in Definition 4.1.4

Properties of Abstraction and Concretisation Maps

The abstraction maps we have defined are bottom-reflecting, so we have the following lemma, which is important for subsequent discussion.

Lemma 4.1.6

1. *For all types σ, α_σ is strict.*
2. *For all types σ, α_σ is bottom-reflecting.*
3. *γ_σ is strict for all types σ, i.e.*

$$\gamma_\sigma\ \bot_{\mathbf{A}_\sigma} = \bot_{\mathbf{P}\ \mathbf{S}_\sigma} = \{\bot_{\mathbf{S}_\sigma}\}.$$

Proof

1. The abstraction maps for *bool*, *int*, (*list* τ) and (*tree* τ) are strict, so by Lemma 3.2.4(1) α_σ is strict for all types σ.
2. The abstraction maps for *bool*, *int*, (*list* τ) and (*tree* τ) are bottom-reflecting, so by Lemma 3.2.9 α_σ is bottom-reflecting for all types σ.
3. By parts (1) and (2) of this lemma, α_σ is strict and bottom-reflecting for all types, and so the result holds by Lemma 3.2.10.

□

4.1.2 The Abstract Interpretation of Functional Constants

The correctness condition for constants states that, for each constant c_σ, an abstract interpretation must be given which satisfies:

$$\mathbf{K}^{\mathbf{A}}\ [\![c_\sigma]\!] \sqsupseteq \alpha_\sigma\ (\mathbf{K}^{\mathbf{S}}\ [\![c_\sigma]\!]).$$

A simple way to ensure this is to define ($\mathbf{K}^{\mathbf{A}}\ [\![c_\sigma]\!]$) to be equal to ($\alpha_\sigma$ ($\mathbf{K}^{\mathbf{S}}\ [\![c_\sigma]\!]$)). Unfortunately, sometimes this can be very difficult to calculate exactly, and sometimes it cannot be implemented easily, so approximations have to be made. A full discussion of the problem can be found in [Nie84, Nie85, Nie89], particularly [Nie89, Sections 2.5 and 8].

Abstract interpretations for the constants in Λ_T are given in Figure 4.1. We derived the abstract interpretation for each constant c_σ by trying to calculate (α_σ ($\mathbf{K}^{\mathbf{S}}\ [\![c_\sigma]\!]$)), and using the semi-homomorphic property of α_σ (Proposition 3.2.12) to make approximations when necessary. This is an important methodology when defining any abstract interpretation. Therefore, we will show how to derive the abstract interpretations of $\mathbf{if}_{bool\to\sigma\to\sigma\to\sigma}$, $\mathbf{tail}_{(list\ \tau)\to(list\ \tau)}$ and $\mathbf{lcase}_{(list\ \tau)\to\sigma\to(\tau\to(list\ \tau)\to\sigma)\to\sigma}$. Proofs that the abstract interpretations of the other constants satisfy the constant safety condition can be found in Appendix A, Section A.4.

Abstract Interpretation of $\mathbf{if}_{bool\to\sigma\to\sigma\to\sigma}$

Lemma 4.1.7

For all types σ,

$$\mathbf{K}^{\mathbf{A}}\ [\![\mathbf{if}_{bool\to\sigma\to\sigma\to\sigma}]\!] \sqsupseteq \alpha_{bool\to\sigma\to\sigma\to\sigma}\ (\mathbf{K}^{\mathbf{S}}\ [\![if_{bool\to\sigma\to\sigma\to\sigma}]\!])$$

where

$$\mathbf{K}^{\mathbf{A}}\ [\![\mathbf{if}_{bool\to\sigma\to\sigma\to\sigma}]\!] = \lambda\overline{x}\epsilon\mathbf{A}_{bool}.\lambda\overline{y}\epsilon\mathbf{A}_\sigma.\lambda\overline{z}\epsilon\mathbf{A}_\sigma.\begin{cases}\bot_{\mathbf{S}_\sigma} & \text{if } \overline{x} = \bot_{\mathbf{A}_{bool}}\ (=0)\\ \overline{y}\sqcup\overline{z} & \text{otherwise}\end{cases}$$

$$\mathbf{K}^{\mathbf{A}}\ [\![\mathbf{true}_{bool}]\!] = 1 = \mathbf{K}^{\mathbf{A}}\ [\![\mathbf{false}_{bool}]\!]$$

$$\mathbf{K}^{\mathbf{A}}\ [\![\mathbf{and}_{bool\to bool\to bool}]\!]\ x\ y = x \sqcap y = \mathbf{K}^{\mathbf{A}}\ [\![\mathbf{or}_{bool\to bool\to bool}]\!]\ x\ y$$

$$\mathbf{K}^{\mathbf{A}}\ [\![\mathbf{if}_{bool\to\sigma\to\sigma\to\sigma}]\!]\ x\ y\ z = \begin{cases} \bot_{\mathbf{A}_\sigma} & \text{if } x = \bot_{\mathbf{A}_{bool}}\ (=0) \\ y \sqcup z & \text{otherwise} \end{cases}$$

$$\mathbf{K}^{\mathbf{A}}\ [\![\mathbf{0}_{int}]\!] = 1 = \mathbf{K}^{\mathbf{A}}\ [\![\mathbf{1}_{int}]\!] = \ldots$$

$$\mathbf{K}^{\mathbf{A}}\ [\![+_{int\to int\to int}]\!]\ x\ y = x \sqcap y \quad \text{and similarly for } *, -, /, >, \geq, <, \leq, \text{ and } =$$

$$\mathbf{K}^{\mathbf{A}}\ [\![\mathbf{nil}_{(list\ \tau)}]\!] = \top\!\in$$

$$\mathbf{K}^{\mathbf{A}}\ [\![\mathbf{cons}_{\tau\to(list\ \tau)\to(list\ \tau)}]\!]\ u\ l = \begin{cases} \infty & \text{if } l \sqsubseteq \infty \\ \top\!\in & \text{if } l = \top\!\in \text{ and } u \neq \bot_{\mathbf{A}_\tau} \\ \bot\!\in & \text{otherwise} \end{cases}$$

$$\mathbf{K}^{\mathbf{A}}\ [\![\mathbf{head}_{(list\ \tau)\to\tau}]\!]\ l = \begin{cases} \bot_{\mathbf{A}_\tau} & \text{if } l = \bot \\ \top_{\mathbf{A}_\tau} & \text{otherwise} \end{cases}$$

$$\mathbf{K}^{\mathbf{A}}\ [\![\mathbf{tail}_{(list\ \tau)\to(list\ \tau)}]\!]\ l = \begin{cases} \bot & \text{if } l = \bot \\ \infty & \text{if } l = \infty \\ \top\!\in & \text{otherwise} \end{cases}$$

$$\mathbf{K}^{\mathbf{A}}\ [\![\mathbf{lcase}_{(list\ \tau)\to\sigma\to(\tau\to(list\ \tau)\to\sigma)\to\sigma}]\!]\ l\ s\ f = \begin{cases} \bot_{\mathbf{A}_\sigma} & \text{if } l = \bot \\ f\ \top_{\mathbf{A}_\tau}\ \infty & \text{if } l = \infty \\ (f\ \top_{\mathbf{A}_\tau}\ \bot\!\in) \sqcup (f\ \bot_{\mathbf{A}_\tau}\ \top\!\in) & \text{if } l = \bot\!\in \\ s \sqcup (f\ \top_{\mathbf{A}_\tau}\ \top\!\in) & \text{if } l = \top\!\in \end{cases}$$

$$\mathbf{K}^{\mathbf{A}}\ [\![\mathbf{empty}_{(tree\ \tau)}]\!] = \top\!\in$$

$$\mathbf{K}^{\mathbf{A}}\ [\![\mathbf{node}_{(tree\ \tau)\to\tau\to(tree\ \tau)\to(tree\ \tau)}]\!]\ t_1\ n\ t_2 = \begin{cases} \infty & \text{if } (t_1 \sqsubseteq \infty) \text{ or } (t_2 \sqsubseteq \infty) \\ \top\!\in & \text{if } t_1 = \top\!\in \text{ and } u \neq \bot_{\mathbf{A}_\tau} \\ & \quad \text{and } t_2 = \top\!\in \\ \bot\!\in & \text{otherwise} \end{cases}$$

$$\mathbf{K}^{\mathbf{A}}\ [\![\mathbf{value}_{(tree\ \tau)\to\tau}]\!]\ t = \begin{cases} \bot_{\mathbf{A}_\tau} & \text{if } t = \bot \\ \top_{\mathbf{A}_\tau} & \text{otherwise} \end{cases}$$

$$\mathbf{K}^{\mathbf{A}}\ [\![\mathbf{left}_{(tree\ \tau)\to(tree\ \tau)}]\!]\ t = \begin{cases} \bot & \text{if } t = \bot \\ \top\!\in & \text{otherwise} \end{cases}$$

$$\mathbf{K}^{\mathbf{A}}\ [\![\mathbf{right}_{(tree\ \tau)\to(tree\ \tau)}]\!]\ t = \begin{cases} \bot & \text{if } t = \bot \\ \top\!\in & \text{otherwise} \end{cases}$$

$$\mathbf{K}^{\mathbf{A}}\ [\![\mathbf{tcase}_{(tree\ \tau)\to\sigma\to((tree\ \tau)\to\tau\to(tree\ \tau)\to\sigma)\to\sigma}]\!]\ t\ s\ f$$
$$= \begin{cases} \bot_{\mathbf{A}_\sigma} & \text{if } t = \bot \\ (f\ \top\!\in\ \top_{\mathbf{A}_\tau}\ \infty) \sqcup (f\ \infty\ \top_{\mathbf{A}_\tau}\ \top\!\in) & \text{if } t = \infty \\ (f\ \top\!\in\ \top_{\mathbf{A}_\tau}\ \bot\!\in) \sqcup (f\ \bot\!\in\ \top_{\mathbf{A}_\tau}\ \top\!\in) \sqcup (f\ \top\!\in\ \bot_{\mathbf{A}_\tau}\ \top\!\in) & \text{if } t = \bot\!\in \\ s \sqcup (f\ \top\!\in\ \top_{\mathbf{A}_\tau}\ \top\!\in) & \text{if } t = \top\!\in \end{cases}$$

$$\mathbf{K}^{\mathbf{A}}\ [\![\mathbf{take}_{i_{\sigma_1\times\ldots\times\sigma_k\to\sigma_i}}]\!]\ e = e \downarrow i$$

$$\mathbf{K}^{\mathbf{A}}\ [\![\mathbf{takes}_{i_{\sigma_1\otimes\ldots\otimes\sigma_k\to\sigma_i}}]\!]\ e = e \downarrow i$$

$$\mathbf{K}^{\mathbf{A}}\ [\![\mathbf{outs}_{i_{\sigma_1\oplus\ldots\oplus\sigma_k\to\sigma_i}}]\!]\ e = e \downarrow i$$

$$\mathbf{K}^{\mathbf{A}}\ [\![\mathbf{iss}_{i_{\sigma_1\oplus\ldots\oplus\sigma_k\to bool}}]\!]\ e = \begin{cases} \bot_{\mathbf{A}_{bool}}\ (=0) & \text{if } e = \bot_{\mathbf{A}_{\sigma_1\oplus\ldots\oplus\sigma_k}} \\ \top_{\mathbf{A}_{bool}}\ (=1) & \text{otherwise} \end{cases}$$

Figure 4.1: The Abstract Interpretation of Constants in Λ_T

Proof

In this proof we will denote the standard semantics of $\mathbf{if}_{bool \to \sigma \to \sigma \to \sigma}$ by if, and use the form of $\alpha_{bool \to \sigma \to \sigma \to \sigma}$ from Proposition 3.2.6 (1):

$$(\alpha_{bool \to \sigma \to \sigma \to \sigma}\ if)\ \overline{x}\ \overline{y}\ \overline{z} = \bigsqcup\{\alpha_\sigma(if\ x\ y\ z) | (\alpha_{bool}\ x) \sqsubseteq \overline{x}, (\alpha_\sigma\ y) \sqsubseteq \overline{y}, (\alpha_\sigma\ z) \sqsubseteq \overline{z}\}.$$

$$\begin{aligned}
&(\alpha_{bool \to \sigma \to \sigma \to \sigma}\ if)\ 0\ \overline{y}\ \overline{z} \\
&\quad = \bigsqcup\{\alpha_\sigma(if\ \bot_{\mathbf{S}_{bool}}\ y\ z) | (\alpha_\sigma\ y) \sqsubseteq \overline{y}, (\alpha_\sigma\ z) \sqsubseteq \overline{z}\} \\
&\qquad \text{since } \alpha_{bool} \text{ is bottom-reflecting (Lemma 4.1.6 (2))} \\
&\quad = \bigsqcup\{(\alpha_\sigma\ \bot_{\mathbf{S}_\sigma})\} \quad \text{by the standard semantics of the conditional} \\
&\quad = \bigsqcup\{\bot_{\mathbf{A}_\sigma}\} \qquad\quad \text{since } \alpha_\sigma \text{ is strict (Lemma 4.1.6(1))} \\
&\quad = \bot_{\mathbf{A}_\sigma}
\end{aligned}$$

$$\begin{aligned}
&(\alpha_{bool \to \sigma \to \sigma \to \sigma}\ if)\ 1\ \overline{y}\ \overline{z} \\
&\quad = \bigsqcup\{\alpha_\sigma\ (if\ x\ y\ z) | x \in \{\bot_{\mathbf{S}_{bool}}, true, false\}, (\alpha_\sigma\ y) \sqsubseteq \overline{y}, (\alpha_\sigma\ z) \sqsubseteq \overline{z}\} \\
&\quad = \bigsqcup\{(\alpha_\sigma\ \bot_{\mathbf{S}_\sigma}), (\alpha_\sigma\ y), (\alpha_\sigma\ z) | (\alpha_\sigma\ y) \sqsubseteq \overline{y}, (\alpha_\sigma\ z) \sqsubseteq \overline{z}\} \\
&\qquad \text{by the standard semantics of the conditional} \\
&\quad \sqsubseteq \bigsqcup\{\overline{y}, \overline{z}\} \\
&\qquad \text{by monotonicity of } \alpha_\sigma \text{ and since } \alpha_\sigma \text{ may not be onto}
\end{aligned}$$

and so the result holds.

□

The inequality is introduced because there may not be any y such that $(\alpha_\sigma\ y) = \overline{y}$, or any z such that $(\alpha_\sigma\ z) = \overline{z}$. This is due to the fact that the abstraction maps are not in general onto, since the abstraction map for smash sum types is not onto.

Note that if σ is a function space, so that $\overline{y}$ and $\overline{z}$ in the definition of the abstract interpretation of the conditional are functions, we can use the fact that for continuous functions over finite lattices, $(f \sqcup g)\ x = (f\ x) \sqcup (g\ x)$.

We are now able to demonstrate why using a product for the abstract interpretation of $\oplus$ gives more information than using some form of sum construction. Let σ be $int \oplus int$ and f be the function defined by:

$$f = \lambda x^{int}.\lambda y^{int}.\mathbf{if}_{bool \to \sigma \to \sigma \to \sigma}\ (=_{int \to int \to bool}\ x^{int}\ 5_{int})\ (\mathbf{ins1}_{(int,int)}\ y^{int})\ (\mathbf{ins2}_{(int,int)}\ y^{int}).$$

Recalling that $\bot_{\mathbf{A}_{int}} = 0$, and so $(0,0)$ is $\bot_{\mathbf{A}_{int \oplus int}}$, the abstract interpretation of f is:

$$\begin{aligned}
\mathbf{A}\ [\![f]\!]\ \rho^{\mathbf{A}} &= \lambda x \epsilon \mathbf{2}.\lambda y \epsilon \mathbf{2}. \begin{cases} (0,0) & \text{if } x = 0 \\ (y,0) \sqcup (0,y) & \text{otherwise} \end{cases} \\
&= \lambda x \epsilon \mathbf{2}.\lambda y \epsilon \mathbf{2}. \begin{cases} (0,0) & \text{if } x = 0 \\ (y,y) & \text{otherwise} \end{cases}
\end{aligned}$$

Now $(\mathbf{A}\ [\![f]\!]\ \rho^{\mathbf{A}}\ 1\ 0) = (0,0)$, and $(\gamma_{int \oplus int}\ (0,0))$ is $\{\bot_{\mathbf{S}_{int \oplus int}}\}$ (Lemma 3.2.8(3) or Lemma 4.1.6(3)), so that we can conclude that f is strict in its second argument using Theorem 3.3.5.

If one was to try to use some sort of smash sum for the abstract interpretation of the smash sum type, then firstly note that the smash sum of $k > 1$ lattices is not a lattice. There are two ways to create a lattice out of the smash sum of a number of lattices - either add a new top element, or coalesce all of the top elements together. Either way, the above example will have to give the top element of the abstract lattice whenever the first argument of the function is non-bottom, as the least upper bound of two elements from different parts of the sum would be the top element of the abstract domain. We would then be unable to conclude that the function is strict in its second argument because the concretisation of the top of the abstract domain is the whole of $\mathbf{S}_{int \oplus int}$, not $\bot_{\mathbf{S}_{int\oplus int}}$.

Abstract Interpretation of $\mathbf{tail}_{(list\ \tau)\to(list\ \tau)}$

Lemma 4.1.8

For all types τ,

$$\mathbf{K}^{\mathbf{A}}\ [\![\mathbf{tail}_{(list\ \tau)\to(list\ \tau)}]\!] = \alpha_{(list\ \tau)\to(list\ \tau)}\ (\mathbf{K}^{\mathbf{S}}\ [\![\mathbf{tail}_{(list\ \tau)\to(list\ \tau)}]\!])$$

where

$$\mathbf{K}^{\mathbf{A}}\ [\![\mathbf{tail}_{(list\ \tau)\to(list\ \tau)}]\!]\ \bar{l} = \begin{cases} \bot & \text{if } \bar{l} = \bot \\ \infty & \text{if } \bar{l} = \infty \\ \top\!\in & \text{otherwise} \end{cases}$$

Proof

Recall that $\mathbf{K}^{\mathbf{S}}\ [\![\mathbf{tail}_{(list\ \tau)\to(list\ \tau)}]\!] = tail$, where $tail$ is defined in Figure 2.15. We use the form of $\alpha_{(list\ \tau)\to(list\ \tau)}$ from Proposition 3.2.6 (2):

$$(\alpha_{(list\ \tau)\to(list\ \tau)}\ tail)\ \bar{l} = \bigsqcup\{\alpha_{(list\ \tau)}\ (tail\ l) | l \in (\gamma_{(list\ \tau)}\ \bar{l})\}$$

There are four cases to consider.

1. If $\bar{l}$ is $\bot$, $(\gamma\ \bot) = \{\bot_{\mathbf{S}_{(list\ \tau)}}\}$ (Lemma 4.1.6 (3)), and so

$$\begin{aligned} \bigsqcup\{\alpha_{(list\ \tau)}\ (tail\ l) | l \in (\gamma_{(list\ \tau)}\ \bot)\} &= \bigsqcup\{\alpha_{(list\ \tau)}\ (tail\ \bot_{\mathbf{S}_{(list\ \tau)}})\} \\ &= \bigsqcup\{\alpha_{(list\ \tau)}\ \bot_{\mathbf{S}_{(list\ \tau)}}\} \\ &= \bigsqcup\{\bot_{\mathbf{A}_{(list\ \tau)}}\} \\ &\quad \text{Lemma 4.1.6(1)} \\ &= \bot_{\mathbf{A}_{(list\ \tau)}} \end{aligned}$$

2. If $\bar{l}$ is ∞, then $l \in (\gamma_{(list\ \tau)}\ \bar{l})$ if and only if $l \in \{\bot_{\mathbf{S}_{(list\ \tau)}}\} \cup List_\tau^\infty$. Taking the tail of such a list returns a list in the same set, and the least upper bound of the abstraction of these things is ∞.

3. If $\bar{l}$ is $\bot\!\in$, then $(\gamma_{(list\ \tau)}\ \bar{l})$ is $\{\bot_{\mathbf{S}_{(list\ \tau)}}\} \cup List_\tau^\infty \cup List_\tau^{\bot\in}$. This contains, amongst other things, lists of the form $(cons\ u\ l)$ where $u = \bot_{\mathbf{S}_\tau}$ and $l \in List_\tau^{\top\in}$, that is, lists whose only bottom element is their head. Given such a list,

$$\begin{aligned} \alpha_{(list\ \tau)}\ (tail\ (cons\ u\ l)) &= \alpha_{(list\ \tau)}\ l \\ &= \top\!\in \end{aligned}$$

Since $\top\in$ is the top of the abstract domain for lists, and is contained in $\{\alpha_{(list\ \tau)}\ (tail\ l) | l \in (\gamma_{(list\ \tau)}\ \bot\in)\}$, the least upper bound of this set is $\top\in$, as required.

4. If $\bar{l}$ is $\top\in$, then $(\gamma_{(list\ \tau)}\ \bar{l})$ contains, besides other things, lists of the form $(cons\ u\ l)$ where $l \in List_\tau^{\top\in}$. For such a list,

$$\begin{aligned} \alpha_{(list\ \tau)}\ (tail\ (cons\ u\ l)) &= \alpha_{(list\ \tau)}\ l \\ &= \top\in \end{aligned}$$

and hence the required result.

□

Abstract Interpretation of $\mathbf{lcase}_{(list\ \tau)\to\sigma\to(\tau\to(list\ \tau)\to\sigma)\to\sigma}$

Lemma 4.1.9

For all types σ and all types τ,

$$\begin{aligned} &\mathbf{K^A}\ [\![\mathbf{lcase}_{(list\ \tau)\to\sigma\to(\tau\to(list\ \tau)\to\sigma)\to\sigma}]\!] \\ &\sqsupseteq\ \alpha_{(list\ \tau)\to\sigma\to(\tau\to(list\ \tau)\to\sigma)\to\sigma}\ (\mathbf{K^S}\ [\![\mathbf{lcase}_{(list\ \tau)\to\sigma\to(\tau\to(list\ \tau)\to\sigma)\to\sigma}]\!]) \\ &\textit{where}\ \mathbf{K^A}\ [\![\mathbf{lcase}_{(list\ \tau)\to\sigma\to(\tau\to(list\ \tau)\to\sigma)\to\sigma}]\!]\ l\ s\ f \\ &= \begin{cases} \bot_{\mathbf{A}_\sigma} & \textit{if}\ l = \bot \\ f\ \top_{\mathbf{A}_\tau}\ \infty & \textit{if}\ l = \infty \\ (f\ \top_{\mathbf{A}_\tau}\ \bot\in) \sqcup (f\ \bot_{\mathbf{A}_\tau}\ \top\in) & \textit{if}\ l = \bot\in \\ s \sqcup (f\ \top_{\mathbf{A}_\tau}\ \top\in) & \textit{if}\ l = \top\in \end{cases} \end{aligned}$$

Proof

Recall that $(\mathbf{K^S}\ [\![\mathbf{lcase}_{(list\ \tau)\to\sigma\to(\tau\to(list\ \tau)\to\sigma)\to\sigma}]\!]) = lcase$. We will use the form of $\alpha_{(list\ \tau)\to\sigma\to(\tau\to(list\ \tau)\to\sigma)\to\sigma}$ given in Proposition 3.2.6 (1):

$$\begin{aligned} &(\alpha_{(list\ \tau)\to\sigma\to(\tau\to(list\ \tau)\to\sigma)\to\sigma}\ \bar{s}\ \bar{f}\ \bar{l} \\ &= \bigsqcup\{\alpha_\sigma\ (lcase\ l\ s\ f) | (\alpha_\sigma\ s) \sqsubseteq \bar{s}, (\alpha_{\tau\to(list\ \tau)\to\sigma}\ f) \sqsubseteq \bar{f}, (\alpha_{(list\ \tau)}\ l) \sqsubseteq \bar{l}\} \end{aligned}$$

There are four cases to consider:

1. If $\bar{l}$ is $\bot$, $(\alpha_{(list\ \tau)}\ l) \sqsubseteq \bar{l}$ only if $l = \bot_{\mathbf{S}_{(list\ \tau)}}$ since $\alpha_{(list\ \tau)}$ is bottom-reflecting (Lemma 4.1.6 (2)), and so

$$\begin{aligned} &\bigsqcup\{\alpha_\sigma\ (lcase\ l\ s\ f) | (\alpha_\sigma\ s) \sqsubseteq \bar{s}, (\alpha_{\tau\to(list\ \tau)\to\sigma}\ f) \sqsubseteq \bar{f}, (\alpha_{(list\ \tau)}\ l) \sqsubseteq \bot\} \\ &= \bigsqcup\{\alpha_\sigma\ (lcase\ \bot_{\mathbf{S}_{(list\ \tau)}}\ s\ f) | (\alpha_\sigma\ s) \sqsubseteq \bar{s}, (\alpha_{\tau\to(list\ \tau)\to\sigma}\ f) \sqsubseteq \bar{f}\} \\ &= \bigsqcup\{\alpha_\sigma\ \bot_{\mathbf{S}_\sigma}\} \\ &= \bigsqcup\{\bot_{\mathbf{A}_\sigma}\} \quad \text{Lemma 4.1.6(1)} \\ &= \bot_{\mathbf{A}_\sigma} \end{aligned}$$

2. If $\overline{l} = \infty$, then $(\alpha_{(list\ \tau)}\ l) \sqsubseteq \infty$ only if $l \in \{\perp_{S_{(list\ \tau)}}\} \bigcup List_\tau^\infty$. Elements of the set $List_\tau^\infty$ are of the form $(cons\ u\ l')$, where $u \in S_\tau$ and $l' \in List_\tau^\infty$. From the definition of *lcase*, we have that $(lcase\ \perp_{S_{(list\ \tau)}}\ s\ f) = \perp_{S_\sigma}$, and $(lcase\ (cons\ u\ l')\ s\ f) = (f\ u\ l')$. Clearly $\perp_{S_\sigma} \sqsubseteq (f\ u\ l')$, and so

$$\begin{aligned}&\bigsqcup\{\alpha_\sigma\ (lcase\ l\ s\ f) | (\alpha_\sigma\ s) \sqsubseteq \overline{s}, (\alpha_{\tau\to(list\ \tau)\to\sigma}\ f) \sqsubseteq \overline{f}, (\alpha_{(list\ \tau)}\ l) \sqsubseteq \infty\}\\ &= \bigsqcup\{\alpha_\sigma\ (f\ u\ l') | (\alpha_{\tau\to(list\ \tau)\to\sigma}\ f) \sqsubseteq \overline{f}, u \in S_\tau, l' \in List_\tau^\infty\}\end{aligned}$$

The value of $\alpha_\sigma\ (f\ u\ l')$ depends on the function f, which is a parameter to *lcase*. The only property we know of f is that $(\alpha_{\tau\to(list\ \tau)\to\sigma}\ f) \sqsubseteq \overline{f}$, and so there is no other way to proceed than expanding $\alpha_\sigma\ (f\ u\ l')$ using the semi-homomorphic property of abstraction (Proposition 3.2.12), replacing $=$ by $\sqsubseteq$, to obtain

$$\begin{aligned}&\bigsqcup\{\alpha_\sigma\ (f\ u\ l') | (\alpha_{\tau\to(list\ \tau)\to\sigma}\ f) \sqsubseteq \overline{f}, u \in S_\tau, l' \in List_\tau^\infty)\}\\ &\sqsubseteq \bigsqcup\{(\alpha_{\tau\to(list\ \tau)\to\sigma}\ f)\ (\alpha_\tau\ u)\ (\alpha_{(list\ \tau)}\ l') | (\alpha_{\tau\to(list\ \tau)\to\sigma}\ f) \sqsubseteq \overline{f}, u \in S_\tau,\\ &\quad l' \in List_\tau^\infty)\}\end{aligned}$$

The maximum value of this is when $(\alpha_\tau\ u) = \top_{A_\tau}$ and $(\alpha_{(list\ \tau)}\ l) = \infty$, hence the above reduces to:

$$\bigsqcup\{\overline{f}\ \top_{A_\tau}\ \infty\} = \overline{f}\ \top_{A_\tau}\ \infty$$

3. If $\overline{l} = \perp\in$, then $(\alpha_{(list\ \tau)}\ l) \sqsubseteq \perp\in$ only if $l \in \{\perp_{S_{(list\ \tau)}}\} \bigcup List_\tau^\infty \bigcup List_\tau^{\perp\in}$. Elements of the set $List_\tau^\infty \bigcup List_\tau^{\perp\in}$ are of the form $(cons\ u\ l')$, where either $u \in S_\tau$ and $l' \in (List_\tau^\infty \bigcup List_\tau^{\perp\in})$, or $u = \perp_{S_\tau}$ and $l' \in List_\tau^{\top\in}$. From the definition of *lcase*, we have that $(lcase\ \perp_{S_{(list\ \tau)}}\ s\ f) = \perp_{S_\sigma}$, and $(lcase\ (cons\ u\ l')\ s\ f) = (f\ u\ l')$. Clearly $\perp_{S_\sigma} \sqsubseteq (f\ u\ l')$, and so

$$\begin{aligned}&\bigsqcup\{\alpha_\sigma\ (lcase\ l\ s\ f) | (\alpha_\sigma\ s) \sqsubseteq \overline{s}, (\alpha_{\tau\to(list\ \tau)\to\sigma}\ f) \sqsubseteq \overline{f}, (\alpha_{(list\ \tau)}\ l) \sqsubseteq \perp\in\}\\ &= \bigsqcup\{\{\alpha_\sigma\ (f\ u\ l') | (\alpha_{\tau\to(list\ \tau)\to\sigma}\ f) \sqsubseteq \overline{f}, u \in S_\tau, l' \in (List_\tau^\infty \bigcup List_\tau^{\perp\in})\}\\ &\quad \bigcup\{\alpha_\sigma\ (f\ u\ l') | (\alpha_{\tau\to(list\ \tau)\to\sigma}\ f) \sqsubseteq \overline{f}, u = \perp_{S_\tau}, l' \in List_\tau^{\top\in}\}\}\end{aligned}$$

As with the second case, we can only proceed by using the semi-homomorphic property of abstraction (Proposition 3.2.12), replacing $=$ by $\sqsubseteq$, to obtain

$$\begin{aligned}&\bigsqcup\{\alpha_\sigma\ (lcase\ l\ s\ f) | (\alpha_\sigma\ s) \sqsubseteq \overline{s}, (\alpha_{\tau\to(list\ \tau)\to\sigma}\ f) \sqsubseteq \overline{f}, (\alpha_{(list\ \tau)}\ l) \sqsubseteq \perp\in\}\\ &\sqsubseteq \bigsqcup\{\{(\alpha_{\tau\to(list\ \tau)\to\sigma}\ f)\ (\alpha_\tau\ u)\ (\alpha_{(list\ \tau)}\ l') | (\alpha_{\tau\to(list\ \tau)\to\sigma}\ f) \sqsubseteq \overline{f}, u \in S_\tau,\\ &\qquad l' \in (List_\tau^\infty \bigcup List_\tau^{\perp\in})\}\\ &\quad \bigcup\{(\alpha_{\tau\to(list\ \tau)\to\sigma}\ f)\ (\alpha_\tau\ u)\ (\alpha_{(list\ \tau)}\ l') | (\alpha_{\tau\to(list\ \tau)\to\sigma}\ f) \sqsubseteq \overline{f}, u = \perp_{S_\tau},\\ &\qquad l' \in List_\tau^{\top\in}\}\}\\ &= \bigsqcup\{(\overline{f}\ \top_{A_\tau}\ \infty), (\overline{f}\ \top_{A_\tau}\ \perp\in), (\overline{f}\ \perp_{A_\tau}\ \top\in)\}\\ &= (\overline{f}\ \top_{A_\tau}\ \perp\in) \sqcup (\overline{f}\ \perp_{A_\tau}\ \top\in)\end{aligned}$$

4. If $\overline{l} = \top\in$, then $\forall l \in S_{(list\ \tau)}, (\alpha_{(list\ \tau)}\ l) \sqsubseteq \top\in$. In particular,

$$(\alpha_{(list\ \tau)}\ nil) = \top\in$$

and for any $u \neq \bot_{\mathbf{S}_\tau}$ and $l' \in List_\tau^{\top\!\in}$, $(\alpha_{(list\ \tau)}\ (cons\ u\ l')) = \top\!\in$. Now

$$(lcase\ nil\ s\ f) = s,$$

and

$$lcase\ (cons\ u\ l') = f\ u\ l'.$$

In the first case, we know that $\alpha_\sigma\ s \sqsubseteq \overline{s}$, and in the second we must use the semi-homomorphic property of abstraction as above to calculate that

$$\begin{array}{l} \bigsqcup\{\alpha_\sigma\ (lcase\ l\ s\ f) | (\alpha_\sigma\ s) \sqsubseteq \overline{s}, (\alpha_{\tau\to(list\ \tau)\to\sigma}\ f) \sqsubseteq \overline{f}, (\alpha_{(list\ \tau)}\ l) \sqsubseteq \top\!\in\} \\ \quad \sqsubseteq \overline{s} \sqcup (\overline{f}\ \top_{\mathbf{A}_\tau}\ \top\!\in) \end{array}$$

□

The Correctness of this Abstract Interpretation

All the conditions for the Correctness Theorem for Abstract Interpretation hold, and so this particular abstract interpretation is correct.

4.1.3 Some Examples of the Abstract Interpretation of User-Defined Functions

In order to make the process of abstract interpretation more concrete, we will show how to calculate the abstract interpretation of the function `sumlist`. We then give the abstract interpretations of all of the functions defined in Figure 1.1, which can be calculated in a similar way.

The function `sumlist` was defined by:

```
> sumlist Nil          = 0
> sumlist (Cons x xs)  = x + (sumlist xs)
```

and we saw in Section 2.1.7 that the result of translating this into the language Λ_T is:

$$\mathbf{fix}_\tau\ (\lambda g^{(list\ int)\to int}.\lambda l^{int}.\mathbf{lcase}_\sigma\ l\ \mathbf{0}_{int}\ (\lambda x^{int}.\lambda xs^{(list\ int)\to int}.+_{int\to int\to int}\ x\ (g\ xs)))$$

where $\sigma = (list\ int) \to int \to (int \to (list\ int) \to int) \to int$ and $\tau = (((list\ int) \to int) \to ((list\ int) \to int)) \to ((list\ int) \to int)$. Using the interpretation rules of Figure 3.1, we can determine the abstract interpretation of *sumlist* as follows. If we denote

$$\mathbf{lcase}_\sigma\ l\ \mathbf{0}_{int}\ (\lambda x^{int}.\lambda xs^{(list\ int)}.+_{int\to int\to int}\ x\ (g\ xs))$$

by e, and the empty environment by $\{\}$, then

$$\begin{array}{rcl} \mathbf{A}\ [\![sumlist]\!]\ \{\} & = & \mathbf{A}\ [\![\mathrm{fix}_\tau\ (\lambda g^{(list\ int)\to int}.\lambda l^{int}.e)]\!]\ \{\} \\ & = & \bigsqcup_{i\geq 0}(\mathbf{A}\ [\![\lambda g^{(list\ int)\to int}.\lambda l^{int}.e]\!]\ \{\})^i\ \bot_{\mathbf{A}_{(list\ int)\to int}} \\ & = & \bigsqcup_{i\geq 0}(\lambda \overline{g}\in\mathbf{A}_{(list\ int)\to int}.\lambda \overline{l}\in\mathbf{A}_{(list\ int)}.\mathbf{A}\ [\![e]\!]\ \{\}[\overline{l}/l, \overline{g}/g])^i\ \bot_{\mathbf{A}_{(list\ int)\to int}} \end{array}$$

If we denote $\{\}[\bar{l}/l,\bar{g}/g]$ by $\rho^{\mathbf{A}}$ and $(\lambda x^{int}.\lambda xs^{(list\ int)}.+_{int\to int\to int}\ x\ (g\ xs))$ by e', then

$$\begin{array}{rcl}\mathbf{A}\ [\![e]\!]\ \rho^{\mathbf{A}} & = & (\mathbf{A}\ [\![\mathrm{lcase}_\sigma]\!]\ \rho^{\mathbf{A}})\ (\mathbf{A}\ [\![l]\!]\ \rho^{\mathbf{A}})\ (\mathbf{A}\ [\![0_{int}]\!]\ \rho^{\mathbf{A}})\ (\mathbf{A}\ [\![e']\!]\ \rho^{\mathbf{A}}) \\ & = & (\mathbf{K}^{\mathbf{A}}\ [\![\mathrm{lcase}_\sigma]\!])\ (\rho^{\mathbf{A}}\ l)\ 1\ (\mathbf{A}\ [\![e']\!]\ \rho^{\mathbf{A}}) \\ & = & (\mathbf{K}^{\mathbf{A}}\ [\![\mathrm{lcase}_\sigma]\!])\ \bar{l}\ 1\ (\mathbf{A}\ [\![e']\!]\ \rho^{\mathbf{A}})\end{array}$$

Finally,

$$\begin{array}{rl}\mathbf{A}\ [\![e']\!]\ \rho^{\mathbf{A}} & \\ = & \mathbf{A}\ [\![\lambda x^{int}.\lambda xs^{(list\ int)}.+_{int\to int\to int}\ x\ (g\ xs)]\!]\ \rho^{\mathbf{A}} \\ = & \lambda\bar{x}\epsilon\mathbf{A}_{int}.\lambda\overline{xs}\epsilon\mathbf{A}_{(list\ int)}.\mathbf{A}\ [\![+_{int\to int\to int}\ x\ (g\ xs)]\!]\ \rho^{\mathbf{A}}[\overline{xs}/xs,\bar{x}/x] \\ = & \lambda\bar{x}\epsilon\mathbf{A}_{int}.\lambda\overline{xs}\epsilon\mathbf{A}_{(list\ int)}.(\mathbf{A}\ [\![x]\!]\ \rho^{\mathbf{A}}[\overline{xs}/xs,\bar{x}/x])\sqcap(\mathbf{A}\ [\![g\ xs]\!]\ \rho^{\mathbf{A}}[\overline{xs}/xs,\bar{x}/x]) \\ & \text{using the abstract interpretation of } +_{int\to int\to int} \text{ from Figure 4.1} \\ = & \lambda\bar{x}\epsilon\mathbf{A}_{int}.\lambda\overline{xs}\epsilon\mathbf{A}_{(list\ int)}.\bar{x}\sqcap(\bar{g}\ \overline{xs})\end{array}$$

Drawing all these results together, if we denote

$$\lambda\bar{g}\epsilon\mathbf{A}_{(list\ int)\to int}.\lambda\bar{l}\epsilon\mathbf{A}_{(list\ int)}.(\mathbf{K}^{\mathbf{A}}\ [\![\mathrm{lcase}_\sigma]\!])\ \bar{l}\ 1\ (\lambda\bar{x}\epsilon\mathbf{A}_{int}.\lambda\overline{xs}\epsilon\mathbf{A}_{(list\ int)}.\bar{x}\sqcap(\bar{g}\ \overline{xs}))$$

by F, then we find that

$$\overline{sumlist} = \mathbf{A}\ [\![sumlist]\!]\ \{\} = \bigsqcup_{i\geq 0} F^i\ \bot_{\mathbf{A}_{(list\ int)\to int}}.$$

To calculate $\bigsqcup_{i\geq 0} F^i\ \bot_{\mathbf{A}_{(list\ int)\to int}}$, we generate the sequence of terms

$$F^0\ \bot_{\mathbf{A}_{(list\ int)\to int}}, F^1\ \bot_{\mathbf{A}_{(list\ int)\to int}}, F^2\ \bot_{\mathbf{A}_{(list\ int)\to int}}, \ldots$$

until, for some n, $F^n\ \bot_{\mathbf{A}_{(list\ int)\to int}} = F^{n+1}\ \bot_{\mathbf{A}_{(list\ int)\to int}}$, which is then the least fixed point of F. Our restriction that abstract domains be finite lattices means that the process must terminate after a finite number of iterations, and testing the equality of two approximations to the least fixed point can be done in finite time.

Denoting $F^i\ \bot_{\mathbf{A}_{(list\ int)\to int}}$ by $\overline{sumlist_i}$, we have

$$\overline{sumlist_0} = F^0\ \bot_{\mathbf{A}_{(list\ int)\to int}} = \bot_{\mathbf{A}_{(list\ int)\to int}} = \lambda l\epsilon\mathbf{A}_{(list\ int)}.\bot_{\mathbf{A}_{int}} = \lambda l\epsilon\mathbf{A}_{(list\ int)}.0$$

Given $F^i\ \bot_{\mathbf{A}_{(list\ int)\to int}}$, $F^{i+1}\ \bot_{\mathbf{A}_{(list\ int)\to int}}$ is calculated by applying F to $F^i\ \bot_{\mathbf{A}_{(list\ int)\to int}}$. Thus

$$\overline{sumlist_1} = F\ \overline{sumlist_0}.$$

As $\overline{sumlist}$ is a function, to see if two approximations to the fixed point are equal, we need to make sure they are equal at each of the values that the argument to $\overline{sumlist}$ can take. We now calculate the next approximation of the value of $\overline{sumlist}$, where $(\mathbf{K}^{\mathbf{A}}\ [\![\mathrm{lcase}_\sigma]\!])$

is defined in Figure 4.1.

$$
\begin{aligned}
\overline{sumlist_1}\ \bot &= (\mathbf{K^A}\ [\![\mathrm{lcase}_\sigma]\!])\ \bot\ 1\ (\lambda\overline{x}\epsilon\mathbf{A}_{int}.\lambda\overline{xs}\epsilon\mathbf{A}_{(list\ int)}.\overline{x} \sqcap (\overline{sumlist_0}\ \overline{xs}))\\
&= \bot_{\mathbf{A}_{int}}\\
&= 0
\end{aligned}
$$

$$
\begin{aligned}
\overline{sumlist_1}\ \infty &= (\mathbf{K^A}\ [\![\mathrm{lcase}_\sigma]\!])\ \infty\ 1\ (\lambda\overline{x}\epsilon\mathbf{A}_{int}.\lambda\overline{xs}\epsilon\mathbf{A}_{(list\ int)}.\overline{x} \sqcap (\overline{sumlist_0}\ \overline{xs}))\\
&= 1 \sqcap (\overline{sumlist_0}\ \infty)\\
&= 1 \sqcap 0\\
&= 0
\end{aligned}
$$

$$
\begin{aligned}
\overline{sumlist_1}\ \bot\!\in &= (\mathbf{K^A}\ [\![\mathrm{lcase}_\sigma]\!])\ \bot\!\in\ 1\ (\lambda\overline{x}\epsilon\mathbf{A}_{int}.\lambda\overline{xs}\epsilon\mathbf{A}_{(list\ int)}.\overline{x} \sqcap (\overline{sumlist_0}\ \overline{xs}))\\
&= (1 \sqcap (\overline{sumlist_0}\ \bot\!\in)) \sqcup (0 \sqcap (\overline{sumlist_0}\ \top\!\in))\\
&= (1 \sqcap 0) \sqcup (0 \sqcap 0)\\
&= 0
\end{aligned}
$$

$$
\begin{aligned}
\overline{sumlist_1}\ \top\!\in &= (\mathbf{K^A}\ [\![\mathrm{lcase}_\sigma]\!])\ \top\!\in\ 1\ (\lambda\overline{x}\epsilon\mathbf{A}_{int}.\lambda\overline{xs}\epsilon\mathbf{A}_{(list\ int)}.\overline{x} \sqcap (\overline{sumlist_0}\ \overline{xs}))\\
&= 1 \sqcup (1 \sqcap (\overline{sumlist_0}\ \top\!\in))\\
&= 1
\end{aligned}
$$

Clearly $\overline{sumlist_1} \neq \overline{sumlist_0}$, so we must calculate $\overline{sumlist_2} = F\ \overline{sumlist_1}$.

$$
\begin{aligned}
\overline{sumlist_2}\ \bot &= (\mathbf{K^A}\ [\![\mathrm{lcase}_\sigma]\!])\ \bot\ 1\ (\lambda\overline{x}\epsilon\mathbf{A}_{int}.\lambda\overline{xs}\epsilon\mathbf{A}_{(list\ int)}.\overline{x} \sqcap (\overline{sumlist_1}\ \overline{xs}))\\
&= \bot_{\mathbf{A}_{int}}\\
&= 0
\end{aligned}
$$

$$
\begin{aligned}
\overline{sumlist_2}\ \infty &= (\mathbf{K^A}\ [\![\mathrm{lcase}_\sigma]\!])\ \infty\ 1\ (\lambda\overline{x}\epsilon\mathbf{A}_{int}.\lambda\overline{xs}\epsilon\mathbf{A}_{(list\ int)}.\overline{x} \sqcap (\overline{sumlist_1}\ \overline{xs}))\\
&= 1 \sqcap (\overline{sumlist_1}\ \infty)\\
&= 1 \sqcap 0\\
&= 0
\end{aligned}
$$

$$
\begin{aligned}
\overline{sumlist_2}\ \bot\!\in &= (\mathbf{K^A}\ [\![\mathrm{lcase}_\sigma]\!])\ \bot\!\in\ 1\ (\lambda\overline{x}\epsilon\mathbf{A}_{int}.\lambda\overline{xs}\epsilon\mathbf{A}_{(list\ int)}.\overline{x} \sqcap (\overline{sumlist_1}\ \overline{xs}))\\
&= (1 \sqcap (\overline{sumlist_1}\ \bot\!\in)) \sqcup (0 \sqcap (\overline{sumlist_1}\ \top\!\in))\\
&= (1 \sqcap 0) \sqcup (0 \sqcap 1)\\
&= 0
\end{aligned}
$$

$$
\begin{aligned}
\overline{sumlist_2}\ \top\!\in &= (\mathbf{K^A}\ [\![\mathrm{lcase}_\sigma]\!])\ \top\!\in\ 1\ (\lambda\overline{x}\epsilon\mathbf{A}_{int}.\lambda\overline{xs}\epsilon\mathbf{A}_{(list\ int)}.\overline{x} \sqcap (\overline{sumlist_1}\ \overline{xs}))\\
&= 1 \sqcup (1 \sqcap (\overline{sumlist_1}\ \top\!\in))\\
&= 1
\end{aligned}
$$

The values of $\overline{sumlist_1}$ and $\overline{sumlist_2}$ are equal, and so $\overline{sumlist}$ is $\overline{sumlist_1}$.

For large abstract domains, testing each iteration of the fixed point at each value in the abstract domain can be an expensive operation. Hunt and Hankin [Hun89, HH90] have built on some earlier work by Clack and Peyton Jones [CP85] for determining fixed points more efficiently.

Abstract interpretations for all of the functions given in Figure 1.1 can be calculated in a similar manner, and are given in Figure 4.2.

$\overline{u}$	$\overline{length}\ \overline{u}$	$\overline{sumlist}\ \overline{u}$	$\overline{reverse}\ \overline{u}$	$\overline{before0}\ \overline{u}$	$\overline{doubles}\ \overline{u}$	$\overline{size}\overline{u}$	$\overline{sumtree}\ \overline{u}$
$\bot$	0	0	$\bot$	$\bot$	$\bot$	0	0
∞	0	0	$\bot$	$\top\!\in$	∞	0	0
$\bot\!\in$	1	0	$\bot\!\in$	$\top\!\in$	$\bot\!\in$	1	0
$\top\!\in$	1	1	$\top\!\in$	$\top\!\in$	$\top\!\in$	1	1

For all types τ, $append : (list\ \tau) \rightarrow (list\ \tau) \rightarrow (list\ \tau)$

$\overline{append}\ \overline{xs}\ \overline{ys}$:

$\overline{ys}$ / $\overline{xs}$	$\bot$	∞	$\bot\!\in$	$\top\!\in$
$\bot$	$\bot$	$\bot$	$\bot$	$\bot$
∞	∞	∞	∞	∞
$\bot\!\in$	∞	∞	$\bot\!\in$	$\bot\!\in$
$\top\!\in$	∞	∞	$\bot\!\in$	$\top\!\in$

$map : (int \rightarrow int) \rightarrow (list\ int) \rightarrow (list\ int)$

$\overline{map}\ \overline{f}\ \overline{xs}$:

$\overline{xs}$ / $\overline{f}$	$\bot$	∞	$\bot\!\in$	$\top\!\in$
$\lambda x \epsilon \mathbf{A}_{int}.0$	$\bot$	∞	$\bot\!\in$	$\top\!\in$
$\lambda x \epsilon \mathbf{A}_{int}.x$	$\bot$	∞	$\bot\!\in$	$\top\!\in$
$\lambda x \epsilon \mathbf{A}_{int}.1$	$\bot$	∞	$\top\!\in$	$\top\!\in$

$$\overline{join}\ \overline{t_1}\ \overline{n}\ \overline{t_2} = \begin{cases} \infty & \text{if } \overline{t_1} \sqsubseteq \infty \text{ or } \overline{t_2} \sqsubseteq \infty \\ \top\!\in & \text{if } \overline{t_1} = \top\!\in \text{ and } \overline{n} = 1 \text{ and } \overline{t_2} = \top\!\in \\ \bot\!\in & \text{otherwise} \end{cases}$$

Figure 4.2: Abstract Interpretation of Functions in Figure 1.1

4.2 On Defining Abstract Domains

One of the themes running through this book is that abstract interpretation can be used to find out the information needed to determine evaluation transformers. In the next chapter we will see that the four point domain of Wadler is sufficient to determine the evaluation transformers introduced intuitively in Section 1.2.2. However, the framework of Chapter 3 is more general than these examples. In this section we give another example of choosing an abstract domain to capture a particular property, and discuss how to build abstract domains from smaller ones in order to capture more properties. The new property that we investigate is *one-level head-strictness.*

4.2.1 An Abstract Domain For One-Level Head-Strictness

Intuitively, the result of applying a one-level head-strict function to a list with a bottom head is bottom. If a function is one-level head-strict, then we can conclude that its argument not only needs to be evaluated to HNF, but if the result is an application of $\mathbf{cons}_{\tau \to (list\ \tau) \to (list\ \tau)}$, then the first argument of $\mathbf{cons}_{\tau \to (list\ \tau) \to (list\ \tau)}$, the head of the list, needs to be evaluated to HNF as well. Let us now formally define one-level head-strictness.

Definition 4.2.1

A function $f : (list\ \tau) \to \sigma$ is *one-level head-strict*[1] if for all $l \in \mathbf{S}_{(list\ \tau)}$,

$$(\mathbf{S}\ [\![f]\!]\ \{\})\ (cons\ \bot_{\mathbf{S}_\tau}\ l) = \bot_{\mathbf{S}_\sigma}.$$

The four point abstract domain for lists, $\mathbf{A}_{(list\ \tau)}$, that we have been discussing so far, is not sufficient for determining one-level head-strictness information, as there is no abstract domain point which captures the idea of a list having a bottom head. An abstract domain for one-level head-strictness should distinguish between lists according to whether they have an undefined head or not. To do this, we make the following definition.

Definition 4.2.2

For all types τ, the domain $\mathbf{A}^{hs}_{(list\ \tau)}$ contains the three elements $\{0, 1, 2\}$, where the ordering is defined by $0 \sqsubseteq 1 \sqsubseteq 2$.

The abstraction map is defined by:

$$\alpha^{hs}_{(list\ \tau)} : \mathbf{S}_{(list\ \tau)} \to \mathbf{A}^{hs}_{(list\ \tau)}$$

$$\alpha^{hs}_{(list\ \tau)}\ u = \begin{cases} 0 & \text{if } \ u = \bot_{\mathbf{S}_{(list\ \tau)}} \\ 1 & \text{if } \ u \in \{cons\ u\ l \mid u = \bot_{\mathbf{S}_\tau}, l \in \mathbf{S}_{(list\ \tau)}\} \\ 2 & \text{otherwise} \end{cases}$$

[1] This should not be confused with the notion of head-neededness of [BKKS86], which discusses whether the head redex is reduced in the head reduction sequence to head normal form. As well, one-level head-strictness is weaker than the notion of head-strictness defined in [WH87]. This latter notion gives information about how all the heads in the list are going to be used, whilst one-level head-strictness only tells about the first element in the list, hence 'one-level'.

We have decorated $\mathbf{A}_{(list\ \tau)}$ and $\alpha_{(list\ \tau)}$ with hs to remind us that that they are the three point abstract domain and abstraction map for one-level *h*ead-*s*trictness. The abstraction map sends the bottom list to 0, any list with an bottom head to 1 and any other list to 2, and so distinguishes between lists according to whether or not they have a bottom head.

Since $\alpha^{hs}_{(list\ \tau)}$ is strict and bottom-reflecting for each type τ, we have the following lemma.

Lemma 4.2.3

1. *For all types σ, α_σ is strict.*
2. *For all types σ, α_σ is bottom-reflecting.*
3. *γ_σ is strict for all types σ, i.e.*

$$\gamma_\sigma\ \bot_{\mathbf{A}_\sigma} = \bot_{\mathbf{P}\ \mathbf{S}_\sigma} = \{\bot_{\mathbf{S}_\sigma}\}.$$

Proof

These results follow immediately from Lemmata 3.2.4, 3.2.9 and 3.2.10 respectively.

□

So that the reader is able to determine the abstract interpretation of functions using the abstract domain $\mathbf{A}^{hs}_{(list\ \tau)}$, in Figure 4.3 we give abstract interpretations satisfying the constant safety condition for the constants of Λ_T whose type involves $(list\ \tau)$. We leave it as an exercise to prove that they do in fact satisfy the constant safety condition.

All the conditions are now met for the Correctness Theorem for Abstract Interpretation, and so we can conclude that for any $f : \sigma \rightarrow \tau$, whenever

$$(\mathbf{A}\ [\![f]\!]\ \rho^{\mathbf{A}})\ \overline{s} \sqsubseteq \overline{t},$$

then $\forall s \in (\gamma_\sigma\ \overline{s})$,

$$(\mathbf{S}\ [\![f]\!]\ \rho^{\mathbf{S}})\ s \in (\gamma_\tau\ \overline{t}).$$

Using the abstract interpretations of the constants given in Figure 4.3, we are able to determine the abstract interpretation of those functions in Figure 1.1 whose type involves $(list\ \tau)$, and these are recorded in Figure 4.4.

It can be seen that the domain captures what we expect. For example, our intuition about `before0` is that it is one-level head-strict. All lists with bottom heads abstract to the point 1, and from Figure 4.4 we find that

$$\overline{before0}\ 1 = 0.$$

Since the abstract interpretation is correct, we have that

$$\forall l \in (\gamma_{(list\ \tau)}\ 1),\ (\mathbf{S}\ [\![before0]\!]\ \rho^{\mathbf{S}})\ l \in (\gamma_{(list\ \tau)}\ 0),$$

and $(\gamma_{(list\ \tau)}\ 0) = \{\bot_{\mathbf{S}_{(list\ \tau)}}\}$ by Lemma 4.2.3, and so the above says that `before0` maps all lists with bottom heads to bottom.

$$\mathbf{K^A}\ [\![\mathbf{nil}_{(list\ \tau)}]\!] = 2$$

$$\mathbf{K^A}\ [\![\mathbf{cons}_{\tau\to(list\ \tau)\to(list\ \tau)}]\!]\ u\ l = \begin{cases} 1 & \text{if } u = \bot_{\mathbf{A}_\tau} \\ 2 & \text{otherwise} \end{cases}$$

$$\mathbf{K^A}\ [\![\mathbf{head}_{(list\ \tau)\to\tau}]\!]\ l = \begin{cases} \bot_{\mathbf{A}_\tau} & \text{if } l \sqsubseteq 1 \\ \top_{\mathbf{A}_\tau} & \text{otherwise} \end{cases}$$

$$\mathbf{K^A}\ [\![\mathbf{tail}_{(list\ \tau)\to(list\ \tau)}]\!]\ l = \begin{cases} 0 & \text{if } l = 0 \\ 2 & \text{otherwise} \end{cases}$$

$$\mathbf{K^A}\ [\![\mathbf{lcase}_{(list\ \tau)\to\sigma\to(\tau\to(list\ \tau)\to\sigma)\to\sigma}]\!]\ l\ s\ f = \begin{cases} \bot_{\mathbf{A}_\sigma} & \text{if } l = 0 \\ f\ \bot_{\mathbf{A}_\tau}\ 2 & \text{if } l = 1 \\ s \sqcup (f\ \top_{\mathbf{A}_\tau}\ 2) & \text{if } l = 2 \end{cases}$$

Figure 4.3: The Abstract Interpretation of Some Constants Using $\mathbf{A}^{hs}_{(list\ \tau)}$

$\overline{u}$	$\overline{length}\,\overline{u}$	$\overline{sumlist}\ \overline{u}$	$\overline{reverse}\ \overline{u}$	$\overline{before0}\ \overline{u}$	$\overline{doubles}\ \overline{u}$
0	0	0	0	0	0
1	1	0	2	0	1
2	1	1	2	2	2

For all types τ, $append : (list\ \tau) \to (list\ \tau) \to (list\ \tau)$

$\overline{append}\ \overline{xs}\ \overline{ys}$:

$\overline{ys}$ / $\overline{xs}$	0	1	2
0	0	0	0
1	1	1	1
2	2	2	2

$map : (int \to int) \to (list\ int) \to (list\ int)$

$\overline{map}\ \overline{f}\ \overline{xs}$:

$\overline{xs}$ / $\overline{f}$	0	1	2
$\lambda x \epsilon \mathbf{2}.0$	0	1	2
$\lambda x \epsilon \mathbf{2}.x$	0	1	2
$\lambda x \epsilon \mathbf{2}.1$	0	2	2

Figure 4.4: Abstract Interpretation of the List Functions in Figure 1.1 using $\mathbf{A}^{hs}_{(list\ \tau)}$

4.2.2 Combining Abstract Domains

Just as we defined one-level head-strictness, we can define the property of being *tail-strict*.

Definition 4.2.4

A function $f : (list\ \tau) \rightarrow \sigma$ is *tail-strict* if $\forall l \in (List_\tau^\infty \bigcup \{\perp_{\mathbf{S}_{(list\ \tau)}}\})$,

$$(\mathbf{S}\ [\![f]\!]\ \rho^{\mathbf{S}})\ l = \perp_{\mathbf{S}_\sigma}.$$

Tail-strictness can be determined using the abstract domain $\mathbf{A}_{(list\ \tau)}$: if for some function $f : (list\ \tau) \rightarrow \sigma$,

$$(\mathbf{A}\ [\![f]\!]\ \rho^{\mathbf{A}})\ \infty = \perp_{\mathbf{A}_\sigma},$$

then, recalling that $(\gamma_{(list\ \tau)}\ \infty) = (List_\tau^\infty \bigcup \{\perp_{\mathbf{S}_{(list\ \tau)}}\})$, the Correctness Theorem for Abstract Interpretation assures us that

$$\forall l \in (List_\tau^\infty \bigcup \{\perp_{\mathbf{S}_{(list\ \tau)}}\}),\ (\mathbf{S}\ [\![f]\!]\ \rho^{\mathbf{S}})\ l \in (\gamma_\sigma\ \perp_{\mathbf{S}_\sigma})$$

By Lemma 4.1.6(3), $(\gamma_\sigma\ \perp_{\mathbf{S}_\sigma}) = \{\perp_{\mathbf{S}_\sigma}\}$, and so we can conclude that f is tail-strict.

Now that we have an abstract domain for one-level head-strictness, and an abstract domain for tail-strictness, can we use one when we want to find out about one-level head-strictness, and the other when we want to find out about tail-strictness? Unfortunately the answer is no, because, for example, the one-level head-strictness of one function may depend on the tail-strictness of another. Without an abstract domain which captures both properties, we cannot determine the one-level head-strictness of such a function. For example, consider the functions f and g defined by:

```
> f Nil          = 5
> f (Cons x xs)  = length (Cons 1 (g x))
>
> g n = if n=0 then Nil else Nil
```

Translating this into the language Λ_T, we have:

$$f = \lambda l^\tau.\mathrm{lcase}_\sigma\ l^\tau\ 5_{int}\ (\lambda x^{int}.\lambda xs^\tau.length\ (\mathbf{cons}_{int \rightarrow \tau \rightarrow \tau}\ 1_{int}\ (g\ x^{int}))$$
$$g = \lambda n^{int}.\mathrm{if}_{bool \rightarrow \tau \rightarrow \tau \rightarrow \tau}\ (=_{int \rightarrow int \rightarrow bool}\ n^{int}\ 0_{int})\ \mathrm{nil}_\tau\ \mathrm{nil}_\tau$$

where

$$\sigma = \tau \rightarrow int \rightarrow (int \rightarrow \tau \rightarrow int) \rightarrow int$$
$$\tau = (list\ int)$$

The standard interpretations of f and g are:

$$\mathbf{S}\ [\![f]\!]\ \{\} = \lambda l \epsilon \mathbf{S}_\tau.lcase\ l\ 5\ (\lambda x \epsilon \mathbf{S}_{int}.\lambda xs \epsilon \mathbf{S}_\tau.(\mathbf{S}\ [\![length]\!]\ \{\})\ (cons\ 1\ ((\mathbf{S}\ [\![g]\!]\ \{\})\ x)))$$
$$\mathbf{S}\ [\![g]\!]\ \{\} = \lambda n \epsilon \mathbf{S}_{int}.\mathbf{K}^{\mathbf{S}}\ [\![\mathrm{if}_{bool \rightarrow \tau \rightarrow \tau \rightarrow \tau}]\!]\ (n = 0)\ nil\ nil$$

We can see that (S $[\![f]\!]$ {}) is one-level head-strict by the following calculation, if e is any element of $\mathbf{S}_{(list\ \tau)}$:

$$\begin{array}{l}
(\mathbf{S}\ [\![f]\!]\ \{\})\ (cons\ \bot_{\mathbf{S}_{int}}\ e) \\
\quad = lcase\ (cons\ \bot_{\mathbf{S}_{int}}\ e)\ 5\ (\lambda x\epsilon\mathbf{S}_{int}.\lambda xs\epsilon\mathbf{S}_{\tau}.(\mathbf{S}\ [\![length]\!]\ \{\})\ (cons\ 1\ ((\mathbf{S}\ [\![g]\!]\ \{\})\ x))) \\
\quad = (\mathbf{S}\ [\![length]\!]\ \{\})\ (cons\ 1\ ((\mathbf{S}\ [\![g]\!]\ \{\})\ \bot_{\mathbf{S}_{int}})) \\
\\
\quad = 1 + (\mathbf{S}\ [\![length]\!]\ \{\})\ ((\mathbf{S}\ [\![g]\!]\ \{\})\ \bot_{\mathbf{S}_{int}}) \\
\quad = 1 + (\mathbf{S}\ [\![length]\!]\ \{\})\ (\mathbf{K^S}\ [\![\mathbf{if}_{bool\to\tau\to\tau\to\tau}]\!]\ (=_{int\to int\to bool}\bot_{\mathbf{S}_{int}}\ 0)\ nil\ nil) \\
\quad = 1 + (\mathbf{S}\ [\![length]\!]\ \{\})\ (\mathbf{K^S}\ [\![\mathbf{if}_{bool\to\tau\to\tau\to\tau}]\!]\ \bot_{\mathbf{S}_{bool}}\ nil\ nil) \\
\quad = 1 + (\mathbf{S}\ [\![length]\!]\ \{\})\ \bot_{\mathbf{S}_{\tau}} \\
\\
\quad = 1 + \bot_{\mathbf{S}_{int}} \\
\quad = \bot_{\mathbf{S}_{int}}
\end{array}$$

However, using the abstract domain $\mathbf{A}^{hs}_{(list\ \tau)}$ for lists and the abstract interpretation of the list constants from Figure 4.3, we can determine the abstract interpretation of f, $\overline{f}$, and find that

$$(\overline{f}\ 1) = 1$$

and so we cannot conclude that (S $[\![f]\!]$ {}) is one-level head-strict by using this abstract interpretation.

This example points out the problem:

> *The one-level head-strictness of a function may depend on tail-strictness information (or vice versa), and without an abstract domain to capture* both *properties, in general it will not be possible to find out the one-level head-strictness of that function.*

Is there a systematic way to combine two abstract domains, that give information about different properties, to get an abstract domain which captures both properties? Fortunately there is. The Cousots showed how to do this with a construction on the two domains [CC79]. If $\mathbf{A}^1_\sigma$ and $\mathbf{A}^2_\sigma$ are two abstract domains for the type σ, their *reduced product*, which we will denote by $\mathbf{A}^1_\sigma \times_{rp} \mathbf{A}^2_\sigma$, is obtained by quotienting $\mathbf{A}^1_\sigma \times \mathbf{A}^2_\sigma$ with the relation R defined by :

$$(d_1, d_2)\ R\ (d_1', d_2') \text{ if } (\gamma^1_\sigma\ d_1) \cap (\gamma^2_\sigma\ d_2) = (\gamma^1_\sigma\ d_1') \cap (\gamma^2_\sigma\ d_2')$$

where γ^i_σ is the concretisation function associated with the abstract domain $\mathbf{A}^i_\sigma$. If (d_1, d_2) and (d_1', d_2') are representatives of two equivalence classes, then the equivalence class containing (d_1, d_2) is less defined or equal to the equivalence class containing (d_1', d_2') if and only if

$$(\gamma^1_\sigma\ d_1) \cap (\gamma^2_\sigma\ d_2) \subseteq (\gamma^1_\sigma\ d_1') \cap (\gamma^2_\sigma\ d_2'),$$

where $\subseteq$ is subset inclusion, the ordering on the Hoare powerdomain. Behind this definition is the intuition that taking the intersection of concretisations of the two abstract values gives us the set of values which have both of the properties represented by the two

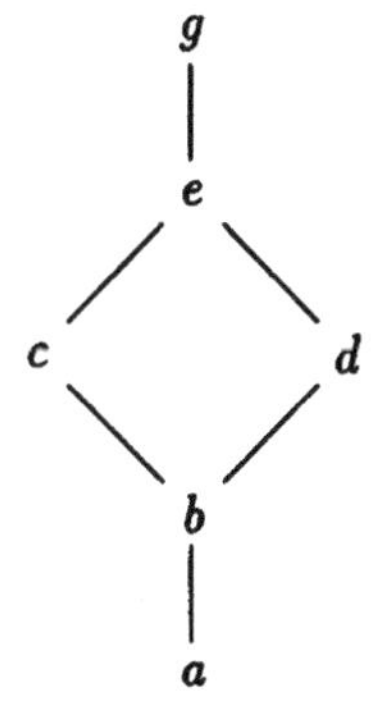

For all types τ, $\alpha^{rp}_{(list\ \tau)} : \mathbf{S}_{(list\ \tau)} \rightarrow \mathbf{A}^{rp}_{(list\ \tau)}$

$$\alpha^{rp}_{(list\ \tau)}\ u = \begin{cases} a & if\ \ u = \bot_{\mathbf{S}_{(list\ \tau)}} \\ b & if\ \ u \in \{cons\ u\ l | u = \bot_{\mathbf{S}_\tau}, l \in List^{\infty}_{\tau}\} \\ c & if\ \ u \in \{cons\ u\ l | u \neq \bot_{\mathbf{S}_\tau}, l \in List^{\infty}_{\tau}\} \\ d & if\ \ u \in \{cons\ u\ l | u = \bot_{\mathbf{S}_\tau}, l \in (List^{\bot\in}_{\tau} \cup List^{\top\in}_{\tau})\} \\ e & if\ \ u \in \{cons\ u\ l | u \neq \bot_{\mathbf{S}_\tau}, l \in List^{\bot\in}_{\tau}\} \\ g & if\ \ u \in List^{\top\in}_{\tau} \end{cases}$$

$$\mathbf{K}^{\mathbf{A}}\ [\![\mathbf{nil}_{(list\ \tau)}]\!] = g$$

$$\mathbf{K}^{\mathbf{A}}\ [\![\mathbf{cons}_{\tau\rightarrow(list\ \tau)\rightarrow(list\ \tau)}]\!]\ u\ l = \begin{cases} b & \text{if } u = \bot_{\mathbf{A}_\tau} \wedge l \in \{a,b,c\} \\ c & \text{if } u \neq \bot_{\mathbf{A}_\tau} \wedge l \in \{a,b,c\} \\ d & \text{if } u = \bot_{\mathbf{A}_\tau} \wedge l \in \{d,e,g\} \\ e & \text{if } u \neq \bot_{\mathbf{A}_\tau} \wedge l \in \{d,e\} \\ g & \text{if } u \neq \bot_{\mathbf{A}_\tau} \wedge l = g \end{cases}$$

$$\mathbf{K}^{\mathbf{A}}\ [\![\mathbf{head}_{(list\ \tau)\rightarrow\tau}]\!]\ l = \begin{cases} \bot_{\mathbf{A}_\tau} & \text{if } l \sqsubseteq d \\ \top_{\mathbf{A}_\tau} & \text{otherwise} \end{cases}$$

$$\mathbf{K}^{\mathbf{A}}\ [\![\mathbf{tail}_{(list\ \tau)\rightarrow(list\ \tau)}]\!]\ l = \begin{cases} a & \text{if } l = a \\ c & \text{if } l \in \{b,c\} \\ g & \text{otherwise} \end{cases}$$

$$\mathbf{K}^{\mathbf{A}}\ [\![\mathbf{lcase}_{(list\ \tau)\rightarrow\sigma\rightarrow(\tau\rightarrow(list\ \tau)\rightarrow\sigma)\rightarrow\sigma}]\!]\ l\ s\ f = \begin{cases} \bot_{\mathbf{A}_\sigma} & \text{if } l = a \\ f\ \bot_{\mathbf{A}_\tau}\ c & \text{if } l = b \\ f\ \top_{\mathbf{A}_\tau}\ c & \text{if } l = c \\ f\ \bot_{\mathbf{A}_\tau}\ g & \text{if } l = d \\ (f\ \bot_{\mathbf{A}_\tau}\ g) \sqcup (f\ \top_{\mathbf{A}_\tau}\ e) & \text{if } l = e \\ s \sqcup (f\ \top_{\mathbf{A}_\tau}\ g) & \text{if } l = g \end{cases}$$

Figure 4.5: The Domain $\mathbf{A}^{rp}_{(list\ \tau)}$, its Abstraction Map and the Abstract Interpretation of Some Constants

abstract values. We take equivalence classes over the relation R because there may be several pairs of values which represent the same sets.

Given two abstraction maps, $\alpha_\sigma^i : \mathbf{S}_\sigma^i \to \mathbf{A}_\sigma^i$ for $i \in \{1,2\}$, the abstraction map for the reduced product, α_σ^{rp}, is defined by

$$\alpha_\sigma^{rp}\ u = [(\alpha_\sigma^1\ u, \alpha_\sigma^2\ u)]$$

where $[(\alpha_\sigma^1\ u, \alpha_\sigma^2\ u)]$ means the equivalence class containing the pair $(\alpha_\sigma^1\ u, \alpha_\sigma^2\ u)$. If both α_σ^1 and α_σ^2 are strict (respectively bottom-reflecting), then α_σ^{rp} is strict (respectively bottom-reflecting), and the concretisation function is strict if both α_σ^1 and α_σ^2 are strict and bottom-reflecting.

The domain we obtain by taking the reduced product of $\mathbf{A}_{(list\ \tau)}$ and $\mathbf{A}_{(list\ \tau)}^{hs}$ is isomorphic to $\mathbf{A}_{(list\ \tau)}^{rp}$, given in Figure 4.5. That this is so can be seen by the fact that any pair (d_1, d_2) where either d_1 is $\perp$ or d_2 is 0 will be in the same equivalence class (Lemma 4.1.6(3)), that $(\perp\in, 1)$ and $(\top\in, 1)$ are in the same equivalence class, and that all other members of the product are in singleton equivalence classes. As an exercise, the reader can show that, for the function f defined earlier in this section, $\overline{f}\ d \sqsubseteq a$, and so we can conclude that f is one-level head-strict if we use this abstract domain (noting that Lemma 4.2.3 is also true when $\mathbf{A}_{(list\ \tau)}^{rp}$ is used for the abstract interpretation of $(list\ \tau)$, and using the Correctness Theorem for Abstract Interpretation).

The problem with this domain is that it still does not give us as much information as we would expect. For example, the following function will be undefined if the tail of the argument list is not finite, or if it contains any bottom elements:

```
> h xs = sumlist (tail xs)
```

but we cannot determine this by using the abstract domain that arises from the reduced product. To see this, note that the abstract interpretation of this function is:

$$\overline{h}\ \overline{xs} = \overline{sumlist}\ (\mathrm{K}^{\mathbf{A}}\ [\![\mathbf{tail}_{(list\ int)\to(list\ int)}]\!]\ \overline{xs}),$$

that the point in the reduced product domain that represents all the lists which are not finite or have bottom elements is e, and it can be determined that $\overline{h}\ e$ is $\top_{\mathbf{A}_{int}}$, not $\perp_{\mathbf{A}_{int}}$. In this case, the information loss is due to the abstract interpretation we have had to give to $\mathbf{tail}_{(list\ int)\to(list\ int)}$. Since the point d represents any finite list with an undefined head, we have to set the abstract interpretation of $\mathbf{tail}_{(list\ int)\to(list\ int)}$ to give g when applied to d, since the head of the list might be the only undefined element of the list. This then forces us to give $\overline{tail}\ e$ to be g, since $d \sqsubseteq e$ in the domain ordering, and this loses information because it is impossible to take the tail of a list whose head is not $\perp$, but containing a bottom element, and get a list not containing any bottom elements. If we therefore split the set of finite lists which have bottom heads into two subsets, those containing at least one other bottom element, and those containing no other bottom elements, then we get the abstract domain given in Figure 4.6, which was first presented in [Bur90a]. Using this domain and the abstract interpretation of the constants from the same figure, which satisfy the constant safety condition, we can determine that the h defined above has an abstract interpretation such that $\overline{h}\ E = A$, and $\overline{h}\ F = A$, and so the application of h applied to any list which is not finite or contains a bottom element is undefined (noting that Lemma 4.2.3 is true when $\mathbf{A}_{(list\ \tau)}^{hts}$ is used for the abstract interpretation of $(list\ \tau)$, and using the Correctness Theorem for Abstract Interpretation).

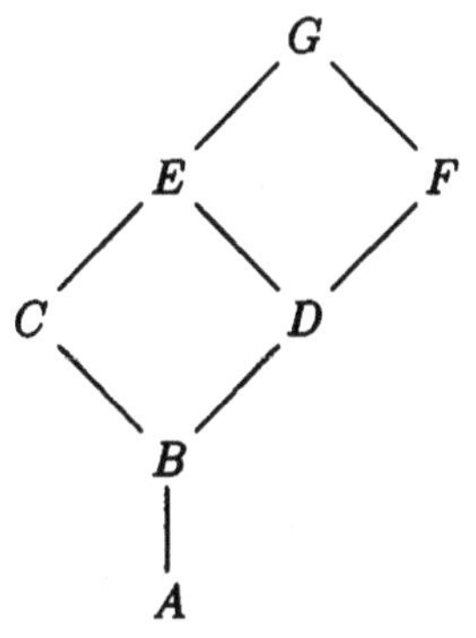

For all types τ, $\alpha^{hts}_{(list\ \tau)} : \mathbf{S}_{(list\ \tau)} \rightarrow \mathbf{A}^{hts}_{(list\ \tau)}$

$$\alpha^{hts}_{(list\ \tau)}\ u = \begin{cases} A & if \quad u\ = \bot_{\mathbf{S}_{(list\ \tau)}} \\ B & if \quad u \in \{cons\ u\ l | u = \bot_{\mathbf{S}_\tau}, u \in List^{\infty}_{\tau}\} \\ C & if \quad u \in \{cons\ u\ l | u \neq \bot_{\mathbf{S}_\tau}, u \in List^{\infty}_{\tau}\} \\ D & if \quad u \in \{cons\ u\ l | u = \bot_{\mathbf{S}_\tau}, l \in List^{\bot\in}_{\tau}\} \\ E & if \quad u \in \{cons\ u\ l | u \neq \bot_{\mathbf{S}_\tau}, l \in List^{\bot\in}_{\tau}\} \\ F & if \quad u \in \{cons\ u\ l | u = \bot_{\mathbf{S}_\tau}, l \in List^{\top\in}_{\tau}\} \\ G & if \quad u \in List^{\top\in}_{\tau} \end{cases}$$

$$\mathbf{K}^{\mathbf{A}}\ [\![\mathbf{nil}_{(list\ \tau)}]\!] = G$$

$$\mathbf{K}^{\mathbf{A}}\ [\![\mathbf{cons}_{\tau\rightarrow(list\ \tau)\rightarrow(list\ \tau)}]\!]\ u\ l = \begin{cases} B & \text{if } u = \bot_{\mathbf{A}_\tau} \wedge l \in \{A, B, C\} \\ C & \text{if } u \neq \bot_{\mathbf{A}_\tau} \wedge l \in \{A, B, C\} \\ D & \text{if } u = \bot_{\mathbf{A}_\tau} \wedge l \in \{D, E, F\} \\ E & \text{if } u \neq \bot_{\mathbf{A}_\tau} \wedge l \in \{D, E, F\} \\ F & \text{if } u = \bot_{\mathbf{A}_\tau} \wedge l = G \\ G & \text{if } u \neq \bot_{\mathbf{A}_\tau} \wedge l = G \end{cases}$$

$$\mathbf{K}^{\mathbf{A}}\ [\![\mathbf{head}_{(list\ \tau)\rightarrow\tau}]\!]\ l = \begin{cases} \bot_{\mathbf{A}_\tau} & \text{if } l \sqsubseteq F \\ \top_{\mathbf{A}_\tau} & \text{otherwise} \end{cases}$$

$$\mathbf{K}^{\mathbf{A}}\ [\![\mathbf{tail}_{(list\ \tau)\rightarrow(list\ \tau)}]\!]\ l = \begin{cases} A & \text{if } l = A \\ C & \text{if } l \in \{B, C\} \\ E & \text{if } l \in \{D, E\} \\ G & \text{if } l \in \{F, G\} \end{cases}$$

$$\mathbf{K}^{\mathbf{A}}\ [\![\mathbf{lcase}_{(list\ \tau)\rightarrow\sigma\rightarrow(\tau\rightarrow(list\ \tau)\rightarrow\sigma)\rightarrow\sigma}]\!]\ l\ s\ f = \begin{cases} \bot_{\mathbf{A}_\sigma} & \text{if } l = A \\ f\ \bot_{\mathbf{A}_\tau}\ C & \text{if } l = B \\ f\ \top_{\mathbf{A}_\tau}\ C & \text{if } l = C \\ f\ \bot_{\mathbf{A}_\tau}\ E & \text{if } l = D \\ (f\ \top_{\mathbf{A}_\tau}\ F) \sqcup (f\ \top_{\mathbf{A}_\tau}\ E) & \text{if } l = E \\ f\ \bot_{\mathbf{A}_\tau}\ G & \text{if } l = F \\ s \sqcup (f\ \top_{\mathbf{A}_\tau}\ G) & \text{if } l = G \end{cases}$$

Figure 4.6: The Domain $\mathbf{A}^{hts}_{(list\ \tau)}$, its Abstraction Map and the Abstract Interpretation of Some Constants

4.2.3 Choosing Optimal Abstract Domains For Base Types

Can we ever define an abstract domain for a data type which is in some sense 'canonical' in that it is the smallest, finite domain which, for every function, captures the properties in which we are interested? By comparison with the halting problem, we should not expect there to be such a domain. The key problem, exemplified by the discussion in the previous section, is that the fact that a function has some property captured by an abstract domain may be a result of some property not captured by the abstract domain, and so it will not be detected by an abstract interpretation using that domain. The old dictum "You get what you pay for" seems to be true in choosing abstract domains — if you pay the cost of finding fixed points in a bigger domain, then you can get more information. Are there any heuristics for choosing a good abstract domain? We have no evidence for this, but would like to suggest that a good heuristic would be to choose a domain such that for all the constants in the language, apart from higher-order ones, we can set the abstract interpretation of the constant to be equal to the abstraction of its standard interpretation. We except higher-order constants, because we may have to make some approximation in giving them an abstract interpretation. Examples of this were given in determining the abstract interpretation of $\mathbf{if}_{bool \rightarrow \sigma \rightarrow \sigma \rightarrow \sigma}$ and $\mathbf{lcase}_{(list\ \tau) \rightarrow \sigma \rightarrow (\tau \rightarrow (list\ \tau) \rightarrow \sigma) \rightarrow \sigma}$ in Section 4.1.2. The problem with the $\mathbf{A}^{rp}_{(list\ \tau)}$ was that we had to set the abstract interpretation of $\mathbf{tail}_{(list\ \tau) \rightarrow (list\ \tau)}$ at the point e to be g to make it monotonic, whereas we would have liked it to be e. By adding the extra point we remove this problem.

4.3 A Systematic Approach to Deriving Abstract Domains for Lists and Trees

One of the motivations for the abstract domains defined so far was to try to capture the behaviour of evaluators. With the evaluators that we have been considering, the only one which does any evaluation to elements of a list is $\xi^{(list\ \tau)}_{\perp\in}$, and the intuition is that it evaluates the elements of a list to HNF. Similarly, $\xi^{(tree\ \tau)}_{\perp\in}$ only evaluates the second argument to $\mathbf{node}_{(tree\ \tau) \rightarrow \tau \rightarrow (tree\ \tau) \rightarrow (tree\ \tau)}$ to HNF.

When the elements of a list or a tree are themselves structured data objects, or functions, then it may be useful to give more precise information about these objects in an abstract interpretation, so that a more informative abstract interpretation can be given. If the elements are structured data objects, this extra information corresponds to saying how much extra evaluation can be done to elements of the list or tree. How can we define abstract domains to give this information?

Let us consider the type $(list\ int)$ and the abstract domain $\mathbf{A}_{(list\ int)}$. We can think of $\mathbf{A}_{(list\ int)}$ as being made up of two parts:

1. $\perp_{\mathbf{A}_{(list\ int)}}$ and ∞: representing respectively the bottom list and lists which are either infinite or end in the bottom list; and

2. $\perp\in$ and $\top\in$: representing finite lists. All the lists which abstract to $\perp\in$ have at least one bottom element, that is, the minimum element in the each list is $\perp_{\mathbf{S}_{int}}$,

$$\mathbf{K^A}\ [\![\mathbf{nil}_{(list\ \tau)}]\!] = lift\ (lift\ \top_{\mathbf{A}_\tau})$$

$$\mathbf{K^A}\ [\![\mathbf{cons}_{\tau\to(list\ \tau)\to(list\ \tau)}]\!]\ u\ l = \begin{cases} lift\ \bot_{\mathbf{A}_{(lift\ \tau)}} & \text{if } l \sqsubseteq lift\ \bot_{\mathbf{A}_{(lift\ \tau)}} \\ lift\ (lift\ (u \sqcap u')) & \text{if } l = lift\ (lift\ u') \end{cases}$$

$$\mathbf{K^A}\ [\![\mathbf{head}_{(list\ \tau)\to\tau}]\!]\ l = \begin{cases} \bot_{\mathbf{A}_\tau} & \text{if } l = \bot_{\mathbf{A}_{(list\ \tau)}} \\ \top_{\mathbf{A}_\tau} & \text{otherwise} \end{cases}$$

$$\mathbf{K^A}\ [\![\mathbf{tail}_{(list\ \tau)\to(list\ \tau)}]\!]\ l = \begin{cases} \bot_{\mathbf{A}_{(list\ \tau)}} & \text{if } l = \bot_{\mathbf{A}_{(list\ \tau)}} \\ lift\ \bot_{\mathbf{A}_{(lift\ \tau)}} & \text{if } l = lift\ \bot_{\mathbf{A}_{(lift\ \tau)}} \\ lift\ (lift\ l'') & \text{otherwise} \end{cases}$$

where

$$l'' = \bigsqcup\{\alpha_{(list\ \tau)}\ l' | u' \in \mathbf{S}_\tau, l' \in \mathbf{S}_{(list\ \tau)}, \alpha_{(list\ \tau)}\ (cons\ u'\ l') \sqsubseteq l\}$$

$$\mathbf{K^A}\ [\![\mathbf{lcase}_{(list\ \tau)\to\sigma\to(\tau\to(list\ \tau)\to\sigma)\to\sigma}]\!]\ l\ s\ f = \begin{cases} \bot_{\mathbf{A}_\sigma} & \text{if } l = \bot_{\mathbf{A}_{(list\ \tau)}} \\ s \sqcup (f\ \top_{\mathbf{A}_\tau}\ \top_{\mathbf{A}_{(list\ \tau)}}) & \text{if } l = \top_{\mathbf{A}_{(list\ \tau)}} \\ v & \text{otherwise} \end{cases}$$

where

$$v = \bigsqcup\{f\ (\alpha_\tau\ u')\ (\alpha_{(list\ \tau)}\ l') | u' \in \mathbf{S}_\tau, l' \in \mathbf{S}_{(list\ \tau)}, \alpha_{(list\ \tau)}\ (cons\ u'\ l') \sqsubseteq l\}$$

Figure 4.7: Abstract Interpretation of List Constants Using $\mathbf{A}_{(list\ \tau)} = lift\ (lift\ \mathbf{A}_\tau)$

which abstracts to $\bot_{\mathbf{A}_{int}}$. All the elements in the lists represented by $\top\in$ abstract to $\top_{\mathbf{A}_{int}}$.

In fact, $\mathbf{A}_{(list\ int)}$ is just a copy of $\mathbf{A}_{int}$ which has two new elements underneath it. This can be formalised by saying that:

$$\mathbf{A}_{(list\ int)} \cong lift\ (lift\ \mathbf{A}_{int});$$

the double lifting adds points for the bottom list and lists which are infinite or ending in the bottom list below the abstract domain for *int*.

This methodology can be generalised, defining

$$\mathbf{A}_{(list\ \tau)} = lift\ (lift\ \mathbf{A}_\tau)$$

where τ is any type. Again, the abstract interpretation of $\bot_{\mathbf{S}_{(list\ \tau)}}$ is $\bot_{\mathbf{A}_{(list\ \tau)}}$, the abstract interpretation of an infinite list or a list ending in the bottom list is $lift\ (\bot_{\mathbf{A}_{lift\ \tau}})$, and a list has $lift\ (lift\ \overline{u})$ as its abstract interpretation if it is finite and the greatest lower bound (c.f. minimum) of the abstract interpretation of any of the elements in the list is $\overline{u}$.

The use of a doubly-lifted domain as the abstract interpretation of lists was first suggested by Wadler in [Wad87], and has been implemented by Hunt in his abstract interpreter [Hun89, HH90]. It can also be used for trees. We can now give the formal definitions of the abstract domains and abstraction map for any type of the form (*list* τ).

Definition 4.3.1

For all types τ, $\mathbf{A}_{(list\ \tau)} = lift\ (lift\ \mathbf{A}_\tau)$.

For all types τ,

$$\alpha_{(list\ \tau)} l = \begin{cases} \bot_{\mathbf{A}_{(list\ \tau)}} & \text{if } l = \bot_{\mathbf{S}_\tau} \\ lift\ \bot_{\mathbf{A}_{(lift\ \tau)}} & \text{if } l \in List_\tau^\infty \\ lift\ (lift\ \overline{u}) & \text{otherwise} \end{cases}$$

where

$\overline{u} = \bigsqcap\{\alpha_\tau\ u | member\ u\ l\}$

$member\ u\ nil = false$

$$member\ u\ (cons\ u'\ l') = \begin{cases} true & \text{if } (u = u') \\ (member\ u\ l') & \text{otherwise} \end{cases}$$

Abstract interpretations of constants over $(list\ \tau)$ which satisfy the constant safety condition are given in Figure 4.7. The reader is encouraged to show that these definitions are equivalent to those given in Figure 4.1 when τ is *bool* (or *int*), where $\mathbf{A}_{(list\ \tau)}$ is isomorphic to the four point domain introduced in Definition 4.1.3.

We leave it as an exercise for the reader to repeat the process for types of the form $(tree\ \tau)$, and to show that the abstract interpretations given for the constants do in fact satisfy the constant safety condition.

4.4 Drawing It Together

Abstract domains have to be chosen which capture some property of interest. The abstract domains we have described have all been motivated by finding out how functions behave on various types of arguments, information which we will be able to use for determining evaluation transformers.

We showed in detail how to define an abstract domain which captured our intuitions about the evaluators described informally in Chapter 1, and how the abstract interpretations of constants could be derived by abstracting their standard interpretations. As well, we showed how to construct an abstract domain to find out one-level head-strictness information, and how to give abstract domains for lists and trees which took into account the structure of their elements. These latter domains could be used to find out evaluation transformer information for evaluators which did more evaluation of the elements of a list or tree than to HNF.

Using the Cousot's reduced product construction on abstract domains, we showed how to combine two abstract domains to get a new one. This new domain captured both the properties that were captured by the constituent domains. Sometimes, the abstract interpretation using the constructed domain is able to find out more information than using the abstract domains separately, as the fact that a function has one property may rely on the fact that another function has the other property, and so one needs an abstract domain which captures both properties. Given some property, we saw that it was not possible in general to define a finite abstract domain which could definitely determine whether or not a function had that property. A larger abstract domain may capture a larger proportion of functions with a property. We gave a heuristic for choosing the size of an abstract domain.

Chapter 5

Evaluation Transformers

The evaluation transformer model of reduction was introduced in Section 1.2. We argued informally that certain functions needed to evaluate their arguments, that sometimes their arguments needed more evaluation than just to HNF, and that the amount of evaluation needed of the arguments depended on the amount of evaluation required of an application of a function. How can this intuition be formalised? To use this information means changing the reduction strategy from being the leftmost strategy. How can we be sure that it is *safe* to change the evaluation strategy in this way?

The Head-Normalisation Theorem gives an important clue about how we can proceed. It states that the leftmost reduction sequence fails to terminate with a head normal form for a program if and only if the program has no HNF. Since each $\beta\delta$-reduction step preserves the semantics of a program, in changing the evaluation order we have only to preserve the termination properties of a program. This will lead us to the definition of a *safe* evaluation strategy.

One of the abstract interpretations developed in Chapter 4 was motivated by trying to capture the intuitive behaviour of some example evaluators. We change our perspective a little in this chapter, so that abstract domain points become the important entities, and formally define evaluators *related to* an abstract domain point. We will see that an *evaluator* is a *reduction strategy* which is guaranteed to terminate for a certain class of expressions of a particular type, and may fail to terminate for all other expressions of that type. Evaluation transformers can then be determined from any correct abstract interpretation, using a theorem which follows from the correctness of the interpretation. The evaluation strategy which uses the evaluation transformer information is provably safe.

Unfortunately, in a program which uses higher-order functions, the function being applied in some applications cannot be determined until run-time. We also show how the abstract interpretation can be used to determine evaluation transformer information that can be used at run-time. The use of such information in an implementation requires extra run-time support.

All the definitions and theorems given in this chapter are independent of any particular abstract domains. However, all examples will be given using Mycroft's two-point abstract domain for *bool* and *int* (Section 4.1.1), and Wadler's four point domain for (*list* τ) (Section 4.1.1) and (*tree* τ) (Section 4.1.1).

5.1 Safe Changes to the Evaluation Strategy

Most works on the semantics of programming languages have only one concept of an *infinite computation*, namely that which never terminates, and produces no result. In denotational semantics, this is usually given the value $\perp$ (from the appropriate domain). In order to deal with evaluators, we need a more general concept of a non-terminating computation. Consider the evaluator $\xi_\infty^{(list\ \tau)}$ informally introduced in Section 1.2.1. The intuition about this evaluator is that it needs to evaluate the structure of its argument list, that is, if it evaluates an expression to the form (*cons u l*), then it needs to evaluate l with $\xi_\infty^{(list\ \tau)}$. One way of implementing this evaluator is to evaluate the whole of the structure of the list before returning any result. If the list is infinite, or has an undefined tail at some point, then this implementation of the evaluator will fail in the classical way – it will produce no output. Another way to implement the evaluator is to evaluate the expression to the form (*cons u l*), return this much of the result, and then begin evaluating l with $\xi_\infty^{(list\ \tau)}$. Thus, at any finite time, the infinite computation can have produced a finite approximation to the expression being evaluated. We therefore make the following definition.

Definition 5.1.1

> An *infinite computation* is an infinite reduction sequence. We will also say that a reduction sequence *fails to terminate* if it is an infinite reduction sequence.

We will be very careful in our use of these phrases, so that an infinite computation refers only to the property that it is an infinite reduction sequence, and does not determine the amount of the result that has been produced.

For the language Λ_T, the leftmost reduction strategy has the property that it fails to terminate if and only if the program has no HNF (Computational Adequacy Theorem). Any change in the reduction model should preserve this property. With this in mind, we make the following definition.

Definition 5.1.2

> A reduction strategy is *safe* for a program if it initiates an infinite computation if and only if the program has no HNF.
>
> We will say it is safe to evaluate some term (with a particular evaluator) if the resulting reduction strategy is safe.

We say 'initiates' in the above definition because the definition must cover both sequential and parallel implementations. In a sequential implementation, there will be only one reduction sequence, and so 'initiates an infinite reduction sequence' is equivalent to 'consists of an infinite reduction sequence'. A parallel reduction strategy allows one reduction sequence to initiate the parallel reduction of some other expression. On a parallel machine, it is still possible that the HNF of a program could be reached even if some processor was performing an infinite reduction sequence. This is ruled out by the above definition of safety. Sometimes what we have called a safe reduction strategy is called *conservative*, to distinguish them from *speculative* ones, which might do some evaluation of expressions which do not need to be evaluated in order to produce the HNF of a program. Peyton Jones discusses some of the issues involved in choosing between a conservative and speculative evaluation model [Pey89]. It is much simpler to implement a conservative parallel evaluation strategy than a speculative one because there are no useless processes which have to be garbage collected. A complete specification of an abstract machine employing speculative evaluation can be found in [Par90].

5.2 Definition of Evaluators

An evaluator captures the intuitive notion of doing a certain amount of evaluation to an expression. The important property of an evaluator is the way it divides the expressions of a type into two classes: those for which it terminates, and those for which it initiates an infinite computation.

Definition 5.2.1

> An *evaluator* is a reduction strategy. An evaluator and an abstract domain point, $\overline{s} \in \mathbf{A}_\sigma$, are *related* if for all expressions $e : \sigma$, it terminates if $(\mathrm{S}\ [\![e]\!]\ \rho^{\mathrm{S}}) \notin (\gamma_\sigma\ \overline{s})$. When an evaluator has the further property that it definitely fails to terminate when evaluating $e : \sigma$ if $(\mathrm{S}\ [\![e]\!]\ \rho^{\mathrm{S}}) \in (\gamma_\sigma\ \overline{s})$, then we will write it as $\xi^\sigma_{\overline{s}}$. The symbol ξ is used because it looks like a curly E, reminding us of ξvaluator. For completeness, the evaluator ξ_{NO} performs no reductions on expressions of any type.

Recalling that reduction preserves the standard interpretation of expressions, if the evaluator terminates, then the standard interpretation of the expression will be unchanged. Even though there may be several reduction strategies which fail to terminate when evaluating an expression if and only if its standard interpretation is in the concretisation of some abstract domain point $\overline{s} \in \mathbf{A}_\sigma$, they all have the essential property that they fail to terminate, or terminate with a result whose standard interpretation is the same as that of the original expression. We therefore feel justified in writing *the* evaluator $\xi^\sigma_{\overline{s}}$.

The reason for referring to $\xi^\sigma_{\overline{s}}$ rather than to any evaluator related to $\overline{s}$ is that it represents the most evaluation that is allowed of an expression, whilst staying within the constraint that it must terminate for all expressions whose standard interpretation is not in the concretisation of $\overline{s}$; to do any more evaluation would introduce the possibility of a non-terminating computation. Other evaluators related to an abstract domain point may do less evaluation.

Not every abstract domain point has a corresponding (sequential) evaluator. For example, all of the abstract domains we considered in Chapter 4 have the property that the concretisation map is strict for all types σ, that is,

$$\gamma_\sigma\ \bot_{\mathbf{A}_\sigma} = \{\bot_{\mathbf{S}_\sigma}\}$$

(Lemma 4.1.6). Therefore, the evaluator $\xi^{\sigma_1 \times \ldots \times \sigma_k}_{\bot_{\mathbf{A}_{\sigma_1 \times \ldots \times \sigma_k}}}$ must fail to terminate if and only if the expression being reduced has $\bot_{\mathbf{S}_{\sigma_1 \times \ldots \times \sigma_k}} = (\bot_{\mathbf{S}_{\sigma_1}}, \ldots, \bot_{\mathbf{S}_{\sigma_k}})$ as its standard interpretation. As we discussed in Section 2.4, it is not possible to define a sequential reduction strategy which will do this.

Even though the definition of an evaluator is quite abstract, it is sometimes easy to give reduction strategies which implement particular evaluators. For example, if σ is some type for which the notion of HNF is well-defined, and concretisation is strict for the type σ in some particular abstract interpretation, then an evaluator related to $\perp_{\mathbf{A}_\sigma}$ may only fail to terminate if the standard interpretation of the program is $\perp_{\mathbf{S}_\sigma}$. The Computational Adequacy Theorem says that the leftmost reduction strategy fails to terminate if and only if the standard interpretation of the program being executed is the bottom of the appropriate domain. For such a type then, leftmost reduction is an example of an evaluator related to $\perp_{\mathbf{A}_\sigma}$. Furthermore, it is $\xi^{\sigma}_{\perp_{\mathbf{A}_\sigma}}$. As another example, when an application of $\mathbf{cons}_{\tau \to (list\ \tau) \to (list\ \tau)}$ is to be evaluated with $\xi_{\infty}^{(list\ \tau)}$, then we will find that its second argument has to be evaluated with $\xi_{\infty}^{(list\ \tau)}$. Therefore the evaluator $\xi_{\infty}^{(list\ \tau)}$ can be implemented by firstly evaluating an expression to HNF. If the result is $\mathbf{nil}_{(list\ \tau)}$, then it terminates. Otherwise it is an application of $\mathbf{cons}_{\tau \to (list\ \tau) \to (list\ \tau)}$, and the second argument is evaluated with $\xi_{\infty}^{(list\ \tau)}$. This still leaves some freedom in how the evaluator can be implemented. In a sequential machine the evaluation of the second argument to $\mathbf{cons}_{\tau \to (list\ \tau) \to (list\ \tau)}$ could be done straight away, whilst a parallel machine might create a process to evaluate it with $\xi_{\infty}^{(list\ \tau)}$.

5.3 Determining Evaluation Transformers

Ideally, given any function application that appears in the program, and the amount of evaluation that is allowed of the application, we would like to be able to say how much evaluation could be done to each argument expression in the application. This will be studied in the first subsection. Unfortunately, in a program which uses higher-order functions, sometimes the function being applied is unknown, and so we are unable to determine, at compile time, how much evaluation can be done to the argument expressions. However, at run-time, when the function being applied does become known, then we would like to be able to cause the evaluation of some of its arguments. For this we need evaluation transformer information which is true about a function in any context in which it can be applied. This is studied in the second subsection. In the next chapter, we will see how to use both sorts of information in compiling code for functional programs.

5.3.1 Annotating Applications With Evaluation Transformers

The following theorem uses the results from the abstract interpretation to tell how much evaluation can be done to an argument expression, given the amount of evaluation allowed of a function application.

Theorem 5.3.1 (Context-Sensitive Evaluation Transformer Theorem)

Suppose that $f : \sigma_1 \to \ldots \to \sigma_n \to \tau$, that $\forall j \in \{1, \ldots, n\}, j \neq i$, $(\mathbf{A}\ [\![e_j]\!]\ \rho^{\mathbf{A}}) \sqsubseteq \overline{v}_j$, and that

$$(\mathbf{A}\ [\![f]\!]\ \rho^{\mathbf{A}})\ \overline{v}_1\ \ldots\ \overline{v}_{i-1}\ \overline{s}_i\ \overline{v}_{i+1}\ \ldots\ \overline{v}_n \sqsubseteq \overline{t}.$$

Then when it is safe to evaluate the application $(f\ e_1\ \ldots\ e_n)$ with $\xi^{\tau}_{\overline{t}}$, it is safe to evaluate e_i with $\xi^{\sigma_i}_{\overline{s}_i}$.

Proof

There are two cases to consider:

1. **Evaluation of e_i with $\xi^{\sigma_i}_{\overline{s}_i}$ terminates: This is trivially safe.**
2. Evaluation of e_i with $\xi^{\sigma_i}_{\overline{s}_i}$ initiates an infinite computation: From the definition of $\xi^{\sigma_i}_{\overline{s}_i}$, evaluating e_i with $\xi^{\sigma_i}_{\overline{s}_i}$ can only have caused an infinite computation because $(\mathbf{S}\ [\![e_i]\!]\ \rho^{\mathbf{S}}) \in (\gamma_{\sigma_i}\ \overline{s}_i)$. Since we have that $\forall j \in \{1,\ldots,n\}$, $j \neq i$, $(\mathbf{A}\ [\![e_j]\!]\ \rho^{\mathbf{A}}) \sqsubseteq \overline{v}_j$, and

$$(\mathbf{A}\ [\![f]\!]\ \rho^{\mathbf{A}})\ \overline{v}_1\ \ldots\ \overline{v}_{i-1}\ \overline{s}_i\ \overline{v}_{i+1}\ \ldots\ \overline{v}_n\ \sqsubseteq\ \overline{t},$$

Theorem 3.3.5 tells us that $\forall s_i \in (\gamma_{\sigma_i}\ \overline{s}_i)$,

$$(\mathbf{S}\ [\![f]\!]\ \rho^{\mathbf{S}})\ (\mathbf{S}\ [\![e_1]\!]\ \rho^{\mathbf{S}})\ldots(\mathbf{S}\ [\![e_{i-1}]\!]\ \rho^{\mathbf{S}})\ s_i\ (\mathbf{S}\ [\![e_{i+1}]\!]\ \rho^{\mathbf{S}})\ldots(\mathbf{S}\ [\![e_n]\!]\ \rho^{\mathbf{S}}) \in (\gamma_\tau\ \overline{t}).$$

Since the result of the application is in $(\gamma_\tau\ \overline{t})$, we know that its evaluation with $\xi^{\tau}_{\overline{t}}$ will initiate an infinite computation. As it was safe to evaluate the application with $\xi^{\tau}_{\overline{t}}$, this means that the program has no HNF, and so it was safe to initiate an infinite computation when evaluating the expression e_i with $\xi^{\sigma_i}_{\overline{s}_i}$.

□

We will now give some examples of using this theorem. Recall that for all the examples we are using the abstract interpretation developed in Section 4.1.

Our first example will be to consider the application

$$size\ (join\ t_1\ n\ t_2)$$

where t_1, n and t_2 are formal parameters of the function in whose body this application occurs. An example similar to this was used to motivate evaluation transformers in Section 1.2.

Suppose that the application of *size* to $(join\ t_1\ n\ t_2)$ has to be evaluated with ξ^{int}_0, that is, $\xi^{int}_{\perp_{\mathbf{A}_{int}}}$. How much evaluation can be done to the expression $(join\ t_1\ n\ t_2)$? The evaluator ξ^{int}_0 is related to the abstract domain point 0. The above theorem says that we have to see if there is some $\overline{s}$ such that

$$(\mathbf{A}\ [\![size]\!]\ \rho^{\mathbf{A}})\ \overline{s} \sqsubseteq 0.$$

Using the convention introduced in Chapter 4, that the abstract interpretation of functions are denoted by putting a bar over the function name, this can be rewritten

$$\overline{size}\ \overline{s} \sqsubseteq 0.$$

Looking up the abstract interpretation of *size* in Figure 4.2, we find that:

$$\begin{aligned} \overline{size}\ \perp\ &\sqsubseteq\ 0 \\ \overline{size}\ \infty\ &\sqsubseteq\ 0 \end{aligned}$$

and so both of $\xi_{\perp}^{(tree\ \tau)}$ and $\xi_{\infty}^{(tree\ \tau)}$ can be used to evaluate the argument to *size*. The four point domain we are using as an abstract domain for lists is a chain, and so if there is any $\overline{s}_i$ satisfying Theorem 5.3.1, then there is a greatest one. We make the following decision in the discussion throughout the rest of the chapter:

When there is more than one $\overline{s}_i$ which satisfies the condition of Theorem 5.3.1, we will choose the greatest one, since its evaluator will do the most evaluation.

Therefore, we will say that the application (*join* t_1 n t_2) can be evaluated with $\xi_{\infty}^{(tree\ \tau)}$.

When a non-chain domain is used, it is possible that there is not a greatest one, and so Theorem 5.3.1 may give several different $\xi_{\overline{s}_i}^{\sigma_i}$ which could be used to evaluate an expression.

Which evaluator can be used to evaluate the argument expressions that will be bound to t_1? We have no way of knowing what expressions the variables n and t_2 will be bound to, but we do know that the abstract interpretation of whatever they are bound to must be less than the tops of the respective abstract domains. Therefore, using Theorem 5.3.1, we must find the maximum value of $\overline{s}$ such that

$$\overline{join}\ \overline{s}\ 1\ \top\!\in\ \sqsubseteq \infty$$

where 1 is $\top_{\mathbf{A}_{int}}$, $\top\!\in$ is $\top_{\mathbf{A}_{(tree\ \tau)}}$, and $\overline{t}$ is ∞ because the application can be evaluated with $\xi_{\infty}^{(tree\ \tau)}$, and ∞ is the abstract domain point related to $\xi_{\infty}^{(tree\ \tau)}$. From Figure 4.2, it is ∞, and so Theorem 5.3.1 allows us to conclude that the expression bound to t_1 can be evaluated with $\xi_{\infty}^{(tree\ \tau)}$. In a similar way we can determine that the expression bound to t_2 can also be evaluated with $\xi_{\infty}^{(tree\ \tau)}$. What about the argument n? We must find the maximum value of $\overline{s}$ such that

$$\overline{join}\ \top\!\in\ \overline{s}\ \top\!\in\ \sqsubseteq \infty.$$

From Figure 4.2, there is no such $\overline{s}$ which satisfies this condition, and so it is not safe to do any evaluation of the expression bound to n.

All these results coincide with intuitions given in Section 1.2.

The above example is fairly simple because an application of *size* can only be evaluated to HNF. When the result of a function application is a list or a tree, the annotations on the nodes have to be evaluation transformers, as different amounts of evaluation may be requested of the function application. As a second example of using Theorem 5.3.1, we will analyse the application

$$append\ (map\ (\lambda y^{int}.y^{int})\ e_1)\ \mathbf{nil}_{(list\ int)},$$

where e_1 is some arbitrary expression. The application of *append* can be evaluated with $\xi_{\perp}^{(list\ \tau)}$, $\xi_{\infty}^{(list\ \tau)}$ and $\xi_{\perp\!\in}^{(list\ \tau)}$. In each of these three cases, how much evaluation can be done to the argument expression (*map* $(\lambda y^{int}.y^{int})$ e_1)?

Suppose that the application of *append* has to be evaluated with $\xi_{\perp}^{(list\ \tau)}$. To find out how much evaluation can be performed on the expression (*map* $(\lambda y^{int}.y^{int})$ e_1), Theorem 5.3.1 tells us we must find an $\overline{s}$ such that

$$\overline{append}\ \overline{s}\ (\mathbf{A}\ [\![\mathbf{nil}_{(list\ int)}]\!]\ \rho^{\mathbf{A}}) \sqsubseteq \perp,$$

and our convention above says that we want to find the *maximum* $\overline{s}$ which satisfies this condition. Recalling that, as $\mathbf{nil}_{(list\ int)} \in List_\tau^{\top\!\in}$, $(\mathbf{A}\ [\![\mathbf{nil}_{(list\ int)}]\!]\ \rho^{\mathbf{A}}) = \top\!\in$ (Section 4.1.1 and Figure 4.1), this condition reduces to finding the maximum $\overline{s}$ such that

$$\overline{append}\ \overline{s}\ \top\!\in\ \sqsubseteq \bot.$$

From Figure 4.2, we find that the maximum value of $\overline{s}$ satisfying this inequation is $\bot$, and so $(map\ (\lambda y^{int}.y^{int})\ e_1)$ can be evaluated with $\xi_\bot^{(list\ \tau)}$. When the application of *append* can be evaluated with $\xi_\infty^{(list\ \tau)}$, we set $\overline{t}$ to ∞ in the test of Theorem 5.3.1, and using the information from Figure 4.2, find that the maximum $\overline{s}$ that satisfies the inequation is ∞, and so $(map\ (\lambda y^{int}.y^{int})\ e_1)$ can be evaluated with $\xi_\infty^{(list\ \tau)}$. In a similar way we can determine that $(map\ (\lambda y^{int}.y^{int})\ e_1)$ can be evaluated with $\xi_{\bot\!\in}^{(list\ \tau)}$ when the application of *append* is being evaluated with $\xi_{\bot\!\in}^{(list\ \tau)}$.

How much evaluation can be done to the expression e_1? From the above discussion, we can see that the application $(map\ (\lambda y^{int}.y^{int})\ e_1)$ could possibly be evaluated by any one of the evaluators $\xi_\bot^{(list\ \tau)}$, $\xi_\infty^{(list\ \tau)}$ and $\xi_{\bot\!\in}^{(list\ \tau)}$. Repeating the above process, noting that $(\mathbf{A}\ [\![\lambda y^{int}.y^{int}]\!]\ \rho^{\mathbf{A}}) = \lambda y_\epsilon \mathbf{A}_{int}.y$, Theorem 5.3.1 tells us that we must find (the maximum) $\overline{s}$ such that

$$\overline{map}\ (\lambda y_\epsilon \mathbf{A}_{int}.y)\ \overline{s} \sqsubseteq \overline{t}$$

where $\overline{t}$ is respectively bound to $\bot$, ∞ and $\bot\!\in$. Again using the abstract interpretations from Figure 4.2, we find that the evaluation transformer for e_1 sends $\xi_\bot^{(list\ \tau)}$ to $\xi_\bot^{(list\ \tau)}$, $\xi_\infty^{(list\ \tau)}$ to $\xi_\infty^{(list\ \tau)}$, and $\xi_{\bot\!\in}^{(list\ \tau)}$ to $\xi_{\bot\!\in}^{(list\ \tau)}$. We will return to this example near the end of the next subsection.

5.3.2 A Complication of Higher-Order Functions

We were able to give the above examples because we always knew what function was being applied. Suppose that x_j is a formal parameter and that we are analysing the application

$$x_j\ e_1\ \ldots\ e_n : \tau,$$

where $\forall k \in \{1,\ldots,n\}$, $e_k : \sigma_k$. Suppose we are trying to find out which evaluator can be used to evaluate e_i when $\xi_{\overline{t}}^\tau$ is a safe evaluator for the application. Since x_j could be bound to any function, it can only be guaranteed that $(\mathbf{A}\ [\![x_j]\!]\ \rho^{\mathbf{A}}) \sqsubseteq \top_{\mathbf{A}_{\sigma_1 \to \ldots \to \sigma_n \to \tau}}$ (c.f. the application $(join\ t_1\ n\ t_2)$ in the first example of the previous subsection), and so using Theorem 5.3.1 we want to find the maximum $\overline{s}_i$ such that

$$\top_{\mathbf{A}_{\sigma_1 \to \ldots \to \sigma_n \to \tau}}\ (\mathbf{A}\ [\![e_1]\!]\ \rho^{\mathbf{A}})\ \ldots\ (\mathbf{A}\ [\![e_{i-1}]\!]\ \rho^{\mathbf{A}})\ \overline{s}_i\ (\mathbf{A}\ [\![e_{i+1}]\!]\ \rho^{\mathbf{A}})\ \ldots\ (\mathbf{A}\ [\![e_n]\!]\ \rho^{\mathbf{A}}) \sqsubseteq \overline{t}.$$

However, $\top_{\mathbf{A}_{\sigma_1 \to \ldots \to \sigma_n \to \tau}} = \lambda y_{1\epsilon} \mathbf{A}_{\sigma_1}.\ldots.\lambda y_{n\epsilon} \mathbf{A}_{\sigma_n}.\top_{\mathbf{A}_\tau}$, and so $\forall \overline{s}_i \in \mathbf{A}_{\sigma_i}$,

$$\top_{\mathbf{A}_{\sigma_1 \to \ldots \to \sigma_n \to \tau}}\ (\mathbf{A}\ [\![e_1]\!]\ \rho^{\mathbf{A}})\ \ldots\ (\mathbf{A}\ [\![e_{i-1}]\!]\ \rho^{\mathbf{A}})\ \overline{s}_i\ (\mathbf{A}\ [\![e_{i+1}]\!]\ \rho^{\mathbf{A}})\ \ldots\ (\mathbf{A}\ [\![e_n]\!]\ \rho^{\mathbf{A}}) = \top_{\mathbf{A}_\tau}.$$

This tells us that the only possible value of $\overline{t}$ for which the formula can be satisfied is $\top_{\mathbf{A}_\tau}$. How does the evaluator $\xi_{\top_{\mathbf{A}_\tau}}^\tau$ behave? It is the evaluator which initiates an infinite computation when trying to evaluate any expression of type τ (since for all $e : \tau$,

$(\mathcal{S}\ [\![e]\!]\ \rho^{\mathcal{S}}) \in (\gamma_\tau\ \top_{\mathbf{A}_\tau})$). Safety only allows this evaluator to be used to evaluate the application $(x_j\ e_1\ \ldots\ e_n)$ when it is impossible for the execution of the program to terminate! Only in this situation are we allowed to do any evaluation of the expression e_i. At compile time therefore, we cannot say anything useful about how the expression e_i can be evaluated. However, during the execution of the program, the parameter x_j will become bound to some argument expression, which will be reduced to some partial application (i.e. a function). It is probably impractical to perform a run-time analysis to determine the evaluation transformers, using Theorem 5.3.1 when the function becomes known. Can we find out any useful information at compile-time? Fortunately, we can. Since the information could be used in any application of the function, the evaluation transformer for an argument of a function must give safe amounts of evaluation no matter what values the other argument expressions take. The following corollary of Theorem 5.3.1 gives the method for determining evaluation transformers which satisfy this condition.

Theorem 5.3.2 (Context-Free Evaluation Transformer Theorem)

Suppose that $f\ :\ \sigma_1 \rightarrow \ldots \sigma_n \rightarrow \tau$ *and that*

$$(\mathbf{A}\ [\![f]\!]\ \rho^{\mathbf{A}})\ \top_{\mathbf{A}_{\sigma_1}}\ \ldots\ \top_{\mathbf{A}_{\sigma_{i-1}}}\ \overline{s}_i\ \top_{\mathbf{A}_{\sigma_{i+1}}}\ \ldots\ \top_{\mathbf{A}_{\sigma_n}} \sqsubseteq \overline{t}.$$

Then for any application $(f\ e_1\ \ldots\ e_n)$*, when it is safe to evaluate the application with* $\xi^{\tau}_{\overline{t}}$*, it is safe to evaluate* e_i *with* $\xi^{\sigma}_{\overline{s}_i}$*.*

Proof

The corollary follows directly from Theorem 5.3.1 since $\forall j \in \{1,\ldots,i-1,i+1,\ldots n\}$, $\forall e_j : \sigma_j$, $(\mathbf{A}\ [\![e_j]\!]\ \rho^{\mathbf{A}}) \sqsubseteq \top_{\mathbf{A}_{\sigma_j}}$.

□

The intuition behind using the value $\top_{\mathbf{A}_{\sigma_j}}$ for each $j \neq i$ is that it represents any possible expression $e : \sigma_j$ in the sense that $(\mathcal{S}\ [\![e_j]\!]\ \rho^{\mathcal{S}}) \in (\gamma_{\sigma_j}\ \top_{\mathbf{A}_{\sigma_j}})$.

We call the evaluation transformers determined using Theorem 5.3.2 *context-free* evaluation transformers because they are safe in any context. The concept of context-free information was first introduced in [HBJ86, HBJ88], and context-free evaluation transformers in [Bur87b]. In a similar way, we say that the evaluation transformers determined using Theorem 5.3.1 are *context-sensitive* since they depend on the context of the other arguments in the function application.

We now give two examples of determining context-free evaluation transformers for functions.

The function *reverse* has a list as its result and therefore an application of *reverse* may appear in the context of being evaluated by any of the evaluators ξ_{NO} to $\xi^{(list\ \tau)}_{\perp\!\!\!\in}$. The evaluator ξ_{NO} says that it is not safe to do any evaluation of an application, and so it is not safe to do any evaluation of any arguments in the application. All evaluation transformers therefore return ξ_{NO} at ξ_{NO}. We will denote the context-free evaluation transformer for the ith argument of a function f by F_i, that is, the name of the function in upper case letters, subscripted by the argument number. Thus we have determined that

$$REVERSE_1\ \xi_{NO} = \xi_{NO}$$

We must determine the values for the other possible evaluators.

The evaluator $\xi_{\perp}^{(list\ \tau)}$ is related to the point $\perp$ and so we put in the value $\perp$ on the right-hand side of the above test and determine the maximum $\overline{s}$ such that

$$\overline{reverse}\ \overline{s} \sqsubseteq \perp$$

From the abstract interpretation of *reverse* in Figure 4.2 we find that the maximum value is ∞, which is related to $\xi_{\infty}^{(list\ \tau)}$, and so

$$REVERSE_1\ \xi_{\perp}^{(list\ \tau)} = \xi_{\infty}^{(list\ \tau)}$$

We can see that this is intuitively true by noting that $\xi_{\perp}^{(list\ \tau)}$ is asking for an expression to be evaluated to head normal form and that *reverse* must traverse the entire list before it can create the first *cons* cell, so the list must be finite if it is to be able to give a result in head normal form.

Related to the evaluator $\xi_{\infty}^{(list\ \tau)}$ we have the point ∞, and from the abstract interpretation we see the maximum point satisfying the condition is again ∞, and thus the evaluation transformer is $\xi_{\infty}^{(list\ \tau)}$ at $\xi_{\infty}^{(list\ \tau)}$. Note that in this case we have that $\overline{reverse}\ \infty$ is $\perp$, which is strictly less defined than ∞. This says that it is impossible for *reverse* to return a list which is partial or infinite.

Finally, the point $\perp\!\in$ is related to the evaluator $\xi_{\perp\in}^{(list\ \tau)}$, and the abstract interpretation says that the maximum $\overline{s}$ satisfying the criterion is $\perp\!\in$, and so $\xi_{\perp\in}^{(list\ \tau)}$ is a safe evaluator for the argument in this case. We interpret this as saying that for an application of *reverse* to return a finite list with at least one bottom element, then it must be given a finite list with at least bottom element in it as an argument. The evaluation transformer for *reverse* is given in Figure 5.1.

For functions such as *length* and *sumlist*, which have results which come from flat domains like integers and booleans, there is only ever one sensible evaluator for an application which does any work, namely $\xi_{\perp}^{(list\ \tau)}$, and so we have only to determine the evaluation transformer at that point. The evaluation transformers of these functions are given in Figure 5.1.

As an example of the use of Theorem 5.3.2 for a function of more than one argument, we find the evaluation transformer for the first argument of *append* when a safe evaluator for the application is $\xi_{\infty}^{(list\ \tau)}$. Using the above test, we find the maximum $\overline{s}$ such that

$$\overline{append}\ \overline{s}\ \top\!\in\ \sqsubseteq \infty,$$

noting that $\top\!\in$ is the top of the abstract domain for lists, and that ∞ is related to the evaluator $\xi_{\infty}^{(list\ \tau)}$. From the abstract interpretation of *append* given in Figure 4.2 we find that the maximum value of $\overline{s}$ is ∞, and thus

$$APPEND_1\ \xi_{\infty}^{(list\ \tau)} = \xi_{\infty}^{(list\ \tau)}.$$

E	$LENGTH_1\ E$	$SUMLIST_1\ E$	$SIZE_1\ E$	$SUMTREE_1\ E$
ξ_{NO}	ξ_{NO}	ξ_{NO}	ξ_{NO}	ξ_{NO}
ξ_0^{int}	$\xi_\infty^{(list\ \tau)}$	$\xi_{\perp\in}^{(list\ \tau)}$	$\xi_\infty^{(tree\ \tau)}$	$\xi_{\perp\in}^{(tree\ \tau)}$

E	$HEAD_1\ E$	$VALUE_1\ E$
ξ_{NO}	ξ_{NO}	ξ_{NO}
$\xi^\tau_{\perp_{A_\tau}}$	$\xi_\perp^{(list\ \tau)}$	$\xi_\perp^{(tree\ \tau)}$

E	$CONS_1\ E$	$CONS_2\ E$	$TAIL_1\ E$	$REVERSE_1\ E$	$BEFORE0_1\ E$
ξ_{NO}	ξ_{NO}	ξ_{NO}	ξ_{NO}	ξ_{NO}	ξ_{NO}
$\xi_\perp^{(list\ \tau)}$	ξ_{NO}	ξ_{NO}	$\xi_\perp^{(list\ \tau)}$	$\xi_\infty^{(list\ \tau)}$	$\xi_\perp^{(list\ \tau)}$
$\xi_\infty^{(list\ \tau)}$	ξ_{NO}	$\xi_\infty^{(list\ \tau)}$	$\xi_\infty^{(list\ \tau)}$	$\xi_\infty^{(list\ \tau)}$	$\xi_\perp^{(list\ \tau)}$
$\xi_{\perp\in}^{(list\ \tau)}$	$\xi^\tau_{\perp_{A_\tau}}$	$\xi_{\perp\in}^{(list\ \tau)}$	$\xi_\infty^{(list\ \tau)}$	$\xi_{\perp\in}^{(list\ \tau)}$	$\xi_\perp^{(list\ \tau)}$

E	$DOUBLES_1\ E$	$APPEND_1\ E$	$APPEND_2\ E$	$MAP_1\ E$	$MAP_2\ E$
ξ_{NO}	ξ_{NO}	ξ_{NO}	ξ_{NO}	ξ_{NO}	ξ_{NO}
$\xi_\perp^{(list\ \tau)}$	$\xi_\perp^{(list\ \tau)}$	$\xi_\perp^{(list\ \tau)}$	ξ_{NO}	ξ_{NO}	$\xi_\perp^{(list\ \tau)}$
$\xi_\infty^{(list\ \tau)}$	$\xi_\infty^{(list\ \tau)}$	$\xi_\infty^{(list\ \tau)}$	$\xi_\infty^{(list\ \tau)}$	ξ_{NO}	$\xi_\infty^{(list\ \tau)}$
$\xi_{\perp\in}^{(list\ \tau)}$	$\xi_{\perp\in}^{(list\ \tau)}$	$\xi_{\perp\in}^{(list\ \tau)}$	$\xi_{\perp\in}^{(list\ \tau)}$	ξ_{NO}	$\xi_\infty^{(list\ \tau)}$

E	$NODE_1\ E$	$NODE_2\ E$	$NODE_3\ E$	$LEFT_1\ E$/ $RIGHT_1\ E$	$JOIN_1\ E$	$JOIN_2\ E$	$JOIN_3\ E$
ξ_{NO}	ξ_{NO}	ξ_{NO}	ξ_{NO}	ξ_{NO}	ξ_{NO}	ξ_{NO}	ξ_{NO}
$\xi_\perp^{(tree\ \tau)}$	ξ_{NO}	ξ_{NO}	ξ_{NO}	$\xi_\perp^{(tree\ \tau)}$	ξ_{NO}	ξ_{NO}	ξ_{NO}
$\xi_\infty^{(tree\ \tau)}$	$\xi_\infty^{(tree\ \tau)}$	ξ_{NO}	$\xi_\infty^{(tree\ \tau)}$	$\xi_\perp^{(tree\ \tau)}$	$\xi_\infty^{(tree\ \tau)}$	ξ_{NO}	$\xi_\infty^{(tree\ \tau)}$
$\xi_{\perp\in}^{(tree\ \tau)}$	$\xi_{\perp\in}^{(tree\ \tau)}$	$\xi^\tau_{\perp_{A_\tau}}$	$\xi_{\perp\in}^{(tree\ \tau)}$	$\xi_\perp^{(tree\ \tau)}$	$\xi_{\perp\in}^{(tree\ \tau)}$	$\xi^\tau_{\perp_{A_\tau}}$	$\xi_{\perp\in}^{(tree\ \tau)}$

Figure 5.1: Context-Free Evaluation Transformers for the Functional Constants and Functions in Figure 1.1 Using the Abstract Interpretation From Section 4.1

The rest of the evaluation transformer for the first argument and the evaluation transformer for the second argument can be determined in a similar manner, and are given in Figure 5.1, along with the context-free evaluation transformers for many of the functional constants in Λ_T and the rest of the functions in Figure 1.1.

At this stage, it is worth considering whether or not context-free information is sufficient. It turns out not to be; taking into account the information available from the abstract interpretation of the other arguments in a function application may allow a stronger evaluator to be used for a particular argument expression. Consider again the application

$$map\ (\lambda y^{int}.y^{int})\ e_1$$

discussed in the previous subsection, and suppose that it is being evaluated with $\xi_{\perp\in}^{(list\ \tau)}$. Looking up the context-free evaluation transformer information for the second argument to *map* in Figure 5.1, we find that $(MAP_2\ \xi_{\perp\in}^{(list\ \tau)}) = \xi_{\infty}^{(list\ \tau)}$, and so e_1 can be evaluated with $\xi_{\infty}^{(list\ \tau)}$. However, in the previous subsection we saw that Theorem 5.3.1 allowed us to use the contextual information that the first argument to *map* is $\lambda y^{int}.y^{int}$, and so e_1 could in fact be evaluated with $\xi_{\perp\in}^{(list\ \tau)}$.

There is one final issue that must be resolved with context-free evaluation transformers. Given the definition of some function $f : \sigma_1 \rightarrow \sigma'$, what evaluators can applications of the function f be evaluated with? If σ' is not one of *bool*, *int*, $(list\ \tau)$ and $(tree\ \tau)$, recall that the type of f can be expanded out into a canonical form: $\sigma_1 \rightarrow \ldots \rightarrow \sigma_n \rightarrow \tau'$, where τ' is one of *int*, *bool*, $(list\ \tau)$ and $(tree\ \tau)$. For example, the function f defined by:

$$f = \lambda g^{int\rightarrow int}.map\ g^{int\rightarrow int}$$

has type $(int \rightarrow int) \rightarrow ((list\ int) \rightarrow (list\ int))$, and τ' is $(list\ int)$. In this case, an application of f can appear in a context where it will be evaluated with any one of $\xi_{\perp}^{(list\ \tau)}$, $\xi_{\infty}^{(list\ \tau)}$ and $\xi_{\perp\in}^{(list\ \tau)}$, and so context-free evaluation transformers have to be determined for each of those evaluators. A similar situation holds for $(tree\ \tau)$. If τ' is *int* (or *bool*), an application of the function can only be evaluated with ξ_0^{int} (or ξ_0^{bool}), and so the values of the evaluation transformers need only to be given at ξ_0^{int} (or ξ_0^{bool}).

5.4 Drawing it Together

The critical property that we require of any reduction strategy is that it does not initiate an infinite computation unless the program has no head normal form. Moreover, if a program has a head normal form, then the reduction strategy must find one. Such a reduction strategy has been called *safe* in this chapter. The Computational Adequacy Theorem tells us that leftmost reduction is such a strategy, and it is the default strategy for executing a program. The purpose of the evaluation transformer model is to only make changes to the leftmost reduction strategy that result in a new, safe reduction strategy. We have shown in this chapter how to use abstract interpretation information to determine evaluation transformers which preserve the safety of a reduction strategy.

In the chapter we have twice chosen to find the maximum amount of evaluation that is allowed of an expression – for any abstract domain value $\overline{s} \in \mathbf{A}_\sigma$ always discussing the evaluator $\xi^{\sigma}_{\overline{s}}$, and always finding the maximum $\overline{s}_i$ which satisfied the conditions of Theorem 5.3.1. We regard such information as *permissive*, in that it says that this is the maximum amount of evaluation that is allowed of an expression (because eventually this amount of evaluation of the expression will have to be done). An implementor may choose to ignore this information, or to do less evaluation, or even to do the evaluation in several goes, for example, implement $\xi^{(list\ \tau)}_{\infty}$ by evaluating the list ten *cons* nodes at a time.

We have found that it is important to determine both context-free and context-sensitive evaluation transformers.

There is still some freedom left in implementing the evaluation transformer model of reduction. The evaluation transformer model of reduction says that an argument expression can be evaluated with a particular evaluator. We shall see in the next chapter, that this information is used in a sequential machine to save the cost of building a closure for the argument expression, evaluating the argument before continuing with the leftmost reduction strategy. In a parallel machine, a closure can be built for the argument expression and a task created to evaluate it in parallel with the leftmost reduction of the application of which it was a part.

Chapter 6

Implementing Functional Languages on Sequential and Parallel Machines

The introduction to this book described the implementation of lazy functional languages in terms of reduction, a process which was formalised in terms of $\beta\delta$-reduction of the typed lambda calculus. The Head-Normalisation Theorem gives us a reduction strategy which is guaranteed to terminate with an answer from a program if the program has one. In the last chapter we saw how abstract interpretation could be used to determine evaluation transformers, which told us how the leftmost reduction strategy could be changed in a safe way. The purpose of this chapter is to take this evaluation transformer information, and use it to generate more efficient code. On a sequential machine, this information is used to save the cost of building *closures* for some expressions by evaluating them straight away. A parallel machine uses it to know which expressions can be evaluated as parallel processes.

To implement reduction on a computer, we need some data structure to store expressions, and a way of modifying that structure to represent the reduction steps which have been performed. Trees are typically used in Computer Science to store expressions. To support laziness, we need the more general notion of graphs, so that the subgraphs for subexpressions can be shared and subexpressions need only ever be evaluated once. Reduction is then modelled by replacing the graph representing the redex by the graph which represents the result of the reduction. Executing programs using this data structure is often called *graph reduction*.

An abstract machine can be defined to support the process of graph reduction, and the process of implementing functional languages automated by compiling programs to run on this machine. One such machine, the Spineless G-machine[BPJR88], a simplification of the G-machine [Aug87, Joh87], will be described. Compiling programs through the Spineless G-machine does not produce the fastest possible code for functional programs, but is a suitable level of abstraction for describing how evaluation transformer information can be used to compile more efficient code. The ideas can then be incorporated into other compilers, examples of which can be found in [Arg89, Arg90, Aug87, AJ89, BHY89, FW87, FH88, Gol88, Joh87, KKR+86, Kra88, Les89, LB89, Pey87, JCSH87, PS89, Rea89, Tra89, WW87, WSWW87].

Unfortunately, there is a disparity between the theoretical foundations of the implementation of lazy functional languages in terms of the typed lambda calculus with $\beta\delta$-reduction, and the way they are implemented using combinator reduction. In combinator reduction, a function:

```
> f x1     xn = E
```

(recall we are using the inverse comment convention) is regarded as a function of n arguments, and an application of f is not reduced unless it has at least that many arguments, whereas the equivalent term in the typed lambda calculus could have at least k β-reduction steps performed on it if f was applied to k arguments. Effectively implementations are regarding each function definition as a δ-rule, and extending the definition of head normal form to say that an application of a function is in HNF if it is applied to fewer arguments than its arity (c.f. the δ-rules for functional constants in Λ_T). Fortunately, this does not affect the answers from programs, and so this chapter will discuss implementations as they are usually made.

With the foundations laid, we are then able to show how evaluation transformer information can be used to generate more efficient code. Context-sensitive evaluation transformers can be used without modification to the abstract machine, whilst the use of context-free information needs some run-time support.

To make our discussion simpler, and to enable us to concentrate on the main issues concerning the use of evaluation transformer information, we will restrict our attention to the data types integers and lists, and to evaluation transformers using the evaluators ξ_{NO}, ξ_0^{int}, and $\xi_\perp^{(list\ \tau)}$ to $\xi_{\perp\in}^{(list\ \tau)}$. Implementing programs using other data types is only a matter of choosing suitable data structures to support them, and then using the evaluation transformer information in a similar way to how it is used in this chapter.

As mentioned earlier, we will be discussing the implementation of programs which have been translated into the form:

```
> f1 x1 ... xn1 = E1; /* function definitions */
> ...
> fm x1 ... xnm = Em;
```

where each of the fi are combinators. Any standard text on implementing lazy functional languages gives an algorithm to take functional programs and convert them to this form – see [FH88, Pey87, Rea89] for example.

Entire books can be, and have been, written on the material in the first two sections of this chapter; examples are referred to in the last paragraph. Some of the issues we discuss are rather subtle, but we hope that, along with Appendix B, which gives a complete, executable specification of the Spineless G-machine, and compilation rules to produce code for it, that the material is accessible. In a way, the details are not as important as getting a feel for how the implementation is changed in using the evaluation transformer information. For those who wish to find out more about implementations, we again refer them to one of [FH88, Pey87, Rea89].

6.1 Graph Reduction

In Section 1.1 we introduced the execution of lazy functional languages in terms of rewriting an expression. Further discussion showed that programs should be evaluated lazily. Lazy evaluation is the evaluation mechanism that was defined in the following way:

1. At each reduction step the leftmost redex is reduced.
2. Reduction of an expression proceeds only as far as head normal form; application of base functions such as **head** may force further evaluation of an expression.
3. Any expression which is bound to a formal parameter in a function application must only be evaluated once.

In this section we introduce a graphical data structure which can be used for supporting lazy evaluation.

Consider the functions defined by:

```
> f x = g x x
> g a b = + a b
```

Using lazy evaluation, the evaluation of the application (f `(* 5 2))` proceeds as follows:

$$\begin{aligned} \texttt{f (* 5 2)} &\rightarrow \texttt{g (* 5 2)} & (6.1)\\ &\rightarrow \texttt{+ (* 5 2) (* 5 2)} & (6.2)\\ &\rightarrow \texttt{+ 10 10} & (6.3)\\ &\rightarrow \texttt{20} & (6.4)\end{aligned}$$

In the application `(f (* 5 2))` there are two redexes, and lazy evaluation says to choose the leftmost one to do first, so the application of `f` is reduced in the step labelled 6.1. Similarly, the application of g is reduced in the next step. To reduce the application of `+`, its arguments must first be reduced to HNF. The two expressions `(* 5 2)` come from the same formal parameter, and laziness says that when one of them is reduced, the other copy must share the reduced expression so that it will not have to reduce it too. This is why both occurrences of `(* 5 2)` are replaced by `10` in the step to the line marked 6.3. One more reduction is then performed to obtain the result.

What sort of data structure can be used to represent expressions? In computing, trees are often used to represent the structure of expressions. However, we need to represent sharing, so that a *graph* is the sensible data structure. Graph reduction was first invented by Wadsworth in order to implement the lambda calculus [Wad71, Chapter 4]. Let us see how we can represent programs as graphs, and rewriting as graph modification by again considering the above example. The graph for the expression `(f (* 5 2))` is given in Figure 6.1*(a)*. It contains two different sorts of nodes:

`Vap`: these contain function applications, and `Vap` stands for `Variable-sized application node`. They are of variable size because `Vap`s must be created to hold applications of functions to differing numbers of arguments. `Vap` nodes are called *closures* by many authors. In an implementation, they would need to have some extra information to say how big they are.

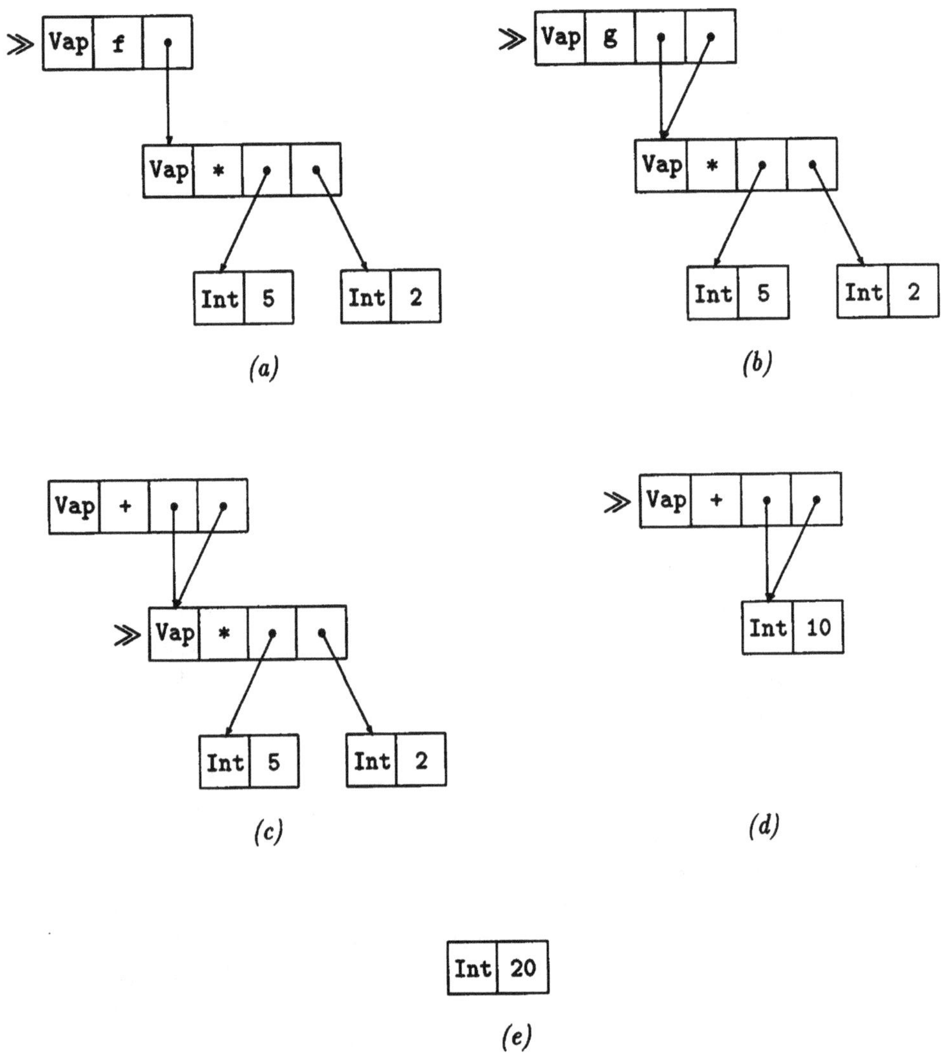

Figure 6.1: Graph Reduction of the Expression `f (* 5 2)`

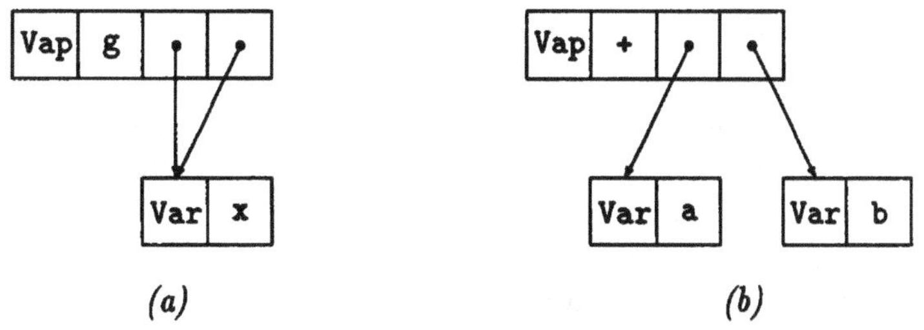

Figure 6.2: Graphs for the Functions f and g

Int: these store an integer.

Usually Vap and Int are called *tags*.

Expressions can be turned into graphs using the following two rules:

1. if the expression is an application, (f E1 ... En), then a Vap node with n+1 slots is created, graphs are built for each of the argument expressions, E1 to En, and for each $1 \leq i \leq n$, the i+1st slot in the Vap node is filled with a pointer to the graph for Ei. The first slot contains the information necessary to be able to access the (code for the) function being applied. In our diagrams, this will be represented by putting the name of the function in the first slot of the Vap node.

2. if the expression is an integer, an Int node is created to contain the integer.

As examples of this, graphs for each of the expressions in the lines marked 6.1 to 6.4 can be found in Figure 6.1.

Bodies of functions can also be represented by graphs, with the graphs for f and g being given in Figure 6.2*(a)* and 6.2*(b)* respectively. The new node type, Var indicates that such a node is a formal parameter to a function. Note how the Var node for the argument x is shared in the graph for f. It is here that we get the sharing that is required to implement laziness. To see how it works, we must first show how to perform a reduction step.

In the graph being reduced, there is a distinguished node, marked with $\gg$ in Figure 6.1, which is the node to be reduced at the next reduction step. To reduce an expression to HNF, the following algorithm is performed:

1. move the mark $\gg$ to point at the root node of the redex to be reduced.

2. reduce the redex which is marked with $\gg$. This involves making a copy of the graph of the function being applied, substituting pointers to the Var nodes with pointers to the graphs which are the actual parameters of the function.

3. If the result of the reduction step is a node in HNF, then overwrite the original expression with this node, and return to the code which caused this expression to be reduced. Otherwise, move the mark to point at the root of the newly created graph, and jump to step (2).

When a result in HNF is obtained, it is used to overwrite the original expression, so that all expressions which had it as a subexpression will share the result of the reduction, implementing that part of laziness.

The graph reduction of the expression `f (* 5 2)`, written out in steps 6.1 to 6.4 is represented pictorially in Figure 6.1. Initially, the application `f (* 5 2)` is marked with $\gg$ (Figure 6.1*(a)*). The application of `f` is reduced, building a copy of the graph for `f` (Figure 6.2*(a)*), with the pointers to the `Var` node being made to point to the graph of `(* 5 2)`, the actual parameter to `f` (Figure 6.1*(b)*). An application of g results from the reduction step, which is not in HNF, and so the mark is moved to the application of g, and another reduction step is performed, to produce the graph in Figure 6.1*(c)*. At this stage we have a problem: the result of the previous reduction step is not in HNF, and we are unable to reduce the application of `+` because all the δ-rules for `+` require its arguments to be reduced to HNF before the application can be reduced. Therefore both arguments of `+` have to be reduced to HNF, so that the application of `+` is reduced using the algorithm:

1. reduce the first argument to HNF

2. reduce the second argument to HNF

3. add the results.

To do this, we can use the reduction algorithm again, moving $\gg$ to point to the root of the graph which is the first argument to `+`, and then beginning to reduce the expression. We must remember, when the first argument has been reduced, to return to reduce the second argument, and then to move $\gg$ back to the application of `+` to reduce it. Figure 6.1*(c)* shows the graph with $\gg$ moved so that the first argument of `+` can be reduced. The function `*` is like `+`, but in this application, both of its arguments are in HNF, and so the δ-rule for `*` can be used to reduce the expression to the value `10`, which must be stored in an `Int` node, and by step (3) of the reduction algorithm, the result must overwrite the application of `*`, resulting in Figure 6.1*(d)*. Because the second argument to `+` is a pointer to the same expression, $\gg$ can be moved back to point at the application of `+`, which can be reduced to `20` and the result stored in an `Int` node, which overwrites the root node of the original application of `f`.

Graph reduction of lazy functional languages can be formalised using *term graph rewriting* [BvEG+87].

The next section describes how to generate Spineless G-machine code for the reduction process.

6.2 The Spineless G-machine

6.2.1 The State of the Spineless G-machine

The Spineless G-machine is a stack-based abstract machine for graph reduction. It was originally described in [BPJR88], and was defined using binary application nodes to store function applications, so that it could be compared with the normal G-machine [Aug87, Joh83, Joh87]. Here however, we will store function applications using Vaps. We will write out parts of the specification of the abstract machine using the functional language Miranda. A complete, annotated specification of the Spineless G-machine can be found in Appendix B.

The state of the Spineless G-machine is given by the six-tuple:

```
> state == (output, code_sequence, stack, graph, dump, environment)
```

which are:

- output: a representation of the answer produced by a program. This is of no further concern in the present chapter.

- code_sequence: the sequence of instructions which must be executed. In the specification we represent it as a list of Spineless G-machine instructions.

- stack: the stack contains pointers into the graph, and is used for two purposes:

  - to store the pointers to the arguments of the function application currently being reduced (the one marked by $\gg$ in our previous discussion); and
  - to store pointers to subexpressions of the body of a function as it is being built.

  ```
  > stack          == [label]
  ```

  In our specification we represent the stack as a list of labels, which would probably be the addresses of graph nodes (i.e. pointers) in a real implementation. In the specification a label is just an integer.

- graph: stores the graphical data structure described in the previous section.

  ```
  > graph          == [graph_node]
  > graph_node     == (label, tagged_exp)
  ```

  Graph nodes are a pair containing their label and a tagged expression, such as a Vap or an Int node.

- dump: used to save the current code sequence and stack when the reduction process must recursively evaluate some subexpression, as was the case in Figure 6.1*(c)*. We will see how this is used when we discuss the EVAL instruction.

- environment: used to access the code for functions. This will not be discussed further in this chapter.

6.2.2 Expression Evaluation – The EVAL Instruction

The EVAL instruction causes the evaluation of an expression to HNF. Its action is represented by the function eval, which takes the current state of the machine, and returns the new state of the machine after the execution of the instruction:

```
> eval (o, c, s, g, d, e)
>    = (o, c', s', g, d', e), isVap te
>    = (o, c, s, g, d, e),     otherwise
>      where
>      c'        = [LOAD]
>      s'        = ns
>      d'        = (UPDATE 1:c, s):d
>      te        = g_lookup g n
>      (Vap ns) = te
>      n         = top s
```

In all of the code sequences that we write, we will adopt the convention that the parts of the state which change will be primed in the result state, so that for EVAL the code sequence (c), stack (s) and dump (d) are changed in the case that (isVap te) is true, and the other components of the state are unchanged.

What does the EVAL instruction do? The variable n is bound to the top label (pointer) on the stack, and (g_lookup g n) gets the contents of the node with label n from the graph g. There are two cases to consider:

- If it points to an object already in HNF ((isVap te) is false), then no evaluation has to be done, and so the state of the machine remains unchanged.
- If it points to a Vap node, then the Vap node must be evaluated to HNF. The reduction algorithm given in the previous section said that the first step was to mark the graph node to be reduced with $\gg$. In the machine this is done by notionally creating a new stack containing ns, the contents of the Vap node, which we have seen is a pointer to the code of the function being applied and pointers to its arguments. A real implementation may just create a new stack *frame* on the top of the current stack (c.f. the entry to a function in a procedural language). The EVAL instruction also sets up the return, saving the current code sequence and stack on the top of the dump to give a new dump d'. An UPDATE 1 instruction is added to the front of the saved instruction stream so that the Vap node can be updated with the HNF of the expression when it has been evaluated, as required by step (3) of the reduction algorithm. Finally, the new instruction sequence is LOAD, which causes the reduction of the expression to begin.

6.2.3 Generating Code for Function Definitions – The $\mathcal{F}$ and $\mathcal{R}$ Compilation Rules

The EVAL instruction is responsible for setting up the evaluation of an expression. Code for a function must perform one reduction step, that is, build a copy of the graph of the body of a function and either:

- jump to the code to perform the next reduction step (if its body is an application of another function, so performing the next leftmost reduction); or
- pop the information off the dump and return (if its body is in HNF).

We maintain the following *stack invariants* at the entry point of the code for a function:

1. *pointers to the argument graphs are on the top of the stack, so that the first argument is on the top of the stack, the second is the next to top, and so on; and*
2. *If the function takes* n *arguments, then there are at least* n *pointers on the stack at the point of entry.*

Suppose that a function is defined by:

```
> f x1 ... xn = E
```

Function definitions are compiled using the $\mathcal{F}$ compilation scheme, defined by:

$$\mathcal{F}\ [\![\texttt{f x1 ... xn = E}]\!] = \mathcal{R}\ [\![\texttt{E}]\!]\ \{\texttt{x1} \mapsto n, \ldots, \texttt{xn} \mapsto 1\}\ \texttt{n},$$

where the $\mathcal{R}$ compilation scheme is used to compile $\mathcal{R}$ight-hand sides of function definitions. When making a copy of the expression E, the code needs to have access to the pointers to the actual parameters to f, which have become bound to the formal parameters x1 to xn. At the point of entry to the code for f, the first invariant ensures that the pointers to the arguments are all available on the stack, with x1 on the top of the stack, x2 next to top, and so on, so that xn is (n-1) places from the top of stack. The second and third arguments to the $\mathcal{R}$ compilation scheme are used to access the pointers to the actual parameters to f, and all the compilation rules maintain the following invariant:

> *If $\mathcal{A}$ is some compilation rule, in the expression*
>
> $$\mathcal{A}\ [\![\texttt{E}]\!]\ \texttt{r n}$$
>
> *if* x *is some formal parameter, then* (n-(r x)) *is the index into the stack of the pointer to the corresponding actual parameter to the function*[1].

Clearly this invariant holds when $\mathcal{R}$ is used to start compiling the right-hand side of a function definition. It is maintained by incrementing n every time a pointer is pushed onto the stack, and decrementing it when a pointer is popped from the stack.

We saw that there are two types of right-hand sides that a function can have, either an application of another function, or a result in HNF. Different code is generated for each case.

[1]Note that we are using a zero-indexed stack, so that the top of stack is 0 items from the top of the stack, and the nth item on the stack is at index (n-1).

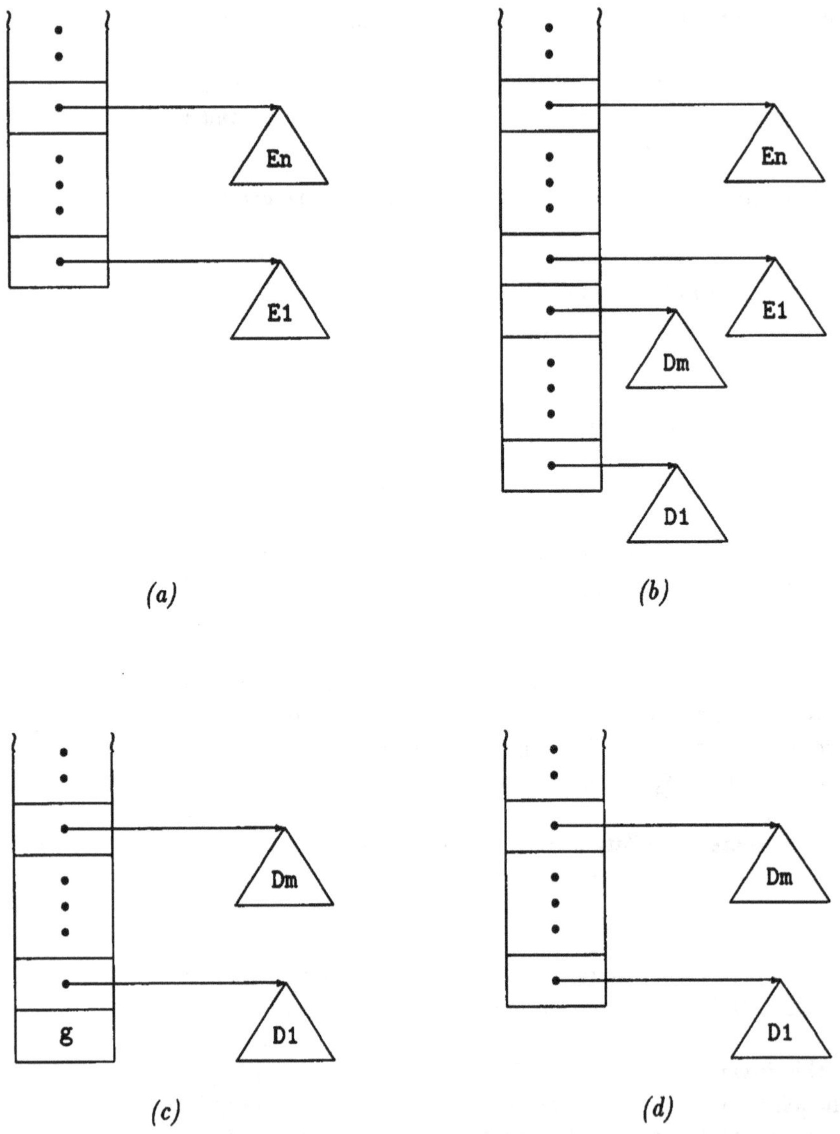

Figure 6.3: Points During the Execution of Code Generated by the $\mathcal{R}$ Compilation Rule

Generating Code for Right-hand Sides Which are Function Applications

Let us tackle generating code for the first case, supposing that the function `f` was defined by:

```
> f x1 ... xn = g D1 ... Dm
```

Using the $\mathcal{F}$ compilation rule, we need to define

$$\mathcal{R}\ [\![\texttt{g D1 ... Dm}]\!]\ \texttt{r n}$$

where `r` is bound to $\{\texttt{x1} \mapsto n, \ldots, \texttt{xn} \mapsto 1\}$ in this case. How should this be done? If the actual parameters to `f` were `E1` to `En`, then the situation before executing any of the code generated by $\mathcal{R}\ [\![\texttt{g D1 ... Dm}]\!]\ \texttt{r n}$ is shown pictorially in Figure 6.3*(a)*, where the stack is growing downwards, an `Ei` in a triangle represents the graph for the expression `Ei`, and the pointers on the stack point to the root node for the argument graphs. The code should build the graph for `Dm`, leaving a pointer to it on the stack, build the graph for `Dm-1`, leaving a pointer to it on the top of the stack, and so on, until the stack is as shown in Figure 6.3*(b)*. At this stage, the pointers to the arguments of `f` are no longer needed, so they can be squeezed out, and a way of accessing the code for g pushed onto the stack, shown in Figure 6.3*(c)*. Now we again have a representation of the node on the stack which would have been marked with $\gg$ in the previous section. All the code has to do now is to arrange for the next reduction step to occur by checking to see if there are enough arguments on the stack for the application of g to be reduced (to maintain the second invariant on the stack), removing the pointer to g if there are (to maintain the first invariant on the stack), and jump to the code generated by $\mathcal{R}$ for g, with the stack as shown in Figure 6.3*(d)*, so completing a full cycle. We will treat the case of when there are not enough arguments on the stack after showing how to generate code for right-hand sides in HNF.

Supposing that we have a compilation scheme called $\mathcal{C}$, for generating code which builds graphs of expressions, leaving a pointer to the newly-created graph on the top of the stack, then the process we have described in words is defined by:

$$\begin{aligned}\mathcal{R}\ [\![\texttt{g D1 ... Dm}]\!]\ \texttt{r n} = {} & \mathcal{C}\ [\![\texttt{Dm}]\!]\ \texttt{r n};\ \ldots;\ \mathcal{C}\ [\![\texttt{D1}]\!]\ \texttt{r}\ (\texttt{n}+\texttt{m}-1);\\ & \texttt{SQUEEZE m n; PUSHFUN g; ENTER}\end{aligned}$$

The `SQUEEZE m n` instruction moves the `m` pointers to the arguments to g down the stack `n` places, squeezing out the pointers to the arguments to `f`, `PUSHFUN g` pushes a way to access the code for g onto the top of the stack, and the `ENTER` instruction tests to see if there are enough arguments on the stack for the function to perform a reduction step. If there are, it removes the top element from the stack and enters the code for the function. The action of `SQUEEZE m n` on the state of the machine is given by the function squeeze:

```
> squeeze m n (o, c, s, g, d, e)
>   = (o, c, s', g, d, e)
>     where
>     s' = (take m s) ++ (stack_pop (m+n) s)
```

Generating Code for Right-hand Sides Which are in HNF

Suppose that the function `f` was defined by:

```
> f x1 ... xn = Cons D1 D2.
```

The result of applying this function is in HNF, and so the reduction algorithm says that a return must be made to continue the reduction of the expression which was suspended whilst this subexpression was being reduced to HNF. This is achieved by the following code:

$$\mathcal{R}\, [\![\texttt{Cons D1 D2}]\!]\ \mathrm{r}\ \mathrm{n} = \mathcal{C}\ [\![\texttt{D2}]\!]\ \mathrm{r}\ \mathrm{n};\ \mathcal{C}\ [\![\texttt{D1}]\!]\ \mathrm{r}\ (\mathrm{n}+1); \texttt{CONS};\ \ \texttt{SQUEEZE 1 n};\ \ \texttt{RETURN}.$$

Here the `CONS` instruction creates a new type of graph node, with label `Cons`, which has two slots in it. The first slot contains a pointer to the graph which was created for `D1`, the head of the list, and the second contains a pointer to the graph for `D2`, the tail of the list. As well, it removes the top two pointers from the stack, and replaces them with a pointer to the newly created `Cons` node. The action of `CONS` on the state is defined by the function `cons`:

```
> cons (o, c, s, g, d, e)
>    = (o, c, s', g', d, e)
>      where
>      n = newlabel g
>      s' = stack_push n (stack_pop 2 s)
>      n1 = top s
>      n2 = next_to_top s
>      g' = (n, Cons n1 n2):g
```

The function `newlabel` models calling a heap allocator which returns a label of (pointer to) an area of memory which has been allocated to store the new `Cons` node. A return to the previous stack and code is achieved by the `RETURN` instruction, whose action on the state is defined by the `return` function:

```
> return (o, c, s, g, d, e)
>    = (o, c', s', g, d', e)
>      where
>      ((c',s''):d') = d
>      s' = stack_push (top s) s''
```

Notice how the old code sequence, `c'`, has been restored from the dump, and that the new stack, `s'`, consists of the old stack, `s''`, with a pointer to the node which was left from evaluating the subexpression, `(top s)`. Recalling that the `EVAL` instruction put an `UPDATE 1` instruction at the beginning of the code sequence which was saved on the dump, the next instruction will be to update the graph node pointed to by the top of the old stack, which is a pointer to the `Vap` node that had to be reduced, with the result of evaluating it, which is what was required.

Functions Applied to too Few Arguments

In the introduction to this chapter, we noted that function definitions like:

```
> f x1 ... xn = E
```

are effectively treated as new δ-rules in a combinator-based implementation, so that the application of the above function to less than n arguments cannot be reduced – it is in HNF. Recall that the reduction algorithm requires a return to the code which initiated the evaluation of an expression when the expression has been reduced to HNF. Therefore, when the ENTER instruction encounters a function applied to too few arguments, it creates a new Wvap node, a node type to hold applications in HNF, to store the application[2], and returns to the previous code and stack frame. Any arguments on the previous stack frame are available to f to be used. Since a program has to have valid type, in particular it cannot have a functional type, we are assured that a stack frame will eventually be found containing enough arguments to reduce the application of the function.

6.2.4 Compiling Code to Build Graphs – The $\mathcal{C}$ Compilation Scheme

The $\mathcal{C}$ compilation scheme compiles code to $\mathcal{C}$onstruct graphs of expressions. Suppose that a graph for the expression (g D1 ... Dm) has to be constructed. This can be done by firstly constructing the graph for Dm, with a pointer to it left on the top of the stack, then the graph for Dm-1, leaving a pointer to it on the top of the stack, and so on, till the graph for D1 has been constructed, leaving a pointer to it on the top of the stack. During this process, the stack has gained m extra pointers. A pointer to the code for g can then be pushed onto the stack, and then the construction of the graph can be completed by creating a new Vap node to contain the top m+1 pointers from the stack, removing these pointers from the stack, and leaving a pointer to the new Vap node on the top of the stack. This process is expressed by the following compilation rule:

$$\mathcal{C}\,[\![\mathtt{g\ D1\ \ldots\ Dm}]\!]\ \mathtt{r}\ \mathtt{n} = \mathcal{C}\,[\![\mathtt{Dm}]\!]\ \mathtt{r}\ \mathtt{n};\ \ldots;\ \mathcal{C}\,[\![\mathtt{D1}]\!]\ \mathtt{r}\ (\mathtt{n}+\mathtt{m}-1);$$
$$\mathtt{PUSHFUN}\ \mathtt{g};\ \mathtt{STORE}\ (\mathtt{m}+1)$$

The instruction STORE (m+1) creates a new Vap node containing the top m+1 pointers from the stack, removes them from the stack, and leaves a pointer to the new Vap node on the top of the stack. Its action on the state is defined by the function store:

```
> store m (o, c, s, g, d, e)
>   = (o, c, s', g', d, e)
>     where
>     n = newlabel g
>     s' = stack_push n (stack_pop m s)
>     g' = (n, Vap (take m s)):g
```

[2]Applications of combinators to fewer arguments than their arity are often called *partial applications*.

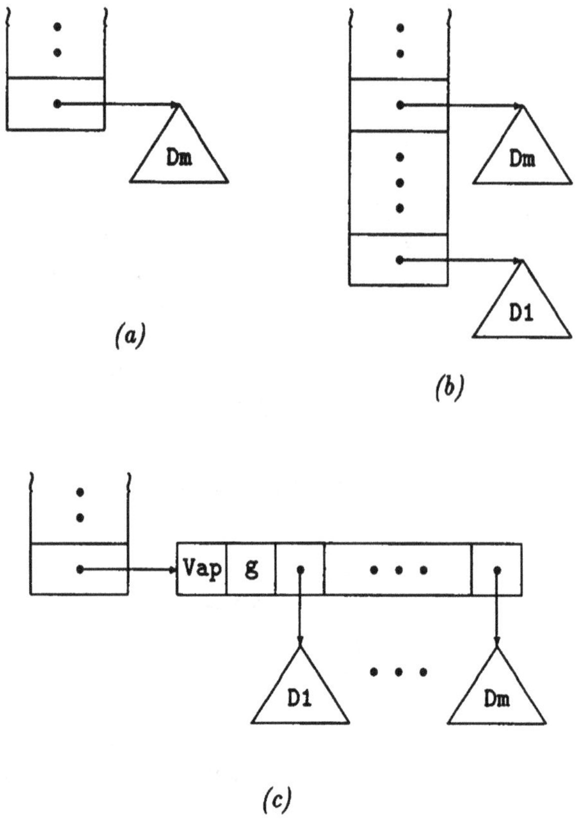

Figure 6.4: Constructing the Graph of (g D1 ... Dm)

Figure 6.4 shows the process of constructing the graph for the expression at three different stages:

(a) after the code $\mathcal{C}$ [[Dm]] r n has been executed, where the triangle represents the graph for Dm;

(b) after the code sequence $\mathcal{C}$ [[Dm]] r n; ...; $\mathcal{C}$ [[D1]] r (n + m − 1) has been executed; and

(c) after the entire code sequence has been completed, that is, after the construction of the application.

A formal parameter may be one of the argument expressions when constructing the graph of an application. What should be done in this case? The stack is being used to build up the current Vap node. Recall that a formal parameter, x, in the body of the function is to be replaced by a pointer to the graph of the actual parameter, and that the index into the stack of that pointer is given by (n-(r x)), so the $\mathcal{C}$ compilation rule for variables is:

$$\mathcal{C} [\![\texttt{x}]\!] \ \texttt{r n} = \texttt{PUSH (n} - \texttt{(r x))}.$$

The PUSH instruction takes a stack index and pushes a copy of the pointer at that index onto the top of the stack. Using this rule, all occurrences of a particular formal parameter in the body of a function will be replaced by pointers to the same piece of graph, implementing the sharing required by laziness.

We can now generate code which will implement the steps from *(a)* to *(c)* in Figure 6.1. How can we implement the application of +?

6.2.5 Compiling Applications of +

An application of + can only be reduced when both of its arguments have been reduced to HNF. In Section 6.2.2, we saw that the EVAL instruction causes the evaluation of a graph that is pointed to by the top element of the stack. So the code for + is the following:

$$\mathcal{R} [\![\texttt{+ x y}]\!] \ \texttt{r n} = \texttt{PUSH 0; EVAL; PUSH 2; EVAL; ADD; SQUEEZE 1 2; RETURN.}$$

At the point of entry to the code for +, the first stack invariant says that the two arguments to + are on the top of the stack. The PUSH 0 instruction pushes a pointer to the first argument graph onto the top of the stack, and EVAL evaluates it to HNF, overwriting the original graph with the result. In the same way, the second argument to + is evaluated. The ADD instruction adds together the integers stored in the nodes which are pointed at from the top two locations on the stack, creates a new Int node containing their value, and replaces the top two pointers with a pointer to the new Int node. Its action on the state is given by the function add[3]:

```
> add (o, c, s, g, d, e)
>    = (o, c, s', g', d, e)
>      where
>      n = newlabel g
>      s' = stack_push n (stack_pop 2 s)
>      (Int i2) = g_lookup g (top s)
>      (Int i1) = g_lookup g (next_to_top s)
>      g' = (n, Int (i1 + i2)):g
```

Since the result is in HNF, a RETURN is made to the code which caused the evaluation of this expression. Similar code sequences can be written for the other binary arithmetic functions.

Executing this code sequence will get from *(c)* to *(e)* in Figure 6.1.

The reader may like to try to define a more efficient code sequence for +, and consider whether it would also work for -, which is not a commutative function.

[3]In the specification in Appendix B, the action of ADD is specified by a call to the higher-order function arithmetic_op.

6.2.6 Compilation and Optimisation

Now that graph reduction is being expressed in terms of compilation rules, a number of optimisations become obvious. For example, the $\mathcal{R}$ compilation rule for function applications:

$$\mathcal{R}\ [\![\texttt{g D1 ... Dm}]\!]\ \texttt{r n} = \mathcal{C}\ [\![\texttt{Dm}]\!]\ \texttt{r n; ...; } \mathcal{C}\ [\![\texttt{D1}]\!]\ \texttt{r (n+m-1);}$$
$$\texttt{SQUEEZE m n; PUSHFUN g; ENTER}$$

makes no use of any known properties of the function g. Consider the function g defined by:

```
> g a b = + D1 D2.
```

Using the $\mathcal{R}$ compilation scheme given above, the code generated for g is:

$$\mathcal{C}\ [\![\texttt{D2}]\!]\ \texttt{r n; } \mathcal{C}\ [\![\texttt{D1}]\!]\ \texttt{r (n+1); SQUEEZE 2 n; PUSHFUN +; ENTER}$$

Combining this with the code for + given in the previous subsection, the code that will be executed in evaluating an application of g is:

$$\mathcal{C}\ [\![\texttt{D2}]\!]\ \texttt{r n; } \mathcal{C}\ [\![\texttt{D1}]\!]\ \texttt{r (n+1); SQUEEZE 2 n; PUSHFUN +; ENTER;}$$
$$\texttt{PUSH 0; EVAL; PUSH 2; EVAL; ADD; SQUEEZE 1 2; RETURN.}$$

The code can be thought of as performing three steps:

1. assemble the arguments to + so that the two top pointers on the stack point to the arguments to +;

2. checking that there are enough arguments on the stack, and jumping to the code for +; and

3. executing the code for +, which evaluates each of the arguments in turn, adds the results, cleans up the stack, and returns (as the result is in HNF).

Clearly, the middle step is redundant, as + is applied to two arguments in the definition of g. Removing this step, the other two steps can be interleaved, to generate a more efficient algorithm:

1. assemble first argument to +, leave a pointer to it on the top of the stack, and evaluate it.

2. repeat the process for the second argument.

3. add the results, clean up the stack, and return.

By defining a new $\mathcal{R}$ compilation rule to capture this algorithm:

$$\mathcal{R}\ [\![\texttt{+ D1 D2}]\!]\ \texttt{r n} = \mathcal{C}\ [\![\texttt{D1}]\!]\ \texttt{r n; EVAL; } \mathcal{C}\ [\![\texttt{D2}]\!]\ \texttt{r (n+1); EVAL;}$$
$$\texttt{ADD; SQUEEZE 1 n; RETURN}$$

more efficient code is generated, saving one SQUEEZE, an ENTER and two PUSH instructions.

6.2.7 Optimising Applications of Strict Functions – The $\mathcal{E}$ Compilation Scheme

We know that both of the arguments to + need to be evaluated. In the case that one of the arguments is itself an application of a function which needs to evaluate some of its arguments, then we can save some of the cost of building the graph of the argument expression, generating code to evaluate it straight away. An extreme example of this is the function defined by:

```
> f x1 ... xn = (1 + 5) * (xi - 7),
```

where no graph needs to be built for the body of `f`; the code for `f` only needs to force the evaluation of the graph bound to the formal parameter `xi`, and then perform some simple arithmetic.

To use this information, the designer of the original G-machine, Thomas Johnsson, introduced the $\mathcal{E}$ compilation scheme. The code generated by $\mathcal{E}$ ⟦E⟧ `r n` produces the same answer as the code generated by $\mathcal{C}$ ⟦E⟧ `r n; EVAL`, that is, the code will leave a pointer to the HNF of `E` on the top of the stack. The $\mathcal{R}$ compilation scheme for applications of + is changed so that each of its arguments are compiled with the $\mathcal{E}$ scheme, to indicate that they need to be evaluated:

$$\mathcal{R}\ [\![\texttt{+ D1 D2}]\!]\ \texttt{r n} = \mathcal{E}\ [\![\texttt{D1}]\!]\ \texttt{r n};\ \mathcal{E}\ [\![\texttt{D2}]\!]\ \texttt{r (n} + \texttt{1);}\ \texttt{ADD;}\ \texttt{SQUEEZE 1 n;}\ \texttt{RETURN.}$$

The $\mathcal{E}$ scheme is then used whenever it is known that a function needs to evaluate its arguments. For example, the $\mathcal{E}$ scheme rule for an application of + is:

$$\mathcal{E}\ [\![\texttt{+ D1 D2}]\!]\ \texttt{r n} = \mathcal{E}\ [\![\texttt{D1}]\!]\ \texttt{r}\ ;\ \mathcal{E}\ [\![\texttt{D2}]\!]\ \texttt{r}\ ;\ \texttt{ADD,}$$

and similar compilation rules can be defined for all the other strict functions. When an application (`g D1 ... Dm`) is being compiled using the $\mathcal{E}$ scheme, and nothing is known about the function `g`, then the default rule constructs the graph of the expression and then evaluates it:

$$\mathcal{E}\ [\![\texttt{g D1 ... Dm}]\!]\ \texttt{r n} = \mathcal{C}\ [\![\texttt{g D1 ... Dm}]\!]\ \texttt{r n; EVAL.}$$

In actual fact, the compilation rules for the Spineless G-machine make one further optimisation. Rather than constructing a `Vap` node for the application, and then having all the pointers to the arguments read back onto the stack again by the `EVAL` instruction, the following code is generated instead:

$$\begin{aligned}\mathcal{E}\ [\![\texttt{g D1 ... Dm}]\!]\ \texttt{r n} = \ & \mathcal{C}\ [\![\texttt{Dm}]\!]\ \texttt{r n;}\ \ldots;\ \mathcal{C}\ [\![\texttt{D1}]\!]\ \texttt{r (n} + \texttt{m} - \texttt{1);} \\ & \texttt{PUSHFUN g;}\ \texttt{CALL (m} + \texttt{1)}\end{aligned}$$

and produces the same answer.

Once one starts introducing optimisations, there seems to be an endless stream of them that could be introduced. The purpose of this chapter is not to describe all the tricks to get the fastest possible implementation, but to show how to introduce evaluation transformer information into code for sequential and parallel machines. However, we give one more optimisation which is simple, but very important.

Suppose that some function is defined by:

```
> f x1    xn = if E1 E2 E3.
```

Clearly, only one of E2 and E3 is going to be evaluated, and which depends on whether E1 reduces to true or false. Therefore, the code for the $\mathcal{R}$ scheme for the conditional is:

$$\mathcal{R}\ [\![\texttt{if E1 E2 E3}]\!]\ \texttt{r n} = \ \mathcal{E}\ [\![\texttt{E1}]\!]\ \texttt{r n; JFALSE 1;}\ \mathcal{R}\ [\![\texttt{E2}]\!]\ \texttt{r n; LABEL 1;}\ \mathcal{R}\ [\![\texttt{E3}]\!]\ \texttt{r n}$$

It first evaluates E1 to HNF. If the result is false, then it jumps to the code following the label LABEL 1, which executes the code for E3, otherwise it executes the code for E2 (which will not fall through to LABEL 1).

The correctness of all of the optimisations mentioned in this section was proved by Lester in [Les88], by representing instructions as functions over the state and then using equational reasoning.

An astute reader will have noticed that we switched from using the $\mathcal{C}$ scheme to the $\mathcal{E}$ scheme for the arguments to + because we know that the arguments to + need to be evaluated, and that this is exactly the sort of information which is provided for arguments of user-defined functions by evaluation transformers. We will see that this information can be used in a sequential machine to save the cost of building the graphs for arguments which we know need to be evaluated, just as we saved the cost of building graphs for the arguments to +. In a parallel machine, we will still build the graphs, but spawn parallel processes to evaluate the argument graphs.

All the compilation rules we will use in our subsequent discussion are gathered together in Figure 6.5. The complete set of compilation rules for, and a specification of the Spineless G-machine can be found in Appendix B. Being written in Miranda, the specification can be copied and executed. Furthermore, it can be used as a basis for developing the complete specification of either a sequential or parallel machine which makes use of the evaluation transformer information, as outlined in Section 6.4.

6.2.8 Comparing the Function Call Mechanisms of Lazy Functional and Imperative Languages

If we step back from the details of the code we have produced for the Spineless G-machine, the code for the function defined by

```
> f x1 ... xn = g D1 ... Dm
```

does the following:

1. prepares the arguments to g on the stack; and

2. jumps to the code for g.

This is similar to how function calls are compiled in imperative languages. The main differences are:

- pointers to the graphs of the argument expressions are pushed onto the stack, rather than the values of the arguments, in order to support laziness; and

$$\mathcal{R}[\![\texttt{g D1 ... Dm}]\!]\ \texttt{r n} = \mathcal{C}[\![\texttt{Dm}]\!]\ \texttt{r n; ...;}\ \mathcal{C}[\![\texttt{D1}]\!]\ \texttt{r (n+m-1);}$$
$$\texttt{SQUEEZE m n; PUSHFUN g; ENTER}$$
$$\mathcal{E}[\![\texttt{g D1 ... Dm}]\!]\ \texttt{r n} = \mathcal{C}[\![\texttt{Dm}]\!]\ \texttt{r n; ...;}\ \mathcal{C}[\![\texttt{D1}]\!]\ \texttt{r (n+m-1);}$$
$$\texttt{PUSHFUN g; CALL (m+1)}$$
$$\mathcal{C}[\![\texttt{g D1 ... Dm}]\!]\ \texttt{r n} = \mathcal{C}[\![\texttt{Dm}]\!]\ \texttt{r n; ...;}\ \mathcal{C}[\![\texttt{D1}]\!]\ \texttt{r (n+m-1);}$$
$$\texttt{PUSHFUN g; STORE (m+1)}$$

Rules for General Function Applications

$$\mathcal{R}[\![\texttt{Cons D1 D2}]\!]\ \texttt{r n} = \mathcal{C}[\![\texttt{D2}]\!]\ \texttt{r n;}\ \mathcal{C}[\![\texttt{D1}]\!]\ \texttt{r (n+1);}$$
$$\texttt{CONS; SQUEEZE 1 n; RETURN}$$
$$\mathcal{E}[\![\texttt{Cons D1 D2}]\!]\ \texttt{r n} = \mathcal{C}[\![\texttt{D2}]\!]\ \texttt{r n;}\ \mathcal{C}[\![\texttt{D1}]\!]\ \texttt{r (n+1);}$$
$$\texttt{CONS}$$
$$\mathcal{C}[\![\texttt{Cons D1 D2}]\!]\ \texttt{r n} = \mathcal{C}[\![\texttt{D2}]\!]\ \texttt{r n;}\ \mathcal{C}[\![\texttt{D1}]\!]\ \texttt{r (n+1);}$$
$$\texttt{CONS}$$

Rules for Cons

$$\mathcal{R}[\![\texttt{if D1 D2 D3}]\!]\ \texttt{r n} = \mathcal{E}[\![\texttt{D1}]\!]\ \texttt{r n; JFALSE l;}\ \mathcal{R}[\![\texttt{D2}]\!]\ \texttt{r n}$$
$$\texttt{LABEL l;}\ \mathcal{R}[\![\texttt{D3}]\!]\ \texttt{r n}$$
$$\mathcal{E}[\![\texttt{if D1 D2 D3}]\!]\ \texttt{r n} = \mathcal{E}[\![\texttt{D1}]\!]\ \texttt{r n; JFALSE l1;}\ \mathcal{E}[\![\texttt{D2}]\!]\ \texttt{r n; JMP l2}$$
$$\texttt{LABEL l1;}\ \mathcal{E}[\![\texttt{D3}]\!]\ \texttt{r n; LABEL l2}$$

Rules for `if`

Figure 6.5: Compilation Rules for the Spineless G-machine

- functions like `f` are *tail-recursive*, and there is no more work for the application of `f` to do when the application of `g` has been evaluated. Therefore, its evaluation does not need to take place on a new stack frame, but the old stack frame can be reused, hence the `SQUEEZE` instruction. In an imperative language, the next statement must be executed, which requires the creation of a new stack frame for each (non tail-recursive) function call.

Due to the similarity between the function call mechanism of the two language styles, we can expect an increasing use of standard compiler technology in the implementation of lazy functional languages. The important, language-specific issues are data structures to store the graphs of expressions and data types allowed in functional languages, so that they can be stored and retrieved with minimum overhead.

6.3 Relating the Graph Reduction Model to the Typed Lambda Calculus

There are two main differences between the combinator reduction approach to implementing lazy functional languages and the $\beta\delta$-reduction of the typed lambda calculus:

- combinator reduction effectively does several $\beta\delta$-reduction steps at once; and
- combinators applied to insufficient arguments are in HNF whilst their equivalent typed lambda calculus terms are not.

The obvious question to ask is, given a program (i.e. a closed term of valid type), do the two methods give the same answer? Fortunately, Lester has proved that they do [Les88]. Moreover, in the same work he proved that the G-machine was a correct implementation of lazy functional programming languages.

6.4 Compiling Code for Evaluation Transformers

In Chapter 5 we saw that two types of evaluation transformer information could be determined: context-sensitive information, which is true in the context of a particular function application, which was used to annotate function applications, and context-free information which could be used in any application of a function.

Context-sensitive evaluation transformer information is easily incorporated into the compilation rules for the Spineless G-machine, and requires no modification to the abstract machine (or its parallel equivalent). We show how this can be done in the next two subsections, firstly for sequential machines, and then for parallel machines.

Context-free evaluation transformers were introduced because sometimes more information about expressions is available at run-time. The use of this information is discussed in the third subsection, and requires some modifications to the basic abstract machine.

6.4.1 Compiling Code for Sequential Machines

The most important feature of the evaluation transformer model is that the amount of evaluation allowed of arguments in a function application depends on the amount of evaluation required of the application. Therefore, for each function, a different sequence of code must be generated for each possible evaluator that could evaluate an application of the function. We will call each sequence of code which is generated a *version*, and the version corresponding to the evaluator $\xi_{\bar{s}}^{\sigma}$ will be called the $\xi_{\bar{s}}^{\sigma}$ version.

We assume that the Context-Sensitive Evaluation Transformer Theorem has been used in some pass of the compiler to annotate all function applications with evaluation transformers, as discussed in Section 5.3.1. If the evaluation transformer for the ith argument in a function application is called ETi, then we will represent the application (g D1 ... Dm) annotated with evaluation transformers by:

$$\texttt{g \{ET1\} D1 ... \{ETm\} Dm.}$$

The compilation rules for a sequential machine supporting the evaluation transformer model, corresponding to those in Figure 6.5 for the Spineless G-machine, are given in Figure 6.6. In the compilation rules, ξ is any evaluator. Each group of rules will be discussed in turn.

Compilation of General Function Applications

Let us first consider the compilation rule:

$$\begin{aligned}&\mathcal{R}\,\xi\,[\![\texttt{g \{ET1\} D1 ... \{ETm\} Dm}]\!]\;\texttt{r n}\\ &= \mathcal{A}\,(\texttt{ETm}\;\xi)\,[\![\texttt{Dm}]\!]\;\texttt{r n; ...; }\mathcal{A}\,(\texttt{ET1}\;\xi)\,[\![\texttt{D1}]\!]\;\texttt{r}\;(\texttt{n}+\texttt{m}-\texttt{1});\\ &\quad\texttt{SQUEEZE m n; PUSHFUN }\texttt{g}_{\xi}\texttt{; ENTER}\end{aligned}$$

There are four main differences between this code and the code for the Spineless G-machine:

- Each compilation rule now takes an evaluator as an extra argument. For the $\mathcal{R}$ compilation rule, this indicates which version of the code is being generated, that is, the extent to which the result of applying the function has to be evaluated.
- The evaluation transformer information tells how much evaluation can be done to an expression in a function application, given the amount of evaluation being performed on the application. For example, the amount of evaluation allowed of Dm when the application is being evaluated with ξ is given by (ETm ξ).
- We have already seen that the $\mathcal{E}$ compilation scheme is used in the Spineless G-machine when it is known that an expression has to be evaluated. In the same way, if an evaluation transformer says that an expression needs to be evaluated, then it can be compiled using the $\mathcal{E}$ scheme, passing it the evaluator which gives the amount of evaluation that must be done. Otherwise, code must be generated by the $\mathcal{C}$ scheme to build the graph of the expression. This is expressed by writing the compilation of each argument expression in the form:

$$\mathcal{A}\,(\texttt{ETi}\;\xi)\,[\![\texttt{Di}]\!]\;\texttt{r}\;(\texttt{n}+\texttt{i}-\texttt{1})$$

$$\mathcal{A}\ \xi = \begin{cases} \mathcal{E}\ \xi & \text{if } \xi \neq \xi_{NO} \\ \mathcal{C}\ \xi & \text{otherwise} \end{cases}$$

$$\texttt{g} : \sigma_1 \rightarrow \ldots \rightarrow \sigma_m \rightarrow \tau$$

$$\begin{aligned}
&\mathcal{R}\ \xi\ [\![\texttt{g \{ET1\} D1 ... \{ETm\} Dm}]\!]\ \texttt{r n} \\
&\quad = \mathcal{A}\ (\texttt{ETm}\ \xi)\ [\![\texttt{Dm}]\!]\ \texttt{r n};\ \ldots;\ \mathcal{A}\ (\texttt{ET1}\ \xi)\ [\![\texttt{D1}]\!]\ \texttt{r}\ (\texttt{n} + \texttt{m} - 1); \\
&\quad\quad \texttt{SQUEEZE m n; PUSHFUN}\ \texttt{g}_{\xi}\texttt{; ENTER} \\
&\mathcal{E}\ \xi\ [\![\texttt{g \{ET1\} D1 ... \{ETm\} Dm}]\!]\ \texttt{r n} \\
&\quad = \mathcal{A}\ (\texttt{ETm}\ \xi)\ [\![\texttt{Dm}]\!]\ \texttt{r n};\ \ldots;\ \mathcal{A}\ (\texttt{ET1}\ \xi)\ [\![\texttt{D1}]\!]\ \texttt{r}\ (\texttt{n} + \texttt{m} - 1); \\
&\quad\quad \texttt{PUSHFUN}\ \texttt{g}_{\xi}\texttt{; CALL}\ (\texttt{m} + 1) \\
&\mathcal{C}\ \xi_{NO}\ [\![\texttt{g \{ET1\} D1 ... \{ETm\} Dm}]\!]\ \texttt{r n} \\
&\quad = \mathcal{C}\ (\texttt{ETm}\ \xi^{\tau}_{\bot_{A_\tau}})\ [\![\texttt{Dm}]\!]\ \texttt{r n};\ \ldots;\ \mathcal{C}\ (\texttt{ET1}\ \xi^{\tau}_{\bot_{A_\tau}})\ [\![\texttt{D1}]\!]\ \texttt{r}\ (\texttt{n} + \texttt{m} - 1); \\
&\quad\quad \texttt{PUSHFUN}\ \texttt{g}_{\xi^{\tau}_{\bot_{A_\tau}}}\texttt{; STORE}\ (\texttt{m} + 1) \\
&\mathcal{C}\ \xi\ [\![\texttt{g \{ET1\} D1 ... \{ETm\} Dm}]\!]\ \texttt{r n} \\
&\quad = \mathcal{C}\ (\texttt{ETm}\ \xi)\ [\![\texttt{Dm}]\!]\ \texttt{r n};\ \ldots;\ \mathcal{C}\ (\texttt{ET1}\ \xi)\ [\![\texttt{D1}]\!]\ \texttt{r}\ (\texttt{n} + \texttt{m} - 1); \\
&\quad\quad \texttt{PUSHFUN}\ \texttt{g}_{\xi}\texttt{; STORE}\ (\texttt{m} + 1)
\end{aligned}$$

Rules for General Function Applications

$$\texttt{Cons} : \tau \rightarrow (list\ \tau) \rightarrow (list\ \tau)$$

$$\begin{aligned}
\mathcal{R}\ \xi^{(list\ \tau)}_{\bot}\ [\![\texttt{Cons D1 D2}]\!]\ \texttt{r n} &= \mathcal{C}\ \xi_{NO}\ [\![\texttt{D2}]\!]\ \texttt{r n};\ \mathcal{C}\ \xi_{NO}\ [\![\texttt{D1}]\!]\ \texttt{r}\ (\texttt{n} + 1); \\
&\quad \texttt{CONS; SQUEEZE 1 n; RETURN} \\
\mathcal{R}\ \xi^{(list\ \tau)}_{\infty}\ [\![\texttt{Cons D1 D2}]\!]\ \texttt{r n} &= \mathcal{E}\ \xi^{(list\ \tau)}_{\infty}\ [\![\texttt{D2}]\!]\ \texttt{r n};\ \mathcal{C}\ \xi_{NO}\ [\![\texttt{D1}]\!]\ \texttt{r}\ (\texttt{n} + 1); \\
&\quad \texttt{CONS; SQUEEZE 1 n; RETURN} \\
\mathcal{R}\ \xi^{(list\ \tau)}_{\bot\in}\ [\![\texttt{Cons D1 D2}]\!]\ \texttt{r n} &= \mathcal{E}\ \xi^{(list\ \tau)}_{\bot\in}\ [\![\texttt{D2}]\!]\ \texttt{r n};\ \mathcal{E}\ \xi^{\tau}_{\bot_{A_\tau}}\ [\![\texttt{D1}]\!]\ \texttt{r}\ (\texttt{n} + 1); \\
&\quad \texttt{CONS; SQUEEZE 1 n; RETURN}
\end{aligned}$$

Rules for `Cons`

$$\texttt{if} : bool \rightarrow \sigma \rightarrow \sigma \rightarrow \sigma$$

$$\begin{aligned}
\mathcal{R}\ \xi\ [\![\texttt{if D1 D2 D3}]\!]\ \texttt{r n} &= \mathcal{E}\ \xi^{bool}_{0}\ [\![\texttt{D1}]\!]\ \texttt{r n; JFALSE 1;}\ \mathcal{R}\ \xi\ [\![\texttt{D2}]\!]\ \texttt{r n} \\
&\quad \texttt{LABEL 1;}\ \mathcal{R}\ \xi\ [\![\texttt{D3}]\!]\ \texttt{r n} \\
\mathcal{E}\ \xi\ [\![\texttt{if D1 D2 D3}]\!]\ \texttt{r n} &= \mathcal{E}\ \xi^{bool}_{0}\ [\![\texttt{D1}]\!]\ \texttt{r n; JFALSE 11;}\ \mathcal{E}\ \xi\ [\![\texttt{D2}]\!]\ \texttt{r n; JMP 12} \\
&\quad \texttt{LABEL 11;}\ \mathcal{E}\ \xi\ [\![\texttt{D3}]\!]\ \texttt{r n; LABEL 12}
\end{aligned}$$

Rules for `if`

Figure 6.6: Compilation Rules for a Sequential Machine

where $\mathcal{A}$ is defined by:

$$\mathcal{A}\,\xi = \begin{cases} \mathcal{E}\,\xi & \text{if } \xi \neq \xi_{NO} \\ \mathcal{C}\,\xi & \text{otherwise} \end{cases}$$

When some evaluation is allowed, so that (`ETi` ξ) is not ξ_{NO}, the expression `Di` can be compiled using $\mathcal{E}$ (`ETi` ξ), otherwise it is compiled with $\mathcal{C}\ \xi_{NO}$.

- When the pointer to the code for g is pushed onto the stack, a pointer to the correct version must be pushed. The expression is being evaluated with ξ, and so a pointer to the ξ version of g, g_ξ, is pushed.

Stepping back from the details, the evaluation transformer information is being used to show where the $\mathcal{E}$ scheme can be used instead of the $\mathcal{C}$ scheme, changing the evaluation strategy and saving the cost of building a graph which would only have to be evaluated some time in the future. It also specifies the amount of evaluation which must be done.

There are two rules for compiling code to build graphs of expressions using $\mathcal{C}$. The first is to be used when the evaluator argument to the rule is ξ_{NO}, indicating that there is no guarantee that the expression will ever be evaluated. If it is ever evaluated, then we are only guaranteed that it will be evaluated at least to HNF, that is, if

$$g : \sigma_1 \rightarrow \ldots \rightarrow \sigma_m \rightarrow \tau,$$

then it will be evaluated with at least $\xi^{\tau}_{\bot_{A_\tau}}$, and so a pointer to this version of the code for g is stored in the graph for the expression. Since the expression being compiled cannot be evaluated, it is not safe to evaluate any of its subexpressions either, and so the $\mathcal{C}$ compilation rule must be used for them too. However, if the expression ever does need to be evaluated, then the evaluation transformers annotating the application may indicate that some of the subexpressions will need to get evaluated too. The second $\mathcal{C}$ compilation rule is used to compile code to build graphs for expressions which need to be evaluated if their parent expression needs to be evaluated, and the amount of evaluation they need is given by the evaluator ξ passed as an argument to the compilation rule. It has the effect of storing a pointer to this version of the code in the graph built for the expression, and is used to propagate evaluation information to subexpressions. Note that in the first compilation rule, the evaluator given to the $\mathcal{C}$ rule when compiling the expression `Di` is (`ETi` $\xi^{\tau}_{\bot_{A_\tau}}$) because we can only be guaranteed that, if the parent expression is ever evaluated, then the parent expression will be evaluated with at least $\xi^{\tau}_{\bot_{A_\tau}}$.

A Program Transformation for Generating More Efficient Code

When the graph for some function application (`g D1 ... Dm`) has to be created, it has the effect that graphs for all of the `Di` have to be created, even if the evaluation transformers annotating the application say that, if the expression is ever evaluated, then some of the `Di` have to be evaluated. Even though the code generated above will choose the appropriate version of the function being applied in each `Di` that could be evaluated, we have still had to pay the price of building graphs for all of the `Di`. A program transformation, attributed in the folklore to Augustsson and Johnsson, but also present implicitly in the compilation rules for the abstract machine called Tim [FW87], removes this problem. The application (g D1 ... Dm) is replaced by an application (h xi1 ... xik) of a new function h, where {xi1, ..., xik} are the formal parameters which occur in (g D1 ... Dm), and h is defined by:

```
> h xi1 ... xik = g D1 ... Dm
```

Now the code for this expression will construct the graph of the application of h, and if it is ever evaluated, then the evaluation transformer information for g will ensure that graphs will not have to be built for the Di which need to be evaluated.

Compiling Applications of Cons

So far evaluators have only been used to say how much evaluation is to be done to subexpressions, and to choose the appropriate version of the code for a function. It is not until we consider compiling code for the constructors of a data type that we see how the amounts of evaluation are actually achieved. Consider the $\mathcal{R}$ compilation rule for Cons from the Spineless G-machine:

$$\mathcal{R}\ [\![\texttt{Cons D1 D2}]\!]\ \texttt{r n} = \mathcal{C}\ [\![\texttt{D2}]\!]\ \texttt{r n};\ \mathcal{C}\ [\![\texttt{D1}]\!]\ \texttt{r (n + 1)};\texttt{CONS};\ \texttt{SQUEEZE 1 n};\ \texttt{RETURN}.$$

and suppose we are generating code for the $\xi_{\infty}^{(list\ \tau)}$ version of Cons. The context-free evaluation transformers for Cons, from Figure 5.1, say that the second argument to Cons can be evaluated with $\xi_{\infty}^{(list\ \tau)}$, and that no evaluation can be done to the first argument. With our methodology of using the $\mathcal{E}$ scheme for compiling expressions which need to be evaluated, and the $\mathcal{C}$ scheme when this cannot be determined, the code for Cons in this case is:

$$\begin{aligned}\mathcal{R}\ \xi_{\infty}^{(list\ \tau)}\ [\![\texttt{Cons D1 D2}]\!]\ \texttt{r n} \ &= \ \mathcal{E}\ \xi_{\infty}^{(list\ \tau)}\ [\![\texttt{D2}]\!]\ \texttt{r n};\ \mathcal{C}\ \xi_{NO}\ [\![\texttt{D1}]\!]\ \texttt{r (n + 1)};\\ &\quad\ \texttt{CONS; SQUEEZE 1 n; RETURN}\end{aligned}$$

Notice how this naturally implements our intuitions about how $\xi_{\infty}^{(list\ \tau)}$ should be implemented: all the tails of the list (its structure) are evaluated, and graphs are created for the unevaluated elements of the list. The $\mathcal{R}$ compilation rules for applications of Cons are recorded in Figure 6.6.

The $\mathcal{E}$ compilation rules for applications of Cons are identical to the $\mathcal{R}$ rules, except that there are no SQUEEZE and RETURN instructions. The $\mathcal{C}$ rules have the same structure as the $\mathcal{E}$ rules, with all uses of $\mathcal{E}$ being replaced by uses of $\mathcal{C}$.

Compilation rules for node can be determined in the same way as the ones for Cons.

Compiling Applications of if

Suppose that some evaluator ξ is evaluating the application if D1 D2 D3. The expression D1 needs to be reduced to HNF, and then one of D2 and D3 needs to be evaluated, depending on the reduced value of D1. Clearly D1 has to be evaluated to HNF (i.e. with ξ_0^{bool}), and the evaluator which is evaluating the application of if is the one to evaluate whichever one of D2 and D3 is chosen to be evaluated. This is expressed by the compilation rules for if in Figure 6.6. In the same way, the evaluator for the chosen expression in an application of lcase (or tcase) is the same as the evaluator for the application, whilst the discriminating list-valued (or tree-valued) expression only needs to be evaluated with $\xi_{\perp}^{(list\ \tau)}$ (or $\xi_{\perp}^{(tree\ \tau)}$).

6.4.2 Compiling Code for Parallel Machines

The design of a parallel reduction machine can be broken into two fairly distinct parts [Bur88a]:

- design of a sequential reduction machine; and
- design of a parallel harness, which provides the facility for creating tasks, and does all the task management.

A similar approach has been taken by Warren in the case of Prolog [War87] and by the group working at CSELT on the integration of logic and functional languages [BBC+90]. We assume that such a parallel harness has been designed, and that it provides the SPAWN instruction which creates a new task to evaluate the graph pointed to by the top of the stack. Such a machine is described in [LB89].

For a sequential machine, the information that an argument expression could be evaluated was used to generate code which evaluated it, rather than creating a piece of graph which would be evaluated some time in the future. In a parallel machine, we use the information to introduce parallelism: the graph for the argument is built and a process is created to evaluate the expression. The compilation rules for a parallel machine are given in Figure 6.7. It is well worth comparing them with the rules in Figure 6.6 for a sequential machine.

To generate code for a parallel machine, we introduce a new compilation scheme called $\mathcal{P}$, for $\mathcal{P}$arallel, which uses the evaluator information in a different way to the $\mathcal{E}$ scheme: where the $\mathcal{E}$ scheme generated code to evaluate an argument expression, the $\mathcal{P}$ scheme constructs the graph of the expression, and creates a process to evaluate it using the SPAWN instruction. This is specified by the $\mathcal{P}$-rule for compiling general function applications in Figure 6.7. Apart from `if`, the compilation rules for the parallel machine are obtained from those for the sequential machine by replacing the occurrences of $\mathcal{E}$ with $\mathcal{P}$.

The evaluation transformers for `if` allow a parallel process to be created to evaluate its first argument. However, there is no point in doing this as the evaluation of the application cannot proceed until its first argument has been evaluated, and so the $\mathcal{R}$ and $\mathcal{E}$ compilation schemes for the conditional are identical to those for the sequential machine. Should there be a special $\mathcal{P}$ compilation rule for `if`? Using the $\mathcal{P}$ rules for a general function application, the following code will be produced for an application of `if`:

$$\begin{array}{lcl}\mathcal{P}\ \xi\ [\![\texttt{if D1 D2 D3}]\!]\ \texttt{r n} & = & \mathcal{C}\ \xi_{NO}\ [\![\texttt{D3}]\!]\ \texttt{r n};\ \mathcal{C}\ \xi_{NO}\ [\![\texttt{D2}]\!]\ \texttt{r (n+1)};\\ & & \mathcal{P}\ \xi_0^{bool}\ [\![\texttt{D1}]\!]\ \texttt{r (n+2); PUSHFUN if}_\xi\texttt{; STORE 4; SPAWN}\end{array}$$

Clearly it is a waste to build the graphs of both of the expressions D2 and D3, and it is also wasteful to use the $\mathcal{P}$ compilation scheme to generate code which will create a parallel process for evaluating D1, as the process which is spawned to evaluate the application of `if` can do no more work until D1 has been reduced to HNF. To overcome this problem, we can use the program transformation introduced in Section 6.4.1. The application `(if D1 D2 D3)` is replaced by `(h xi1 ... xik)`, where h is a new function, `{xi1,...,xik}` are the formal parameters which occur in `(if D1 D2 D3)`, and h is defined by:

$$\mathcal{A}\ \xi = \begin{cases} \mathcal{P}\ \xi & \text{if } \xi \neq \xi_{NO} \\ \mathcal{C}\ \xi & \text{otherwise} \end{cases}$$

$$\texttt{g} : \sigma_1 \rightarrow \ldots \rightarrow \sigma_k \rightarrow \tau$$

$\mathcal{R}\ \xi$ ⟦g {ET1} D1 ... {ETm} Dm⟧ r n
  $=$ $\mathcal{A}$ (ETm ξ) ⟦Dm⟧ r n; ...; $\mathcal{A}$ (ET1 ξ) ⟦D1⟧ r $(\mathtt{n}+\mathtt{m}-1)$;
  SQUEEZE m n; PUSHFUN $\mathtt{g}_\xi$; ENTER

$\mathcal{E}\ \xi$ ⟦g {ET1} D1 ... {ETm} Dm⟧ r n
  $=$ $\mathcal{A}$ (ETm ξ) ⟦Dm⟧ r n; ...; $\mathcal{A}$ (ET1 ξ) ⟦D1⟧ r $(\mathtt{n}+\mathtt{m}-1)$;
  PUSHFUN $\mathtt{g}_\xi$; CALL $(\mathtt{m}+1)$

$\mathcal{P}\ \xi$ ⟦g {ET1} D1 ... {ETm} Dm⟧ r n
  $=$ $\mathcal{A}$ (ETm ξ) ⟦Dm⟧ r n; ...; $\mathcal{A}$ (ET1 ξ) ⟦D1⟧ r $(\mathtt{n}+\mathtt{m}-1)$;
  PUSHFUN $\mathtt{g}_\xi$; STORE $(\mathtt{m}+1)$; SPAWN

$\mathcal{C}\ \xi_{NO}$ ⟦g {ET1} D1 ... {ETm} Dm⟧ r n
  $=$ $\mathcal{C}$ (ETm $\xi^{\tau}_{\perp_{\mathbf{A}_\tau}}$) ⟦Dm⟧ r n; ...; $\mathcal{C}$ (ET1 $\xi^{\tau}_{\perp_{\mathbf{A}_\tau}}$) ⟦D1⟧ r $(\mathtt{n}+\mathtt{m}-1)$;
  PUSHFUN $\mathtt{g}_{\xi^{\tau}_{\perp_{\mathbf{A}_\tau}}}$; STORE $(\mathtt{m}+1)$

$\mathcal{C}\ \xi$ ⟦g {ET1} D1 ... {ETm} Dm⟧ r n
  $=$ $\mathcal{C}$ (ETm ξ) ⟦Dm⟧ r n; ...; $\mathcal{C}$ (ET1 ξ) ⟦D1⟧ r $(\mathtt{n}+\mathtt{m}-1)$;
  PUSHFUN $\mathtt{g}_\xi$; STORE $(\mathtt{m}+1)$

Rules for General Function Applications

$$\texttt{Cons} : \tau \rightarrow (list\ \tau) \rightarrow (list\ \tau)$$

$\mathcal{R}\ \xi_{\perp}^{(list\ \tau)}$ ⟦Cons D1 D2⟧ r n $=$ $\mathcal{C}\ \xi_{NO}$ ⟦D2⟧ r n; $\mathcal{C}\ \xi_{NO}$ ⟦D1⟧ r $(\mathtt{n}+1)$;
  CONS; SQUEEZE 1 n; RETURN

$\mathcal{R}\ \xi_{\infty}^{(list\ \tau)}$ ⟦Cons D1 D2⟧ r n $=$ $\mathcal{P}\ \xi_{\infty}^{(list\ \tau)}$ ⟦D2⟧ r n; $\mathcal{C}\ \xi_{NO}$ ⟦D1⟧ r $(\mathtt{n}+1)$;
  CONS; SQUEEZE 1 n; RETURN

$\mathcal{R}\ \xi_{\perp\in}^{(list\ \tau)}$ ⟦Cons D1 D2⟧ r n $=$ $\mathcal{P}\ \xi_{\perp\in}^{(list\ \tau)}$ ⟦D2⟧ r n; $\mathcal{P}\ \xi^{\tau}_{\perp_{\mathbf{A}_\tau}}$ ⟦D1⟧ r $(\mathtt{n}+1)$;
  CONS; SQUEEZE 1 n; RETURN

Rules for Cons

$$\texttt{if} : bool \rightarrow \sigma \rightarrow \sigma \rightarrow \sigma$$

$\mathcal{R}\ \xi$ ⟦if D1 D2 D3⟧ r n $=$ $\mathcal{E}\ \xi_0^{bool}$ ⟦D1⟧ r n; JFALSE 1; $\mathcal{R}\ \xi$ ⟦D2⟧ r n
  LABEL 1; $\mathcal{R}\ \xi$ ⟦D3⟧ r n

$\mathcal{E}\ \xi$ ⟦if D1 D2 D3⟧ r n $=$ $\mathcal{E}\ \xi_0^{bool}$ ⟦D1⟧ r n; JFALSE 11; $\mathcal{E}\ \xi$ ⟦D2⟧ r n; JMP 12
  LABEL 11; $\mathcal{E}\ \xi$ ⟦D3⟧ r n; LABEL 12

Rules for if

Figure 6.7: Compilation Rules for a Parallel Machine

```
> h xil      xik = if D1 D2 D3
```

Now the code will create the graph of the application of h and spawn a parallel process for it. When the process to evaluate the application for h begins, it will start executing the code for h. Because h is a function definition, its body will have been compiled using the $\mathcal{R}$ compilation scheme, which will evaluate D1 and then one of D2 or D3, depending on the value of D1.

Sometimes it is not worth creating a parallel task to evaluate some expression, for the amount of work in evaluating the expression may not warrant the overheads of managing a task for its evaluation. In that case, the $\mathcal{E}$ scheme from the sequential machine could be used to compile the expression rather than $\mathcal{P}$.

Notice that the evaluators have been implemented in a different way to the way they were in the sequential machine. For example, $\xi_{\infty}^{(list\ \tau)}$ builds a graph for the second argument to Cons and spawns a process to evaluate it. This means that the Cons node becomes available to a consumer as soon as it is created, rather than waiting for the structure of the whole list to be created before it can be consumed, as occurs on the sequential machine.

6.4.3 Run-Time Choice of Versions

In the compilation rules discussed in the previous two subsections, the version of the code that will be used to evaluate a function application is chosen at compile-time, and so is sometimes called *compile-time choice of version.* Sometimes more information is available at run-time, which allows further evaluation of an expression. The following two examples typify the ways we lose information by fixing the version at compile-time:

- Consider the function defined by:

  ```
  > f x ys = if (x=0) then (sumlist ys) else (length ys).
  ```

  In any application of f, the code produced by the compilation rules from Figure 6.6 for a sequential machine will cause the evaluation of the argument to f with $\xi_{\infty}^{(list\ \tau)}$. If the evaluation terminates, then it will have constructed the structure of the list, which points to graphs for each of the elements in the list. When the code for f is executed, if the value of its first parameter is 0, then its second argument could be further evaluated, so that all of the elements in the list are in HNF[4]. Code produced for the parallel machine, using the rules in Figure 6.7, constructs a graph for the argument to f and spawns a parallel process to evaluate it. The graph which is constructed has a pointer to the $\xi_{\infty}^{(list\ \tau)}$ version of the code for the argument to f. If

[4]This might not be worth doing because the main advantage of of $\xi_{\perp\epsilon}^{(list\ \tau)}$ over $\xi_{\infty}^{(list\ \tau)}$ is that it does not have to create graphs for the elements of a list. In this case, the list has already been evaluated with $\xi_{\infty}^{(list\ \tau)}$, so that these graphs have already been constructed. However, when evaluated to HNF, the elements of the list may take less memory space, so the trade-off is not clear; only experiments will enable us to see what should be done in general. We also note that if optimisations are put into the compiler assuming that, if an expression *could* be evaluated with a particular evaluator, then it *has* been, then the expression must always have the extra evaluation done to it.

the first parameter to f evaluates to 0, again we would like to cause the expression to be evaluated with $\xi_{\perp\!\in}^{(list\ \tau)}$.

- More pernicious are higher-order functions, for example the function defined by:

  ```
  > g x1 ... xn = xi D1 ... Dm
  ```

  where no information is known at compile-time about how the arguments D1 to Dm will be used, and so they must be compiled with $\mathcal{C}\ \xi_{NO}$. This example was introduced in Section 5.3.2 to motivate the need for context-free evaluation transformers. When the expression bound to xi has been evaluated to HNF, the function being applied is known, and so its context-free evaluation transformer information can be used to cause the evaluation of some of the Di.

These two examples require different solutions. We will treat examples such as the function f first, and then return to the problems exemplified by the function g.

Run-Time Updating of Evaluators

Let us consider the function f that was defined by:

```
> f x ys = if (x=0) then (sumlist ys) else (length ys).
```

An application of f returns an integer, and so can only be evaluated with ξ_0^{int}, meaning there is only one version of the code f. From the compilation rules in Figures 6.6 and 6.7, the application (sumlist ys) will be compiled with $\mathcal{R}$ rule, with the evaluator ξ_0^{int} as its first argument. Using the compilation rules from Figure 6.6, the code produced for this application for a sequential machine is:

$$\mathcal{E}\ \xi_{\perp\!\in}^{(list\ \tau)}\ [\![ys]\!]\ \mathtt{r\ n;\ SQUEEZE\ 1\ 2;\ PUSHFUN\ sumlist}_{\xi_0^{int}}\mathtt{;\ ENTER}$$

and for a parallel machine, using Figure 6.7 is:

$$\mathcal{P}\ \xi_{\perp\!\in}^{(list\ \tau)}\ [\![ys]\!]\ \mathtt{r\ n;\ SQUEEZE\ 1\ 2;\ PUSHFUN\ sumlist}_{\xi_0^{int}}\mathtt{;\ ENTER.}$$

What code should be produced by $\mathcal{E}\ \xi_{\perp\!\in}^{(list\ \tau)}\ [\![ys]\!]\ \mathtt{r\ n}$ and $\mathcal{P}\ \xi_{\perp\!\in}^{(list\ \tau)}\ [\![ys]\!]\ \mathtt{r\ n}$ in order to ensure that the expression bound to ys is evaluated with $\xi_{\perp\!\in}^{(list\ \tau)}$?

All problems like this can be solved by giving appropriate rules for compiling formal parameters to a function. To find the solution, we begin by looking at the compilation rules for formal parameters from the Spineless G-machine, which are equivalent to those given in the first part of Figure 6.8. Consider the $\mathcal{E}$ compilation rule. The PUSH instruction pushes a pointer to the graph of the expression to be evaluated. This graph can be in one of three states:

- a Cons node, with no further evaluation of any of its subgraphs in progress, although some evaluation may have been completed on some subgraphs.
- a Vap node.

$$\begin{aligned}
\mathcal{R}\ [\![\mathtt{x}]\!]\ \mathtt{r}\ \mathtt{n} &= \mathtt{PUSH\ (n-(r\ x));\ EVAL}\\
\mathcal{E}\ [\![\mathtt{x}]\!]\ \mathtt{r}\ \mathtt{n} &= \mathtt{PUSH\ (n-(r\ x));\ EVAL}\\
\mathcal{C}\ [\![\mathtt{x}]\!]\ \mathtt{r}\ \mathtt{n} &= \mathtt{PUSH\ (n-(r\ x))}
\end{aligned}$$

Compilation Rules for the Spineless G-machine

$$\begin{aligned}
\mathcal{R}\ \xi\ [\![\mathtt{x}]\!]\ \mathtt{r}\ \mathtt{n} &= \mathtt{PUSH\ (n-(r\ x));UPDATEEV}\ \xi;\ \mathtt{EVAL}\\
\mathcal{E}\ \xi\ [\![\mathtt{x}]\!]\ \mathtt{r}\ \mathtt{n} &= \mathtt{PUSH\ (n-(r\ x));UPDATEEV}\ \xi;\ \mathtt{EVAL}\\
\mathcal{P}\ \xi\ [\![\mathtt{x}]\!]\ \mathtt{r}\ \mathtt{n} &= \mathtt{PUSH\ (n-(r\ x));UPDATEEV}\ \xi;\ \mathtt{SPAWN}\\
\mathcal{C}\ \xi\ [\![\mathtt{x}]\!]\ \mathtt{r}\ \mathtt{n} &= \mathtt{PUSH\ (n-(r\ x))}
\end{aligned}$$

Compilation Rules for the Sequential and Parallel Machines

Figure 6.8: Compilation Rules for Formal Parameters

- a Cons node where further evaluation is being done to some of its subgraphs, or processes have been created to do further evaluation of some subgraphs.

Only the first two are possible in a sequential machine, whilst all three can arise in a parallel machine because of the way that applications of Cons being evaluated with $\xi_{\infty}^{(list\ \tau)}$ and $\xi_{\perp\in}^{(list\ \tau)}$ are compiled (see Figure 6.7).

To know whether more evaluation of a Cons node needs to be done, we need to be able to tell how much evaluation of the subgraphs of the Cons has been done, or is in the process of being done. In a similar manner, to tell whether another version of the function being applied in the Vap node should be chosen in order to do more evaluation, requires that we can find out the version of the function which has already been chosen. At an abstract level, the solution to both of these problems is to keep an evaluator as a field in each Vap and Cons node. It records the maximum amount of evaluation that has been requested of that expression so far[5].

How can this evaluator field be used to cause more evaluation of an expression if more evaluation is required? We introduce a new instruction called UPDATEEV, which takes an evaluator as an argument. Its action depends on whether the pointer on the top of the stack points to a Vap or a Cons node:

- Vap: Here the evaluator field is updated with the new evaluator if it requires more evaluation than the evaluator already there. Note that PUSHFUN instruction no longer pushes a pointer to the code for a particular version of the code for a function, but to a table of code entry points for the various versions of the function. As well,

[5]The evaluators $\xi_{\perp}^{(list\ \tau)}$ to $\xi_{\perp\in}^{(list\ \tau)}$ are in a linear relationship; $\xi_{\perp\in}^{(list\ \tau)}$ does more evaluation than $\xi_{\infty}^{(list\ \tau)}$, and $\xi_{\infty}^{(list\ \tau)}$ does more evaluation than $\xi_{\perp}^{(list\ \tau)}$. When there is no linear relationship like this between evaluators, there may need to be more than one evaluator field on a node in order to record all of the available evaluation information.

the STORE instruction must be modified to take an evaluator as an argument, and it sets the evaluator field to this argument, and the ENTER instruction also takes an evaluator as an argument, to say which version of the code must be used.

- Cons: Here the evaluator field is updated with the new evaluator, and any further evaluation required of subexpressions can be done. A parallel machine may create parallel processes to evaluate the subexpressions which require further evaluation. In a parallel machine, some of the subexpressions may not be evaluated yet, they are Vap nodes, and so the evaluator fields are treated as above.

The code for compiling formal parameters, using this instruction is given in the second half of Figure 6.8. To complete the description of how these compilation rules cause the required extra evaluation, we note that when the evaluation of expressions begin, either because of an EVAL instruction, or because the process to evaluate an expression begins executing, the version of the code to be executed is chosen by looking in the evaluator field of the Vap.

As an aside, we note that the use of UPDATEEV simplifies the definition of the parallel machine of [Bur88b, LB89], where each of the instructions which cause evaluation (EVAL, SPAWN, CALL, LOAD) are given an evaluator, and are each responsible for performing the actions of the UPDATEEV instruction. Also note that there is no point in generating an UPDATEEV instruction unless more evaluation than to HNF is required of an expression.

Using Context-Free Evaluation Transformers

This section began by also giving another problem, that caused by higher-order functions, exemplified by the function g:

```
> g x1 ... xn = xi D1 ... Dm
```

When the actual parameter bound to xi has been evaluated to HNF at run-time, so that the function being applied is known, we would like to make use of evaluation transformer information for that function to cause some evaluation of D1 to Dm. What sort of evaluation transformer information can be used? If no run-time analysis is to be done, then the evaluation transformers used must be allowed in any context, that is, the context-free evaluation transformers should be used.

Suppose that the expression bound to xi is evaluated to an application of the function h, defined by:

```
> h x1      xj = E
```

At the point of entry to the code for h, the first stack invariant assures us that the top j pointers on the stack are pointing to the arguments to h, some of which will be D1 to Dm. As the function is known, and pointers to its arguments are available on the stack, it is an appropriate time to force the evaluation of the arguments allowed by the context-free evaluation transformer information for h, before executing the usual code for h. Supposing that the context-free evaluation transformers for h are $H_1, \ldots H_j$, and that we are generating code for the ξ version of the code for h. The code sequence to achieve the desired affect on a sequential machine is:

PUSH (j − 1); UPDATEEV (H_j ξ); EVAL; POP 1; ...; PUSH 0;
UPDATEEV (H_1 ξ); EVAL; POP 1

Clearly, if any of the (H_i ξ) are ξ_{NO}, then no evaluation is allowed, and the sequence of four instructions:

PUSH (i − 1); UPDATEEV (H_i ξ); EVAL; POP 1

is omitted.

This code sequence needs to be used whenever a return has been made from evaluating an expression to a partial application. It can also be used when beginning the evaluation of an expression, as more evaluation may have been requested of the application since its graph was created, meaning that more evaluation may be allowed of the argument expressions. However, we do not want to execute code sequences like this every time the code for a function is executed. Consider the function definitions:

```
> f x1 ... xi = g D1 ... Dj
> g y1 ... ym = h E1 ... En
```

The code produced by $\mathcal{R}$ ⟦g D1 ... Dj⟧ r i will cause the evaluation of some of D1 to Dj, according to the context-sensitive evaluation transformer information available on the application. There is no reason to then enter the code for g at the point where the context-free information is used to cause the evaluation of its arguments, as at least as much evaluation will have already been caused in the code for the body of f using the context-sensitive evaluation transformers. Therefore, the code for a function has two entry points for each evaluator ξ, ENTRY ξ 1 and ENTRY ξ 2. For the function h defined above, the following code is produced:

ENTRY ξ 1; PUSH (j − 1); UPDATEEV (H_j ξ); EVAL; POP 1; ...; PUSH 0;
UPDATEEV (H_1 ξ); EVAL; POP 1; ENTRY ξ 2; $\mathcal{R}$ ξ ⟦E⟧ r j

It is entered at ENTRY ξ 1 when returning from evaluating an expression to a partial application of the function, or when beginning the evaluation of an expression. This then falls through to the code sequence after ENTRY ξ 2, which is the entry point for the ENTER instruction.

There are a number of other minor modifications which must be made to support run-time choice of versions. A complete (executable) specification of a parallel machine using run-time choice of versions can be found in [LB89], where a slightly different instruction set is used.

6.5 Drawing It Together

In this chapter, we have shown how to take the operational notion of evaluating functional programs using reduction and the evaluation transformer model of reduction, and shown how to implement them on a computer. Specifically, we have covered the following topics:

- a graphical data structure was introduced to support lazy evaluation, and it was shown how to use this data structure to execute programs. The process of executing programs with such a data structure is often called graph reduction.

- an abstract machine, the Spineless G-machine, which supports graph reduction, was described. We showed how to compile code for functional programs to run on it.

- there are three main compilation rules for the Spineless G-machine:

  - $\mathcal{R}$ – used to compile the right-hand side of function definitions;
  - $\mathcal{E}$ – used to compile code which will evaluate an expression when it needs to be evaluated; and
  - $\mathcal{C}$ – used to construct the graphs of expressions.

- When there are a number of different evaluators that can evaluate an application of a function, a number of different versions of the code for the function need to be generated. Generating code which chooses the version of a function at compile-time requires no modification to the Spineless G-machine, just to the compilation rules.

- For a sequential machine with compile-time choice of versions, the compilation rules take an extra argument – the amount of evaluation which is to be done to the expression. For the $\mathcal{R}$ and $\mathcal{E}$ compilation schemes, this is the amount of evaluation which must be done now, whilst for the $\mathcal{C}$ scheme it is the amount of evaluation which must be done if the expression is ever evaluated. The sequential machine uses the evaluation transformer information to evaluate an argument expression straight away, saving the cost of building a graph for it.

- The compilation rules for a parallel machine with compile-time choice of version have the same structure as those of the sequential machine. Evaluation transformer information is used to say when the graph of an expression can be constructed and a parallel process spawned for it, rather than evaluating it straight away as in the sequential machine. Obviously, if it could be determined that the amount of work required to evaluate the expression was not worth the overheads of creating a parallel process, then the expression could just be evaluated instead.

- Choosing the version of a function at compile-time may not make maximal use of the evaluation transformer information available from an abstract interpretation. By modifying the abstract machine slightly, to keep information about how much evaluation has been requested of, or been done to an expression, and choosing the version of a function which is to be used at run-time, we are able to generate more efficient code. This extra information is used in the way formal parameters are compiled, and by adding a code prelude which is executed when the evaluation of an expression is begun.

A complete specification of the Spineless G-machine and compilation rules for it is given in Appendix B. The interested reader is invited to use this as a basis for complete specifications of sequential and parallel machines which incorporate evaluation transformer information.

This completes the main development of the book. Now we have seen how functional programs can be executed, how the abstract interpretation technique can be used to determine evaluation transformers, and how to use this information to generate more efficient code for lazy functional programs to run on sequential and parallel machines.

Chapter 7

Relationship to Other Work

There is a large amount of literature on each of the topics addressed in this book. Consequently this chapter is not much more than an annotated bibliography, containing pointers to some of the literature covering the topics of this book, and discussing the relationship of some of the key pieces of work to this book. The list is not exhaustive, and the interested reader is encouraged to follow up these references to find others. Often work in this field is published in one of the following conferences: ACM Conference on Lisp and Functional Programming, Conference on Functional Programming Languages and Computer Architecture (FPCA), Principles of Programming Languages (POPL) and Parallel Architectures and Languages Europe (PARLE).

7.1 Abstract Interpretation

Optimising compilers for imperative languages have been around for a long time now. They perform analyses such as finding when statements can be moved out of loops, to see whether values that are computed are ever used, finding if certain statements in a program can be reached or not, and finding out which parts of Fortran programs can be run in parallel.

The Cousots produced seminal work on formalising these analysis techniques in terms of abstract interpretation or *flow analysis* [Cou78, CC79]. A good, early book in the area covers a number of aspects of flow analysis [MJ81], and a collection of papers covering a wider class of programming languages is contained in [AH87].

Abstract Interpretation of Lazy Functional Languages

Mycroft pioneered the work on the abstract interpretation of lazy functional languages with his work on the *strictness analysis* and *update analysis* of first-order functional programs [Myc80, Myc81]. Strictness analysis is a technique for finding out which arguments a function is strict in. His aim was much the same as ours, finding out strictness information so that programs could be executed more efficiently. Mycroft also developed an analysis which could be used to determine whether or not the evaluation of an expression would terminate [Myc81]. There were some problems in its correctness proof, which were fixed in [MN83].

The work of Mycroft was generalised in two ways. Firstly Burn, Hankin and Abramsky developed a strictness analysis for higher-order functions [BHA85, BHA86], and secondly Wadler invented the four point abstract domain for finding out more information about functions over lists [Wad87]. All these strands were drawn together and tidied up in [Bur87b], which presented a more general framework for the abstract interpretation of higher-order functional programs and also included product, sum and lifted types. In order to get a working analysis for higher-order programs, the abstract interpretation of [BHA85, BHA86] was restricted to monomorphically typed programs. Abramsky recast this work in terms of *logical relations* [Abr90].

Evaluation transformers were first discovered by Burn, and reported in [Bur87a, Bur87b]. It was also in [Bur87b] that the first serious attempt was made to prove that using the abstract interpretation information to change the reduction strategy did not change the meaning of a program.

A group led by Hudak at Yale has worked on analyses of untyped languages, and has a number of publications in the area, [Blo89a, Blo89b, BH86, BH88, BHY89, Gol87, Gol88, HY86, You89] for example. The *path analysis* abstract interpretation of [Blo89a] has been used for finding strictness information [BH86] and for finding out when parts of data structures can be updated in place [Blo89b]. Goldberg developed an analysis for detecting how many times a function is applied to each subset of its arguments [Gol87, Gol88]. They have also implemented an abstract interpretation in their compiler [BHY89].

Maurer also did some early work on the strictness analysis of the untyped lambda calculus [Mau85].

Abstract Interpretation of Denotational Definitions

In parallel with the work being done on functional languages, Nielson has been developing a general framework for the abstract interpretation of denotational definitions of languages. References to most of the papers he has published in the area can be found in [Nie89]. By giving a meta-language in which to give the denotational semantics of programming languages, Nielson is able to develop a framework for abstract interpretation which can, at least in theory, be used for any programming language. A distinctive feature of the meta-language is that it has two levels of type information, roughly so that a distinction can be made between run-time and compile-time objects in the language.

The framework Nielson has developed allows the interpretations of all of the type constructors to be varied in every interpretation, and hence the interpretations of all of the language constructs can also vary. Proofs of the correctness of the framework are in terms of proving that relations hold between two interpretations, reminiscent of the work of Abramsky using logical relations [Abr90]. A gentler introduction to the work can be found in [JN91].

Abstract Interpretation of Prolog

The abstract interpretation of Prolog has also been a subject of study. A typical question asked of a clause is: "Which arguments are always bound when the clause is invoked?". Some early work on this is given in [JS87, Mel87]. More recently, a group at the University of Pisa has produced a framework for the abstract interpretation of Prolog [BGL89], which is based on a new model for Prolog programs that allows variables in the terms of the model [FLMP88]. It has been used to determine the polymorphic typing of Prolog programs [BG89], and to generate efficient code for parallel machines [Ric90].

7.2 Polymorphism

A problem with the abstract interpretation framework developed in Chapter 3 is that it requires all functions to be monotyped, whereas polymorphic typing is one of the joys of writing programs in functional languages. Whilst this is not a restriction in terms of the power of the technique, as any polymorphic program can be translated into a monomorphic one [Hol83], it would be better if an analysis technique could be developed which dealt with polymorphic functions directly.

What we would like is an analysis for a polymorphic function which, for any type, would give an expression for the abstract interpretation of the function at that type. Unfortunately, this problem has not been solved completely, but there are two partial solutions to the problem, corresponding roughly to the problems of finding context-free and context-sensitive evaluation transformers.

Strictness analysis can be performed by choosing the domain **2** (see Definition 4.1.1) as the abstract interpretation of all of the types *bool*, *int*, (*list* τ) and(*tree* τ), and using the abstract interpretation framework given in Chapter 3. Abramsky has shown that strictness analysis is *polymorphically invariant*, by which he means that if strictness analysis can find that a function is strict for any instantiation of the type variables, then it is strict for all possible instantiations of the type variables [Abr85, AJ91]. In particular, if it is found to be strict when all of the type variables are replaced by the domain **2**, which will involve the least computation, then it is strict for all possible instantiations. If the result could be generalised to analyses using other base domains, then this would be sufficient for finding out the context-free evaluation transformers for a function.

To determine context-sensitive evaluation transformers using Theorem 5.3.1, a formula is needed for the abstract interpretation of the subexpressions in a function application. For first-order functions, Baraki and Hughes have developed a way of inferring a safe approximation to the abstract interpretation of an expression from its abstract interpretation where the type variables have been replaced by **2** [Bar91a].

As an aside, we note that when the four point domain (Definition 4.1.3) is used as the abstract interpretation of (*list* τ) and (*tree* τ) for any type τ, the abstract interpretations of all of the constants over lists and trees (Figure 4.1) are true for all types τ. The abstract interpretations of such functions are essentially polymorphic, and so should give polymorphic expressions for the abstract interpretation of functions. It may be possible to adapt the theory in Chapter 3 to deal with such cases.

7.3 Other Program Analysis Techniques

We will briefly mention four other semantically based program analysis techniques: projection analysis, inverse image analysis, the analysis of streams, and strictness analysis using type inference.

An evaluation transformer says how much evaluation of an argument to a function is allowed, given the amount of evaluation allowed of a function application. Another way of thinking about this is to say that we want to 'do something' to an argument to a function, given that we are allowed to 'do something' to the output of the function. How is 'doing something' modelled mathematically? It is modelled by applying a function to a value. Suppose that we have some function $f : \sigma \rightarrow \tau$, and that we are allowed to do β to the result of the function, then we would like to find the maximum α to apply to the argument such that

$$\beta \circ f \circ \alpha = \beta \circ f.$$

If the above condition holds, then we are assured that 'doing α' to the argument does not change the result of 'doing β' to the answer from the application of f.

What properties should such functions have? Firstly, they should actually do something, and so

$$\beta \sqsubseteq id_{\mathbf{S}_\tau}.$$

Secondly, it would be useful that if something had to be done, then it only had to be done once. This is achieved by requiring that

$$\beta \circ \beta = \beta$$

(and so β is *idempotent*). Such functions are sometimes called *projections*. Wadler and Hughes developed a *projection analysis* to find out projection information for functions [WH87]. It is a *backwards* analysis because it asks questions of the form: "Given that the projection β can be applied to the result of applying a function, what projection α can be applied to its argument so that $\beta \circ f \circ \alpha = \beta \circ f$?". Davis and Wadler have produced a more accurate projection analysis, and proved its correctness [DW90]. A *forwards* projection analysis has been developed by Launchbury [Lau89]. It asks the question the opposite way around: "Given that a certain amount of information is known about the arguments to a function, what is definitely known about the result from a function?" Hughes and Launchbury have started to formally investigate the relationship between forwards and backwards analyses [HL90].

So far, projection analysis has only been developed for first-order programs, but Hunt has been working on an analysis based on partial equivalence relations [Hun90, AP90].

The answers obtained from projection analysis seem to be very similar to those obtained from abstract interpretation. We are only aware of one paper which attempts to relate the two techniques [Bur90a], and there is much more work to be done in this area. Burn has also showed how to use the results of projection analysis to determine evaluation transformers, and to compile code using it [Bur90b].

Dybjer has done some preliminary work on an analysis technique called *inverse image analysis* [Dyb87] which also finds information like that available from abstract interpretation.

Hall uses a domain of list strictness patterns to identify what is known about the strictness of a list, and uses a backwards analysis to annotate both arguments to every application of cons, to indicate which ones can be evaluated [HW87, HW89]. For each different usage pattern of the result of a function, a different version of the code for a function could be generated. These ideas are similar to evaluation transformers, where the 'evaluators' (i.e. strictness patterns) could be program dependent.

Type inference [Mil78, DM82] is intuitively very much like an abstract interpretation – it abstracts away from the values of expressions, and considers a property of terms which has been called their type. Conceivably, types could contain more information about the behaviour of terms. For example, their could be separate types for strict and non-strict functions with the normal type $\sigma \rightarrow \tau$. Proofs of the correctness of such information would have to be made against some model for the typed lambda calculus. Some promising work has been done in this area by Kuo and Mishra [KM89], Jensen [Jen90] and Wright [Wri89].

7.4 Implementation of Lazy Functional Languages

There is a vast amount of literature on the implementation of lazy functional languages on sequential and parallel machines – see [Arg89, Arg90, Aug87, AJ89, BHY89, Bur88a, Bur88b, BPJR88, FW87, FH88, Gol88, Joh87, Kra88, KKR+86, Les89, LB89, Pey87, JCSH87, PS89, Rea89, Tra89, WSWW87, WW87] for example. As we wrote in the preamble to Chapter 6, our aim in this book was not to develop the fastest sequential or parallel implementation, but to demonstrate how evaluation transformer information can be used to increase the speed of both sequential and parallel implementations. With this in mind, we mention only two other pieces of work that are related to ours.

Loogen has also developed an abstract machine to support the evaluation transformer model of reduction [LKID89]. It has been specified to a much lower architectural level than we have discussed in this book, and simulated in occam.

A completely different approach have been taken by Hertzberger and his colleagues [HV89]. They require that the programmer explicitly annotate parts of the program which can be evaluated in parallel. The evaluation model evaluates to normal form all the subexpressions of the application that is to be evaluated on a remote processor before they are transported, so lazy semantics is not preserved. When an expression is transferred to another processor, a complete copy of all of its subgraphs (which have been reduced to normal form) are sent to the recipient processor.

Recently there has also been a number of papers on provably correct implementations of lazy functional languages [GM90, HM90, Les88, NN90].

Chapter 8

Epilogue

This book has spanned a wide range of topics:

- foundational material on the operational and denotational semantics of lazy functional languages;
- the abstract interpretation of functional languages – a semantically sound analysis technique;
- using the information from the abstract interpretation to change the operational semantics of a program whilst retaining its denotational semantics, to give more efficient implementations on sequential and parallel machines; and
- compiling code for this alternative operational model to run on sequential and parallel machines.

In this final chapter, we bring together the main line of reasoning which has been running through the book, making explicit the distinction between the generality of the theory and the specificity of the examples that have been used.

All functional programming languages can be translated into a typed lambda calculus with constants, and so it is, in some sense, the canonical functional programming language. Therefore, the theoretical development in Chapters 2 to 5 has been done in terms of the typed lambda calculus, and is applicable to any lazy functional programming language.

The typed lambda calculus can be studied from two viewpoints:

- an *operational* one, which tells us how to execute functional programs. The two most important theorems about the operational semantics are:
  - The Church-Rosser Theorem which says that in any finite reduction sequence, the order of the reduction steps can be changed without affecting the meaning of the program. Therefore, any change in the reduction strategy which preserves the termination properties of a program will not change the meaning of the program.
  - The Head-Normalisation Theorem which says that the strategy of reducing the leftmost redex will always obtain an answer from a program if it has one.

- a *denotational* one, where the meanings of programs are given in some mathematical domain.

An important theorem, the Computational Adequacy Theorem (Theorem 2.4.1), gave a relationship between the two views of the typed lambda calculus – the leftmost reduction sequence fails to terminate when executing a program if and only if the semantics of the program is bottom. The leftmost reduction strategy is an example of what we called a *safe* reduction strategy, which causes an infinite reduction sequence, producing no answer for a program if and only if the semantics of the program is bottom.

Rather than just giving the semantics of a programming language, we have developed a semantic framework where different *interpretations* of a program can be given. Different interpretations are defined by giving alternative interpretations to the types in a program, some of the syntactic constructs of the language, and the constants in the language. The *standard* interpretation is just the normal denotational semantics that would be given to the program, whilst the purpose of an *abstract* interpretation is to find out information about the standard interpretation of a program.

In order to determine when it is safe to change the reduction strategy for a program, we developed an abstract interpretation framework to give us this information. To use the framework, the following must be given:

- finite lattices as the abstract interpretation of the types *bool*, *int*, (*list* τ) and (*tree* τ) for any type τ;

- an abstract interpretation for each of the constants in Λ_T which satisfies the Constant Safety Condition (Definition 3.3.1); and

- a strict, continuous abstraction map for each of the types *bool*, *int*, (*list* τ) and (*tree* τ) from the standard interpretation of the type to its abstract interpretation.

The purpose of singling out the types *bool*, *int*, (*list* τ) and (*tree* τ) was that the first two are typical of any type which has a flat domain as its standard interpretation, whilst the second two are typical of recursively defined types. Similar techniques could be used for other recursively defined types.

Abstract domains and abstraction maps should be chosen to pick out some property of the standard interpretation which is of interest. Our use of the framework was to find out about how much evaluation functions need to do to their arguments. In Chapter 4, we gave several examples of abstract domains for determining information about differing amounts of evaluation. We also showed how to combine two abstract domains which found out different information, to make an abstract domain which found out both types of information. In the same chapter, we demonstrated a methodology for determining the abstract interpretation of constants, and proved the safety of the abstract interpretations that we gave for the constants when the four point abstract domain of Definitions 4.1.3 and 4.1.5 was used for the abstract interpretation of the types (*list* τ) and (*tree* τ). The reader should be able to use the methods demonstrated in the chapter to do the same for any abstract domain. We gave some examples of the abstract interpretation of programmer-defined functions.

Chapter 5 returned to the abstract interpretation framework and asked how it could be used to show when the reduction strategy for a program could be safely changed. Given any particular abstract interpretation which gives the three items required above, it defines the notion of an *evaluator* (Definition 5.2.1). An evaluator is a reduction strategy for an expression. It is related to an abstract domain point if it always terminates when evaluating an expression if the standard interpretation of the expression is not contained in the concretisation of the abstract domain point. It was then shown how to use the Correctness Theorem for Abstract Interpretation (Theorem 3.3.4) to determine *evaluation transformers* for functions from their abstract interpretations. We found that two types of evaluation transformer information were needed in order to maximise the information that could be obtained from abstract interpretation:

- *context-sensitive*: which takes into account the context of a function application; and
- *context-free*: which is true in any application of the function.

The first gives more information in general, but the second is necessary in order to generate more efficient code for functions like:

```
> f x1 ... xn = xi D1 ... Dm
```

where the function being applied, which will be bound to `xi`, is not known until run-time. Using the context-free information, some evaluation of the expressions `D1` to `Dm` may be allowed once the function being applied is known. Again we gave examples of determining evaluation transformers when the four point abstract domain was used for lists and trees.

Finally, we showed how to use the evaluation transformer information to generate more efficient code for sequential and parallel machines. When an argument expression is known to need a certain amount of evaluation:

- code is generated for a *sequential* machine which evaluates the expression, rather than creating a closure for it; and
- code is generated for a *parallel* machine which builds a closure for the expression and spawns a parallel process for its evaluation.

Obviously, if it can be determined that the overheads of creating a parallel process for evaluating an expression outweigh the advantage of doing so, code can be generated to evaluate it straight away.

In generating code, we found that the version of the code for a function could be chosen at *compile-time* or at *run-time*. The former method lost information available from the evaluation transformers in two ways:

- When an argument expression is shared, we may subsequently discover that it needs to have more evaluation than could be determined at compile-time; and
- In cases like the higher-order function given above, the function being applied is not known until run-time. Here the context-free evaluation transformer information could be used to generate code which performed some evaluation of the `Di` when the function became known.

Our description of the compilation of functional programs was based on the Spineless G-machine, a full specification of which can be found in Appendix B. The specification can be adapted in the ways indicated in Chapter 6 to give an implementation of the evaluation transformer model of reduction on sequential and parallel machines. Supporting compile-time choice of versions did not require any modifications to the abstract machine model, only the compilation rules need changing, but some changes to the abstract machine were needed to support run-time choice of versions.

Whilst this book tells a complete story, from the semantic foundations of functional languages, through a semantically sound analysis technique, to implementations on sequential and parallel machines, we hope that it has been of use to those interested in only one or two of these topics. Being a research monograph, the presentation has been somewhat parochial, but we have endeavoured to set this right by giving the wider context of the work in Chapter 7. The interested reader is encouraged to follow up some of the references recorded there and throughout the text.

Appendix A

Proofs Omitted in Earlier Chapters

This appendix contains the proofs omitted from Chapters 2 to 4. To make the proofs easier to find, the proofs from Chapter 2 appear in Section A.2, from Chapter 3 in Section A.3, and from Chapter 4 in Section A.4; there is no Section A.1. Where relevant, we have repeated the statement of the lemma (or proposition or theorem), with the same numbering as appears in the body of the book.

A.2 Proofs From Chapter 2

The Language Λ_2 has the Church-Rosser property

Corollary 2.1.9

$\beta\delta$-reduction for Λ_2 has the Church-Rosser property.

Proof

Using Theorem 2.1.8, we can see that $\twoheadrightarrow_{\beta\delta}$, where $\rightarrow_\delta$ is defined in Table 2.4, is Church-Rosser. Each of the δ-rules for $+_{int\rightarrow int\rightarrow int}$ that results from the δ-rule schemata given in Table 2.4 trivially satisfies the conditions on the R_i because there are no R_i. The same is true of the rules for $\mathbf{if}_{bool\rightarrow\sigma\rightarrow\sigma\rightarrow\sigma}$.

□

The Reduction Strategy F_ℓ is Head-normalising for Λ_T

To prove that F_ℓ is head-normalising, we show that any reduction sequence is *strongly equivalent* to a *strongly standard* reduction sequence. We will see that leftmost reduction is a strongly standard reduction sequence, and so that, if any reduction sequence terminates in an HNF, then F_ℓ will terminate with an HNF. Our proof is obtained by adapting that of Theorem 4 from [Hin78b], extending it to cover all of the δ-rules for Λ_T. The crucial step is extending Lemma 4 of the same paper; to give the full proof of this extension would require the reproduction of a large proof from that paper, and so we only sketch the modifications of the proof necessary for our purposes.

Suppose that there are at least two redexes in a term of Λ_T. Reducing one redex may affect the other redex. For example, in the term

$$(\lambda x^\sigma.(\lambda y^\sigma.y^\sigma)\ x^\sigma)\ z^\sigma,$$

there are two redexes – $(\lambda x^\sigma.(\lambda y^\sigma.y^\sigma)\ x^\sigma)\ z^\sigma$ and $(\lambda y^\sigma.y^\sigma)\ x^\sigma$. Reducing the second redex leaves

$$(\lambda x^\sigma.x^\sigma)\ z^\sigma$$

as the *residual* of the redex $(\lambda x^\sigma.(\lambda y^\sigma.y^\sigma)\ x^\sigma)\ z^\sigma$. Informally, a residual of a redex is what is left of a redex after some other redex has been reduced. There may be many residuals of a redex. For example, in the reduction:

$$\begin{aligned}&(\lambda x^{int}.+_{int\to int\to int}\ x^{int}\ x^{int})\ (+_{int\to int\to int}\ 0_{int}\ 1_{int})\\ &\quad\to_{\beta\delta} +_{int\to int\to int}\ (+_{int\to int\to int}\ 0_{int}\ 1_{int})\ (+_{int\to int\to int}\ 0_{int}\ 1_{int})\end{aligned}$$

there are two residuals of the redex $(+_{int\to int\to int}\ 0_{int}\ 1_{int})$. Sometimes there may be no residuals of a redex, and from the above examples we see that sometimes each residual of a redex is an unchanged copy of the redex, whilst at others they may be changed. Residuals are formally defined as follows (from [Hin77], but see also [Bar84, p. 284]).

Definition A.2.1

Let e_1 and e_2 be $\beta\delta$-redexes occurring in a term. Then the residuals of e_1 when e_2 is reduced, written e_1/e_2, are defined by the following cases:

1. $e_1 = e_2$: There are no residuals of e_1.
2. e_1 and e_2 are disjoint: The only residual is e_1, occurring in the same place as in the term before the reduction of e_2.
3. e_1 properly contains e_2: The residual of e_1 is obtained by replacing the occurrence of e_2 in e_1 with the result of its reduction.
4. e_2 properly contains e_1: There are three cases to consider.
   (a) $e_2 = (\lambda x^\sigma.e)\ e'$: e_2 is either in e or e'. If it is in e, then the residual of the term e_1 is the one occurrence of e_1 in $e[x^\sigma := e']$. Otherwise e_2 is in e', then there will be a residual of e_1 for each free occurrence of x^σ in e.
   (b) $e_2 = c_\sigma\ d_1\ \ldots\ d_k$: Here c_σ is some constant from Λ^T and the d_i are terms from Λ_T. In this case e_1 occurs in one of the d_i, and there will be one occurrence of the redex e_1 for every occurrence of d_i in the result of the reduction of e_2.
   (c) $e_2 =$ **let** $x^\sigma = e'$ **in** e'': If e_1 is in e', then a copy of e_1 will be a residual of e_1 for each free occurrence of x^σ in e_2. Otherwise, if e_1 is in e'', then e_1 is its own residual in $e''[x^\sigma := e']$.

The reason for defining residuals is that it enables us to define *strongly standard reduction* sequences.

Definition A.2.2

The reduction sequence

$$e_0 \rightarrow_{\beta\delta} e_1 \rightarrow_{\beta\delta} \dots \rightarrow_{\beta\delta} e_n$$

is *strongly standard* if and only if for each i and each $j < i$, the redex reduced in the step $e_i \rightarrow_{\beta\delta} e_{i+1}$ is not a residual of a redex in e_j which is to the left of the redex which was reduced in the reduction step $e_j \rightarrow_{\beta\delta} e_{j+1}$.

We will say that a finite reduction sequence is *strongly equivalent* to another finite reduction sequence if the two reduction sequences terminate with the same residuals of any redex.

Hindley calls this *strongly* standard, as distinct from *standard* because it insists on the property for all $j < i$, whereas a standard reduction sequence only requires that this hold for $j = i - 1$. It is important to make the distinction because for some constants and δ-rules, there may be a standard reduction sequence which is strongly equivalent to a reduction sequence, but not a strongly standard one, and it is the existence of a strongly standard reduction sequence which will give us that F_ℓ is head-normalising. An example of a reduction sequence for which there is a strongly equivalent standard reduction sequence, but for which there is no strongly equivalent strongly standard one is given in [Hin78b, p. 261]. Unfortunately, many authors do not make the distinction, and so care must be taken when using results from the literature. For example, the definition of standard reduction sequence in [Bar84, p. 296] is what Hindley has called strongly standard.

Now we can state the very important Standardisation Theorem.

Theorem A.2.3 (Standardisation Theorem)

Every finite $\beta\delta$-reduction sequence in Λ_T is strongly equivalent to a strongly standard reduction sequence.

Proof

The proof of this theorem is based on extending the proof of Theorem 4 from [Hin78b].

The δ-rules of Figure 2.7 can easily be seen to satisfy conditions (D1)–(D7) from [Hin78a, p. 358], and so by Theorem 1 (i) of [Hin78b], we can conclude that every finite reduction sequence is strongly equivalent to a standard reduction sequence (but not strongly standard as yet).

Theorem 4 of [Hin78b] says that for certain δ-rules, strong standardness is equivalent to standardness, and so our theorem would then hold by appealing to Theorem 1 (i) of the same paper. Unfortunately, our δ-rule schema do not satisfy the restricted set of conditions. They fail because we have schema representing rules of the form:

$$c_\sigma \; e_1 \; \dots \; e_n \rightarrow_\delta e$$

where some of the e_i may contain redexes. However, the proof of Theorem 4 relies solely on the proof of Lemma 4 of the same paper. If we can prove that Lemma 4 also holds for the δ-rules of Λ_T, then we can conclude that Theorem 4 is also true, and we have the desired result.

The proof of Lemma 4 proceeds by a lengthy case analysis, and the only relevant case is the last one, which occurs part way down page 263 of [Hin78b]. It is the case where we are trying to prove that it is impossible, using the notation of the paper, for ξ and η_0 to be two redexes in some term T_0, ξ is proper subterm of T_0, that is, it is not T_0, ξ to the left of η_0, and the contraction of η_0 in T_0 produces a new redex T_1, where T_1 properly contains ξ', the residual of ξ, and ξ' is to the left of $C(\eta_0)$, the contraction of η_0. For example, this is not possible if the new redex is an application of a λ-abstraction, say

$$T_1 = (\lambda x^\sigma.e_1)\ e_2$$

because then we would have that T_0 must be $\eta_0\ e_2$ (recall that ξ is a proper subterm of T_0) and $C(\eta_0) = (\lambda x^\sigma.e_1)$. In T_0, η_0 is the leftmost redex, contradicting the fact that ξ was to the left of η_0. We can show that this also is not possible for all of the δ-rules in Λ_T, and so conclude that Lemma 4 holds for Λ_T, and hence that this theorem is true. For example, if the new redex is of the form:

$$T_1 = \mathbf{if}_{bool\rightarrow\sigma\rightarrow\sigma\rightarrow\sigma}\ \mathbf{true}_{bool}\ e_1\ e_2,$$

then T_0 must be of the form:

$$T_0 = \mathbf{if}_{bool\rightarrow\sigma\rightarrow\sigma\rightarrow\sigma}\ \eta_0\ e_1\ e_2$$

where $\eta_0 \rightarrow_{\beta\delta} \mathbf{true}_{bool}$, and it is impossible for there to be any redex ξ in T_0 which is to the left of η_0.

□

Theorem A.2.4

A term e of Λ_T has an HNF if and only if the reduction of e using F_ℓ terminates (with an HNF).

Proof

($\Rightarrow$) Suppose that e_0 has an HNF, that is, there is some $\lambda x_1^{\sigma_1} \ldots \lambda x_n^{\sigma_n}.v\ d_1\ \ldots\ d_k$ such that

$$e_0 \twoheadrightarrow_{\beta\delta} \lambda x_1^{\sigma_1} \ldots \lambda x_n^{\sigma_n}.v\ d_1\ \ldots\ d_k$$

(from a corollary of the Church-Rosser Theorem – see [Bar84, Corollary 11.4.8, p. 300]). Then by the Standardisation Theorem (Theorem A.2.3), there is a strongly standard reduction sequence

$$e_0 \rightarrow_{\beta\delta} e_1 \rightarrow_{\beta\delta} \ldots \rightarrow_{\beta\delta} \lambda x_1^{\sigma_1} \ldots \lambda x_n^{\sigma_n}.v\ d_1\ \ldots\ d_k.$$

There must be a first term in this which is in HNF. Up to the point of reaching an HNF, F_ℓ reduces the same redexes as the standard reduction sequence, and so it must terminate with an HNF.

($\Leftarrow$) Trivial.

□

Theorem 2.1.14, repeated below, is important for implementation of lazy functional languages because it gives a mechanical procedure for choosing the next redex to reduce.

Theorem 2.1.14

For Λ^T with $\beta\delta$-reduction, F_ℓ is head-normalising.

Proof

This follows directly from Theorem A.2.4.

□

The Relationship Between the Operational Semantics and Standard Interpretation of Λ_T

Theorem 2.4.1

Given any program $e : \sigma$, F_ℓ, the leftmost reduction strategy, fails to terminate if and only if $\mathbf{S}\ [\![e]\!]\ \{\} = \bot_{\mathbf{S}_\sigma}$. *Moreover, if the reduction sequence terminates in some HNF e', then*

$$\mathbf{S}\ [\![e]\!]\ \{\} = \mathbf{S}\ [\![e']\!]\ \{\}.$$

Proof

We will prove this by proving the equivalent statements:

1. If the evaluation of an expression $e : \sigma$ using F_ℓ terminates in some HNF e', then $\mathbf{S}\ [\![e]\!]\ \{\} = \mathbf{S}\ [\![e']\!]\ \{\}$.
2. For any program $e : \sigma$ such that $\mathbf{S}\ [\![e]\!]\ \{\} = v$, $v \neq \bot_{\mathbf{S}_\sigma}$, the reduction of e using F_ℓ terminates with an expression e' in HNF such that $\mathbf{S}\ [\![e']\!]\ \{\} = v$.

We prove this by adapting the proof of Theorem 3.1 of [Plo77], found on pages 230–232. A key difference between our result and that of [Plo77] is that the language of the paper, PCF, has only boolean and arithmetic constants, and so the result of a program in HNF is also in normal form. This means that our statement of the adequacy result is slightly different. As well, we have a number of extra type constructors.

A sketch of the proof of this theorem is as follows.

1. This follows from the fact that we can show that if $e \rightarrow_{\beta\delta} e'$, then S $[\![e]\!]$ $\{\}$ = S $[\![e']\!]$ $\{\}$, and so for any terminating reduction sequence, $e \twoheadrightarrow_{\beta\delta} e''$, we can prove, by induction on the length of the reduction sequence, that S $[\![e]\!]$ $\{\}$ = S $[\![e'']\!]$ $\{\}$, and hence the required result holds. The proof that $e \rightarrow_{\beta\delta} e'$ implies S $[\![e]\!]$ $\{\}$ = S $[\![e']\!]$ $\{\}$ is an easy case analysis on all the ways that it is possible for $e \rightarrow_{\beta\delta} e'$.
2. To prove this we need a predicate $Comp_\sigma$ for each type σ. It is defined by:
   (a) If B is one of *bool* or *int*, and e : B is a program then e has the property $Comp_B$ if and only if S $[\![e]\!]$ $\{\} = v$, $v \neq \bot_{S_B}$ implies F_ℓ terminates with an HNF e' such that S $[\![e']\!]$ $\{\} = v$.
   (b) If e : $\sigma \rightarrow \tau$ is a closed term it has the property $Comp_{\sigma\rightarrow\tau}$ if and only if whenever e' : σ is a closed term with property $Comp_\sigma$, (e e') has property $Comp_\tau$.
   (c) If e : $\sigma_1 \times \ldots \times \sigma_k$ is a closed term it has the property $Comp_{\sigma_1\times\ldots\times\sigma_k}$ if and only if S $[\![e]\!]$ $\{\} = v$, $v \neq \bot_{S_{\sigma_1\times\ldots\times\sigma_k}}$ implies

$$e \twoheadrightarrow_{\beta\delta} \mathbf{tuple}_{(\sigma_1,\ldots,\sigma_k)}(e_1, \ldots e_k),$$

   using F_ℓ, and $\forall i \in \{1, \ldots, k\} : e_i$ has property $Comp_{\sigma_i}$.
   (d) If e : $\sigma_1 \otimes \ldots \otimes \sigma_k$ is a closed term it has the property $Comp_{\sigma_1\otimes\ldots\otimes\sigma_k}$ if and only if S $[\![e]\!]$ $\{\} = v$, $v \neq \bot_{S_{\sigma_1\otimes\ldots\otimes\sigma_k}}$ implies

$$e \twoheadrightarrow_{\beta\delta} \mathbf{tuples}_{(\sigma_1,\ldots,\sigma_k)}(e_1, \ldots e_k),$$

   using F_ℓ and $\forall i \in \{1, \ldots, k\} : e_i$ has property $Comp_{\sigma_i}$.
   (e) If e : $\sigma_1 \oplus \ldots \oplus \sigma_k$ is a closed term it has the property $Comp_{\sigma_1\oplus\ldots\oplus\sigma_k}$ if and only if S $[\![e]\!]$ $\{\} = v$, $v \neq \bot_{S_{\sigma_1\oplus\ldots\oplus\sigma_k}}$ implies

$$e \twoheadrightarrow_{\beta\delta} \mathbf{ins}_{\mathbf{i}(\sigma_1,\ldots,\sigma_k)}(e'),$$

   and e' has property $Comp_{\sigma_i}$.
   (f) If e : *lift* σ is a closed term it has the property $Comp_{(lift\ \sigma)}$ if and only if S $[\![e]\!]$ $\{\} = v$, $v \neq \bot_{S_{(lift\ \sigma)}}$

$$e \twoheadrightarrow_{\beta\delta} (\mathbf{lift}_\sigma\ e'),$$

   using F_ℓ, and e' has property $Comp_{\sigma_i}$.
   (g) If e : *list* σ is a closed term it has the property $Comp_{(list\ \sigma)}$ if and only if S $[\![e]\!]$ $\{\} = v$, $v \neq \bot_{S_{(list\ \sigma)}}$ implies

$$e \twoheadrightarrow_{\beta\delta} \mathbf{nil}_{list\ \sigma} \text{ or } e \twoheadrightarrow_{\beta\delta} \mathbf{cons}_{\sigma\rightarrow(list\ \sigma)\rightarrow(list\ \sigma)}\ e_1\ e_2,$$

   using F_ℓ, and e_1 has property $Comp_\sigma$ and e_2 has property $Comp_{(list\ \sigma)}$.
   (h) If e : *tree* σ is a closed term it has the property $Comp_{(tree\ \sigma)}$ if and only if S $[\![e]\!]$ $\{\} = v$, $v \neq \bot_{S_{(tree\ \sigma)}}$ implies

$$e \twoheadrightarrow_{\beta\delta} \mathbf{empty}_{tree\ \sigma} \text{ or } e \twoheadrightarrow_{\beta\delta} \mathbf{node}_{(tree\ \sigma)\rightarrow\sigma\rightarrow(tree\ \sigma)\rightarrow(tree\ \sigma)}\ e_1\ e_2\ e_3,$$

   using F_ℓ, and e_1 has property $Comp_{(tree\ \sigma)}$, e_2 has property $Comp_\sigma$ and e_3 has property $Comp_{(tree\ \sigma)}$.

(i) If $e : \sigma$ is an open term with free variables $x_1^{\sigma_1}, \ldots x_n^{\sigma_n}$ then it has the property $Comp_\sigma$ if and only if $e[x_1^{\sigma_1} := e_1] \ldots [x_n^{\sigma_n} := e_n]$ has the property $Comp_\sigma$ whenever $e_1, \ldots e_n$ are closed terms having properties $Comp_{\sigma_1}, \ldots,$ $Comp_{\sigma_n}$ respectively.

We will say that $e : \sigma$ is *computable* if and only if it has property $Comp_\sigma$.

To finish the proof, we need the following Lemma.

Lemma A.2.5

Every term in Λ_T *is computable.*

Proof

The proof is done by structural induction over the terms in Λ_T, and is an adaptation of Lemma 3.3 of [Plo77].

(a) Every variable x^σ is computable since any closed instantiation of the variable by a computable term is computable.

(b) Every constant is computable: This is clear for constants of ground type. The proof for the other constants follows as in case (2) of the proof of Lemma 3.3 in [Plo77]. For example, consider $\mathbf{head}_{(list\ \tau)\rightarrow\tau}$. It is enough to show $\mathbf{head}_{(list\ \tau)\rightarrow\tau}\ e$ is computable when $e : \tau$ is a closed computable term. Suppose $\mathrm{S}\ [\![\mathbf{head}_{(list\ \tau)\rightarrow\tau}\ e]\!]\ \{\} = v,\ v \neq \bot_{\mathrm{S}_\tau}$. Then we must have that $\mathrm{S}\ [\![e]\!]\ \{\} = cons\ v\ l$ for some l (from the standard interpretation of $\mathbf{head}_{(list\ \tau)\rightarrow\tau}$). Since e is computable, $e \twoheadrightarrow_{\beta\delta} e'$ using F_ℓ where e' is in HNF, and $\mathrm{S}\ [\![e']\!]\ \{\} = cons\ v\ l$. The only terms e' in Λ_T satisfying this condition are of the form $\mathbf{cons}_{\tau\rightarrow(list\ \tau)\rightarrow(list\ \tau)}\ e_1\ e_2$ where $\mathrm{S}\ [\![e_1]\!]\ \{\} = v$ and $\mathrm{S}\ [\![e_2]\!]\ \{\} = l$, and the δ-rule for $\mathbf{head}_{(list\ \tau)\rightarrow\tau}$ states that

$$\mathbf{head}_{(list\ \tau)\rightarrow\tau}\ (\mathbf{cons}_{\tau\rightarrow(list\ \tau)\rightarrow(list\ \tau)}\ e_1\ e_2) \rightarrow_\delta e_1$$

and so we have that $\mathbf{head}_{(list\ \tau)\rightarrow\tau}\ e \twoheadrightarrow_{\beta\delta} e_1$ and $\mathrm{S}\ [\![e_1]\!]\ \{\} = v$ as required.

(c) If $e_1 : \sigma \rightarrow \tau$ and $e_2 : \sigma$ are computable, then so is $(e_1\ e_2)$: This is case (3) of the proof of Lemma 3.3 in [Plo77].

(d) If $e : \tau$ is computable so is $\lambda x^\sigma.e$: This is case (4) of the proof of Lemma 3.3 in [Plo77].

(e) Each $\mathbf{fix}_{(\sigma\rightarrow\sigma)\rightarrow\sigma}$ is computable: This is case (5) of the proof of Lemma 3.3 in [Plo77].

(f) If e_1 and e_2 are computable, then so is $\mathbf{let}\ x^\sigma = e_1\ \mathbf{in}\ e_2$: We prove it for when the term $\mathbf{let}\ x^\sigma = e_1\ \mathbf{in}\ e_2$ is closed. The case for when it is not closed follows from the case for when it is, using the same observations made for the case of application in [Plo77]. There are two cases to consider:

i. F_ℓ fails to terminate when evaluating e_1: By the induction hypothesis this happens if and only if $(\mathrm{S}\ [\![e_1]\!]\ \rho^{\mathrm{S}}) = \bot_{\mathrm{S}_\sigma}$, and so

$$\mathrm{S}\ [\![(\mathbf{let}\ x^\sigma = e_1\ \mathbf{in}\ e_2) : \tau]\!]\ \rho^{\mathrm{S}} = \bot_{\mathrm{S}_\tau}$$

by definition, and so the term is computable.

ii. F_ℓ terminates when evaluating e_1: This means that $e_1 \twoheadrightarrow_{\beta\delta} e_1'$ using F_ℓ, where e_1' is in HNF. Now,

$$\mathbf{let}\ x^\sigma = e_1'\ \mathbf{in}\ e_2 \rightarrow_\delta e_2[x^\sigma := e_1']$$

since e_1' is in HNF, and so the term $\mathbf{let}\ x^\sigma = e_1\ \mathbf{in}\ e_2$ is computable if $e_2[x^\sigma := e_1']$ is, which it is by the induction hypothesis.

(g) If $\forall i \in \{1,\ldots,k\} : e_i : \sigma_i$ is computable, then $\mathbf{tuple}_{(\sigma_1,\ldots,\sigma_k)}(e_1,\ldots e_k)$ is computable: For closed terms, this follows directly from the definition of computability for product types. For open terms, the similar observations can be made as in applications, case (3) of [Plo77], and the result follows from the definition of computability for product types.

The cases for smash products, smash sums, lifting, lists and trees follow as for products.

□

The required result then follows as any program $e : \sigma$ must be computable, and for each of the possible types that a program can take, being computable implies the required result. For example, if $e : \sigma_1 \otimes \ldots \otimes \sigma_k$ and

$$\mathrm{S}\ [\![e]\!]\ \{\} =< s_1,\ldots,s_k > \text{ where } \forall i \in \{1,\ldots,k\} : s_i \neq \bot_{\mathrm{S}_{\sigma_i}},$$

that is, $\mathrm{S}\ [\![e]\!]\ \{\} \neq \bot_{\mathrm{S}_{\sigma_1 \otimes \ldots \otimes \sigma_k}}$, then e having property $Comp_{\sigma_1 \otimes \ldots \otimes \sigma_k}$ means that $e \twoheadrightarrow_{\beta\delta} \mathbf{tuples}_{(\sigma_1,\ldots,\sigma_k)}(e_1,\ldots,e_k)$ using F_ℓ and that each e_i, for $i \in \{1,\ldots,k\}$, has property $Comp_{\sigma_i}$. If $\forall i \in \{1,\ldots,k\}$, e_i is in HNF, then we are done because $\mathbf{tuples}_{(\sigma_1,\ldots,\sigma_k)}(e_1,\ldots,e_k)$ is in HNF, and, since $\beta\delta$-reduction preserves semantics,

$$\mathrm{S}\ [\![\mathbf{tuples}_{(\sigma_1,\ldots,\sigma_k)}(e_1,\ldots,e_k)]\!]\ \rho^{\mathrm{S}} =< s_1,\ldots,s_k >$$

as required. If some e_i is not in HNF, then

$$\begin{array}{ll}\mathbf{tuples}_{(\sigma_1,\ldots,\sigma_k)}(e_1,\ldots,e_k) \rightarrow_\delta & \mathbf{let}\ x_1 = e_1\ \mathbf{in} \\ & \quad \mathbf{let}\ x_2 = e_2\ \mathbf{in} \\ & \quad\quad \ddots \\ & \quad\quad\quad \mathbf{let}\ x_k = e_k\ \mathbf{in}\ \mathbf{tuples}_{(\sigma_1,\ldots,\sigma_k)}(x_1,\ldots,x_k)\end{array}$$

For all $i \in \{1,\ldots,k\}$, from the computability of e_i, since $\mathrm{S}\ [\![e_i]\!]\ \rho^{\mathrm{S}} = s_i \neq \bot_{\mathrm{S}_{\sigma_i}}$, the evaluation of each of the e_i using F_ℓ results in an expression e_i' which is in HNF. Using the δ-rule for let-expressions k times, we get

$$\mathbf{tuples}_{(\sigma_1,\ldots,\sigma_k)}(e_1,\ldots,e_k) \twoheadrightarrow_{\beta\delta} \mathbf{tuples}_{(\sigma_1,\ldots,\sigma_k)}(e_1',\ldots,e_k')$$

which is in HNF, and

$$\mathrm{S}\ [\![e]\!]\ \rho^{\mathrm{S}} =< s_1,\ldots,s_k >= \mathrm{S}\ [\![\mathbf{tuples}_{(\sigma_1,\ldots,\sigma_k)}(e_1',\ldots,e_k')]\!]\ \rho^{\mathrm{S}}$$

as required, since $\beta\delta$-reduction preserves semantics.

□

We can now see the reason for δ-rules like

$$\mathbf{head}_{(list\ \tau)\to\tau}\ \mathbf{nil}_{(list\ \tau)} \to_\delta \mathbf{head}_{(list\ \tau)\to\tau}\ \mathbf{nil}_{(list\ \tau)}.$$

They are needed firstly because each δ-reduction step must preserve the standard interpretation of a term. Secondly,

$$\mathbf{S}\ [\![\mathbf{head}_{(list\ \tau)\to\tau}\ \mathbf{nil}_{(list\ \tau)}]\!]\ \rho^{\mathbf{S}} = \bot_{\mathbf{S}_\tau}$$

and so the reduction sequence evaluating $\mathbf{head}_{(list\ \tau)\to\tau}\ \mathbf{nil}_{(list\ \tau)}$ must fail to terminate, which it clearly does with the δ-rule we have given above.

A.3 Proofs From Chapter 3

Lemma A.3.1

If $f \in \mathbf{I}_\sigma \to \mathbf{I}_\tau$ is strict and $\mathbf{I}_\tau$ is a complete lattice, then $\bigsqcup \circ \mathbf{P}f$ is strict.

Proof

$$\begin{array}{rcll} (\bigsqcup \circ \mathbf{P}f)\ \{\bot_{\mathbf{I}_\sigma}\} & = & \bigsqcup\{f\ x \mid x \in \{\bot_{\mathbf{I}_\sigma}\}\}^* & \text{definition of } \mathbf{P} \text{ on morphisms} \\ & = & \bigsqcup\{f\ \bot_{\mathbf{I}_\sigma}\}^* & \\ & = & \bigsqcup\{\bot_{\mathbf{I}_\tau}\}^* & \text{since } f \text{ is strict} \\ & = & \bot_{\mathbf{I}} & \text{(P10)} \end{array}$$

□

Lemma 3.2.4

If for each of the types bool, int, and if τ is any type, for (list τ) and (tree τ), strict and continuous abstraction maps from the standard interpretation of the type to the abstract interpretation of the type are given, then for all types σ

1. *α_σ and Abs_σ are continuous.*
2. *α_σ and Abs_σ are strict.*
3. *γ_σ is well-defined and continuous.*

Proof

We prove this by induction on the type structure.

1. α_{bool} and α_{int} are continuous by the condition of the lemma. Abs_{bool} and Abs_{int} are continuous because $\bigsqcup$ is continuous, $\mathbf{P}f$ is continuous if f is (P2), and the composition of continuous functions is continuous.

2. This holds for *bool* and *int* by the conditions of the lemma and Lemma A.3.1.
3. If B is one of *bool* and *int*, we have to prove that γ_B is well-defined and monotonic, for its source is a finite domain and hence is continuous if it is monotonic.

   To prove well definedness, we must show that $\{T | Abs_B\ T \sqsubseteq \overline{a}\}$ is a non-empty Scott-closed subset of $\mathbf{PPS}_B$. Since we have that Abs_B is strict (part 2 of induction), we have that the set $\{T | Abs_B\ T \sqsubseteq \overline{a}\}$ is non-empty. Denoting $\{T | Abs_B\ T \sqsubseteq \overline{a}\}$ by Θ, to show that Θ is Scott-closed we need to show that *(a)* Θ is left-closed and that *(b)* Θ is closed under least upper bounds of directed sets. The first is true since if $Y \sqsubseteq X \in \Theta$, then $Abs_B\ Y \sqsubseteq Abs_B\ X \sqsubseteq \overline{a}$ and so $Y \in \Theta$. The second is true for if $\Delta \subseteq \Theta$ is a directed set, then $Abs_B(\bigsqcup \Delta) = \bigsqcup\{Abs_B\ X | X \in \Delta\}$ (continuity of Abs_B) and since $Abs_B\ X \sqsubseteq \overline{a}$ for all $X \in \Delta$, $\bigsqcup\{Abs_B\ X | X \in \Delta\} \sqsubseteq \overline{a}$.

   To show monotonicity of γ_B, let $s_1, s_2 \in \mathbf{A}_B$, $s_1 \sqsubseteq s_2$. Then

   $$\gamma_B\ s_1 = \bigcup\{T \mid Abs_B\ T \sqsubseteq s_1\}$$

   and

   $$\gamma_B\ s_2 = \bigcup\{T | Abs_B\ T \sqsubseteq s_2\}.$$

   Clearly, $\{T | Abs_B\ T \sqsubseteq s_1\} \subseteq \{T | Abs_B\ T \sqsubseteq s_2\}$ since $s_1 \sqsubseteq s_2$ and so $(\gamma_B\ s_1) \sqsubseteq (\gamma_B\ s_2)$. Thus γ_B is monotonic and hence continuous.

Assuming (1) to (4) are true for types σ, σ_1, ..., σ_k, and τ we prove them for each of the constructed types.

1. $\alpha_{\sigma\to\tau}\ f(= Abs_\tau \circ \mathbf{P}f \circ \gamma_\sigma)$ is continuous because by the induction hypothesis it is the composition of continuous functions, $\alpha_{\sigma_1\times\ldots\times\sigma_k}$, $\alpha_{\sigma_1\otimes\ldots\otimes\sigma_k}$, and $\alpha_{lift\ \sigma}$ are continuous because they are respectively the product, smash product and lifting of what are, by the induction hypothesis, continuous functions, and $\alpha_{(list\ \tau)}$ and $\alpha_{(tree\ \tau)}$ are continuous by a condition of the Lemma. For $\alpha_{\sigma_1\oplus\ldots\oplus\sigma_k}$, any argument chain must either be of the form:

   $$\{\bot_{\mathbf{S}_{\sigma_1\oplus\ldots\oplus\sigma_k}}, in_i\ e_1, in_i\ e_2, \ldots\}$$

   or

   $$\{in_i\ e_1, in_i\ e_2, \ldots\}$$

   for some i, where the e_k form a chain in $\mathbf{S}_{\sigma_i}$, and then the continuity of $\alpha_{\sigma_1\oplus\ldots\oplus\sigma_k}$ follows from the continuity of α_{σ_i}.

   The continuity of Abs_σ follows as for the base case.
2. For $\alpha_{\sigma\to\tau}$ we make the following calculation, where $\overline{s} \in \mathbf{A}_\sigma$:

   $$\begin{aligned}(\alpha_{\sigma\to\tau}\ \bot_{\mathbf{S}_{\sigma\to\tau}})\ \overline{s} &= (\bigsqcup \circ \mathbf{P}\ \alpha_\tau \circ \mathbf{P}(\bot_{\mathbf{S}_{\sigma\to\tau}}) \circ \gamma_\sigma)\ \overline{s} \\ &= (\bigsqcup \circ \mathbf{P}(\alpha_\tau \circ \bot_{\mathbf{S}_{\sigma\to\tau}}) \circ \gamma_\sigma)\ \overline{s} \quad \text{(P3)} \\ &= (\bigsqcup \circ \mathbf{P}(\alpha_\tau \circ \bot_{\mathbf{S}_{\sigma\to\tau}}))\ \{s | s \in \gamma_\sigma\ \overline{s}\}\end{aligned}$$

$$
\begin{aligned}
&= \bigsqcup\{\alpha_\tau(\bot_{S_{\sigma\to\tau}}\ s) | s \in \gamma_\sigma\ \overline{s}\} \\
&\quad \text{definition of } \mathbf{P} \text{ on morphisms and (P11)} \\
&= \bigsqcup\{\alpha_\tau\ \bot_{S_\tau}\} \\
&= \bigsqcup\{\bot_{A_\tau}\} \qquad \text{by induction hypothesis (2)} \\
&= \bot_{A_\tau}
\end{aligned}
$$

and so $\alpha_{\sigma\to\tau}\ \bot_{S_{\sigma\to\tau}} = \bot_{A_{\sigma\to\tau}}$.

For $\alpha_{\sigma_1\times\ldots\times\sigma_k}$ we make the following calculation:

$$
\begin{aligned}
\alpha_{\sigma_1\times\ldots\times\sigma_k}\ \bot_{S_{\sigma_1\times\ldots\times\sigma_k}} &= \alpha_{\sigma_1\times\ldots\times\sigma_k}\ (\bot_{S_{\sigma_1}},\ldots,\bot_{S_{\sigma_k}}) \\
&= (\alpha_{\sigma_1}\ \bot_{S_{\sigma_1}},\ldots,\alpha_{\sigma_k}\ \bot_{S_{\sigma_k}}) \\
&= (\bot_{A_{\sigma_1}},\ldots,\bot_{A_{\sigma_k}}) \qquad \text{by induction hypothesis (2)} \\
&= \bot_{A_{\sigma_1\times\ldots\times\sigma_k}}
\end{aligned}
$$

The strictness of $\alpha_{\sigma_1\otimes\ldots\otimes\sigma_k}$, $\alpha_{\sigma_1\oplus\ldots\oplus\sigma_k}$, and $\alpha_{lift\ \sigma}$ is immediate from their definitions, and the strictness of $\alpha_{(list\ \tau)}$ and $\alpha_{(tree\ \tau)}$ is a condition of the Lemma The result holds for Abs_σ by Lemma A.3.1.

3. Follows as for the base case.

□

Proposition 3.2.5

For all types σ, $(\alpha_\sigma\ s) \sqsubseteq \overline{s}$ if and only if $s \in (\gamma_\sigma\ \overline{s})$.

Proof

($\Rightarrow$) Suppose $\alpha_\sigma\ s \sqsubseteq \overline{s}$. Then

$$
\begin{aligned}
\gamma_\sigma\ \overline{s} &= \bigcup\{T | (Abs_\sigma\ T) \sqsubseteq \overline{s}\} \\
&= \bigcup\{T | \bigsqcup\{(\alpha_\sigma\ t) | t \in T\} \sqsubseteq \overline{s}\} \\
&\quad \text{definition of } Abs_\sigma \text{ and definition of } \mathbf{P} \text{ on morphisms}
\end{aligned}
$$

and certainly $\bigsqcup\{(\alpha_\sigma\ t) | t \in \{\!\{s\}\!\}\} \sqsubseteq \overline{s}$ since $(\alpha_\sigma\ s) \sqsubseteq \overline{s}$, and thus $s \in (\gamma_\sigma\ \overline{s})$.

$$
\begin{aligned}
(\Leftarrow)\quad \gamma_\sigma\ \overline{s} &= \bigcup\{S | (Abs_\sigma\ S) \sqsubseteq \overline{s}\} \\
&= \bigcup\{S | \bigsqcup\{(\alpha_\sigma\ s) | s \in S\} \sqsubseteq \overline{s}\} \\
&\quad \text{definition of } Abs_\sigma \text{ and definition of } \mathbf{P} \text{ on morphisms} \\
&= \bigcup\{S | \forall s \in S : (\alpha_\sigma\ s) \sqsubseteq \overline{s}\} \\
&= \{s | (\alpha_\sigma\ s) \sqsubseteq \overline{s}\}
\end{aligned}
$$

and so $s \in (\gamma_\sigma\ \overline{s})$ only if $(\alpha_\sigma\ s) \sqsubseteq \overline{s}$.

□

Proposition 3.2.6

Suppose $f \in \mathbf{S}_{\sigma_1} \to \ldots \to \mathbf{S}_{\sigma_n} \to \mathbf{S}_\tau$. *Then*

1. $(\alpha_{\sigma_1 \to \ldots \to \sigma_n \to \tau}\ f)\ \overline{s}_1\ \ldots\ \overline{s}_k = \bigsqcup\{\alpha_\tau(f\ s_1 \quad s_n) | \forall i \in \{1,\ldots,n\} : (\alpha_{\sigma_i}\ s_i) \sqsubseteq \overline{s}_i\}$
2. $(\alpha_{\sigma_1 \to \ldots \to \sigma_n \to \tau}\ f)\ \overline{s}_1 \quad \overline{s}_k = \bigsqcup\{\alpha_\tau(f\ s_1 \quad s_n) | \forall i \in \{1,\ldots,n\} : s_i \in (\gamma_{\sigma_i}\ \overline{s}_i)\}$.

Proof

1. Follows from the trivial expansion of the definition of $(\alpha_{\sigma_1 \to \ldots \to \sigma_k \to \tau}\ f)\ \overline{s}_1\ \ldots\ \overline{s}_k$, noting (P10), and using Proposition 3.2.5.
2. Follows from the trivial expansion of the definition of $(\alpha_{\sigma_1 \to \ldots \to \sigma_k \to \tau}\ f)\ \overline{s}_1\ \ldots\ \overline{s}_k$, noting (P10).

□

Proposition 3.2.7

For all types σ, $\gamma_\sigma\ \overline{s} = \{s | (\alpha_\sigma\ s) \sqsubseteq \overline{s}\}$.

Proof

This was proved as part of the proof of Proposition 3.2.5.

□

Proposition 3.2.8

For all types $\sigma, \sigma_1, \ldots, \sigma_k$,

1. $\gamma_{\sigma_1 \times \ldots \times \sigma_k}\ (\overline{s_1}, \ldots, \overline{s_k}) = (\gamma_{\sigma_1}\ \overline{s_1}) \times \ldots \times (\gamma_{\sigma_k}\ \overline{s_k})$.
2. $\gamma_{\sigma_1 \otimes \ldots \otimes \sigma_k}\ < \overline{s_1}, \ldots, \overline{s_k} >= (\gamma_{\sigma_1}\ \overline{s_1}) \otimes \ldots \otimes (\gamma_{\sigma_k}\ \overline{s_k})$.
3. $\gamma_{\sigma_1 \oplus \ldots \oplus \sigma_k}\ (\overline{s_1}, \ldots, \overline{s_k}) = inject\ (\gamma_{\sigma_1}\ \overline{s_1}, \ldots, \gamma_{\sigma_k}\ \overline{s_k})$ *where*

$$inject\ (S_1, \ldots, S_k) = \{mk\_sum_1\ s_1 | s_1 \in S_1\} \bigcup \ldots \bigcup \{mk\_sum_k\ s_k | s_k \in S_k\}$$

4. $\gamma_{(lift\ \sigma)}\ \overline{a} = \begin{cases} \{\bot_{\mathbf{S}_{(lift\ \sigma)}}\} & if\ \overline{a} = \bot_{\mathbf{A}_{(lift\ \sigma)}} \\ (\mathbf{P}\ lift)\ (\gamma_\sigma\ \overline{s}) & if\ \overline{a} = (0, \overline{s}) \end{cases}$

Proof

1. $\gamma_{\sigma_1 \times \ldots \times \sigma_k}\ (\bar{s}_1, \ldots, \bar{s}_k)$
   $= \{(s_1, \ldots, s_k) | (\alpha_{\sigma_1 \times \ldots \times \sigma_k}\ (s_1, \ldots, s_k)) \sqsubseteq (\bar{s}_1, \ldots, \bar{s}_k)\}$
   Proposition 3.2.6(1)
   $= \{(s_1, \ldots, s_k) | \forall i \in \{1, \ldots, k\} : (\alpha_{\sigma_i}\ s_i) \sqsubseteq \bar{s}_i\}$
   definition of $\alpha_{\sigma_1 \times \ldots \times \sigma_k}$
   $= \{(s_1, \ldots, s_k) | \forall i \in \{1, \ldots, k\} : s_i \in (\gamma_{s_i}\ \bar{s}_i)\}$
   Proposition 3.2.5
   $= (\gamma_{\sigma_1}\ \bar{s}_1) \times \ldots \times (\gamma_{\sigma_k}\ \bar{s}_k)$

2. $\gamma_{\sigma_1 \otimes \ldots \otimes \sigma_k}\ < \bar{s}_1, \ldots, \bar{s}_k >$
   $= \{< s_1, \ldots, s_k > | (\alpha_{\sigma_1 \otimes \ldots \otimes \sigma_k}\ < s_1, \ldots, s_k >) \sqsubseteq < \bar{s}_1, \ldots, \bar{s}_k >\} \cup \{\bot_{\mathbf{S}_{\sigma_1 \otimes \ldots \otimes \sigma_k}}\}$
   where $\forall i \in \{1, \ldots, k\} : s_i \neq \bot_{\mathbf{S}_{\sigma_i}}$
   Proposition 3.2.6(1)
   $= \{< s_1, \ldots, s_k > | \forall i \in \{1, \ldots, k\} : (\alpha_{\sigma_i}\ s_i) \sqsubseteq \bar{s}_i, s_i \neq \bot_{\mathbf{S}_{\sigma_i}}\} \cup \{\bot_{\mathbf{S}_{\sigma_1 \otimes \ldots \otimes \sigma_k}}\}$
   definition of $\alpha_{\sigma_1 \otimes \ldots \otimes \sigma_k}$
   $= \{< s_1, \ldots, s_k > | \forall i \in \{1, \ldots, k\} : s_i \in (\gamma_{\sigma_i}\ \bar{s}_i), s_i \neq \bot_{\mathbf{S}_{\sigma_i}}\} \cup \{\bot_{\mathbf{S}_{\sigma_1 \otimes \ldots \otimes \sigma_k}}\}$
   Proposition 3.2.5
   $= (\gamma_{\sigma_1}\ \bar{s}_1) \otimes \ldots \otimes (\gamma_{\sigma_k}\ \bar{s}_k)$

3. $\gamma_{\sigma_1 \oplus \ldots \oplus \sigma_k}\ (\bar{s}_1, \ldots, \bar{s}_k)$
   $= \{s | (\alpha_{\sigma_1 \oplus \ldots \oplus \sigma_k}\ s) \sqsubseteq (\bar{s}_1, \ldots, \bar{s}_k)\}$ Proposition 3.2.7
   $= \{mk\_sum_1\ s_1 | (\alpha_{\sigma_1}\ s_1) \sqsubseteq \bar{s}_1\} \cup \ldots \cup \{mk\_sum_k\ s_k | (\alpha_{\sigma_k}\ s_k) \sqsubseteq \bar{s}_k\}$
   $= inject\ (\{s_1 | (\alpha_{\sigma_1}\ s_1) \sqsubseteq \bar{s}_1\}, \ldots, \{s_k | (\alpha_{\sigma_k}\ s_k) \sqsubseteq \bar{s}_k\})$
   $= inject\ (\gamma_{\sigma_1}\ \bar{s}_1, \ldots, \gamma_{\sigma_k}\ \bar{s}_k)$ Proposition 3.2.7

4. $\gamma_{(lift\ \sigma)}\ \bot_{\mathbf{A}_{(lift\ \sigma)}} = \{s | (\alpha_{(lift\ \sigma)}\ s) \sqsubseteq \bot_{\mathbf{A}_{(lift\ \sigma)}}\} = \{\bot_{\mathbf{S}_{(lift\ \sigma)}}\}$ by the definition of $\alpha_{(lift\ \sigma)}$.
   Let $(0, \bar{s})$ be any other element of $\mathbf{A}_{(lift\ \sigma)}$. Then

$$\begin{aligned}
\gamma_{(lift\ \sigma)}\ (0, \bar{s}) &= \{(0, s) | (\alpha_{(lift\ \sigma)}\ (0, s) \sqsubseteq (0, \bar{s}))\} \bigcup \{\bot_{\mathbf{S}_{(lift\ \sigma)}}\} \\
&\quad \text{Proposition 3.2.7} \\
&= \{(0, s) | (0, \alpha_\sigma\ s) \sqsubseteq (0, \bar{s})\} \bigcup \{\bot_{\mathbf{S}_{(lift\ \sigma)}}\} \\
&\quad \text{Definition of } \alpha_{(lift\ \sigma)} \\
&= \{lift\ s | (\alpha_\sigma\ s) \sqsubseteq \bar{s}\} \bigcup \{\bot_{\mathbf{S}_{(lift\ \sigma)}}\} \\
&= (\mathbf{P}\ lift)\ \{s | (\alpha_\sigma\ s) \sqsubseteq \bar{s}\} \qquad (A.1) \\
&= (\mathbf{P}\ lift)\ (\gamma_\sigma\ \bar{s}) \\
&\quad \text{Proposition 3.2.7}
\end{aligned}$$

The step labelled A.1 is true since $\{s | (\alpha_\sigma\ s) \sqsubseteq \bar{s}\}$ is Scott-closed, as it is $(\gamma_\sigma\ \bar{s})$ (Proposition 3.2.7), and so the Scott-closure of applying $lift$ to everything in the set just adds $\bot_{\mathbf{S}_{(lift\ \sigma)}}$.

□

Lemma A.3.2

If $f \in \mathbf{I}_\sigma \to \mathbf{I}_\tau$ is bottom-reflecting and $\mathbf{I}_\tau$ is a complete lattice, then $\bigsqcup \circ \mathbf{P}f$ is bottom-reflecting.

Proof

Suppose $\bigsqcup\{f\ s|s \in S\}^* = (\bigsqcup \circ \mathbf{P}f)\ S = \bot_{\mathbf{I}_\tau}$. Then we must have for each $s \in S$ that $f\ s = \bot_{\mathbf{I}_\tau}$ (P10), and since f is bottom-reflecting, this means that $s = \bot_{\mathbf{I}_\sigma}$ and so $S = \{\bot_{\mathbf{I}_\sigma}\} = \bot_{\mathbf{P}\ \mathbf{I}_\sigma}$.

□

Lemma 3.2.9

If for each of the types bool, int, and if τ is any type, for (list τ) and (tree τ) the abstraction maps are bottom-reflecting, then α_σ and Abs_σ are bottom-reflecting for each type σ.

Proof

We prove this by induction over the type structure, where the base case is true for α_{bool} and α_{int} by hypothesis and for Abs_{bool} and Abs_{int} by Lemma A.3.2.

1. Assume that the result holds for σ and τ.

$$\begin{aligned} \alpha_{\sigma\to\tau}\ f = \bot_{\mathbf{A}_{\sigma\to\tau}} &\Rightarrow \alpha_{\sigma\to\tau}\ f\ \top_{\mathbf{A}_\sigma} = \bot_{\mathbf{A}_\tau} \\ &\Rightarrow \bigsqcup\{\alpha_\tau\ (f\ s)|s \in (\gamma_\sigma\ \top_{\mathbf{A}_\sigma})\} = \bot_{\mathbf{A}_\tau}\ \text{Proposition 3.2.6(2)} \\ &\Rightarrow \alpha_\tau\ (f\ s) = \bot_{\mathbf{A}_\tau} \forall s \in \mathbf{S}_\sigma \end{aligned}$$

   Since by the induction hypothesis, α_τ is bottom-reflecting, we have that for all $s \in \mathbf{S}_\sigma$

$$f\ s = \bot_{\mathbf{S}_\tau} \Rightarrow f = \bot_{\mathbf{S}_{\sigma\to\tau}}$$

2. Assume that the result holds for $\sigma_1, \ldots, \sigma_k$.

$$\alpha_{\sigma_1 \times \ldots \times \sigma_k}\ (d_1, \ldots, d_k) = (\alpha_{\sigma_1}\ d_1, \ldots, \alpha_{\sigma_k}\ d_k)$$

   which is $(\bot_{\mathbf{A}_{\sigma_1}}, \ldots, \bot_{\mathbf{A}_{\sigma_k}})$ only if $\forall i \in \{1, \ldots k\} : (\alpha_{\sigma_i}\ d_i) = \bot_{\mathbf{A}_{\sigma_i}}$. Since, by the induction hypothesis, α_{σ_i} is bottom-reflecting, this can only be true if $\forall i \in \{1, \ldots k\} : d_i = \bot_{\mathbf{S}_{\sigma_i}}$, and so $\alpha_{\sigma_1 \times \ldots \times \sigma_k}$ is bottom-reflecting.

3. Assume that the result holds for $\sigma_1, \ldots, \sigma_k$. The only non-bottom elements of $\mathbf{S}_{\sigma_1 \otimes \ldots \otimes \sigma_k}$ are of the form $< d_1, \ldots, d_k >$ where $\forall i \in \{1, \ldots, k\} : d_i \neq \bot_{\mathbf{S}_{\sigma_i}}$. Now $\alpha_{\sigma_1 \otimes \ldots \otimes \sigma_k}\ < d_1, \ldots, d_k >= \bot_{\mathbf{A}_{\sigma_1 \otimes \ldots \otimes \sigma_k}}$ only if $\exists i \in \{1, \ldots, k\} : (\alpha_{\sigma_i}\ d_i) = \bot_{\mathbf{A}_{\sigma_i}}$, but since α_{σ_i} is bottom-reflecting, this can hold only if $d_i = \bot_{\mathbf{S}_{\sigma_i}}$, which is not true. Combined with the fact that $\alpha_{\sigma_1 \otimes \ldots \otimes \sigma_k}$ is strict, we can therefore conclude that $\alpha_{\sigma_1 \otimes \ldots \otimes \sigma_k}$ is bottom-reflecting.

4. Assume that the result holds for $\sigma_1, \ldots, \sigma_k$. Let $(ins_i\ e)$ be an arbitrary, non-bottom element of $\mathbf{S}_{\sigma_1 \oplus \ldots \oplus \sigma_k}$, which means that $e \neq \bot_{\mathbf{S}_{\sigma_i}}$. Then

$$\alpha_{\sigma_1 \oplus \ldots \oplus \sigma_k}\ (ins_i\ e) = (\bot_{\mathbf{A}_{\sigma_1}}, \ldots, \bot_{\mathbf{A}_{\sigma_{i-1}}}, \alpha_{\sigma_i}\ e, \bot_{\mathbf{A}_{\sigma_{i+1}}}, \ldots, \bot_{\mathbf{A}_{\sigma_k}})$$

which can only be $\bot_{\mathbf{A}_{\sigma_1 \oplus \ldots \oplus \sigma_k}}$ if $\alpha_{\sigma_i}\ e = \bot_{\mathbf{A}_{\sigma_i}}$, which does not hold since α_{σ_i} is bottom-reflecting and $e \neq \bot_{\mathbf{S}_{\sigma_i}}$. The result follows because $\alpha_{\sigma_1 \oplus \ldots \oplus \sigma_k}$ is also strict.

5. Assume that the result holds for σ. If $d \in \mathbf{S}_{lift\ \sigma}$ and $d \neq \bot_{\mathbf{S}_{lift\ \sigma}}$, then $d = (0, d')$ for some $d' \in \mathbf{S}_\sigma$. Then

$$\begin{aligned} \alpha_{lift\ \sigma}\ d &= \alpha_{lift\ \sigma}\ (0, d') \\ &= (0, \alpha_\sigma\ d') \\ &\neq \bot_{\mathbf{A}_{lift\ \sigma}} \end{aligned}$$

The result follows because $\alpha_{lift\ \sigma}$ is strict.

6. $\alpha_{(list\ \tau)}$ and $\alpha_{(tree\ \tau)}$ are bottom-reflecting by a condition on the lemma.

Abs_σ is $\bot$-reflecting by Lemma A.3.2.

□

Lemma 3.2.10

If for all types σ, α_σ is strict and bottom-reflecting, then γ_σ is strict for all types σ, that is, $\gamma_\sigma\ \bot_{\mathbf{A}_\sigma} = \bot_{\mathbf{P}\ \mathbf{S}_\sigma} = \{\bot_{\mathbf{S}_\sigma}\}$.

Proof

$$\begin{aligned} \gamma_\sigma\ \bot_{\mathbf{A}_\sigma} &= \bigcup\{T \mid Abs_\sigma\ T \sqsubseteq \bot_{\mathbf{A}_\sigma}\} \\ &= \bigcup\{T \mid Abs_\sigma\ T = \bot_{\mathbf{A}_\sigma}\} \\ &= \bigcup\{\{\bot_{\mathbf{S}_\sigma}\}\} \quad \text{since from Lemma 3.2.9 } Abs_\sigma \text{ is bottom-reflecting} \\ &= \{\bot_{\mathbf{S}_\sigma}\} \end{aligned}$$

□

Proposition 3.2.11

Abs_σ and γ_σ are a pair of adjoined functions. i.e.

1. *$\gamma_\sigma \circ Abs_\sigma \sqsupseteq id_{\mathbf{P}\ \mathbf{S}_\sigma}$; and*
2. *$Abs_\sigma \circ \gamma_\sigma \sqsubseteq id_{\mathbf{A}_\sigma}$.*

Proof

1. Let $S \in \mathbf{PS}_\sigma$.

$$\gamma_\sigma(Abs_\sigma\ S) = \bigcup\{T | Abs_\sigma\ T \sqsubseteq Abs_\sigma\ S\}$$

and $Abs_\sigma\ S \sqsubseteq Abs_\sigma\ S$, so $S \in \{T | Abs_\sigma\ T \sqsubseteq Abs_\sigma\ S\}$. Hence the result follows since $\sqsupseteq$ is just $\supseteq$ in the Hoare powerdomain.

2. Let $\overline{s} \in \mathbf{A}_\sigma$.

$$\begin{array}{rcll} (Abs_\sigma \circ \gamma_\sigma)\ \overline{s} & = & (\bigsqcup \circ \mathbf{P}\alpha_\sigma \circ \gamma_\sigma)\ \overline{s} & \\ & = & \bigsqcup\{\alpha_\sigma\ s | s \in (\gamma_\sigma\ \overline{s})\} & \text{definition of } \mathbf{P} \text{ on functions and (P11)} \\ & = & \bigsqcup\{\alpha_\sigma\ s | (\alpha_\sigma\ s) \sqsubseteq \overline{s}\} & \text{Proposition 3.2.5} \\ & \sqsubseteq & \overline{s} & \end{array}$$

□

Proposition 3.2.12

For all types σ, α_σ is a semi-homomorphism of function application.

Proof

$$\begin{array}{rcll} \alpha_{\sigma\to\tau}\ f \circ \alpha_\sigma & = & \bigsqcup \circ \mathbf{P}\alpha_\tau \circ \mathbf{P}f \circ \gamma_\sigma \circ \alpha_\sigma & \\ & = & \bigsqcup \circ \mathbf{P}\alpha_\tau \circ \mathbf{P}f \circ \gamma_\sigma \circ \bigsqcup \circ \{\!\{.\}\!\} \circ \alpha_\sigma & \text{(P10)} \\ & = & \bigsqcup \circ \mathbf{P}\alpha_\tau \circ \mathbf{P}f \circ \gamma_\sigma \circ \bigsqcup \circ \mathbf{P}\alpha_\sigma \circ \{\!\{.\}\!\} & \text{(P6)} \quad . \\ & = & \bigsqcup \circ \mathbf{P}\alpha_\tau \circ \mathbf{P}f \circ \gamma_\sigma \circ Abs_\sigma \circ \{\!\{.\}\!\} & \text{definition of } Abs_\sigma \\ & \sqsupseteq & \bigsqcup \circ \mathbf{P}\alpha_\tau \circ \mathbf{P}f \circ \{\!\{.\}\!\} & \text{Proposition 3.2.11(1)} \\ & = & \bigsqcup \circ \mathbf{P}(\alpha_\tau \circ f) \circ \{\!\{.\}\!\} & \text{(P3)} \\ & = & \bigsqcup \circ \{\!\{.\}\!\} \circ \alpha_\tau \circ f & \text{(P6)} \\ & = & \alpha_\tau \circ f & \text{(P10)} \end{array}$$

□

Proposition 3.2.13

Taking fixed points is a semi-homomorphism of abstraction, that is,

$$(\lambda F \epsilon \mathbf{A}_{\sigma\to\sigma}. \bigsqcup_{i\geq 0} F^i \perp_{\mathbf{A}_\sigma}) \circ \alpha_{\sigma\to\sigma} \sqsupseteq \alpha_\sigma \circ (\lambda F \epsilon \mathbf{S}_{\sigma\to\sigma}. \bigsqcup_{i\geq 0} F^i \perp_{\mathbf{S}_\sigma})$$

Proof

Let $f \in \mathbf{S}_{\sigma\to\sigma}$, and let

$$h_i = (\alpha_{\sigma\to\sigma}\ f)^i\ \bot_{\mathbf{A}_\sigma}$$

and

$$f_i = f^i\ \bot_{\mathbf{S}_\sigma}.$$

Then $h_0 = \bot_{\mathbf{A}_\sigma} = \alpha_\sigma\ \bot_{\mathbf{S}_\sigma}$ (since by Lemma 3.2.4(1) the abstraction maps for all types are strict) $= \alpha_\sigma\ f_0$. Assume that $h_k \sqsupseteq \alpha_\sigma\ f_k$ for all $k \leq i$. Then

$$\begin{array}{rcll} h_{i+1} & = & (\alpha_{\sigma\to\sigma}\ f)\ h_i & \\ & \sqsupseteq & (\alpha_{\sigma\to\sigma}\ f)\ (\alpha_\sigma\ f_i) & \text{induction hypothesis and monotonicity of } \alpha_{\sigma\to\sigma} \\ & \sqsupseteq & \alpha_\sigma\ (f\ f_i) & \text{Proposition 3.2.12} \\ & = & \alpha_\sigma\ f_{i+1} & \end{array}$$

So $h_i \sqsupseteq (\alpha_\sigma\ f_i)$ for all i. Now

$$\begin{array}{rcll} \bigsqcup_{i\geq 0}(\alpha_{\sigma\to\sigma}\ f)^i\ \bot_{\mathbf{A}_\sigma} & = & \bigsqcup_{i\geq 0}\{h_i\} & \\ & \sqsupseteq & \bigsqcup_{i\geq 0}\{\alpha_\sigma\ f_i\} & \text{by above induction} \\ & = & \alpha_\sigma\ (\bigsqcup_{i\geq 0}\ f^i\ \bot_{\mathbf{S}_\sigma}) & \\ & & \text{since } \alpha_\sigma \text{ is continuous and } \{f_i\} \text{ is a chain} & \end{array}$$

□

Proposition 3.2.14

1. $\alpha_{\sigma_1\to\ldots\to\sigma_k\to\tau} = \mathit{curry} \circ \alpha_{\sigma_1\times\ldots\times\sigma_k\to\tau} \circ \mathit{uncurry}$

2. $\alpha_{\sigma_1\times\ldots\times\sigma_k\to\tau} = \mathit{uncurry} \circ \alpha_{\sigma_1\to\ldots\to\sigma_k\to\tau} \circ \mathit{curry}$

Proof

1. Suppose that $f \in \mathbf{S}_{\sigma_1\to\ldots\to\sigma_k\to\tau}$. Then, by Proposition 3.2.6 (1) we have that

$$\begin{array}{l} (\mathit{curry} \circ \alpha_{\sigma_1\times\ldots\times\sigma_k\to\tau} \circ \mathit{uncurry})\ f \\ \quad = \mathit{curry}\ (\lambda(\bar{s}_1,\ldots,\bar{s}_k)\epsilon\mathbf{A}_{\sigma_1\times\ldots\times\sigma_k}.\bigsqcup\{\alpha_\tau\ ((\mathit{uncurry}\ f)\ (s_1,\ldots,s_k)) \\ \qquad |\alpha_{\sigma_1\times\ldots\times\sigma_k}\ (s_1,\ldots,s_k) \sqsubseteq (\bar{s}_1,\ldots,\bar{s}_k)\}) \\ \quad = \lambda\bar{s}_1\epsilon\mathbf{A}_{\sigma_1}\ldots\lambda\bar{s}_k\epsilon\mathbf{A}_{\sigma_k}.\bigsqcup\{\alpha_\tau\ (f\ s_1\ \ldots\ s_k)|\alpha_{\sigma_1\times\ldots\times\sigma_k}\ (s_1,\ldots,s_k) \sqsubseteq (\bar{s}_1,\ldots,\bar{s}_k)\} \\ \qquad \text{from the definitions of } \mathit{curry} \text{ and } \mathit{uncurry} \\ \quad = \lambda\bar{s}_1\epsilon\mathbf{A}_{\sigma_1}\ldots\lambda\bar{s}_k\epsilon\mathbf{A}_{\sigma_k}.\bigsqcup\{\alpha_\tau\ (f\ s_1\ \ldots\ s_k)|\forall i \in \{1,\ldots,k\} : \alpha_{\sigma_i}\ s_i \sqsubseteq \bar{s}_i\} \\ \qquad \text{from the definition of } \alpha_{\sigma_1\times\ldots\times\sigma_k} \\ \quad = \alpha_{\sigma_1\to\ldots\to\sigma_k\to\tau}\ f \\ \qquad \text{Proposition 3.2.6 (1)} \end{array}$$

2. Follows in a similar manner to the first result.

□

Theorem 3.3.2

Suppose that the abstract interpretations of all constants satisfy the constant safety condition. Then for all $\rho^{\mathbf{S}}, \rho^{\mathbf{A}}$ *such that for all* x^τ, $(\rho^{\mathbf{A}}\ x^\tau) \sqsupseteq \alpha_\tau\ (\rho^{\mathbf{S}}\ x^\tau)$, *we have for all* $e\ :\ \sigma$:

$$\mathbf{A}\ [\![e]\!]\ \rho^{\mathbf{A}} \sqsupseteq\ \alpha_\sigma(\mathbf{S}\ [\![e]\!]\ \rho^{\mathbf{S}}).$$

Proof

We prove this by structural induction over the terms in the language Λ^T.

1. $$\begin{aligned} \mathbf{A}\ [\![x]\!]\ \rho^{\mathbf{A}} &= \rho^{\mathbf{A}}\ x \\ &\sqsupseteq \alpha_\sigma(\rho^{\mathbf{S}}\ x) && \text{condition of Theorem} \\ &= \alpha_\sigma\ (\mathbf{S}\ [\![x]\!]\ \rho^{\mathbf{S}}) \end{aligned}$$

2. $$\begin{aligned} \mathbf{A}\ [\![c_\sigma]\!]\ \rho^{\mathbf{A}} &= \mathbf{K}^{\mathbf{A}}\ [\![c_\sigma]\!] \\ &\sqsupseteq \alpha_\sigma(\mathbf{K}^{\mathbf{S}}\ [\![c_\sigma]\!]) && \text{by condition of Theorem} \\ &= \alpha_\sigma\ (\mathbf{S}\ [\![c_\sigma]\!]\ \rho^{\mathbf{S}}) \end{aligned}$$

3. Let $\bar{s} \in \mathbf{A}_\sigma$. Then

$$\begin{aligned} (\mathbf{A}\ [\![\lambda x^\sigma.e]\!]\ \rho^{\mathbf{A}})\ \bar{s} &= (\lambda \bar{y}_\epsilon \mathbf{A}_\sigma.\mathbf{A}\ [\![e]\!]\ \rho^{\mathbf{A}}[\bar{y}/x^\sigma])\ \bar{s} \\ &= \mathbf{A}\ [\![e]\!]\ \rho^{\mathbf{A}}[\bar{s}/x^\sigma] \end{aligned}$$

and

$$\begin{aligned} (\alpha_{\sigma\to\tau}\ (\mathbf{S}\ [\![\lambda x^\sigma.e]\!]\ \rho^{\mathbf{S}}))\ \bar{s} &= (\lambda \bar{s}_\epsilon \mathbf{A}_\sigma.\bigsqcup\{\alpha_\tau\ ((\mathbf{S}\ [\![\lambda x^\sigma.e]\!]\ \rho^{\mathbf{S}})\ s) | (\alpha_\sigma\ s) \sqsubseteq \bar{s}\})\ \bar{s} \\ &= \bigsqcup\{\alpha_\tau((\lambda y_\epsilon \mathbf{S}_\sigma.\mathbf{S}\ [\![e]\!]\ \rho^{\mathbf{S}}[y/x^\sigma])\ s) | (\alpha_\sigma\ s) \sqsubseteq \bar{s}\} \\ &= \bigsqcup\{\alpha_\tau(\mathbf{S}\ [\![e]\!]\ \rho^{\mathbf{S}}[s/x^\sigma]) | (\alpha_\sigma\ s) \sqsubseteq \bar{s}\}^{\bullet} \end{aligned}$$

Now $\rho^{\mathbf{A}}[\bar{s}/x^\sigma]$ and $\rho^{\mathbf{S}}[s/x^\sigma]$ still satisfy the conditions on the environment since $(\alpha_\sigma\ s) \sqsubseteq \bar{s}$, and so by the induction hypothesis, every element in the set:

$$\{\alpha_\tau(\mathbf{S}\ [\![e]\!]\ \rho^{\mathbf{S}}[s/x^\sigma]) | (\alpha_\sigma\ s) \sqsubseteq \bar{s}\}$$

approximates $\mathbf{A}\ [\![e]\!]\ \rho^{\mathbf{A}}[\bar{s}/x^\sigma]$ and hence the required result holds (by the definition of the *least* upper bound).

4. $$\begin{aligned} \mathbf{A}\ [\![e_1\ e_2]\!]\ \rho^{\mathbf{A}} &= (\mathbf{A}\ [\![e_1]\!]\ \rho^{\mathbf{A}})\ (\mathbf{A}\ [\![e_2]\!]\ \rho^{\mathbf{A}}) \\ &\sqsupseteq \alpha_{\sigma\to\tau}(\mathbf{S}\ [\![e_1]\!]\ \rho^{\mathbf{S}})\ (\alpha_\sigma\ (\mathbf{S}\ [\![e_2]\!]\ \rho^{\mathbf{S}})) && \text{induction hypothesis} \\ &\sqsupseteq \alpha_\tau((\mathbf{S}\ [\![e_1]\!]\ \rho^{\mathbf{S}})\ (\mathbf{S}\ [\![e_2]\!]\ \rho^{\mathbf{S}})) && \text{Proposition 3.2.12} \\ &= \alpha_\tau(\mathbf{S}\ [\![e_1\ e_2]\!]\ \rho^{\mathbf{S}}) \end{aligned}$$

5. $$\begin{aligned} \mathbf{A}\ [\![\mathrm{fix}_{(\sigma\to\sigma)\to\sigma}\ e]\!]\ \rho^{\mathbf{A}} &= \bigsqcup_{i\geq 0}\ (\mathbf{A}\ [\![e]\!]\ \rho^{\mathbf{A}})^i\ \bot_{\mathbf{A}_\sigma} \\ &\sqsupseteq \bigsqcup_{i\geq 0}\ (\alpha_{\sigma\to\sigma}\ (\mathbf{S}\ [\![e]\!]\ \rho^{\mathbf{S}}))^i\ \bot_{\mathbf{A}_\sigma} && \text{induction hypothesis} \\ &\sqsupseteq \alpha_\sigma\ (\bigsqcup_{i\geq 0}\ (\mathbf{S}\ [\![e]\!]\ \rho^{\mathbf{S}})^i\ \bot_{\mathbf{S}_\sigma}) && \text{Proposition 3.2.13} \\ &= \alpha_\sigma(\mathbf{S}\ [\![\mathrm{fix}_{(\sigma\to\sigma)\to\sigma}\ e]\!]\ \rho^{\mathbf{S}}) \end{aligned}$$

6. For (let $x^\sigma = e_1$ in e_2) : τ there are two cases to consider:

   (a) α_σ is bottom-reflecting and $\mathbf{A}\ [\![e_1]\!]\ \rho^{\mathbf{A}} = \bot_{\mathbf{A}_\sigma}$: By the induction hypothesis, this means that

   $$\alpha_\sigma\ (\mathbf{S}\ [\![e_1]\!]\ \rho^{\mathbf{S}}) = \bot_{\mathbf{A}_\sigma}$$

   and, since α_σ is bottom-reflecting, we have that

   $$\mathbf{S}\ [\![e_1]\!]\ \rho^{\mathbf{S}} = \bot_{\mathbf{S}_\sigma}.$$

   Therefore,

   $$\begin{aligned} \alpha_\tau\ (\mathbf{S}\ [\![(\text{let } x^\sigma = e_1 \text{ in } e_2 : \tau)]\!]\ \rho^{\mathbf{S}}) &= \alpha_\tau\ \bot_{\mathbf{S}_\tau} \\ &= \bot_{\mathbf{A}_\tau} \end{aligned}$$

   since α_τ is strict for all types (Lemma 3.2.4(1)), and hence we have that

   $$\alpha_\tau\ (\mathbf{S}\ [\![\text{let } x^\sigma = e_1 \text{ in } e_2]\!]\ \rho^{\mathbf{S}}) \sqsubseteq \mathbf{A}\ [\![\text{let } x^\sigma = e_1 \text{ in } e_2]\!]\ \rho^{\mathbf{A}}$$

   in this case.

   (b) $\mathbf{A}\ [\![\text{let } x^\sigma = e_1 \text{ in } e_2]\!]\ \rho^{\mathbf{A}} = \mathbf{A}\ [\![e_2]\!]\ \rho^{\mathbf{A}}[\mathbf{A}\ [\![e_1]\!]\ \rho^{\mathbf{A}}/x^\sigma]$: By the induction hypothesis,

   $$\mathbf{A}\ [\![e_1]\!]\ \rho^{\mathbf{A}} \sqsupseteq \alpha_\sigma\ (\mathbf{S}\ [\![e_1]\!]\ \rho^{\mathbf{S}})$$

   and so $\rho^{\mathbf{A}}[\mathbf{A}\ [\![e_1]\!]\ \rho^{\mathbf{A}}/x^\sigma]$ and $\rho^{\mathbf{S}}[\mathbf{S}\ [\![e_1]\!]\ \rho^{\mathbf{S}}/x^\sigma]$ satisfy the condition on the environments given in the statement of the theorem. Therefore,

   $$\begin{aligned} \alpha_\tau\ (\mathbf{S}\ [\![\text{let } x^\sigma = e_1 \text{ in } e_2]\!]\ \rho^{\mathbf{S}}) &\sqsubseteq \alpha_\tau\ (\mathbf{S}\ [\![e_2]\!]\ \rho^{\mathbf{S}}[\mathbf{S}\ [\![e_1]\!]\ \rho^{\mathbf{S}}/x^\sigma]) \\ &\quad \text{from the standard interpretation of} \\ &\quad \text{let } x^\sigma = e_1 \text{ in } e_2 \\ &\sqsubseteq \mathbf{A}\ [\![e_2]\!]\ \rho^{\mathbf{A}}[\mathbf{A}\ [\![e_1]\!]\ \rho^{\mathbf{A}}/x^\sigma] \\ &\quad \text{induction hypothesis and above} \\ &\quad \text{observation on environments} \\ &= \mathbf{A}\ [\![\text{let } x^\sigma = e_1 \text{ in } e_2]\!]\ \rho^{\mathbf{A}}. \end{aligned}$$

7. $$\begin{aligned} \mathbf{A}\ [\![\mathbf{tuple}_{(\sigma_1,\ldots,\sigma_k)}(e_1,\ldots e_k)]\!]\ \rho^{\mathbf{A}} &= (\mathbf{A}\ [\![e_1]\!]\ \rho^{\mathbf{A}},\ldots,\mathbf{A}\ [\![e_k]\!]\ \rho^{\mathbf{A}}) \\ &\sqsupseteq (\alpha_{\sigma_1}\ (\mathbf{S}\ [\![e_1]\!]\ \rho^{\mathbf{S}}),\ldots,\alpha_{\sigma_k}\ (\mathbf{S}\ [\![e_k]\!]\ \rho^{\mathbf{S}})) \\ &\quad \text{induction hypothesis} \\ &= \alpha_{\sigma_1 \times \ldots \times \sigma_k}\ (\mathbf{S}\ [\![e_1]\!]\ \rho^{\mathbf{S}},\ldots,\mathbf{S}\ [\![e_k]\!]\ \rho^{\mathbf{S}}) \\ &= \alpha_{\sigma_1 \times \ldots \times \sigma_k}\ (\mathbf{S}\ [\![\mathbf{tuple}_{(\sigma_1,\ldots,\sigma_k)}(e_1,\ldots e_k)]\!]\ \rho^{\mathbf{S}} \end{aligned}$$

8. For $\mathbf{tuples}_{(\sigma_1,\ldots,\sigma_k)}$, there are two cases to consider:

   (a) $\forall i \in \{1,\ldots,k\} : \mathbf{A}\ [\![e_i]\!]\ \rho^{\mathbf{A}} \neq \bot_{\mathbf{A}_{\sigma_i}}$:

   $$\mathbf{A}\ [\![\mathbf{tuples}_{(\sigma_1,\ldots,\sigma_k)}(e_1,\ldots e_k)]\!]\ \rho^{\mathbf{A}} = <\mathbf{A}\ [\![e_1]\!]\ \rho^{\mathbf{A}},\ldots,\mathbf{A}\ [\![e_k]\!]\ \rho^{\mathbf{A}}>$$

   Now

   $$\begin{aligned} &\alpha_{\sigma_1 \otimes \ldots \otimes \sigma_k}\ (\mathbf{S}\ [\![\mathbf{tuples}_{(\sigma_1,\ldots,\sigma_k)}(e_1,\ldots e_k)]\!]\ \rho^{\mathbf{S}}) \\ &= \begin{cases} \bot_{\mathbf{A}_{\sigma_1 \otimes \ldots \otimes \sigma_k}} & \text{if } \exists i \in \{1,\ldots,k\} : \alpha_{\sigma_i}\ (\mathbf{S}\ [\![e_i]\!]\ \rho^{\mathbf{S}}) = \bot_{\mathbf{A}_{\sigma_i}} \\ <\alpha_{\sigma_1}\ (\mathbf{S}\ [\![e_1]\!]\ \rho^{\mathbf{S}}),\ldots,\alpha_{\sigma_k}\ (\mathbf{S}\ [\![e_k]\!]\ \rho^{\mathbf{S}})> & \text{otherwise} \end{cases} \end{aligned}$$

   In the first case, the result holds trivially. The desired result holds in the second case by the induction hypothesis.

(b) $\exists i \in \{1,\ldots,k\} : \mathbf{A}\ [\![e_i]\!]\ \rho^{\mathbf{A}} = \bot_{\mathbf{A}_{\sigma_i}}$: This means that

$$\mathbf{A}\ [\![\mathbf{tuples}_{(\sigma_1,\ldots,\sigma_k)}(e_1,\ldots e_k)]\!]\ \rho^{\mathbf{A}} = \bot_{\mathbf{A}_{\sigma_1 \otimes \ldots \otimes \sigma_k}}.$$

$$\begin{array}{l} \alpha_{\sigma_1 \otimes \ldots \otimes \sigma_k}\ (\mathbf{S}\ [\![\mathbf{tuples}_{(\sigma_1,\ldots,\sigma_k)}(e_1,\ldots e_k)]\!]\ \rho^{\mathbf{S}} \\ = \left\{ \begin{array}{ll} \alpha_{\sigma_1 \otimes \ldots \otimes \sigma_k}\ \bot_{\mathbf{S}_{\sigma_1 \otimes \ldots \otimes \sigma_k}} & \text{if } \exists i \in \{1,\ldots,k\} : (\mathbf{S}\ [\![e_i]\!]\ \rho^{\mathbf{S}}) = \bot_{\mathbf{S}_{\sigma_i}} \\ \alpha_{\sigma_1 \otimes \ldots \otimes \sigma_k}\ < \mathbf{S}\ [\![e_1]\!]\ \rho^{\mathbf{S}}, \ldots, \mathbf{S}\ [\![e_k]\!]\ \rho^{\mathbf{S}} > & \text{otherwise} \end{array} \right. \end{array}$$

In the first case, the result holds trivially because all abstraction maps are strict (Lemma 3.2.4(1)). In the second case, since $\exists i \in \{1,\ldots,k\}$: $\mathbf{A}\ [\![e_i]\!]\ \rho^{\mathbf{A}} = \bot_{\mathbf{A}_{\sigma_i}}$, the induction hypothesis implies that $\alpha_{\sigma_i}\ (\mathbf{S}\ [\![e_i]\!]\ \rho^{\mathbf{S}}) = \bot_{\mathbf{A}_{\sigma_i}}$, the bottom-reflexivity of α_{σ_i} implies that $\mathbf{S}\ [\![e_i]\!]\ \rho^{\mathbf{S}} = \bot_{\mathbf{S}_{\sigma_i}}$, and so

$$\alpha_{\sigma_1 \otimes \ldots \otimes \sigma_k}\ (\mathbf{S}\ [\![\mathbf{tuples}_{(\sigma_1,\ldots,\sigma_k)}(e_1,\ldots,e_k)]\!]\ \rho^{\mathbf{S}}) = \bot_{\mathbf{A}_{\sigma_1 \otimes \ldots \otimes \sigma_k}}$$

by the definition of the smash product of functions.

9. $$\begin{array}{l} \mathbf{A}\ [\![\mathbf{ins_i}_{(\sigma_1,\ldots,\sigma_k)}\ e]\!]\ \rho^{\mathbf{A}} \\ \quad = (\bot_{\mathbf{A}_{\sigma_1}}, \ldots, \bot_{\mathbf{A}_{\sigma_{i-1}}}, \mathbf{A}\ [\![e]\!]\ \rho^{\mathbf{A}}, \bot_{\mathbf{A}_{\sigma_{i+1}}}, \ldots, \bot_{\mathbf{A}_{\sigma_k}}) \\ \quad \sqsupseteq (\bot_{\mathbf{A}_{\sigma_1}}, \ldots, \bot_{\mathbf{A}_{\sigma_{i-1}}}, \alpha_{\sigma_i}\ (\mathbf{S}\ [\![e]\!]\ \rho^{\mathbf{S}}), \bot_{\mathbf{A}_{\sigma_{i+1}}}, \ldots, \bot_{\mathbf{A}_{\sigma_k}}) \\ \quad\quad \text{induction hypothesis} \end{array}$$

There are two cases to consider:

(a) $\mathbf{S}\ [\![e]\!]\ \rho^{\mathbf{S}} = \bot_{\mathbf{S}_{\sigma_i}}$:

$$\begin{array}{l} (\bot_{\mathbf{A}_{\sigma_1}}, \ldots, \bot_{\mathbf{A}_{\sigma_{i-1}}}, \alpha_{\sigma_i}\ (\mathbf{S}\ [\![e]\!]\ \rho^{\mathbf{S}}), \bot_{\mathbf{A}_{\sigma_{i+1}}}, \ldots, \bot_{\mathbf{A}_{\sigma_k}}) \\ \quad = (\bot_{\mathbf{A}_{\sigma_1}}, \ldots, \bot_{\mathbf{A}_{\sigma_{i-1}}}, \alpha_{\sigma_i}\ \bot_{\mathbf{S}_{\sigma_i}}, \bot_{\mathbf{A}_{\sigma_{i+1}}}, \ldots, \bot_{\mathbf{A}_{\sigma_k}}) \\ \quad = (\bot_{\mathbf{A}_{\sigma_1}}, \ldots, \bot_{\mathbf{A}_{\sigma_k}}) \\ \quad\quad \text{since } \alpha_{\sigma_i} \text{ is strict by Lemma 3.2.4(1)} \\ \quad = \alpha_{\sigma_1 \oplus \ldots \oplus \sigma_k}\ (mk\_sum_i\ (\mathbf{S}\ [\![e]\!]\ \rho^{\mathbf{S}})) \\ \quad = \alpha_{\sigma_1 \oplus \ldots \oplus \sigma_k}\ (\mathbf{S}\ [\![\mathbf{ins_i}_{(\sigma_1,\ldots,\sigma_k)}\ e]\!]\ \rho^{\mathbf{S}}) \end{array}$$

(b) $\mathbf{S}\ [\![e]\!]\ \rho^{\mathbf{S}} \neq \bot_{\mathbf{S}_{\sigma_i}}$:

$$\begin{array}{l} (\bot_{\mathbf{A}_{\sigma_1}}, \ldots, \bot_{\mathbf{A}_{\sigma_{i-1}}}, \alpha_{\sigma_i}\ (\mathbf{S}\ [\![e]\!]\ \rho^{\mathbf{S}}), \bot_{\mathbf{A}_{\sigma_{i+1}}}, \ldots, \bot_{\mathbf{A}_{\sigma_k}}) \\ \quad = \alpha_{\sigma_1 \oplus \ldots \oplus \sigma_k}\ (ins_i\ (\mathbf{S}\ [\![e]\!]\ \rho^{\mathbf{S}})) \\ \quad = \alpha_{\sigma_1 \oplus \ldots \oplus \sigma_k}\ (mk\_sum_i\ (\mathbf{S}\ [\![e]\!]\ \rho^{\mathbf{S}})) \\ \quad = \alpha_{\sigma_1 \oplus \ldots \oplus \sigma_k}\ (\mathbf{S}\ [\![\mathbf{ins_i}_{(\sigma_1,\ldots,\sigma_k)}\ e]\!]\ \rho^{\mathbf{S}}) \end{array}$$

10. $$\begin{array}{rcll} \mathbf{A}\ [\![\mathbf{lift}_\sigma\ e]\!]\ \rho^{\mathbf{A}} & = & lift\ (\mathbf{A}\ [\![e]\!]\ \rho^{\mathbf{A}}) & \\ & \sqsupseteq & lift\ (\alpha_\sigma\ (\mathbf{S}\ [\![e]\!]\ \rho^{\mathbf{S}})) & \text{induction hypothesis} \\ & = & \alpha_{lift\ \sigma}\ (lift\ (\mathbf{S}\ [\![e]\!]\ \rho^{\mathbf{S}})) & \\ & = & \alpha_{lift\ \sigma}\ (\mathbf{S}\ [\![\mathbf{lift}_\sigma\ e]\!]\ \rho^{\mathbf{S}}) & \end{array}$$

□

Theorem 3.3.5

Suppose that $f : \sigma_1 \to \ldots \to \sigma_n \to \tau$ *and* $(\mathbf{A} [\![f]\!] \rho^{\mathbf{A}})\ \overline{s}_1 \ldots \overline{s}_n \sqsubseteq \overline{t}$. *Then* $\forall j \in \{1,\ldots,n\}, j \neq i, \forall e_j : \sigma_j$ *such that* $(\mathbf{A} [\![e_j]\!] \rho^{\mathbf{A}}) \sqsubseteq \overline{s}_j$, $\forall s_i \in (\gamma_{\sigma_i}\ \overline{s}_i)$,

$$(\mathbf{S} [\![f]\!] \rho^{\mathbf{S}})\ (\mathbf{S} [\![e_1]\!] \rho^{\mathbf{S}}) \ldots (\mathbf{S} [\![e_{i-1}]\!] \rho^{\mathbf{S}})\ s_i\ (\mathbf{S} [\![e_{i+1}]\!] \rho^{\mathbf{S}}) \ldots (\mathbf{S} [\![e_n]\!] \rho^{\mathbf{S}}) \in (\gamma_\tau\ \overline{t}).$$

Proof

$$\begin{aligned}
\overline{t}\ &\sqsupseteq (\mathbf{A} [\![f]\!] \rho^{\mathbf{A}})\ \overline{s}_1 \ldots \overline{s}_n \\
&\sqsupseteq (\mathbf{A} [\![f]\!] \rho^{\mathbf{A}})\ (\mathbf{A} [\![e_1]\!] \rho^{\mathbf{A}}) \ldots (\mathbf{A} [\![e_{i-1}]\!] \rho^{\mathbf{A}})\ \overline{s}_i\ (\mathbf{A} [\![e_{i+1}]\!] \rho^{\mathbf{A}}) \ldots (\mathbf{A} [\![e_n]\!] \rho^{\mathbf{A}}) \\
&\quad \text{since } \forall j \in \{1,\ldots,i-1,i+1,\ldots,n\}, (\mathbf{A} [\![e_j]\!] \rho^{\mathbf{A}}) \sqsubseteq \overline{s}_j \\
&\sqsupseteq (\alpha_{\sigma_1 \to \ldots \to \sigma_n \to \tau}\ (\mathbf{S} [\![f]\!] \rho^{\mathbf{S}}))\ (\alpha_{\sigma_1}\ (\mathbf{S} [\![e_1]\!] \rho^{\mathbf{S}})) \ldots (\alpha_{\sigma_{i-1}}\ (\mathbf{S} [\![e_{i-1}]\!] \rho^{\mathbf{S}}))\ \overline{s}_i \\
&\quad (\alpha_{\sigma_{i+1}}\ (\mathbf{S} [\![e_{i+1}]\!] \rho^{\mathbf{S}})) \ldots (\alpha_{\sigma_n}\ (\mathbf{S} [\![e_n]\!] \rho^{\mathbf{S}})) \\
&\quad \text{Theorem 3.3.2} \\
&\sqsupseteq (\alpha_{\sigma_1 \to \ldots \to \sigma_n \to \tau}\ (\mathbf{S} [\![f]\!] \rho^{\mathbf{S}}))\ (\alpha_{\sigma_1}\ (\mathbf{S} [\![e_1]\!] \rho^{\mathbf{S}})) \ldots (\alpha_{\sigma_{i-1}}\ (\mathbf{S} [\![e_{i-1}]\!] \rho^{\mathbf{S}}))\ (\alpha_{\sigma_i}\ s_i) \\
&\quad (\alpha_{\sigma_{i+1}}\ (\mathbf{S} [\![e_{i+1}]\!] \rho^{\mathbf{S}})) \ldots (\alpha_{\sigma_n}\ (\mathbf{S} [\![e_n]\!] \rho^{\mathbf{S}})) \\
&\quad \forall s_i \in (\gamma_{\sigma_i}\ \overline{s}_i) \text{ by Proposition 3.2.7} \\
&\sqsupseteq \alpha_\tau\ ((\mathbf{S} [\![f]\!] \rho^{\mathbf{S}})\ (\mathbf{S} [\![e_1]\!] \rho^{\mathbf{S}}) \ldots (\mathbf{S} [\![e_{i-1}]\!] \rho^{\mathbf{S}})\ s_i\ (\mathbf{S} [\![e_{i+1}]\!] \rho^{\mathbf{S}}) \quad (\mathbf{S} [\![e_n]\!] \rho^{\mathbf{S}})) \\
&\quad \text{Proposition 3.2.12}
\end{aligned}$$

and Proposition 3.2.5 therefore implies that

$$((\mathbf{S} [\![f]\!] \rho^{\mathbf{S}})\ (\mathbf{S} [\![e_1]\!] \rho^{\mathbf{S}}) \ldots (\mathbf{S} [\![e_{i-1}]\!] \rho^{\mathbf{S}})\ s_i\ (\mathbf{S} [\![e_{i+1}]\!] \rho^{\mathbf{S}}) \ldots (\mathbf{S} [\![e_n]\!] \rho^{\mathbf{S}})) \in (\gamma_\tau\ \overline{t}).$$

□

A.4 Proofs From Chapter 4

A.4.1 Abstract Interpretation of Strict Functions

The fact that the abstract interpretations of $+_{int \to int \to int}$, $*_{int \to int \to int}$, $-_{int \to int \to int}$, $/_{int \to int \to int}$, $<_{int \to int \to bool}$, $\leq_{int \to int \to bool}$, $<_{int \to int \to bool}$, $\leq_{int \to int \to bool}$ and $=_{int \to int \to bool}$ satisfy the constant correctness condition follows immediately from the following Lemma.

Lemma A.4.1

Let $\sigma_1,\ldots,\sigma_k,\tau$ *be any types with abstract interpretation the two point domain. If* $f : \sigma_1 \to \ldots \to \sigma_n \to \tau$ *is such that for all* $i \in \{1,\ldots,n\}$

$$(\mathbf{S} [\![f]\!] \rho^{\mathbf{S}})\ s_1 \ldots s_{i-1}\ \bot_{\mathbf{S}_{\sigma_i}}\ s_{i+1} \ldots s_n = \bot_{\mathbf{S}_\tau}$$

i.e. f *is strict in each of its parameters, and*

$$\mathbf{S} [\![f\ s_1 \ldots s_n]\!] \rho^{\mathbf{S}} = \bot_{\mathbf{S}_\tau} \Rightarrow \mathbf{S} [\![s_i]\!] \rho^{\mathbf{S}} = \bot_{\mathbf{S}_{\sigma_i}}$$

for some i, *then*

$$\alpha_{\sigma_1 \to \ldots \to \sigma_n \to \tau}\ (\mathbf{S} [\![f]\!] \rho^{\mathbf{S}}) = \lambda x_1 \epsilon \mathbf{2}. \ldots .\lambda x_n \epsilon \mathbf{2}. x_1 \sqcap \ldots \sqcap x_n$$

Proof

We prove this by induction with the base case being $n = 1$. In this proof we will denote (S $[\![e]\!]$ ρ^S) by f, and we will use the definition of $\alpha_{\sigma_1 \to \ldots \to \sigma_n \to \tau}$ given in Proposition 3.2.6(2).

$$\begin{aligned}
(\alpha_{\sigma_1 \to \tau}\ f)\ 0 &= \bigsqcup\{\alpha_\tau\ (f\ x) | x \in (\gamma_{\sigma_1}\ 0)\} \\
&= \bigsqcup\{\alpha_\tau (f\ \bot_{S_{\sigma_1}})\} && \text{Lemma 4.1.6(3)} \\
&= \bigsqcup\{0\} && \text{since } f \text{ and } \alpha_{\sigma_1} \text{ are strict} \\
&= 0
\end{aligned}$$

$$\begin{aligned}
(\alpha_{\sigma_1 \to \tau}\ f)\ 1 &= \bigsqcup\{\alpha_\tau (f\ s) | s \in (\gamma_{\sigma_1}\ 1)\} \\
&= \bigsqcup\{\alpha_\tau\ (f\ s) | s \in S_{\sigma_1}\} \\
&= \bigsqcup\{0, 1\} && \text{since } f \text{ is strict and not } \bot_{S_{\sigma_1 \to \tau}} \\
&= 1
\end{aligned}$$

Therefore, $(\alpha_{\sigma_1 \to \tau}\ f) = \lambda x \epsilon \mathbf{2}.x$. In the induction step, we assume the result for all $n < k$.

$$\begin{aligned}
(\alpha_{\sigma_1 \to \ldots \to s_k \to \tau}\ f)\ 0 &= \bigsqcup\{\alpha_{\sigma_2 \to \ldots \to \sigma_k \to \tau} (f\ x) | x \in (\gamma_{\sigma_1}\ 0)\} \\
&= \bigsqcup\{\alpha_{\sigma_2 \to \ldots \to \sigma_k \to \tau} (f\ \bot_{S_{\sigma_1}})\} \\
&\quad \text{Lemma 4.1.6(3)} \\
&= \bigsqcup\{\alpha_{\sigma_2 \to \ldots \to \sigma_k \to \tau} (\lambda x_2 \epsilon S_{\sigma_2} . \ldots . \lambda x_k \epsilon S_{\sigma_k} . \bot_{S_\tau})\} \\
&\quad \text{since } f \text{ is strict} \\
&= \lambda x_2 \epsilon \mathbf{2} \ldots \lambda x_k \epsilon \mathbf{2}.0 \\
&\quad \text{since } \alpha_{\sigma_2 \to \ldots \to \sigma_k \to \tau} \text{ is strict}
\end{aligned}$$

$$\begin{aligned}
(\alpha_{\sigma_1 \to \ldots \to \sigma_k \to \tau}\ f)\ 1 &= \bigsqcup\{\alpha_{\sigma_2 \to \ldots \to \sigma_k \to \tau} (f\ s) | s \in (\gamma_{\sigma_1}\ 1)\} \\
&= \bigsqcup\{\alpha_{\sigma_2 \to \ldots \to \sigma_k \to \tau} (f\ s) | s \in S_{\sigma_1}\} \\
&= \bigsqcup\{\alpha_{\sigma_2 \to \ldots \to \sigma_k \to \tau} (f\ s) | s \neq \bot_{S_{\sigma_1}}, s \in S_{\sigma_1}\} \\
&\quad \text{since } f \text{ is monotonic} \\
&= \bigsqcup\{\lambda x_2 \epsilon \mathbf{2} \ldots \lambda x_k \epsilon \mathbf{2}. x_2 \sqcap \ldots \sqcap x_k\} \\
&\quad \text{by induction hypothesis because } (f\ s) \text{ satisfies the} \\
&\quad \text{condition of the Lemma} \\
&= \lambda x_2 \epsilon \mathbf{2} \ldots \lambda x_k \epsilon \mathbf{2}. x_2 \sqcap \ldots \sqcap x_k
\end{aligned}$$

Hence, $(\alpha_{\sigma_1 \to \ldots \to \sigma_k \to \tau}\ f) = \lambda x_1 \epsilon \mathbf{2} \ldots \lambda x_k \epsilon \mathbf{2}. x_1 \sqcap \ldots \sqcap x_k$.

□

A.4.2 Abstract Interpretation of $\mathbf{head}_{(list\ \tau) \to \tau}$

Lemma A.4.2

For all types τ,

$$K^A\ [\![\mathbf{head}_{(list\ \tau) \to \tau}]\!] \sqsupseteq \alpha_{(list\ \tau) \to \tau}\ (K^S\ [\![\mathbf{head}_{(list\ \tau) \to \tau}]\!])$$

where

$$K^A\ [\![\mathbf{head}_{(list\ \tau) \to \tau}]\!]\ l = \begin{cases} \bot_{A_\tau} & \textit{if } l = \bot \\ \top_{A_\tau} & \textit{otherwise} \end{cases}$$

Proof

Recall that $\mathbf{K}^{\mathbf{S}}$ $[\![\text{head}_{(list\ \tau)\to\tau}]\!] = head$, where *head* is defined in Figure 2.15. We use the definition of $\alpha_{(list\ \tau)\to\tau}$ from Proposition 3.2.6(2):

$$(\alpha_{(list\ \tau)\to\tau}\ head)\ \bar{l} = \bigsqcup\{\alpha_\tau(head\ l) | l \in (\gamma_{(list\ \tau)}\ \bar{l})\}$$

There are two cases to consider:

1. If $\bar{l} = \bot$, then the only $l \in (\gamma_{(list\ \tau)}\ \bot)$ is $\bot_{\mathbf{S}_{(list\ \tau)}}$ (Lemma 4.1.6(3)) and so we obtain $\bot_{\mathbf{A}_\tau}$ for the above as both *head* and α_τ are strict (Figure 2.15 and Lemma 4.1.6(1)).
2. If $\bar{l}$ is any other element of $\mathbf{S}_{(list\ \tau)}$, then the concretisation of $\bar{l}$ contains lists of the form $(cons\ u\ l)$ where $u \neq \bot_{\mathbf{S}_\tau}$, and we can only be assured that $(\alpha_\tau\ u) \sqsubseteq \top_{\mathbf{A}_\tau}$, so that

$$\begin{aligned} \alpha_\tau\ (head\ (cons\ u\ l)) &= \alpha_\tau\ u \\ &\sqsubseteq \top_{\mathbf{A}_\tau} \end{aligned}$$

   and hence the result.

If there is some $u \in \mathbf{S}_\tau$ such that $(\alpha_\tau\ u) = \top_{\mathbf{A}_\tau}$, then the inequality in the lemma becomes an equality.

□

A.4.3 Abstract Interpretation of $\text{cons}_{\tau\to(list\ \tau)\to(list\ \tau)}$

Lemma A.4.3

For all types τ,

$$\mathbf{K}^{\mathbf{A}}\ [\![\text{cons}_{\tau\to(list\ \tau)\to(list\ \tau)}]\!] = \alpha_{\tau\to(list\ \tau)\to(list\ \tau)}\ (\mathbf{K}^{\mathbf{S}}\ [\![\text{cons}_{\tau\to(list\ \tau)\to(list\ \tau)}]\!])$$

$$where\ \mathbf{K}^{\mathbf{A}}\ [\![\text{cons}_{\tau\to(list\ \tau)\to(list\ \tau)}]\!]\ u\ l = \begin{cases} \infty & if\ l \sqsubseteq \infty \\ \top\!\in & if\ l = \top\!\in\ and\ u \neq \bot_{\mathbf{A}_\tau} \\ \bot\!\in & otherwise \end{cases}$$

Proof

Recall that $(\mathbf{K}^{\mathbf{S}}\ [\![\text{cons}_{\tau\to(list\ \tau)\to(list\ \tau)}]\!]) = cons$. We use the form of $\alpha_{\tau\to(list\ \tau)\to(list\ \tau)}$ from Proposition 3.2.6(2):

$$(\alpha_{\tau\to(list\ \tau)\to(list\ \tau)}\ cons)\ \bar{u}\ \bar{l} = \bigsqcup\{\alpha_{(list\ \tau)}\ (cons\ u\ l) | u \in (\gamma_\tau\ \bar{u}), l \in (\gamma_{(list\ \tau)}\ \bar{l})\}$$

We give two examples of the calculation; the others follow in a similar manner.

1. $$\begin{aligned} (\alpha_{\tau\to(list\ \tau)\to(list\ \tau)}\ cons)\ \bot_{\mathbf{A}_\tau}\ \bot &= \bigsqcup\{\alpha_{(list\ \tau)}\ (cons\ \bot_{\mathbf{S}_\tau}\ \bot_{\mathbf{S}_{(list\ \tau)}})\} \\ &\quad \text{Lemma 4.1.6(3)} \\ &= \bigsqcup\{\infty\} \\ &\quad \text{since } (cons\ \bot_{\mathbf{S}_\tau}\ \bot_{\mathbf{S}_{(list\ \tau)}}) \in List_\tau^\infty \\ &= \infty \end{aligned}$$

2. Let $\overline{u} \neq \bot_{\mathbf{A}_\tau}$.

$(\alpha_{\tau \to (list\ \tau) \to (list\ \tau)}\ cons)\ \overline{u}\ \bot\!\!\in\ = \bigsqcup\{\alpha_{(list\ \tau)}\ (cons\ u\ l) | u \in (\gamma_\tau\ \overline{u}), l \in (\gamma_{(list\ \tau)}\ \bot\!\!\in)\}$

No matter what value u takes, since $l \in List_\tau^{\bot\in}$, we have that $(cons\ u\ l) \in List_\tau^{\bot\in}$, and $(\alpha_{(list\ \tau)}\ (cons\ u\ l))$ in this case is $\bot\!\!\in$.

The other six cases follow in a similar manner.

□

A.4.4 Abstract Interpretation of value$_{(tree\ \tau) \to \tau}$

Lemma A.4.4

For all types τ,

$$\mathbf{K}^{\mathbf{A}}\ [\![\text{value}_{(tree\ \tau)\to\tau}]\!] \sqsupseteq \alpha_{(tree\ \tau)\to\tau}\ (\mathbf{K}^{\mathbf{S}}\ [\![\text{value}_{(tree\ \tau)\to\tau}]\!])$$

where

$$\mathbf{K}^{\mathbf{A}}\ [\![\text{value}_{(tree\ \tau)\to\tau}]\!]\ t = \begin{cases} \bot_{\mathbf{A}_\tau} & if\ t = \bot \\ \top_{\mathbf{A}_\tau} & otherwise \end{cases}$$

Proof

Recall that $\mathbf{K}^{\mathbf{S}}\ [\![\text{value}_{(tree\ \tau)\to\tau}]\!] = value$, where *value* is defined in Figure 2.15. We use the definition of $\alpha_{(tree\ \tau)\to\tau}$ from Proposition 3.2.6(2):

$$(\alpha_{(tree\ \tau)\to\tau}\ value)\ \overline{t} = \bigsqcup\{\alpha_\tau(value\ t) | t \in (\gamma_{(tree\ \tau)}\ \overline{t})\}$$

There are two cases to consider.

1. If $\overline{t} = \bot$, then the only $t \in (\gamma_{(tree\ \tau)}\ \bot)$ is $\bot_{\mathbf{S}_{(tree\ \tau)}}$ (Lemma 4.1.6(3)) and so we obtain $\bot_{\mathbf{A}_\tau}$ for the above as both *value* and α_τ are strict (Figure 2.15 and Lemma 4.1.6(1)).
2. If $\overline{t}$ is any other element of $\mathbf{S}_{(tree\ \tau)}$, then the concretisation of $\overline{t}$ contains trees of the form $(node\ t_1\ n\ t_2)$ where $n \neq \bot_{\mathbf{S}_\tau}$, and we can only be assured that $(\alpha_\tau\ n) \sqsubseteq \top_{\mathbf{A}_\tau}$, so that

$$\begin{aligned} \alpha_\tau\ (value\ (node\ t_1\ n\ t_2)) &= \alpha_\tau\ n \\ &\sqsubseteq \top_{\mathbf{A}_\tau} \end{aligned}$$

and hence the result.

If there is some $n \in \mathbf{S}_\tau$ such that $(\alpha_\tau\ n) = \top_{\mathbf{A}_\tau}$, then the inequality in the lemma becomes an equality.

□

A.4.5 Abstract Interpretation of $\mathbf{left}_{(tree\ \tau)\rightarrow(tree\ \tau)}$

Lemma A.4.5

For all types τ,

$$\mathbf{K^A}\ [\![\mathbf{left}_{(tree\ \tau)\rightarrow(tree\ \tau)}]\!] = \alpha_{(tree\ \tau)\rightarrow(tree\ \tau)}\ (\mathbf{K^S}\ [\![\mathbf{left}_{(tree\ \tau)\rightarrow(tree\ \tau)}]\!])$$

where

$$\mathbf{K^A}\ [\![\mathbf{left}_{(tree\ \tau)\rightarrow(tree\ \tau)}]\!]\ t = \begin{cases} \bot & if\ t = \bot \\ \top\!\in & otherwise \end{cases}$$

Proof

Recall that $\mathbf{K^S}\ [\![\mathbf{left}_{(tree\ \tau)\rightarrow(tree\ \tau)}]\!] = left$, where $left$ is defined in Figure 2.15. We use the form of $\alpha_{(tree\ \tau)\rightarrow(tree\ \tau)}$ from Proposition 3.2.6(2):

$$(\alpha_{(tree\ \tau)\rightarrow(tree\ \tau)}\ left)\ \bar{l} = \bigsqcup\{\alpha_{(tree\ \tau)}\ (left\ l) | l \in (\gamma_{(tree\ \tau)}\ \bar{l})\}$$

There are two cases to consider.

1. If $\bar{t}$ is $\bot$, $(\gamma_{(tree\ \tau)}\ \bot) = \{\bot_{\mathbf{S}_{(tree\ \tau)}}\}$ (Lemma 4.1.6(3)), and so

$$\begin{aligned} \bigsqcup\{\alpha_{(tree\ \tau)}\ (left\ t) | t \in (\gamma_{(tree\ \tau)}\ \bot)\} &= \bigsqcup\{\alpha_{(tree\ \tau)}\ (left\ \bot_{\mathbf{S}_{(tree\ \tau)}})\} \\ &= \bigsqcup\{\alpha_{(tree\ \tau)}\ \bot_{\mathbf{S}_{(tree\ \tau)}}\} \\ &= \bigsqcup\{\bot_{\mathbf{A}_{(tree\ \tau)}}\} \quad \text{Lemma 4.1.6(1)} \\ &= \bot_{\mathbf{A}_{(tree\ \tau)}} = \bot \end{aligned}$$

2. If $\bar{t} \neq \bot$, then $(\gamma_{(tree\ \tau)}\ \bar{t})$ contains trees of the form $(node\ t_1\ n\ t_2)$ where $t_1 \in Tree_\tau^{\top\in}$ (see the abstract interpretation of $\mathbf{node}_{(tree\ \tau)\rightarrow\tau\rightarrow(tree\ \tau)\rightarrow(tree\ \tau)}$ in Figure 4.1). For trees of this form,

$$\begin{aligned} \alpha_{(tree\ \tau)}\ (left\ (node\ t_1\ n\ t_2)) &= \alpha_{(tree\ \tau)}\ t_1 \\ &= \top\!\in \end{aligned}$$

As $\top\!\in$ is in the set $\bigsqcup\{\alpha_{(tree\ \tau)}\ (left\ t) | t \in (\gamma_{(tree\ \tau)}\ \bar{l}), \bar{l} \neq \bot)\}$, and is the top element of the domain $\mathbf{A}_{(list\ \tau)}$, it must be the least upper bound of the elements of the set, which is the required result.

□

A.4.6 Abstract Interpretation of $\mathbf{right}_{(tree\ \tau)\rightarrow(tree\ \tau)}$

Lemma A.4.6

For all types τ,

$$\mathbf{K^A}\ [\![\mathbf{right}_{(tree\ \tau)\rightarrow(tree\ \tau)}]\!] = \alpha_{(tree\ \tau)\rightarrow(tree\ \tau)}\ (\mathbf{K^S}\ [\![\mathbf{right}_{(tree\ \tau)\rightarrow(tree\ \tau)}]\!])$$

where

$$\mathbf{K^A}\ [\![\mathbf{right}_{(tree\ \tau)\rightarrow(tree\ \tau)}]\!]\ t = \begin{cases} \bot & if\ t = \bot \\ \top\!\in & otherwise \end{cases}$$

Proof

Follows in the same way as for $\mathbf{left}_{(tree\ \tau)\to(tree\ \tau)}$.

□

A.4.7 Abstract Interpretation of $\mathbf{tcase}_{(tree\ \tau)\to\sigma\to((tree\ \tau)\to\tau\to(tree\ \tau)\to\sigma)\to\sigma}$

Lemma A.4.7

Let σ and τ be any types, and $\beta = (tree\ \tau) \to \sigma \to ((tree\ \tau) \to \tau \to (tree\ \tau) \to \sigma) \to \sigma$. Then

$$\mathbf{K}^{\mathbf{A}}\ [\![\mathbf{tcase}_\beta]\!] \sqsupseteq \alpha_\beta\ (\mathbf{K}^{\mathbf{S}}\ [\![\mathbf{tcase}_\beta]\!])$$

where $\mathbf{K}^{\mathbf{A}}\ [\![\mathbf{tcase}_\beta]\!]\ t\ s\ f$

$$= \begin{cases} \bot_{\mathbf{A}_\sigma} & \textit{if}\ t = \bot \\ (f\ \top\!\in\ \top_{\mathbf{A}_\tau}\ \infty) \sqcup (f\ \infty\ \top_{\mathbf{A}_\tau}\ \top\!\in) & \textit{if}\ t = \infty \\ (f\ \top\!\in\ \top_{\mathbf{A}_\tau}\ \bot\!\in) \sqcup (f\ \bot\!\in\ \top_{\mathbf{A}_\tau}\ \top\!\in) \sqcup (f\ \top\!\in\ \bot_{\mathbf{A}_\tau}\ \top\!\in) & \textit{if}\ t = \bot\!\in \\ s \sqcup (f\ \top\!\in\ \top_{\mathbf{A}_\tau}\ \top\!\in) & \textit{if}\ t = \top\!\in \end{cases}$$

Proof

This is proved in the same was as that $\mathbf{K}^{\mathbf{A}}\ [\![\mathbf{lcase}_{(list\ \tau)\to\sigma\to(\tau\to(list\ \tau)\to\sigma)\to\sigma}]\!]$ was proved to satisfy the constant safety condition (Lemma 4.1.9).

□

A.4.8 Abstract Interpretation of $\mathbf{take}_{\mathbf{i}_{\sigma_1\times\ldots\times\sigma_k\to\sigma_i}}$

Lemma A.4.8

For all types $\sigma_1, \ldots, \sigma_k$,

$$\mathbf{K}^{\mathbf{A}}\ [\![\mathbf{take}_{\mathbf{i}_{\sigma_1\times\ldots\times\sigma_k\to\sigma_i}}]\!] \sqsupseteq \alpha_{\sigma_1\times\ldots\times\sigma_k\to\sigma_i}\ (\mathbf{K}^{\mathbf{S}}\ [\![\mathbf{take}_{\mathbf{i}_{\sigma_1\times\ldots\times\sigma_k\to\sigma_i}}]\!])$$

where

$$\mathbf{K}^{\mathbf{A}}\ [\![\mathbf{take}_{\mathbf{i}_{\sigma_1\times\ldots\times\sigma_k\to\sigma_i}}]\!]\ e = e \downarrow i$$

Proof

Recall that $\mathbf{K}^{\mathbf{S}}\ [\![\mathbf{take}_{\mathbf{i}_{\sigma_1\times\ldots\times\sigma_k\to\sigma_i}}]\!] = (\lambda e \epsilon \mathbf{S}_{\sigma_1\times\ldots\times\sigma_k}.e \downarrow i)$ (Figure 2.12). We use the definition of $\alpha_{\sigma_1\times\ldots\times\sigma_k\to\sigma_i}$ from Proposition 3.2.6(2):

$$(\alpha_{\sigma_1\times\ldots\times\sigma_k\to\sigma_i}\ (\lambda e \epsilon \mathbf{S}_{\sigma_1\times\ldots\times\sigma_k}.e \downarrow i))\ \overline{e} = \bigsqcup\{\alpha_{\sigma_i}\ (e \downarrow i) | e \in (\gamma_{\sigma_1\times\ldots\times\sigma_k}\ \overline{e})\}$$

$$\begin{array}{ll} & (\alpha_{\sigma_1\times\ldots\times\sigma_k\to\sigma_i}\ (\lambda e \epsilon \mathbf{S}_{\sigma_1\times\ldots\times\sigma_k}.e \downarrow i))\ (\overline{s}_1, \ldots, \overline{s}_k) \\ = & \bigsqcup\{\alpha_{\sigma_i}\ (e \downarrow i) | e \in (\gamma_{\sigma_1\times\ldots\times\sigma_k}\ (\overline{s}_1, \ldots, \overline{s}_k))\} \\ \sqsubseteq & \bigsqcup\{\alpha_{\sigma_i}\ ((s_1, \ldots, s_k) \downarrow i) | \forall j \in \{1, \ldots, k\} : s_j \in (\gamma_{\sigma_j}\ \overline{s}_j)\} \\ & \quad \text{Proposition 3.2.8(1)} \\ = & \bigsqcup\{\alpha_{\sigma_i}\ s_i | s_i \in (\gamma_{\sigma_i}\ \overline{s}_i)\} \\ \sqsubseteq & \bigsqcup\{\overline{s}_i\} \qquad \text{Proposition 3.2.5} \\ = & \overline{s}_i \\ = & \mathbf{K}^{\mathbf{A}}\ [\![\mathbf{take}_{\mathbf{i}_{\sigma_1\times\ldots\times\sigma_k\to\sigma_i}}]\!]\ (\overline{s}_1, \ldots, \overline{s}_k) \end{array}$$

□

A.4.9 Abstract Interpretation of $\mathbf{takes}_{i_{\sigma_1 \otimes \ldots \otimes \sigma_k \to \sigma_i}}$

Lemma A.4.9

For all types $\sigma_1, \ldots, \sigma_k$,

$$\begin{array}{l} \mathbf{K}^{\mathbf{A}} [\![\mathbf{takes}_{i_{\sigma_1 \otimes \ldots \otimes \sigma_k \to \sigma_i}}]\!] \sqsupseteq \alpha_{\sigma_1 \otimes \ldots \otimes \sigma_k \to \sigma_i} (\mathbf{K}^{\mathbf{S}} [\![\mathbf{takes}_{i_{\sigma_1 \otimes \ldots \otimes \sigma_k \to \sigma_i}}]\!]) \\ \textit{where} \\ \mathbf{K}^{\mathbf{A}} [\![\mathbf{takes}_{i_{\sigma_1 \otimes \ldots \otimes \sigma_k \to \sigma_i}}]\!]\ e = e \downarrow i \end{array}$$

Proof

Recall that $\mathbf{K}^{\mathbf{S}} [\![\mathbf{takes}_{i_{\sigma_1 \otimes \ldots \otimes \sigma_k \to \sigma_i}}]\!] = (\lambda e \epsilon \mathbf{S}_{\sigma_1 \otimes \ldots \otimes \sigma_k}.e \downarrow i)$ (Figure 2.12). We use the definition of $\alpha_{\sigma_1 \otimes \ldots \otimes \sigma_k \to \sigma_i}$ from Proposition 3.2.6(2):

$$(\alpha_{\sigma_1 \otimes \ldots \otimes \sigma_k \to \sigma_i} (\lambda e \epsilon \mathbf{S}_{\sigma_1 \otimes \ldots \otimes \sigma_k}.e \downarrow i))\ \overline{e} = \bigsqcup \{\alpha_{\sigma_i} (e \downarrow i) | e \in (\gamma_{\sigma_1 \otimes \ldots \otimes \sigma_k}\ \overline{e})\}$$

There are two cases to consider:

1. $\overline{e} = \bot_{\mathbf{A}_{\sigma_1 \otimes \ldots \otimes \sigma_k}}$:

$$\begin{array}{l} (\alpha_{\sigma_1 \otimes \ldots \otimes \sigma_k \to \sigma_i} (\lambda e \epsilon \mathbf{S}_{\sigma_1 \otimes \ldots \otimes \sigma_k}.e \downarrow i))\ \bot_{\mathbf{A}_{\sigma_1 \otimes \ldots \otimes \sigma_k}} \\ \quad = \bigsqcup \{\alpha_{\sigma_i} (e \downarrow i) | e \in (\gamma_{\sigma_1 \otimes \ldots \otimes \sigma_k}\ \bot_{\mathbf{A}_{\sigma_1 \otimes \ldots \otimes \sigma_k}})\} \\ \quad = \bigsqcup \{\alpha_{\sigma_i} (\bot_{\mathbf{S}_{\sigma_1 \otimes \ldots \otimes \sigma_k}} \downarrow i)\} \quad \text{Lemma 4.1.6(3)} \\ \quad = \bigsqcup \{\alpha_{\sigma_i}\ \bot_{\mathbf{S}_{\sigma_i}}\} \quad \text{Figure 2.10} \\ \quad = \bigsqcup \{\bot_{\mathbf{A}_{\sigma_i}}\} \quad \text{Lemma 4.1.6(1)} \\ \quad = \bot_{\mathbf{A}_{\sigma_i}} \\ \quad = \mathbf{K}^{\mathbf{A}} [\![\mathbf{takes}_{i_{\sigma_1 \otimes \ldots \otimes \sigma_k \to \sigma_i}}]\!]\ \bot_{\mathbf{A}_{\sigma_1 \otimes \ldots \otimes \sigma_k}} \end{array}$$

2. $\overline{e} = < \overline{s}_1, \ldots, \overline{s}_k >$:

$$\begin{array}{cl} \multicolumn{2}{l}{(\alpha_{\sigma_1 \otimes \ldots \otimes \sigma_k \to \sigma_i} (\lambda e \epsilon \mathbf{S}_{\sigma_1 \otimes \ldots \otimes \sigma_k}.e \downarrow i))\ < \overline{s}_1, \ldots, \overline{s}_k >} \\ = & \bigsqcup \{\alpha_{\sigma_i} (e \downarrow i) | e \in (\gamma_{\sigma_1 \otimes \ldots \otimes \sigma_k}\ < \overline{s}_1, \ldots, \overline{s}_k >)\} \\ \sqsubseteq & \bigsqcup \{\alpha_{\sigma_i} (< s_1, \ldots, s_k > \downarrow i) | \forall j \in \{1, \ldots, k\} : s_j \in (\gamma_{\sigma_j}\ \overline{s}_j)\} \\ & \text{Proposition 3.2.8(2)} \\ = & \bigsqcup \{\alpha_{\sigma_i}\ s_i | s_i \in (\gamma_{\sigma_i}\ \overline{s}_i)\} \\ \sqsubseteq & \bigsqcup \{\overline{s}_i\} \quad \text{Proposition 3.2.5} \\ = & \overline{s}_i \\ = & \mathbf{K}^{\mathbf{A}} [\![\mathbf{takes}_{i_{\sigma_1 \otimes \ldots \otimes \sigma_k \to \sigma_i}}]\!]\ < \overline{s}_1, \ldots, \overline{s}_k > \end{array}$$

□

A.4.10 Abstract Interpretation of $\mathbf{outs}_{\mathrm{i}_{\sigma_1\oplus\ldots\oplus\sigma_k\rightarrow\sigma_i}}$

Lemma A.4.10

For all types σ_1, ..., σ_k,

$$\begin{array}{l} K^A\ [\![\mathbf{outs}_{\mathrm{i}_{\sigma_1\oplus\ldots\oplus\sigma_k\rightarrow\sigma_i}}]\!] \sqsupseteq \alpha_{\sigma_1\oplus\ldots\oplus\sigma_k\rightarrow\sigma_i}\ (K^S\ [\![\mathbf{outs}_{\mathrm{i}_{\sigma_1\oplus\ldots\oplus\sigma_k\rightarrow\sigma_i}}]\!]) \\ \textit{where} \\ K^A\ [\![\mathbf{outs}_{\mathrm{i}_{\sigma_1\oplus\ldots\oplus\sigma_k\rightarrow\sigma_i}}]\!]\ e = e \downarrow i \end{array}$$

Proof

Recall that $K^S\ [\![\mathbf{outs}_{\mathrm{i}_{\sigma_1\oplus\ldots\oplus\sigma_k\rightarrow\sigma_i}}]\!] = outs_i$ (Figure 2.16). We use the definition of $\alpha_{\sigma_1\oplus\ldots\oplus\sigma_k\rightarrow\sigma_i}$ from Proposition 3.2.6(2):

$$(\alpha_{\sigma_1\oplus\ldots\oplus\sigma_k\rightarrow\sigma_i}\ outs_i)\ \overline{e} = \bigsqcup\{\alpha_{\sigma_i}\ (outs_i\ e) | e \in (\gamma_{\sigma_1\oplus\ldots\oplus\sigma_k}\ \overline{e})\}$$

$$\begin{array}{l} (\alpha_{\sigma_1\oplus\ldots\oplus\sigma_k\rightarrow\sigma_i}\ outs_i)\ (\overline{s}_1,\ldots,\overline{s}_k) \\ \quad = \bigsqcup\{\alpha_{\sigma_i}\ (outs_i\ e) | e \in (\gamma_{\sigma_1\oplus\ldots\oplus\sigma_k}\ (\overline{s}_1,\ldots,\overline{s}_k))\} \\ \quad = \bigsqcup\{\alpha_{\sigma_i}\ (outs_i\ e) | e \in (\{mk\_sum_1\ s_1 | s_1 \in (\gamma_{\sigma_1}\ \overline{s}_1)\} \cup \ldots \\ \qquad\qquad \cup\{mk\_sum_k\ s_k | s_k \in (\gamma_{\sigma_k}\ \overline{s}_k)\})\} \\ \qquad \text{Proposition 3.2.8(3)} \\ \quad = \bigsqcup\{(\alpha_{\sigma_i}\ \bot_{S_{\sigma_i}}), (\alpha_{\sigma_i}\ s_i) | s_i \in (\gamma_{\sigma_i}\ \overline{s}_i)\} \\ \qquad \text{by definition of } outs_i \\ \quad \sqsubseteq \bigsqcup\{\overline{s}_i\} \qquad \text{Proposition 3.2.5} \\ \quad = \overline{s}_i \\ \quad = K^A\ [\![\mathbf{outs}_{\mathrm{i}_{\sigma_1\oplus\ldots\oplus\sigma_k\rightarrow\sigma_i}}]\!]\ (\overline{s}_1,\ldots,\overline{s}_k) \end{array}$$

□

A.4.11 Abstract Interpretation of $\mathbf{iss}_{\mathrm{i}_{\sigma_1\oplus\ldots\oplus\sigma_k\rightarrow bool}}$

Lemma A.4.11

For all types σ_1, ..., σ_k,

$$\begin{array}{l} K^A\ [\![\mathbf{iss}_{\mathrm{i}_{\sigma_1\oplus\ldots\oplus\sigma_k\rightarrow bool}}]\!] = \alpha_{\sigma_1\oplus\ldots\oplus\sigma_k\rightarrow bool}\ (K^S\ [\![\mathbf{iss}_{\mathrm{i}_{\sigma_1\oplus\ldots\oplus\sigma_k\rightarrow bool}}]\!]) \\ \textit{where} \\ K^A\ [\![\mathbf{iss}_{\mathrm{i}_{\sigma_1\oplus\ldots\oplus\sigma_k\rightarrow bool}}]\!]\ \bot_{A_{\sigma_1\oplus\ldots\oplus\sigma_k}} = \bot_{A_{bool}}\ (=0) \\ K^A\ [\![\mathbf{iss}_{\mathrm{i}_{\sigma_1\oplus\ldots\oplus\sigma_k\rightarrow bool}}]\!]\ (s_1,\ldots,s_k) = \top_{A_{bool}}\ (=1) \end{array}$$

Proof

Recall that $K^S\ [\![\mathbf{iss}_{\mathrm{i}_{\sigma_1\oplus\ldots\oplus\sigma_k\rightarrow bool}}]\!] = iss_i$ (Figure 2.16). We use the definition of $\alpha_{\sigma_1\oplus\ldots\oplus\sigma_k\rightarrow bool}$ from Proposition 3.2.6(2):

$$(\alpha_{\sigma_1\oplus\ldots\oplus\sigma_k\rightarrow\sigma_i}\ iss_i)\ \overline{e} = \bigsqcup\{\alpha_{bool}\ (iss_i\ e) | e \in (\gamma_{\sigma_1\oplus\ldots\oplus\sigma_k}\ \overline{e})\}.$$

There are two cases to consider:

1. $\overline{e} = \perp_{\mathbf{A}_{\sigma_1 \oplus \ldots \oplus \sigma_k}}$:

$$
\begin{aligned}
&(\alpha_{\sigma_1 \oplus \ldots \oplus \sigma_k \to bool}\ iss_i)\ \perp_{\mathbf{A}_{\sigma_1 \oplus \ldots \oplus \sigma_k}} \\
&\quad = \bigsqcup\{\alpha_{bool}\ (iss_i\ e) | e \in (\gamma_{\sigma_1 \oplus \ldots \oplus \sigma_k}\ \perp_{\mathbf{A}_{\sigma_1 \oplus \ldots \oplus \sigma_k}})\} \\
&\quad = \bigsqcup\{\alpha_{bool}\ (iss_i\ \perp_{\mathbf{S}_{\sigma_1 \oplus \ldots \oplus \sigma_k}})\} \quad \text{Lemma 4.1.6(3)} \\
&\quad = \bigsqcup\{\alpha_{bool}\ \perp_{\mathbf{S}_{bool}}\} \quad \text{Figure 2.10} \\
&\quad = \bigsqcup\{\perp_{\mathbf{A}_{bool}}\} \quad \text{Lemma 4.1.6(1)} \\
&\quad = \perp_{\mathbf{A}_{bool}} \\
&\quad = \mathbf{K}^{\mathbf{A}}\ [\![\mathbf{iss}_{\mathbf{i}_{\sigma_1 \oplus \ldots \oplus \sigma_k \to bool}}]\!]\ \perp_{\mathbf{A}_{\sigma_1 \oplus \ldots \oplus \sigma_k}}
\end{aligned}
$$

2. $\overline{e} = (\overline{s}_1, \ldots, \overline{s}_k)$ where $\exists j \in \{1, \ldots, k\} : \overline{s}_j \neq \perp_{\mathbf{A}_{\sigma_j}}$:
   Using Proposition 3.2.8(3), we have that

$$
\begin{aligned}
&\gamma_{\sigma_1 \oplus \ldots \oplus \sigma_k}\ (\overline{s}_1, \ldots, \overline{s}_k) \\
&\quad = \{mk\_sum_1\ s_1 | s_1 \in (\gamma_{\sigma_1}\ \overline{s}_1)\} \cup \ldots \cup \{mk\_sum_k\ s_k | s_k \in (\gamma_{\sigma_k}\ \overline{s}_k)\}
\end{aligned}
$$

   When $\overline{s}_j \neq \perp_{\mathbf{A}_{\sigma_j}}$, we have that $(\gamma_{\sigma_j}\ \overline{s}_j)$ contains objects other than $\perp_{\mathbf{S}_{\sigma_j}}$ (since α_{σ_j} is bottom-reflecting by Lemma 4.1.6(2)). If s_j is such an object, then $(mk\_sum_j\ s_j)$ is $(ins_j\ s_j)$, and $(iss_i\ (ins_j\ s_j)$ is one of *true* and *false*. In either case, α_{bool} applied to the result returns 1, which is the required result.

□

Appendix B

The Spineless G-Machine

This appendix contains a complete specification of the Spineless G-machine and compilation rules for a simple combinator language. For simplicity, the only data types it supports are booleans, integers, lists and trees.

B.1 Compilation Rules

The abstract compiler which generates Spineless G-code is given below, and is divided into four compilation schemes. When using each particular scheme, the source program fragment should be matched with each rule of the scheme in turn. The type of an object appearing in the compilation rules can always be deduced from the letter representing it:

r	is an 'environment' indicating where variables reside on the stack		
n	is the current stack depth	x	is a variable
b	is a boolean constant	m	is ≥ 0
i	is an integer constant	f	is a function
l	is a new and unique label	D	is an arbitrary expression

B.1.1 Scheme $\mathcal{F}$ (Function Definition)

This generates code for an entire function definition.

$\mathcal{F}$ ⟦ f x1 ...xm = D ⟧ = $\mathcal{R}$ ⟦ D ⟧ [x1 $\mapsto$ m , ..., xm $\mapsto$ 1] m

At the point of entry for a function, it is guaranteed that its first argument is pointed to by the top of stack, the second argument by the next-to-top element, and so on, so that the mth argument is m-1 elements from the top of the stack.

B.1.2 Scheme $\mathcal{R}$ (Return Value)

$\mathcal{R}$ ⟦ D ⟧ r n generates code to compute the value of D , push it onto the stack, and return from a function.

$\mathcal{R}$ ⟦ i ⟧ r n = $\mathcal{E}$ ⟦ i ⟧ r n; SQUEEZE 1 n; RETURN

```
R [[ b ]] r n       = E [[ b ]] r n; SQUEEZE 1 n; RETURN
R [[ Nil ]] r n     = E [[ Nil ]] r n; SQUEEZE 1 n; RETURN
R [[ Empty ]] r n = E [[ Empty ]] r n; SQUEEZE 1 n; RETURN
R [[ add D1 D2 ]] r n = E [[ add D1 D2 ]] r n; SQUEEZE 1 n; RETURN
   similarly for sub/mul/div/eq/lt/gt/le/ge/Cons
R [[ head D ]] r n = E [[ head D ]] r n; SQUEEZE 1 n; RETURN
   similarly for tail
R [[ Node D1 D2 D3 ]] r n = C [[ D3 ]] r n; C [[ D2 ]] r (n+1); C [[ D1 ]] r (n+2);
                            NODE; SQUEEZE 1 n; RETURN
R [[ if D1 D2 D3 ]] r n = E [[ D1 ]] r n; JFALSE 1;
                          R [[ D2 ]] r n; LABEL 1; R [[ D3 ]] r n
R [[ lcase D1 D2 (λx.λxs.D3) ]] r n = E [[ D1 ]] r n; LCASE 1; R [[ D2 ]] r n;
                     LABEL 1; R [[ D3 ]] r[xs↦(n+1), x↦(n+2)] (n+2)
R [[ tcase D1 D2 (λt1.λu.λt2.D3) ]] r n = E [[ D1 ]] r n; TCASE 1; R [[ D2 ]] r n;
                     LABEL 1; R [[ D3 ]] r[t2↦(n+1), u↦(n+2), t1↦(n+3)] (n+3)
R [[ f D1 ...Dm ]] r n = C [[ Dm ]] r n; ...C [[ D1 ]] r (n+m-1);
                         SQUEEZE m n; PUSHFUN f; ENTER
R [[ x D1 ...Dm ]] r n = C [[ Dm ]] r n; ...C [[ D1 ]] r (n+m-1);
                         PUSH ((n+m)-(r x)); SQUEEZE (m+1) n; LOAD
R [[ let x=e1 in e2 ]] r n = E [[ e1 ]] r n; R [[ e2 ]] r[x ↦ (n+1)] (n+1)
```

B.1.3 Scheme $\mathcal{E}$ (Evaluate)

$\mathcal{E}$ [[D]] r n generates code which computes the value of D , and leaves a pointer to this value on top of the stack. This scheme avoids building graphs where possible.

```
E [[ i ]] r n       = PUSHINT i
E [[ b ]] r n       = PUSHBOOL b
E [[ Nil ]] r n     = PUSHNIL
E [[ Empty ]] r n = PUSHEMPTY
E [[ f ]] r n       = PUSHFUN f; EVAL
E [[ x ]] r n       = PUSH (n-(r x)); EVAL
E [[ add D1 D2 ]] r n = E [[ D1 ]] r n; E [[ D2 ]] r n; ADD
   similarly for sub/mul/div/eq/lt/gt/le/ge
E [[ Cons D1 D2 ]] r n  = C [[ D2 ]] r n; C [[ D1 ]] r (n+1); CONS
E [[ head D ]] r n      = E [[ D ]] r n; HEAD; EVAL
   similarly for tail
E [[ Node D1 D2 D3 ]] r n = C [[ D3 ]] r n; C [[ D2 ]] r (n+1); C [[ D1 ]] r (n+2);
                            NODE
E [[ if D1 D2 D3 ]] r n = E [[ D1 ]] r n; JFALSE 11; E [[ D2 ]] r n; JMP 12;
                          LABEL 11; E [[ D3 ]] r n; LABEL 12
E [[ lcase D1 D2 (λx.λxs.D3) ]] r n = E [[ D1 ]] r n; LCASE 11; E [[ D2 ]] r n;
                     JMP 12; LABEL 11; E [[ D3 ]] r[xs↦(n+1), x↦(n+2)] (n+2);
                     SQUEEZE 1 2; LABEL 12
E [[ tcase D1 D2 (λt1.λu.λt2.D3) ]] r n = E [[ D1 ]] r n; TCASE 11; E [[ D2 ]] r n;
```

```
          JMP l2; LABEL l1; ℰ ⟦ D3 ⟧ r[t2↦(n+1), u↦(n+2), t1↦(n+3)] (n+3);
          SQUEEZE 1 3; LABEL l2
ℰ ⟦ f D1 ...Dm ⟧ r n = 𝒞 ⟦ Dm ⟧ r n; ...𝒞 ⟦ D1 ⟧ r (n+m-1);
                       PUSHFUN f; CALL (m+1)
ℰ ⟦ x D1 ...Dm ⟧ r n   = 𝒞 ⟦ Dm ⟧ r n; ...𝒞 ⟦ D1 ⟧ r (n+m-1);
                       PUSH ((n+m)-(r x)); CALL (m+1)
ℰ ⟦ let x=e1 in e2 ⟧ r n = ℰ ⟦ e1 ⟧ r n; ℰ ⟦ e2 ⟧ r[x ↦ (n+1)] (n+1);
                         SQUEEZE 1 1
```

B.1.4 Scheme 𝒞 (Construct Graph)

𝒞 ⟦ D ⟧ r n generates code which Constructs the graph of D , and leaves a pointer to this graph on the stack.

```
𝒞 ⟦ i ⟧ r n       = PUSHINT i
𝒞 ⟦ b ⟧ r n       = PUSHBOOL b
𝒞 ⟦ Nil ⟧ r n     = PUSHNIL
𝒞 ⟦ Empty ⟧ r n = PUSHEMPTY
𝒞 ⟦ f ⟧ r n       = PUSHFUN f
𝒞 ⟦ x ⟧ r n       = PUSH (n-(r x))
𝒞 ⟦ Cons D1 D2 ⟧ r n = 𝒞 ⟦ D2 ⟧ r n; 𝒞 ⟦ D1 ⟧ r (n+1); CONS
𝒞 ⟦ Node D1 D2 D3 ⟧ r n = 𝒞 ⟦ D3 ⟧ r n; 𝒞 ⟦ D2 ⟧ r (n+1); 𝒞 ⟦ D1 ⟧ r (n+2);
                        NODE
𝒞 ⟦ D1 ...Dm ⟧ r n = 𝒞 ⟦ Dm ⟧ r n; ...𝒞 ⟦ D1 ⟧ r (n+m-1); STORE m
```

B.2 Initial G-machine state

The initial configuration of the G-machine for the program:

```
E0; /* the program value */
f1 x1 ... xn1 = E1; /* function definitions */
...
fm x1 ... xnm = Em;
```

is as follows:

```
> initial_state = ([], c, [], g, [], e)
>                 where
>                 c = ℰ ⟦ E0 ⟧ [] 0; PRINT; STOP
>                 g = [
>                     (0, (Fun f1 n1 (ℱ ⟦ f1 x1 ... xn1 = E1 ⟧))),
>                     ...
>                     (m-1, (Fun fm nm (ℱ ⟦ fm x1 ... xnm = Em ⟧))),
>                     (m, (Fun "add" 2 (ℱ ⟦ add x y = add x y ⟧))),
>                     ... (code for other base functions)
>                     ]
>                 e = [(f1,0), ... , (fm, m-1), ("add", m),     ]
```

It is necessary to represent built-in operators such as $*$ and $-$ in unevaluated expression graphs, and thus the initial graph must contain FUN nodes for the compiled code which performs these operations.

B.3 An Interpreter for the Spineless G-Machine

Definitions of abstract machines for functional languages have traditionally been given as a set of state transition rules, see [Aug87, Joh87, BPJR88, Bur88b] for example. However, Lester wrote a specification of a abstract parallel machine in a functional language [LB89], and we have adopted this approach in specifying the Spineless G-machine. The following specification is written in the language Miranda [Tur86], using the inverse comment convention, so that all lines of program text begin with a '>'. In fact, this section of the book is a valid Miranda program, and we have successfully run it on several test programs, so hopefully the specification is correct!

The specification is broken up into seven parts: a description of the state of the machine, the execution cycle, the instruction decoder, the definitions of the instructions, auxiliary definitions, functions to pretty-print the state, and an example initial state.

To make it easier to find the function definitions, the page on which each function is defined is recorded in the index.

B.3.1 The State of the Spineless G-Machine

```
> state         == (output, code_sequence, stack, graph, dump, environment)
> output        == [char]
> code_sequence == [gcode]
> stack         == [label]
> graph         == [graph_node]
> dump          == [([gcode], stack)]
> environment   == [(function_name, label)]

> label         == num
> arity         == num
> function_name == [char]
> graph_node    == (label, tagged_exp)
```

The Spineless G-machine is a stack-based architecture. We represent the `state` of the Spineless G-machine with a tuple of 6 elements:

- `output`: The output from the machine is represented as a list of characters.
- `code_sequence`: This is the sequence of instructions which is currently being executed. The next instruction to be executed is the head of the list.

- stack: The stack caches the spine of the expression currently being evaluated. We represent it as a list of labels, where a label in a real implementation would be the address of some memory location (i.e. a pointer).

- graph: The graph is represented as a list of graph_nodes, where a graph_node is a pair of a label and a tagged_expression.

  No garbage collection is done in this specification.

- dump: When the evaluation of some subexpression is commenced, the current instruction sequence and stack are saved on the dump so that they can be resumed when the evaluation of the subexpression has been completed.

- environment: In the initial state of the machine, the graph contains a node for each function defined in the program. Each pair in the environment contains a function name and the label of its node in the graph.

```
> tagged_exp ::= Int num                              |
>                Bool bool                            |
>                Vap [label]                          |
>                Wvap [label]                         |
>                Fun arity [gcode]                    |
>                Nil | Cons label label               |
>                Empty | Node label label label
```

Nodes in the graph are tagged to indicate the type of data they contain. Integers have tag Int, booleans Bool, applications are stored with a tag Vap, applications in head normal form with Wvap, Nil and Cons are used for implementing lists, and Empty and Node for trees. A Fun node stores the arity and code sequence for a function.

```
> code_label == [char]
> stack_index == num

> gcode ::= ADD | SUB | MUL | DIV | GE | GT | LE | LT | AND | OR | EQ      |
>           CONS | PUSHNIL | HEAD | TAIL | LCASE code_label               |
>           NODE | PUSHEMPTY |  VALUE | LEFT | RIGHT | TCASE code_label |
>           JFALSE code_label | JMP code_label | LABEL code_label         |
>           PUSH stack_index | PUSHBOOL bool | PUSHINT num                |
>           PUSHFUN function_name | SQUEEZE num num                       |
>           STORE num | WSTORE num                                        |
>           ENTER | LOAD | EVAL | CALL num  | UPDATE num | RETURN         |
>           PRINT | STOP
```

The instruction set of the Spineless G-machine is given by the type gcode.

B.3.2 The Execution Loop

```
> run st = [st],                  if c = STOP
>        = st:run (step st), otherwise
>          where
>          (o, c:cs, s, g, d, e) = st
```

Executing one Spineless G-machine instruction constitutes a cycle of the Spineless G-machine. The machine executes each instruction in the instruction stream until STOP is reached, whereupon the machine stops. Running the simulator on some initial state results in a list of the states that the machine has been in whilst running its program.

B.3.3 The Instruction Decoder

Each instruction is a state transition function, and so is specified by a function of type `state -> state`. The function `step` is an instruction decoder, removing the first instruction and calling the appropriate function to execute the instruction. We have adopted the convention that, except for arithmetic, boolean and comparison instructions, the name of the function defining an instruction is the same as the instruction except that it is in lower-case letters. These are defined in Section B.3.4. Related instructions are grouped together.

```
> step (o, ADD:c, s, g, d, e) = arithmetic_op (+) (o, c, s, g, d, e)
> step (o, SUB:c, s, g, d, e) = arithmetic_op (-) (o, c, s, g, d, e)
> step (o, MUL:c, s, g, d, e) = arithmetic_op (*) (o, c, s, g, d, e)
> step (o, DIV:c, s, g, d, e) = arithmetic_op (/) (o, c, s, g, d, e)

> step (o, AND:c, s, g, d, e) = boolean_op (&) (o, c, s, g, d, e)
> step (o, OR:c, s, g, d, e)  = boolean_op (\/) (o, c, s, g, d, e)

> step (o, GE:c, s, g, d, e) = comparison_op (>=) (o, c, s, g, d, e)
> step (o, GT:c, s, g, d, e) = comparison_op (>) (o, c, s, g, d, e)
> step (o, LE:c, s, g, d, e) = comparison_op (<=) (o, c, s, g, d, e)
> step (o, LT:c, s, g, d, e) = comparison_op (<) (o, c, s, g, d, e)

> step (o, EQ:c, s, g, d, e) = eq (o, c, s, g, d, e)

> step (o, CONS:c, s, g, d, e)    = cons (o, c, s, g, d, e)
> step (o, PUSHNIL:c, s, g, d, e) = pushnil (o, c, s, g, d, e)
> step (o, HEAD:c, s, g, d, e)    = head (o, c, s, g, d, e)
> step (o, TAIL:c, s, g, d, e)    = tail (o, c, s, g, d, e)
> step (o, LCASE l:c, s, g, d, e) = lcase l (o, c, s, g, d, e)
```

```
> step (o, NODE:c, s, g, d, e)      = node (o, c, s, g, d, e)
> step (o, PUSHEMPTY:c, s, g, d, e) = pushempty (o, c, s, g, d, e)
> step (o, VALUE:c, s, g, d, e)     = value (o, c, s, g, d, e)
> step (o, LEFT:c, s, g, d, e)      = left (o, c, s, g, d, e)
> step (o, RIGHT:c, s, g, d, e)     = right (o, c, s, g, d, e)
> step (o, TCASE l:c, s, g, d, e)   = tcase l (o, c, s, g, d, e)

> step (o, JFALSE l:c, s, g, d, e) = jfalse l (o, c, s, g, d, e)
> step (o, JMP l:c, s, g, d, e)    = jmp l (o, c, s, g, d, e)
> step (o, LABEL l:c, s, g, d, e)  = step (o, c, s, g, d, e)

> step (o, PUSH n:c, s, g, d, e)        = push n (o, c, s, g, d, e)
> step (o, PUSHINT n:c, s, g, d, e)     = pushint n (o, c, s, g, d, e)
> step (o, PUSHBOOL b:c, s, g, d, e)    = pushbool b (o, c, s, g, d, e)
> step (o, PUSHFUN f:c, s, g, d, e)     = pushfun f (o, c, s, g, d, e)
> step (o, STORE m:c, s, g, d, e)       = store m (o, c, s, g, d, e)
> step (o, WSTORE m:c, s, g, d, e)      = wstore m (o, c, s, g, d, e)
> step (o, SQUEEZE m n:c, s, g, d, e)   = squeeze m n (o, c, s, g, d, e)

> step (o, ENTER:c, s, g, d, e)      = enter (o, c, s, g, d, e)
> step (o, LOAD:c, s, g, d, e)       = load (o, c, s, g, d, e)
> step (o, EVAL:c, s, g, d, e)       = eval (o, c, s, g, d, e)
> step (o, CALL m:c, s, g, d, e)     = call m (o, c, s, g, d, e)
> step (o, UPDATE m:c, s, g, d, e)   = update m (o, c, s, g, d, e)
> step (o, RETURN:c, s, g, d, e)     = return (o, c, s, g, d, e)

> step (o, PRINT:c, s, g, d, e)  = print (o, c, s, g, d, e)

> step (o, STOP:c, s, g, d, e)  = (o, c, s, g, d, e)
```

B.3.4 State Transition Functions

The instructions of the Spineless G-machine are specified as functions from `state` to `state`. To help show which parts of the state are changed by an instruction, we represent the argument state by the tuple

`(o, c, s, g, d, e)`

and give the result in the same form, priming the parts of the state that have been altered, and defining the primed objects as subdefinitions. For example, in the definition of `arithmetic_op`, only the `stack` and `graph` components of the state are changed, and so the resulting state is given by the tuple

`(o, c, s', g', d, e)`

Arithmetic, Boolean and Comparison Instructions

Arithmetic, boolean and comparison instructions take the top two labels from the stack, perform the specified operation on the values in the nodes with those labels, create a new node in the graph to store the value resulting from the operation, and leave the label of the new node on the top of the stack.

```
> arithmetic_op op (o, c, s, g, d, e)
>   = (o, c, s', g', d, e)
>     where
>     n = newlabel g
>     s' = stack_push n (stack_pop 2 s)
>     (Int i2) = g_lookup g (top s)
>     (Int i1) = g_lookup g (next_to_top s)
>     g' = (n, Int (op i1 i2)):g

> boolean_op op (o, c, s, g, d, e)
>   = (o, c, s', g', d, e)
>     where
>     n = newlabel g
>     s' = stack_push n (stack_pop 2 s)
>     (Bool b2) = g_lookup g (top s)
>     (Bool b1) = g_lookup g (next_to_top s)
>     g' = (n, Bool (op b1 b2)):g

> comparison_op op (o, c, s, g, d, e)
>   = (o, c, s', g', d, e)
>     where
>     n = newlabel g
>     s' = stack_push n (stack_pop 2 s)
>     (Int i2) = g_lookup g (top s)
>     (Int i1) = g_lookup g (next_to_top s)
>     g' = (n, Bool (op i1 i2)):g

> eq (o, c, s, g, d, e)
>   = (o, c, s' g' d, e)
>     where
>     n = newlabel g
>     s' = stack_push n (stack_pop 2 s)
>     te2 = g_lookup g (top s)
>     te1 = g_lookup g (next_to_top s)
>     g' = (n, Bool (te1 = te2)):g
```

List Manipulation Instructions

The CONS instruction creates a Cons node in the graph which has the two top labels from the stack for its respective fields, removes the two top labels from the stack, and leaves the label of the new Cons node on the top of the stack.

```
> cons (o, c, s, g, d, e)
>   = (o, c, s', g', d, e)
>     where
>     n = newlabel g
>     s' = stack_push n (stack_pop 2 s)
>     n1 = top s
>     n2 = next_to_top s
>     g' = (n, Cons n1 n2):g
```

A new Nil node is created in the graph and the label of the new node is put on the top of the stack by the PUSHNIL instruction.

```
> pushnil (o,     s, g, d, e)
>   = (o,     s'  g', d, e)
>     where
>     n = newlabel g
>     s' = (stack_push n s)
>     g' = (n, Nil):g
```

If the node whose label is on the top of the stack is a Cons node, then HEAD replaces the label of the Cons node with the label of its head (the first label in the Cons node), otherwise it gives an error message.

```
> head (o, c, s, g, d, e)
>   = (o, c, s'  g, d, e),              if isCons te
>   = error "Tried to take head of Nil"  otherwise
>     where
>     te = g_lookup g (top s)
>     (Cons n1 n2) = te
>     s' = stack_push n1 (stack_pop 1 s)
```

If the node whose label is on the top of the stack is a Cons node, then TAIL replaces the label of the Cons node with the label of its tail (the second label in the Cons node), otherwise it gives an error message.

```
> tail (o, c, s, g, d, e)
>   = (o, c, s', g, d, e),                if isCons te
>   = error "Tried to take tail of Nil", otherwise
>     where
>     te = g_lookup g (top s)
>     (Cons n1 n2) = te
>     s' = stack_push n2 (stack_pop 1 s)
```

Tree Manipulation Instructions

The NODE instruction creates a Node node in the graph which has the three top labels from the stack for its respective fields, removes the three top labels from the stack, and leaves the label of the new Node node on the top of the stack.

```
> node (o, c, s, g, d, e)
>   = (o, c, s'  g', d, e)
>     where
>     n = newlabel g
>     s' = stack_push n (stack_pop 3 s)
>     n1 = top s
>     n2 = next_to_top s
>     n3 = index_stack 2 s
>     g' = (n, Node n1 n2 n3):g
```

A new Empty node is created in the graph and the label of the new node is put on the top of the stack by the EMPTY instruction.

```
> pushempty (o, c, s, g, d, e)
>   = (o, c, s', g', d, e)
>     where
>     n = newlabel g
>     s' = stack_push n s
>     g' = (n, Empty):g
```

If the node whose label is on the top of the stack is a Node node, then LEFT replaces the label of the Node node with the label of its left subtree (the first label in the Node node), otherwise it gives an error message.

```
> left (o, c, s, g, d, e)
>   = (o, c, s', g, d, e),                     if isNode te
>   = error "Tried to take left of Emtpy", otherwise
>     where
>     te = g_lookup g (top s)
>     (Node n1 n2 n3) = te
>     s' = stack_push n1 (stack_pop 1 s)
```

If the node whose label is on the top of the stack is a Node node, then RIGHT replaces the label of the Node node with the label of its right subtree (the third label in the Node node), otherwise it gives an error message.

```
> right (o, c, s, g, d, e)
>   = (o, c, s', g, d, e),                     if isNode te
>   = error "Tried to take right of Empty", otherwise
>     where
>     te              = g_lookup g (top s)
>     (Node n1 n2 n3) = te
>     s'              = stack_push n3 (stack_pop 1 s)
```

If the node whose label is on the top of the stack is a Node node, then VALUE replaces the label of the Node node with the label of the value (the second label in the Node node), otherwise it gives an error message.

```
> value (o, c, s, g, d, e)
>   = (o, c, s', g, d, e),                     if isNode te
>   = error "Tried to take value of Empty", otherwise
>     where
>     te              = g_lookup g (top s)
>     (Node n1 n2 n3) = te
>     s'              = stack_push n2 (stack_pop 1 s)
```

Jump Instructions

There are two kinds of jumps in the Spineless G-machine. The compiler for given in Section B.1 only generates forwards jumps. A conditional jump is provided by the JFALSE instruction. It tests the value of the boolean stored in the node whose label is on the top of the stack. If it is true then it just discards the top label from the stack and proceeds to the next instruction, otherwise it discards the top label from the stack and jumps to the instruction following its argument label. The JMP instruction is an unconditional jump to the instruction following its argument label.

```
> jfalse l (o, c, s, g, d, e)
>   = (o, c, s', g, d, e),  if b
>   = (o, c', s', g, d, e), otherwise
>     where
>     c'       = find_destination l c
>     s'       = stack_pop 1 s
>     (Bool b) = g_lookup g (top s)

> jmp l (o, c, s, g, d, e)
>   = (o, c'  s, g, d, e)
>     where
>     c' = find_destination l c

> find_destination l (c:cs) = cs,                     if c = LABEL l
>                           = find_destination l cs, otherwise
```

Case Instructions

The LCASE instruction tests the node whose label is on the top of the stack, to see if it is a Nil or a Cons node. In the first case, it just removes the top label from the stack and proceeds with the current code sequence (the code for the Nil case). In the second, it removes the top stack label, places the labels of the tail and head of the list onto the stack, and jumps to the code for the Cons case.

The TCASE instruction behaves in a similar way.

```
> lcase l (o, c, s, g, d, e)
>   = (o, c, s', g, d, e),   if isNil te
>   = (o, c', s'', g, d, e), if isCons te
>     where
>     c'             = find_destination l c
>     s'             = stack_pop 1 s
>     te             = g_lookup g (top s)
>     s''            = stack_push n1 (stack_push n2 (stack_pop 1 s))
>     (Cons n1 n2) = te

> tcase l (o, c, s, g, d, e)
>   = (o, c, s', g, d, e),   if isEmpty te
>   = (o, c', s'', g, d, e), if isNode te
>     where
>     c'                = find_destination l c
>     s'                = stack_pop 1 s
>     te                = g_lookup g (top s)
>     s''               = stack_push t1 (stack_push n (stack_push t2
```

```
>                                             (stack_pop 1 s)))
>       (Node t1 n t2) = te
```

Stack and Heap Operations

The stack is zero-indexed (i.e. the top of the stack has index 0), and PUSH n pushes a copy of the label, at stack index n onto the stack. PUSHINT and PUSHBOOL create new graph nodes containing an integer and a boolean respectively, and leave the label of the new node on the top of the stack.

```
> push n (o, c, s, g, d, e)
>   = (o, c, s', g, d, e)
>     where
>     s' = stack_push (index_stack n s) s

> pushint i (o, c, s, g, d, e)
>   = (o, c, s'  g', d, e)
>     where
>     n = newlabel g
>     s' = stack_push n s
>     g' = (n, Int i):g

> pushbool b (o, c, s, g, d, e)
>   = (o, c, s', g', d, e)
>     where
>     n = newlabel g
>     s' = stack_push n s
>     g' = (n, Bool b):g
```

PUSHFUN pushes onto the stack a pointer to the graph node containing the code for its argument. It finds the node pointer by looking up its value in the environment, using e_lookup

```
> pushfun f (o, c, s, g, d, e)
>   = (o, c, s', g, d, e)
>     where
>     n = e_lookup e f
>     s' = stack_push n s
```

Given an argument m, STORE creates a new Vap node containing the top m pointers from the stack, removes the pointers from the stack, and leaves a pointer to the newly created Vap node on the top of the stack.

```
> store m (o, c, s, g, d, e)
>   = (o, c, s', g', d, e)
>     where
>     n = newlabel g
>     s' = stack_push n (stack_pop m s)
>     g' = (n, Vap (take m s)):g
```

The functionality of WSTORE is the same as STORE except that it creates a Wvap node instead of a Vap node. A Wvap node stores an application of a function to too few arguments, which is in head normal form, and so does not need further evaluation.

```
> wstore m (o, c, s, g, d, e)
>   = (o, c, s', g', d, e)
>     where
>     n = newlabel g
>     s' = stack_push n (stack_pop m s)
>     g' = (n, Wvap (take m s)):g
```

SQUEEZE m n takes the top m pointers on the stack and moves them down n places, squeezing out the n pointers below them.

```
> squeeze m n (o, c, s, g, d, e)
>   = (o, c, s', g, d, e)
>     where
>     s' = (take m s) ++ (stack_pop (m+n) s)
```

Evaluation Instructions

The instruction ENTER is only ever executed when the pointer on the top of the stack points to a Fun node. Code is generated assuming the invariant that the code for a function is only entered if there are enough arguments on the stack to perform a reduction step (see Section 6.2.3). Since the stack is being represented as a list, the number of arguments on the stack, nargs, is one less than the length of the stack. Each Fun node contains the arity of its function (a). There are two cases to consider:

1. there are enough arguments on the stack (nargs >= a): the code for the function, cs, stored in the Fun node, can be entered, after the pointer to the function is popped off the stack.

2. there are not enough arguments on the stack: the result is in head normal form, and so a node is created to store the partial application (WSTORE m), and a return is made to the code which caused the evaluation of this expression (RETURN).

```
> enter (o, c, s, g, d, e)
>   = (o, c', s'  g, d, e)
>     where
>     (Fun a cs) = g_lookup g (top s)
>     c'         = cs,                  if nargs >= a
>                = [WSTORE m, RETURN], otherwise
>     s'         = stack_pop 1 s, if nargs >= a
>                = s,             otherwise
>     m          = #s
>     nargs      = m-1
```

The purpose of the LOAD instruction is to get the stack ready for evaluating an expression. If the pointer on the top of the stack does not point to a Wvap, a Vap or a Fun node, then the expression does not need to be loaded onto the stack, and so a return is made to the code which caused the evaluation of this expression (c''), leaving a pointer to the reduced expression ((top s)) on the top of the restored stack (s'''), to give the new stack s''. There are three other cases to consider:

1. the top of stack points to a Vap node: here the expression may be shared, so it must be evaluated to HNF, and then the result can be loaded onto the stack.
2. the top of stack points to a Wvap node: here the expression has been evaluated to head normal form, and so after removing the pointer to the Wvap node, all the pointers contained in the node can be loaded onto the stack, and the ENTER instruction executed to see if there are enough arguments on the stack for the execution of the code for the function stored in the Wvap.
3. the top of stack points to a Fun node: All the arguments have now been loaded onto the stack, and so an ENTER instruction is executed to see if there are enough arguments on the stack to execute the code for the function.

```
> load (o, c, s, g, d, e)
>   = (o, c', s', g, d, e),     if isWvap te \/ isVap te \/ isFun te
>   = (o, c'', s'', g, d'', e), otherwise
>     where
>     te = g_lookup g (top s)
>     c'                = [EVAL, LOAD], if isVap te
>                       = [ENTER],      if isFun te \/ isWvap te
>     s'                = ns ++ (stack_pop 1 s), if isWvap te
>                       = s,                     if isVap te \/ isFun te
>     (Wvap ns)         = te
>     ((c'',s'''):d'') = d
>     s''               = stack_push (top s) s'''
```

The EVAL instruction causes an expression to be evaluated to head normal form. If the graph pointed to by the top of stack is already in head normal form, then the EVAL instruction does nothing. Otherwise it is a Vap node, which must be evaluated. To do this, the remaining code sequence and the stack are saved on the dump. An UPDATE instruction is prepended to the saved code so that the Vap node will be overwritten with the head normal form of the expression when it has been reduced. The new stack contains all the pointers that were on the Vap node, and the new code sequence consists of the single instruction LOAD, which gets the stack ready to evaluate the expression.

```
> eval (o, c, s, g, d, e)
>   = (o, c', s', g, d', e), if isVap te
>   = (o, c, s, g, d, e),     otherwise
>     where
>     c'         = [LOAD]
>     s'         = ns
>     d'         = (UPDATE 1:c, s):d
>     te         = g_lookup g n
>     (Vap ns) = te
>     n          = top s
```

The CALL instruction is generated as an optimisation for the code:

$$\mathcal{E}\ [\![\texttt{f E1 ... En}]\!]\ \texttt{r n} = \mathcal{C}\ [\![\texttt{f E1 ... En}]\!]\ \texttt{r n};\ \texttt{EVAL}$$

which creates a new Vap node for the application (f E1 ... En), only to have to read all the pointers to the argument expressions back onto the stack again in the EVAL instruction. Instead the following code is generated:

$$\begin{aligned}\mathcal{E}\ [\![\texttt{f E1 ... En}]\!]\ \texttt{r n} \ &= \ \mathcal{C}\ [\![\texttt{En}]\!]\ \texttt{r n};\ldots;\mathcal{C}\ [\![\texttt{E1}]\!]\ \texttt{r}\ (\texttt{n}+\texttt{m}-1);\\ &\quad\ \texttt{PUSHFUN f; CALL}\ (\texttt{m}+1)\end{aligned}$$

Therefore, the CALL m instruction sets up a new stack containing the top m pointers from the current stack, and causes the execution of the LOAD instruction to get the stack ready to evaluate the application.

```
> call m (o, c, s, g, d, e)
>   = (o, c', s', g, d', e)
>     where
>     c' = [LOAD]
>     s' = take m s
>     d' = (c, stack_pop m s):d
```

The UPDATE m instruction updates the node in the graph at index m into the stack with the contents of the node which is pointed at by the top of stack, and removes the top of stack. In the specification the overwriting is done by creating a new graph, g' which differs from g only in that the graph node whose label (n) is at index m in the stack (index_stack m s), which is changed to contain the contents of the node pointed at by the top of stack (te).

```
> update m (o, c, s, g, d, e)
>    = (o, c, s', g', d, e)
>      where
>      te = g_lookup g (top s)
>      n  = index_stack m s
>      s' = stack_pop 1 s
>      g' = (n, te):[(n', te') | (n', te') <- g; n' ~= n]
```

When an expression has been evaluated to head normal form, the RETURN instruction performs a return to the code sequence which caused the evaluation of the expression. The old code sequence and stack are restored from the dump, and the pointer to the node in head normal form is pushed onto the top of the restored stack.

```
> return (o, c, s, g, d, e)
>    = (o, c', s', g, d', e)
>      where
>      ((c',s''):d') = d
>      s' = stack_push (top s) s''
```

Printing

The PRINT instruction translates the internal representation of the result of running a program into a character string, and adds it to the output that has been produced by the program so far. If the result of executing the program was a Cons or a Node node, the subexpressions of this node need to be evaluated further in order to produce the output from the program.

```
> print (o, c, s, g, d, e)
>    = (o', c'  s', g, d, e)
>      where
>      o' = o ++ l
>      l  = shownum i,  if isInt te
>         = showbool b, if isBool te
>         = "",         if isNil te
>         = "Empty",    if isEmpty te
>         = "Node",     if isNode te
>         = ""          otherwise
```

```
>     c' = [EVAL, PRINT, EVAL, PRINT] ++ c, if isCons te
>     c' = [EVAL, PRINT, EVAL, PRINT, EVAL, PRINT] ++ c, if isNode te
>        = c,                               otherwise
>     te = g_lookup g (top s)
>     s' = stack_push n1 (stack_push n2 (stack_pop 1 s)), if isCons te
>        = stack_push m1 (stack_push m2 (stack_push m3
>                                    (stack_pop 1 s))), if isNode te
>        = stack_pop 1 s,                                 otherwise
>     (Int i)          = te, if isInt te
>     (Bool b)         = te, if isBool te
>     (Cons n1 n2)     = te, if isCons te
>     (Node m1 m2 m3) = te, if isNode te

> showbool :: bool -> [char]
> showbool x = show x
```

B.3.5 Auxiliary Definitions

Node Testing Functions

Various parts of the specification need to test the tag on a node to see what sort of value it contains. For each type of node, there is an is function to test whether it is of that type. The functions are not written using very good programming style because, in each one, anything which matches the first pattern will also match the second pattern (and so the patterns are *overlapping*), and we are relying on the fact that Miranda tries to match patterns from top to bottom. If pattern matching was defined so that any matching equation could be chosen, then the equations we have written would violate the Church-Rosser property.

```
> isInt (Int n) = True
> isInt x       = False

> isBool (Bool b) = True
> isBool x        = False

> isVap (Vap xs) = True
> isVap x        = False

> isWvap (Wvap xs) = True
> isWvap x         = False

> isFun (Fun a gs) = True
> isFun x          = False
```

```
> isNil Nil = True
> isNil x   = False

> isCons (Cons n1 n2) = True
> isCons x            = False

> isNode (Node n1 n2 n3) = True
> isNode x               = False

> isEmpty Empty = True
> isEmpty x     = False
```

Stack Manipulation

The application `index_stack i` returns the pointer which is at index `i` in the stack, `top s` returns the pointer from the top of the stack, and `next_to_top s` returns the pointer which is the second item on the stack. The function `stack_pop` removes a number of items from the stack, and `stack_push` pushes a pointer onto the stack.

```
> index_stack i s = s!i
> top s           = index_stack 0 s
> next_to_top s   = index_stack 1 s

> stack_pop n s  = drop n s
> stack_push n s = n:s
```

Graph Manipulation

```
> assoc g i = hd [l | (k,l) <- g; k=i]
> g_lookup g i = assoc g i
```

In the specification, the graph is stored as a list of nodes, and a node is never removed once it has been created. A unique label for a new graph node can be obtained by taking the length of the list representing the graph.

```
> newlabel g = #g
```

Miscellaneous

```
> e_lookup e i = assoc e i
```

B.3.6 Pretty-Printing the State

The function run produces a list of states that results from running the Spineless G-machine from an initial state given by its argument. This can be filtered to produce the desired output from the simulator. Below is the filter which was used when the specification was being tested. It prints out parts of the state that may have changed from one step to another in a readable format.

It may seem strange that we have defined a number of different functions whose names begin with the prefix show_, which just apply show to their argument. This is due to a restriction in Miranda about the use of show; the interested reader is referred to the on-line manual which comes with the Miranda system.

```
> trace st = lay (map (lay . print_state) (run st))

> print_state (o, c, s, g, d, e)
>    = ["****************************************************************",
>       "Output:", ' ':' ':' ':' ':' ':o,
>       "Code:", ' ':' ':' ':' ':' ':show_code c,
>       "Stack:", ' ':' ':' ':' ':' ':show_stack s,
>       "Graph:", ' ':' ':' ':' ':' ':show_graph g,
>       "Dump:", ' ':' ':' ':' ':' ':show_dump d]

> show_stack :: stack -> [char]
> show_stack x = show x

> show_code :: code_sequence -> [char]
> show_code x = show x

> show_graph :: graph -> [char]
> show_graph x = show x

> show_dump :: dump -> [char]
> show_dump x = show x
```

B.3.7 An Example Initial State

As an example of using this specification, the identifier initial_state is bound to an initial state for the following program:

```
> h f = + (f 3) (f 4)
> g x = * x
```

where the expression to be evaluated is `h (g (+ 3 4))`. Code was produced by an implementation of the compiler given in Section B.1. The code for the functions h and g is stored respectively on the nodes with labels 0 and 1 in the initial graph g. Nodes with labels 2 and 3 contain the code for addition and multiplication. These bindings of functions to graph nodes are given in the environment e. The initial code sequence for the expression `h (g (+ 3 4))` is bound to the variable c. It can be executed by typing:

```
run initial_state
```

To pretty-print the state of the machine after each instruction has been executed, type:

```
trace initial_state
```

```
> initial_state = ([], c, [], g, [], e)
>                 where
>                 c = [PUSHINT 4, PUSHINT 3, PUSHFUN "add", STORE 3,
>                      PUSHFUN "g", STORE 2, PUSHFUN "h", CALL 2, PRINT, STOP]
>                 g = [
>                      (0,(Fun 1 [PUSHINT 1, PUSH 1, CALL 2, PUSHINT 3, PUSH 2,
>                                 CALL 2, ADD, SQUEEZE 1 1, RETURN])),
>                      (1,(Fun 1 [PUSH 0, PUSHFUN "mul", SQUEEZE 2 1, ENTER])),
>                      (2,(Fun 2 [PUSH 0, EVAL, PUSH 2, EVAL, ADD, SQUEEZE 1 2,
>                                 RETURN])),
>                      (3,(Fun 2 [PUSH 0, EVAL, PUSH 2, EVAL, MUL, SQUEEZE 1 2,
>                                 RETURN]))
>                      ]
>                 e = [("h",0),("g",1),("add",2),("mul",3)]
```

Bibliography

[Abr85] S. Abramsky. Strictness analysis and polymorphic invariance. In H. Ganzinger and N.D. Jones, editors, *Proceedings of the Workshop on Programs as Data Objects*, number 217 in LNCS, pages 1–23. Springer-Verlag, 17–19 October 1985.

[Abr90] S. Abramsky. Abstract interpretation, logical relations and Kan extensions. *Journal of Logic and Computation*, 1(1):5–39, 1990.

[AH87] S. Abramsky and C.L. Hankin, editors. *Abstract Interpretation of Declarative Languages*. Computers and Their Applications. Ellis Horwood, 1987.

[AJ89] L. Augustsson and T. Johnsson. The $\langle \nu, G \rangle$-machine: An abstract machine for parallel graph reduction. In D.B. MacQueen, editor, *Proceedings of the Functional Programming Languages and Computer Architecture Conference*. ACM, 11–13 September 1989.

[AJ91] S. Abramsky and T.P. Jensen. A relational approach to strictness analysis for higher-order functions. In *Proceedings of the Symposium on Principles of Programming Languages*, January 1991. To appear.

[AM75] M.A. Arbib and E.G. Manes. *Arrows, Structures and Functors: The Categorical Imperative*. Academic Press, 1975.

[AP90] M. Abadi and G.D. Plotkin. A PER model of polymorphism and recursive types. In *Proceedings of the 5th Annual IEEE Symposium on Logic in Computer Science*, pages 355–365. IEEE, 4-7 June 1990.

[Arg89] G. Argo. Improving the three instruction machine. In *Conference on Functional Programming Languages and Computer Architecture*, pages 100–115, London, U.K., 11–13 September 1989. ACM.

[Arg90] G. Argo. *Efficient Laziness*. PhD thesis, Department of Computer Science, University of Glasgow, Lilybank Gardens, Glasgow G12 8QQ, UK, 1990.

[Aug87] L. Augustsson. *Compiling Lazy Functional Languages, Part II*. PhD thesis, Chalmers Tekniska Högskola, Göteborg, Sweden, 1987.

[Bar84] H.P. Barendregt. *The Lambda Calculus*, volume 103 of *Studies in Logic and the Foundations of Mathematics*. Elsevier Science Publishers B.V., P.O. Box 1991, 1000 BZ Amsterdam, The Netherlands, 2nd edition, 1984.

[Bar91a] G. Baraki. *Title to be announced.* PhD thesis, Department of Computer Science, University of Glasgow, Lilybank Gardens, Glasgow G12 8QQ, UK, 1991. In preparation.

[Bar91b] H.P. Barendregt. Lambda calculi with types. In S. Abramsky, D.M. Gabbai, and T.S.E. Maibaum, editors, *Handbook of Logic in Computer Science*, volume 2. Oxford University Press, 1991. To appear.

[BBC+90] G.P. Balboni, P.G. Bosco, C. Cecchi, R. Melen, C. Moiso, and G. Sofi. Implementation of a parallel logic + functional language. In P.C. Treleaven, editor, *Parallel Computers: Object-Oriented, Functional, Logic*, chapter 7, pages 175–214. Wiley and Sons, 1990.

[BCL85] G. Berry, P.-L. Curien, and J.-J Lévy. Full abstraction for sequential languages: the state of the art. In M. Nivat and J. C. Reynolds, editors, *Algebraic Methods in Semantics*, pages 89–132. Cambridge University Press, 1985.

[BG89] R. Barbuti and R. Giacobazzi. A bottom-up polymorphic type inference in logic programming. Technical Report TR-27/89, Dipartimento di Informatica, University of Pisa, 1989.

[BGL89] R. Barbuti, R. Giacobazzi, and G. Levi. A declarative approach to abstract interpretation of logic programs. Technical Report TR-20/89, Dipartimento di Informatica, University of Pisa, May 1989.

[BH86] A. Bloss and P. Hudak. Variations on strictness analysis. In *Proceedings of the 1986 ACM Conference on Lisp and Functional Programming*, pages 132–142. ACM, Cambridge, Massachusetts, August 1986.

[BH88] A. Bloss and P. Hudak. Path semantics. In M. Main et. al., editor, *Third Workshop on Mathematical Foundations of Programming Language Semantics*, pages 476–489. Springer-Verlag LNCS 298, New Orleans, Louisiana, April 1988.

[BHA85] G.L. Burn, C.L. Hankin, and S. Abramsky. The theory of strictness analysis for higher-order functions. In *Proceedings of the Workshop on Programs as Data Objects*, pages 42–62, DIKU, Copenhagen, Denmark, 17–19 October 1985. Springer-Verlag LNCS 217.

[BHA86] G.L. Burn, C.L. Hankin, and S. Abramsky. Strictness analysis of higher-order functions. *Science of Computer Programming*, 7:249–278, November 1986.

[BHY89] A. Bloss, P. Hudak, and J. Young. An optimising compiler for a modern functional language. *The Computer Journal*, 32(2):152–161, April 1989.

[BKKS86] H.P. Barendregt, J.R. Kennaway, J.W. Klop, and M.R. Sleep. Needed reduction and spine strategies for the lambda calculus. Technical Report CS-R8621, CWI, Postbus 4079, 1009 AB Amsterdam, The Netherlands, May 1986.

[Blo89a] A. Bloss. *Path Analysis: Using Order-of-Evaluation Information to Optimize Lazy Functional Languages.* PhD thesis, Department of Computer Science, Yale University, May 1989. YALEU/DCS/RR-704.

[Blo89b] A. Bloss. Update analysis and the efficient implementation of functional aggregates. In *Proceedings of the Conference on Functional Programming Languages and Computer Architecture*, pages 26–38. ACM, London, 11–13 September 1989.

[BPJR88] G.L. Burn, S.L. Peyton Jones, and J.D. Robson. The spineless G-machine. In *Proceedings of the 1988 ACM Symposium on Lisp and Functional Programming*, pages 244–258, Snowbird, Utah, 25–27 July 1988.

[Bur87a] G. L. Burn. Evaluation transformers - A model for the parallel evaluation of functional languages (extended abstract). In G. Kahn, editor, *Proceedings of the Functional Programming Languages and Computer Architecture Conference*, pages 446–470. Springer-Verlag LNCS 274, September 1987.

[Bur87b] G.L. Burn. *Abstract Interpretation and the Parallel Evaluation of Functional Languages.* PhD thesis, Imperial College, University of London, March 1987.

[Bur88a] G.L. Burn. Developing a distributed memory architecture for parallel graph reduction. In *Proceedings of CONPAR 88*, Manchester, United Kingdom, 12–16 September 1988.

[Bur88b] G.L. Burn. A shared memory parallel G-machine based on the evaluation transformer model of computation. In *Proceedings of the Workshop on the Implementation of Lazy Functional Languages*, pages 301–330, Aspenäs, Göteborg, Sweden, 5–8 September 1988.

[Bur90a] G.L. Burn. A relationship between abstract interpretation and projection analysis. In *17th Annual ACM Symposium on the Principles of Programming Languages*, pages 151–156, San Francisco, 17–19 January 1990. ACM.

[Bur90b] G.L. Burn. Using projection analysis in compiling lazy functional programs. In *Proceedings of the 1990 ACM Conference on Lisp and Functional Programming*, pages 227–241, Nice, France, 27–29 June 1990.

[BvEG+87] H.P. Barendregt, M.C.J.D. van Eekelen, J.R.W. Glauert, J.R. Kennaway, M.J. Plasmeijer, and M.R. Sleep. Term graph rewriting. In *Proceedings of PARLE 87*, volume 2, pages 141–158. Springer-Verlag LNCS 259, Eindhoven, The Netherlands, June 1987.

[BW88] R.J. Bird and P.L. Wadler. *An Introduction to Functional Programming.* Prentice-Hall Series in Computer Science. Prentice-Hall International (UK) Ltd., Hemel Hempstead, Hertfordshire, England, 1988.

[CC79] P. Cousot and R. Cousot. Systematic design of program analysis frameworks. In *Proceedings of the Sixth Annual Symposium on Principles of Programming Languages*, pages 269–282. ACM, January 1979.

[Cou78] P. Cousot. *Methodes Iteratives de Construction et D'approximation de Points Fixes D'operateurs Monotones Sur un Trellis, Analyse Semantique des Programmes.* PhD thesis, Université Scientifique et Médicale de Grenoble, 1978.

[CP85] C. Clack and S.L. Peyton Jones. Strictness analysis – a practical approach. In J.-P. Jouannaud, editor, *Proceedings of the Functional Programming Languages and Computer Architecture Conference*, pages 35–49. Springer-Verlag LNCS 201, September 1985.

[DM82] L. Damas and R. Milner. Principal type schemes for functional programs. In *Proceedings of the ACM Symposium on Principles of Programming Languages*, pages 207–212, 1982.

[DW90] K. Davis and P. Wadler. Strictness analysis: Proved and improved. In *Proceedings of the Second Annual Glasgow Workshop on Functional Programming, 21–23 August, 1989, Fraserburgh Scotland*, Springer Workshops in Computing. Springer-Verlag, 1990.

[Dyb87] P. Dybjer. Inverse image analysis. In *Proceedings of the 14th International Colloquium on Automata, Languages and Programming*, Karlsruhe, Germany, July 1987. Springer-Verlag LNCS 267.

[FH88] A.J. Field and P.G. Harrison. *Functional Programming.* Addison-Wesley International Computer Science Series, 1988.

[FLMP88] M. Falaschi, G. Levi, M. Martelli, and C. Palamidessi. Declarative modelling of the operational behaviour of logic languages. Technical Report TR-10/88, Dipartimento di Informatica, University of Pisa, 1988.

[FW76] D.P. Freidman and D.S. Wise. CONS should not evaluate its arguments. In *Proceedings 3rd International Colloquium on Automata Languages and Programming*, pages 257–284. Edinburgh University Press, 1976.

[FW87] J. Fairbairn and S. Wray. TIM: A simple, lazy abstract machine to execute supercombinators. In G. Kahn, editor, *Proceedings of the Functional Programming Languages and Computer Architecture Conference*, pages 34–45. Springer-Verlag LNCS 274, September 1987.

[GHK+80] G. Gierz, K.H. Hofmann, K. Keimel, J.D. Lawson, M. Mislove, and D.S. Scott. *A Compendium of Continuous Lattices.* Springer-Verlag, 1980.

[GM90] J.F. Giorgi and D. Le Métayer. Continuation-based parallel implementation of functional programming languages. In *Proceedings of the 1990 ACM Conference on Lisp and Functional Programming*, pages 227–241, Nice, France, 27–29 June 1990.

[Gol87] B. Goldberg. Detecting sharing of partial applications in functional languages. In G. Kahn, editor, *Proceedings of the Functional Programming Languages and Computer Architecture Conference*, pages 408–425. Springer-Verlag LNCS 274, September 1987.

[Gol88] B.F. Goldberg. *Multiprocessor Execution of Functional Programs.* PhD thesis, Yale University, Department of Computer Science, April 1988.

[Gor88] M.J.C. Gordon. *Programming Language Theory and Its Implementation: Applicative and Imperative Paradigms.* Prentice-Hall International Series in Computer Science, 1988. ISBN 0-13-730417-X.

[GS90] G.A. Gunter and D.S. Scott. Semantic domains. In J. van Leeuwen, editor, *Handbook of Theoretical Computer Science*, volume B: Formal Models and Semantics. North-Holland, 1990.

[HBJ86] C.L. Hankin, G.L. Burn, and S.L. Peyton Jones. A safe approach to parallel combinator reduction (extended abstract). In *Proceedings ESOP 86 (European Symposium on Programming)*, pages 99–110, Saabrucken, Federal Republic of Germany, March 1986. Springer-Verlag LNCS 213.

[HBJ88] C.L. Hankin, G.L. Burn, and S.L. Peyton Jones. A safe approach to parallel combinator reduction. *Theoretical Computer Science*, 56:17–36, 1988.

[HH90] L.S. Hunt and C.L. Hankin. Fixed points and frontiers: a new perspective. *The Journal of Functional Programming*, 1(1), 1990. To appear.

[Hin77] R. Hindley. The equivalence of complete reductions. *Transactions of the American Mathematical Society*, 229:227–248, 1977.

[Hin78a] R. Hindley. Reductions of residuals are finite. *Transactions of the American Mathematical Society*, 240:345–361, June 1978.

[Hin78b] R. Hindley. Standard and normal reductions. *Transactions of the American Mathematical Society*, 241:253–271, July 1978.

[HL90] R.J.M. Hughes and J. Launchbury. Towards relating forwards and backwards analyses. In *Proceedings of the Third Annual Glasgow Workshop on Functional Programming*, pages 145–155, Ullapool, Scotland, 13–15 August 1990.

[HM76] P. Henderson and J.M. Morris. A lazy evaluator. In *Proceedings of the Third ACM Symposium on the Principles of Programming Languages*, pages 95–103, Atlanta Georgia, January 1976.

[HM90] J. Hannan and D. Miller. From operation semantics to abstract machines: Preliminary results. In *Proceedings of the 1990 ACM Conference on Lisp and Functional Programming*, pages 323–331, Nice, France, 27–29 June 1990.

[HMT88] R. Harper, R. Milner, and M. Tofte. The definition of standard ML (version 2). Technical Report ECS-LFCS-88-62, LFCS, Department of Computer Science, University of Edinburgh, The King's Buildings, Edinburgh EH9 3JZ, UK, August 1988.

[Hol83] S. Holmström. *Polymorphic Type Systems and Concurrent Computation in Functional Languages.* PhD thesis, Chalmers Tekniska Högskola, Göteborg, Sweden, 1983.

[HP79] M. Hennessy and G.D. Plotkin. Full abstraction for a simple parallel programming language. In J. Becvar, editor, *Proceedings of the Conference on the Mathematical Foundations of Computer Science 1979.* Springer-Verlag LNCS 74, 1979.

[Hun89] S. Hunt. Frontiers and open sets in abstract interpretation. In *Proceedings of the Conference on Functional Programming Languages and Computer Architecture*, Imperial College, London, 11–13 September 1989.

[Hun90] L.S. Hunt. PERs generalise projections for strictness analysis. In *Proceedings of the Third Annual Glasgow Workshop on Functional Programming*, pages 156–168, Ullapool, Scotland, 13–15 August 1990.

[HV89] L.O. Hertzberger and W.G Vree. A coarse grain parallel architecture for functional languages. In E. Odijk, M. Rem, and J.-C Syre, editors, *Proceedings of PARLE 89*, volume 1, pages 269–285, Eindhoven, The Netherlands, 12–16 June 1989. Springer-Verlag LNCS 365.

[HW87] C.V. Hall and D.S. Wise. Compiling strictness into streams. In *14th Annual ACM Symposium on the Principles of Programming Languages*, pages 132–143. ACM, January 1987.

[HW89] C.V. Hall and D.S. Wise. Generating function versions using rational strictness patters. *Science of Computer Programming*, 12:39–74, 1989.

[HWe90] P. Hudak and P. Wadler (editors). Report on the programming language Haskell, a non-strict purely functional language (Version 1.0). Technical Report YALEU/DCS/RR777, Yale University, Department of Computer Science, April 1990.

[HY86] P Hudak and J Young. Higher order strictness analysis in untyped lambda calculus. In *Proceedings of 12th ACM Symposium on Principles of Programming Languages*, pages 97–109, January 1986.

[JCSH87] S.L. Peyton Jones, C. Clack, J. Salkild, and M. Hardie. GRIP– a high-performance architecture for parallel graph reduction. In G. Kahn, editor, *Proceedings of the Functional Programming Languages and Computer Architecture Conference*, pages 98–112. Springer-Verlag LNCS 274, September 1987.

[Jen90] T.P. Jensen. Abstract interpretation, type inference and stone duality. In *Proceedings of the Third Annual Glasgow Workshop on Functional Programming*, pages 182–187, Ullapool, Scotland, 13–15 August 1990.

[JN91] N.D. Jones and F. Nielson. Abstract interpretation: a semantics-based tool for program analysis. In S. Abramsky, D.M. Gabbai, and T.S.E. Maibaum, editors, *Handbook of Logic in Computer Science*, volume 3. Oxford University Press, 1991. To appear.

[Joh83] T. Johnsson. The G-machine. An abstract machine for graph reduction. In *Declarative Programming Workshop*, pages 1–20, University College London, April 1983.

[Joh87] T. Johnsson. *Compiling Lazy Functional Languages.* PhD thesis, Chalmers Tekniska Högskola, Göteborg, Sweden, 1987.

[JS87] N.D. Jones and H Sondergaard. A semantics-based framework for the abstract interpretation of prolog. In S. Abramsky and C.L. Hankin, editors, *Abstract Interpretation of Declarative Languages*, Computers and Their Applications, pages 123–142. Ellis Horwood, 1987.

[KKR+86] D.A. Kranz, R. Kelsey, J.A. Rees, P. Hudak, J. Philbin, and N.I. Adams. Orbit: An optimising compiler for scheme. In *Proceedings of the SIGPLAN '86 Symposium on Compiler Construction*, pages 219–233. ACM, June 1986.

[KM89] Tsung-Min Kuo and P. Mishra. Strictness analysis: a new perspective based on type inference. In *Proceedings of the Conference on Functional Programming Languages and Computer Architecture*, pages 260–272, London, 11–13 September 1989. ACM.

[Kra88] D.A. Kranz. *Orbit: An Optimising Compiler for Scheme.* PhD thesis, Department of Computer Science, Yale University, February 1988. Report Number YALEU/DCS/RR-632.

[Lau89] J. Launchbury. *Projection Factorisations in Partial Evaluation.* PhD thesis, Department of Computing, University of Glasgow, November 1989.

[LB89] D.R. Lester and G.L. Burn. An executable specification of the HDG-Machine. In *Workshop on Massive Parallelism: Hardware, Programming and Applications*, Amalfi, Italy, 9–15 October 1989. Academic Press. To appear in 1991.

[Les88] D.R. Lester. *Combinator Graph Reduction: A Congruence and its Applications.* DPhil thesis, Oxford University, 1988. *Also* published as Technical Monograph PRG-73.

[Les89] D.R. Lester. Stacklessness: Compiling recursion for a distributed architecture. In *Conference on Functional Programming Languages and Computer Architecture*, pages 116–128, London, U.K., 11–13 September 1989. ACM.

[LKID89] R. Loogen, H. Kuchen, K. Indermark, and W. Damm. Distributed implementation of programmed graph reduction. In E. Odijk, M. Rem, and J.-C Syre, editors, *Proceedings of PARLE 89*, volume 1, pages 136–157, Eindhoven, The Netherlands, 12–16 June 1989. SPRINGER-Verlag LNCS 365.

[Mau85] D Maurer. Strictness computation using special lambda-expressions. In H Ganzinger and N.D. Jones, editors, *Proceedings of the Workshop on Programs as Data Objects*, pages 136–155, DIKU, Copenhagen, Denmark, 17-19 October 1985. Springer-Verlag LNCS 217.

[Mel87] C. Mellish. Abstract interpretation of prolog programs. In S. Abramsky and C.L. Hankin, editors, *Abstract Interpretation of Declarative Languages*, Computers and Their Applications, pages 181–198. Ellis Horwood, 1987.

[Mil78] R. Milner. A theory of type polymorphism in programming. *Journal of Computer and System Science*, 17(3):348–375, 1978.

[Mit76] G. Mitschke. λ-kalkül, δ-konversion und axiomatische rekursionstheorie. Technical Report 274, Fachbereit Mathematik, Technische Hochshule, Darmstadt, 1976. 77 pages.

[MJ81] S.S. Muchnick and N.D. Jones, editors. *Program Flow Analysis: Theory and Applications.* Prentice-Hall Software Series. Prentice-Hall, 1981. ISBN 0-13-729681-9.

[MN83] A. Mycroft and F. Nielson. Strong abstract interpretation using power domains (extended abstract). In *International Colloquium on Automata, Languages and Programming*, pages 536–547. Springer-Verlag LNCS 154, 1983.

[Mos90] P.D. Mosses. Denotational semantics. In J. van Leeuwen, editor, *Handbook of Theoretical Computer Science*, volume B: Formal Models and Semantics. North-Holland, 1990.

[MS76] R.E. Milne and C. Strachey. *A Theory of Programming Language Semantics.* Chapman and Hall, London, 1976.

[MTH90] R. Milner, M. Tofte, and R. Harper. *The Definition of Standard ML.* MIT Press, Cambridge, Mass., 1990.

[Myc80] A. Mycroft. Theory and practice of transforming call-by-need into call-by-value. In *4th International Symposium on Programming*, pages 269 –281, Paris, April 1980. Springer-Verlag LNCS 83.

[Myc81] A. Mycroft. *Abstract Interpretation and Optimising Transformations for Applicative Programs.* PhD thesis, University of Edinburgh, Department of Computer Science, December 1981. *Also* published as CST-15-81.

[Nie84] F. Nielson. *Abstract Interpretation Using Domain Theory.* PhD thesis, Department of Computer Science, University of Edinburgh, October 1984. *Also* CST-31-84.

[Nie85] F. Nielson. Expected forms of data flow analysis. In *Proceedings of the Workshop on Programs as Data Objects*, pages 172–191, DIKU, Copenhagen, Denmark, 17–19 October 1985. Springer-Verlag LNCS 217.

[Nie89] F. Nielson. Two-level semantics and abstract interpretation. *Theoretical Computer Science*, 69:117–242, 1989.

[NN90] H. Nielson and F. Nielson. Context information for lazy code generation. In *Proceedings of the 1990 ACM Conference on Lisp and Functional Programming*, pages 251–263, Nice, France, 27–29 June 1990.

[Par90] A. Partridge. *Dynamic Aspects of Distributed Graph Reduction.* PhD thesis, Department of Electrical Engineering and Computer Science, University of Tasmania, 1990. In preparation.

[Per87] N. Perry. Hope+. Technical Report IC/FPR/LANG/2.5.1/7, Functional Programming Section, Department of Computing, Imperial College, 180 Queen's Gate, LONDON SW7 2BZ, UK, 1987.

[Pey87] S.L. Peyton Jones. *The Implementation of Functional Programming Languages.* Prentice-Hall International Series in Computer Science. Prentice-Hall International (UK) Ltd, London, 1987.

[Pey89] S.L. Peyton Jones. Parallel implementations of functional programming languages. *The Computer Journal*, 32(2):175–186, April 1989.

[Plo76] G.D. Plotkin. A powerdomain construction. *SIAM J. Comput.*, 5(3):452–487, September 1976.

[Plo77] G. Plotkin. LCF considered as a programming language. *Theoretical Computer Science*, 5(3):223–256, 1977.

[PS89] S.L. Peyton Jones and J. Salkild. The Spineles Tagless G-Machine. In D. B. MacQueen, editor, *Proceedings of the Functional Programming Languages and Computer Architecture Conference*, pages 184–201. ACM, 11–13 September 1989.

[Rea89] C. Reade. *Elements of Functional Programming.* International Computer Science Series. Addison-Wesley, 1989.

[Ric90] L. Ricci. *Compilation of Logic Programs for Massively Parallel Systems.* PhD thesis, Dipartimento di Informatica, University of Pisa, 1990.

[Sch86] D.A. Schmidt. *Denotational Semantics.* Allyn and Bacon, Inc., 7 Wells Avenue, Newton, Massachusetts, 1986.

[Sco70] D.S. Scott. Outline of mathematical theory of computation. Technical Monograph PRG-2, Oxford University Computing Laboratory, Programming Research Group, 1970.

[Sco81] D.S. Scott. Lectures on a mathematical theory of computation. Technical Monograph PRG-19, Oxford University Computing Laboratory, Programming Research Group, 1981.

[Sco82] D.S. Scott. Domains for denotational semantics. In M. Nielsen and E.M. Schmidt, editors, *Automata, Languages and Programming, Proc 10th Int. Colloq.*, number 140 in LNCS, pages 577–613. Springer Verlag, 1982.

[Smy78] M.B. Smyth. Power domains. *Journal of Computer and System Sciences*, 16:23–36, 1978.

[SP82] M.B. Smyth and G.D. Plotkin. The category-theoretic solution of recursive domain equations. *SIAM Journal on Computing*, 11(4):761–783, November 1982.

[Sto77] J.E. Stoy. *Denotational Semantics: The Scott-Strachey Approach to Programming Language Theory.* The MIT Press Series in Computer Science. MIT Press, Cambridge, Massachusetts, 1977.

[Tar55] A. Tarski. A lattice-theoretical fixpoint theorem and its applications. *Pacific Journal of Mathematics*, 5, 1955.

[Tra89] K.R. Traub. *Sequential Implementation of Lenient Programming Languages.* PhD thesis, Laboratory of Computer Science, MIT, September 1989. MIT/LCS/TR-417.

[Tur85] D.A. Turner. Miranda: A non-strict functional language with polymorphic types. In J.-P. Jouannaud, editor, *Proceedings of the Functional Programming Languages and Computer Architecture Conference*, pages 1–16. Springer-Verlag LNCS 201, September 1985.

[Tur86] D.A. Turner. An overview of Miranda. *SIGPLAN Notices*, December 1986.

[Vic89] S.J. Vickers. *Topology via Logic.* Number 5 in Cambridge Tracts in Theoretical Computer Science. Cambridge University Press, 1989.

[Wad71] C.P. Wadsworth. *Semantics and Pragmatics of The Lambda Calculus.* DPhil thesis, University of Oxford, 1971.

[Wad87] P.L. Wadler. Strictness analysis on non-flat domains (by abstract interpretation over finite domains). In S. Abramsky and C.L. Hankin, editors, *Abstract Interpretation of Declarative Languages*, chapter 12, pages 266–275. Ellis Horwood Ltd., Chichester, West Sussex, England, 1987.

[War87] D.H.D. Warren. Or-parallel execution models of Prolog. In *TAPSOFT '87*, pages 243–259. Springer-Verlag LNCS 250, 1987.

[WH87] P. Wadler and R. J. M. Hughes. Projections for strictness analysis. In G. Kahn, editor, *Proceedings of the Functional Programming Languages and Computer Architecture Conference*, pages 385–407. Springer-Verlag LNCS 274, September 1987.

[Wik87] A. Wikström. *Functional Programming Using Standard ML*. Prentice-Hall International Series in Computer Science, Hemel Hempstead, UK, 1987.

[Wri89] D.A. Wright. Strictness analysis via type inference. Technical Report R89-3, Department of Electrical Engineering and Computer Science, University of Tasmania, September 1989.

[WSWW87] I. Watson, J. Sargeant, P. Watson, and V. Woods. Flagship computational models and machine architecture. *ICL Technical Journal*, 5:555–574, May 1987.

[WW87] P. Watson and I. Watson. Evaluating functional programs on the FLAGSHIP machine. In G. Kahn, editor, *Proceedings of the Functional Programming Languages and Computer Architecture Conference*, pages 80–97. Springer-Verlag LNCS 274, September 1987.

[You89] J.H. Young. *The Theory and Practice of Semantic Program Analysis for Higher-Order Functional Programming Languages*. PhD thesis, Department of Computer Science, Yale University, May 1989.

Index of Symbols

Most of the symbols used in this book are listed in this index, along with a brief description of their meaning or their definition. The numbers in the third column are the pages where the symbols are defined. As far as possible, related symbols have been grouped together.

Partial Orders

Types

Constructions on Domains and Functions Over Them

id_D	the identity function on D	46
$g \circ f$	the composition of functions g and f, where $$(g \circ f)\ d = g\ (f\ d)$$	46
$D_1 \times \ldots \times D_k$	the product of the domains D_1 to D_k	44
$(d_1, \ldots, d_k)$	an element of the product $D_1 \times \ldots \times D_k$	44
$f_1 \times \ldots \times f_k$	the product of the functions f_1 to f_k	47
$D_1 \otimes \ldots \otimes D_k$	the smash product of the domains D_1 to D_k	45
$< d_1, \ldots, d_k >$	an element of the smash product $D_1 \otimes \ldots \otimes D_k$. N.B.: $\forall i \in \{1, \ldots, k\} : d_i \neq \bot_{D_i}$.	45
$f_1 \otimes \ldots \otimes f_k$	the smash product of the functions f_1 to f_k	47
$D_1 \oplus \ldots \oplus D_k$	the smash sum $D_1 \oplus \ldots \oplus D_k$	45
$ins_i\ d$	an element of the smash sum $D_1 \oplus \ldots \oplus D_k$, where $d \in D_i$, and $d \neq \bot_{D_i}$	45
$f_1 \oplus \ldots \oplus f_k$	the smash sum of the functions f_1 to f_k	48
$lift\ D$	the lifting of the domain D	46
$(0, d)$	an element of $lift\ D$, where $d \in D$	46
$lift\ f$	the lifting of the function f	48
$D \rightarrow E$	the domain of continuous functions from the domain D to the domain E	46
$\downarrow i$	projection of the th component of a (smash) product	47
mk_sum_i	injects an element of a domain into a sum domain	47
$outs_i$	projects an element from a smash sum domain onto the ith component of the smash sum.	47
iss_i	tests to see if an element comes from the ith component of a smash sum	47

Functions on Powerdomains and Their Properties

P	**The Hoare powerdomain functor**	49
$\{\!\{.\}\!\}$	$\{\!\{d\}\!\}_D = \{d' \in D \mid d' \sqsubseteq d\}$	49
X^*	**the Scott-closure of X**	49
(P1)-(P11)	**properties of functions on powerdomains**	49f.

Reduction in the Typed Lambda Calculus

$FV(e)$	the set of free variables occurring in the expression e	23, 35
$e_1[x^\sigma := e_2]$	the result of replacing all free occurrences of x^σ in e_1 with e_2	23, 35
$\rightarrow_\beta$	one-step β-reduction (reduction rule for an application of the form $(\lambda x^\sigma.e_1)\ e_2$)	23
$\twoheadrightarrow_\beta$	the reflexive, transitive closure of one-step β-reduction	24
δ-rule	a reduction rule for a constant	27
$\rightarrow_\delta$	one-step δ-reduction (reduction rules for constants)	27
$\rightarrow_{\beta\delta}$	one-step $\beta\delta$-reduction	29
$\twoheadrightarrow_{\beta\delta}$	the reflexive, transitive closure of one-step $\beta\delta$-reduction	29
F_h	the one-step reduction strategy that reduces the head redex at each step	26
F_ℓ	the one-step reduction strategy that reduces the leftmost redex at each step	37
$\xi^\sigma_{\overline{s}}$	the evaluator for the type σ related to $\overline{s} \in \mathbf{A}_\sigma$	107

Interpretations and Maps Between Interpretations

$\mathbf{I}_\sigma$	the **I**-interpretation of the type σ	51
$\mathbf{S}_\sigma$	the standard interpretation of the type σ	55
$\mathbf{A}_\sigma$	the abstract interpretation of the type σ	64
$\rho^{\mathbf{I}}$	an environment for the **I**-interpretation of Λ_T	53
$\rho^{\mathbf{I}}[e/x^\sigma]$	a modified environment	53
$\mathbf{I}\ [\![e]\!]\ \rho^{\mathbf{I}}$	the **I**-interpretation of the expression e	53
$\mathbf{S}\ [\![e]\!]\ \rho^{\mathbf{S}}$	the standard interpretation of the expression e	55
$\mathbf{A}\ [\![e]\!]\ \rho^{\mathbf{A}}$	the abstract interpretation of the expression e	64
$\mathbf{K}^{\mathbf{I}}\ [\![c_\sigma]\!]$	the **I**-interpretation of the constant c_σ	53
$\mathbf{K}^{\mathbf{S}}\ [\![c_\sigma]\!]$	the standard interpretation of the constant c_σ	60
$\mathbf{K}^{\mathbf{A}}\ [\![c_\sigma]\!]$	the abstract interpretation of the constant c_σ	73
α_σ	the abstraction map for the type σ, taking an object from $\mathbf{S}_\sigma$ and returning an object in $\mathbf{A}_\sigma$	67
Abs_σ	$Abs_\sigma = \bigsqcup \circ \mathbf{P}\ \alpha_\sigma$	69
γ_σ	the concretisation map for the type σ, taking an object from $\mathbf{A}_\sigma$ and returning an object in $\mathbf{P}\ \mathbf{S}_\sigma$	67
$\mathbf{2}$	the two point abstract domain	79
0, 1	elements of the abstract domain for *int* and *bool*	79
$\perp, \infty, \perp\!\in, \top\!\in$	elements in the abstract interpretation of (*list* τ) and (*tree* τ)	80, 81
$\overline{f}$	the abstract interpretation of the function f, shorthand for $\mathbf{A}\ [\![f]\!]\ \{\}$	78

Lists and Trees

$List_\tau^\infty$	infinite lists or lists containing at least one element and whose tail is $\bot_{\mathbf{S}_{(list\ \tau)}}$ at some point	80
$List_\tau^{\bot\in}$	finite lists containing at least one $\bot_{\mathbf{S}_\tau}$	80
$List_\tau^{\top\in}$	finite lists containing no $\bot_{\mathbf{S}_\tau}$	80
head	returns the first element of a list	59
tail	returns the tail of a list	59
lcase	chooses between two expressions depending on whether its first argument is *nil* or an application of *cons*	59
$Tree_\tau^\infty$	infinite trees or trees containing at least one node and one of whose branches ends in $\bot_{\mathbf{S}_{(tree\ \tau)}}$	81
$Tree_\tau^{\bot\in}$	finite trees containing at least one $\bot_{\mathbf{S}_\tau}$	81
$Tree_\tau^{\top\in}$	finite trees containing no $\bot_{\mathbf{S}_\tau}$	81
value	returns the value in the first node of a tree	59
left	returns the left subtree of a node	59
right	returns the right subtree of a node	59
tcase	chooses between two expressions depending on whether its first argument is *empty* or an application of *node*	59

Syntactic Constructs of Λ_T

x^σ	a variable of type σ	21
c_σ	a general constant of type σ	27
$(e_1\ e_2)$	the term e_1 applied to the term e_2	21
$(\lambda x^\sigma.e)$	a lambda abstraction	21
$\mathrm{fix}_{(\sigma\to\sigma)\to\sigma}$	the least fixed point	27ff.
let $x^\sigma = e_1$ in e_2	the let construct forces the evaluation of e_1. If the evaluation terminates, then it returns the value of e_2 with all the free occurrences of x^σ being bound to the HNF of e_1.	33
$\mathrm{tuple}_{(\sigma_1,\ldots,\sigma_k)}$	constructs a term of type $\sigma_1 \times \ldots \times \sigma_k$	31
$\mathrm{tuples}_{(\sigma_1,\ldots,\sigma_k)}$	constructs a term of type $\sigma_1 \otimes \ldots \otimes \sigma_k$	31
$\mathrm{ins}_{\mathrm{i}(\sigma_1,\ldots,\sigma_k)}$	constructs a term of type $\sigma_1 \oplus \ldots \oplus \sigma_k$	31
lift_σ	constructs a term of type *lift* σ	31

Constants from Λ_T

c_σ	a general constant of type σ	27
$\mathbf{m}_{int}$	one for each integer m	27ff.,32
$+_{int \rightarrow int \rightarrow int}$	integer addition	27,32
$\mathbf{true}_{bool}$	the constant for *true*	28,32
$\mathbf{false}_{bool}$	the constant for *false*	28,32
$\mathbf{if}_{bool \rightarrow \sigma \rightarrow \sigma \rightarrow \sigma}$	a conditional for each type	27,32
$\mathbf{nil}_{(list\ \tau)}$	the empty list	32
$\mathbf{cons}_{\tau \rightarrow (list\ \tau) \rightarrow (list\ \tau)}$	takes an element of type τ and a list of elements of type τ, and returns a new list with the new element put on the front of the old list	32
$\mathbf{head}_{(list\ \tau) \rightarrow \tau}$	returns the head of its argument list	32
$\mathbf{tail}_{(list\ \tau) \rightarrow (list\ \tau)}$	returns the tail of its argument list	32
$\mathbf{lcase}_{(list\ \tau) \rightarrow \sigma \rightarrow (\tau \rightarrow (list\ \tau) \rightarrow \sigma) \rightarrow \sigma}$	tests to see if its argument is an empty list or otherwise, and the value it returns depends on the result of the test	32
$\mathbf{emtpy}_{(tree\ \tau)}$	the empty tree	32
$\mathbf{node}_{(tree\ \tau) \rightarrow \tau \rightarrow (tree\ \tau) \rightarrow (tree\ \tau)}$	takes an element of type τ and two trees of elements of type τ, and returns a new tree containing these three items	32
$\mathbf{value}_{(tree\ \tau) \rightarrow \tau}$	returns the value stored in the root node of a tree	32
$\mathbf{left}_{(tree\ \tau) \rightarrow (tree\ \tau)}$	returns the left subtree of its argument	32
$\mathbf{right}_{(tree\ \tau) \rightarrow (tree\ \tau)}$	returns the right subtree of its argument	32
$\mathbf{tcase}_{(tree\ \tau) \rightarrow \sigma \rightarrow ((tree\ \tau) \rightarrow \tau \rightarrow (tree\ \tau) \rightarrow \sigma) \rightarrow \sigma}$	tests to see if its argument is an empty tree or otherwise, and the value it returns depends on the result of the test	32
$\mathbf{takei}_{\sigma_1 \times \ldots \times \sigma_k \rightarrow \sigma_i}$	projects the $\mathbf{i}$th component from an element of a product type	32
$\mathbf{takesi}_{\sigma_1 \otimes \ldots \otimes \sigma_k \rightarrow \sigma_i}$	projects the $\mathbf{i}$th component from an element of a smash product type	32
$\mathbf{outsi}_{\sigma_1 \oplus \ldots \oplus \sigma_k \rightarrow \sigma_i}$	projects an element from a smash sum type to the $\mathbf{i}$th component of the smash sum	32

Index

www.ingramcontent.com/pod-product-compliance
Lightning Source LLC
Chambersburg PA
CBHW060540060326
40690CB00017B/3553